THE JAPANESE AUTOMOBILE INDUSTRY

Harvard East Asian Monographs 122

SUBSERIES ON THE HISTORY OF
JAPANESE BUSINESS AND INDUSTRY

Japan's rise from the destruction and bitter defeat of World War II to its present eminence in world business and industry is perhaps the most striking development in recent world history. This did not occur in a vacuum. It was linked organically to at least a century of prior growth and transformation. To illuminate this growth a new kind of scholarship on Japan is needed: historical study *in the context of a company or industry* of the interrelations among entrepreneurs, managers, engineers, workers, stockholders, bankers, and bureaucrats, and of the institutions and policies they created. Only in such a context can the contribution of particular factors be weighed and understood. It is to promote and encourage such scholarship that this series is established, supported by the Reischauer Institute of Japanese Studies and published by the Council on East Asian Studies at Harvard.

Albert M. Craig

Technology at Nissan

THE JAPANESE AUTOMOBILE INDUSTRY

and Management

and Toyota

Michael A. Cusumano

Published by The Council on East Asian Studies, Harvard University

and distributed by The Harvard University Press

Cambridge (Massachusetts) and London 1985

The Council on East Asian Studies at Harvard University publishes a monograph series and, through the Fairbank Center for East Asian Research and the Reischauer Institute of Japanese Studies, administers research projects designed to further scholarly understanding of China, Japan, Korea, Vietnam, Inner Asia, and adjacent areas. Publication of this volume has been assisted by a grant from the Shell Companies Foundation.

Book and Jacket Design by Eve Jessen Gordon
Photographs courtesy of Nissan and Toyota

Library of Congress Cataloging-in-Publication Data

Cusumano, Michael, A., 1954–
  The Japanese automobile industry.

  (Harvard East Asian mongraphs ; 122)
  Bibliography: p.
  Includes index.
  1. Automobile industry and trade—Japan. 2. Nissan Jidōsha Kabushiki Kaisha. 3. Toyota Jidōsha Kōgyō Kabushiki Kaisha. I. Title. II. Series.
TL105.C77 1985   338.7'6292'0952   85–14033
ISBN 0–674–47255–1

CONTENTS

TABLES

Tables

ACKNOWLEDGMENTS

This book is a modest revision of a doctoral thesis in Japanese History and East Asian Languages submitted to Harvard University in May 1984. I would like to thank Albert Craig of the Department of History, for serving as my dissertation advisor and for suggesting that I choose a topic in Japanese business or economic history. His support made writing a final draft of the thesis far easier than I expected. I also thank Andrew Gordon of Harvard's Department of History (soon to join Duke University) for being my second reader and providing valuable comments on the entire manuscript, especially the chapter involving labor. Others to whom I am most grateful for their comments include Ezra Vogel of Harvard University, Kim Clark of the Harvard Business School, William Wray of the University of British Columbia, and my father, Michael Cusumano, Sr., of Elmwood Park, New Jersey.

In Japan, my foremost thanks go to the Nissan Motor Company. I did most of the research in Nissan's Business Research Department during 1980-1983, where I was treated extremely well, given almost free access to materials in the department, and assisted on many occasions. From this experience I learned much about how the Japanese automobile industry, and large Japanese firms, operate. I am also grateful to Nissan's Department of Public Relations and International Division for their assistance. In particular, I would like to thank Gotō Mitsuya, Kawarada Shigeru, and Itō Michiaki, although I alone am responsible for the statements and conclusions in this study. I must also mention that the Toyota Motor Corporation cooperated fully; I would especially like to thank Ōno Taiichi and Kamio Takashi for their assistance.

Many of the ideas behind the structure of this book came from interviews with current or former engineers and other managers at Nissan and Toyota. I am especially grateful to Matsuzaki Shirō, Okumura Shōji, Katayama Yutaka, and Maeda Riichi, formerly of Nissan, as well as Ōno Taiichi, formerly of Toyota. In fact, all of the gentlemen who granted me interviews contributed enormously to the character and detail of this study, and it would be impossible to thank them adequately. I only hope that I have done justice to their recollections, and to their work.

Several institutions hosted me during my stay in Japan. I must first thank the Faculty of Economics at the University of Tokyo, where I was a researcher during 1980-1982. Hara Akira and Ishii Kanji, my formal advisors, provided assistance and support whenever I required it. The Institute of Social Science hosted me for a third year at the University of Tokyo while I wrote up a rough draft and finished my research on labor relations; I must thank Yamamoto Kiyoshi for his enthusiastic support and suggestions. Several professors from the Japan Business History Society also served as informal advisors and friends. In particular, I need to thank Morikawa Hidemasa of Yokohama National University, Udagawa Masaru of Hōsei University, and Yuzawa Takeshi of Gakushūin University. Professor Udagawa especially gave freely of his time and generously shared his materials on the Nissan combine. Yamamoto Osamu, the chief editor of the *Jidōsha* (Automobile) *Journal*, also provided valuable advice and introductions during the later stages of my research.

During the dissertation phase, funding came from several sources. The Fulbright program provided two grants during 1980-1982 through the Japan-United States Educational Commission and the U.S. Department of Education. I also received Foreign Language and Area Studies Fellowships during 1979-1980 and 1983-1984, and a grant from the Harvard University Graduate School of Arts and Sciences during 1978-1979. The Reischauer Institute of Harvard University provided financial assistance during 1983-1984. I express appreciation to Florence Trefethen for editorial help. I also thank Gregory Ornatowski and Yashushi Toda for their comments and Dr. Zack Deal of Harvard's Office for Information Technology for his help in using the computer.

Lastly, I must express my gratitude to the Harvard Business School—Dean John McArthur, E. Raymond Corey, Director of the Division of Research, and Richard Rosenbloom, my sponsor in the production and operations management area—for bringing me to the school as a postdoctoral fellow. The fellowship provided an opportunity to learn more about the management of technology in general, to revise the manuscript, and to visit Japan again. My deepest thanks go to Professor Rosenbloom for supporting my application with enthusiasm, encouraging me throughout the year, and displaying faith that what I was doing was truly worthwhile. In addition, I must express my appreciation again to Kim Clark for his patient and invaluable advice on refining, interpreting, and correcting the tables on vertical integration, productivity, and fixed investment in Chapter 4.

To Mom and Dad, and Princeton-in-Asia

PREFACE

The growth of the Japanese automobile industry from a production level of 32,000 vehicles in 1950 to over 11,000,000 per year during the early 1980s provides one of the most remarkable success stories in the history of business as well as the transfer and management of technology. After European engineers invented the automobile in the late nineteenth century, American companies, led by Ford and General Motors, found ways to produce and market this new product on a massive scale. Although Japanese engineers began learning how to make military trucks during the 1930s, to complete a transition to small cars took decades and required the modification of American technology to suit the smaller size of the Japanese market as well as the limited skills and resources of Japanese companies.

Yet it was in response to disadvantages at home that Nissan, Toyota, and other automobile manufacturers in Japan became efficient producers at relatively low volumes of output; in fact, by 1965, Nissan and Toyota had already matched or surpassed the productivity levels of American automakers. After the mid-1960s, productivity in Japan doubled in real terms as sales expanded. By 1980, Japan had replaced the United States as the largest automobile-producing nation in the world; in technology as well as production volume, it seemed that these two countries had come a full circle: Japan was now the world leader in high-productivity, low-cost manufacturing, forcing General Motors, Ford, and Chrysler to import Japanese components and complete vehicles. At the same time, American pressures on the Japanese to manufacture in the United States, and to limit exports, reflected the near impossibility of competing with Japan in an open small-car market.

THE STUDY

The general objective of this study is to understand how Japan began manufacturing motor vehicles and eventually passed the United States in productivity while matching the Europeans in small-car design. The discussion begins in the decades prior to World War II and runs through the early 1980s, although the main period under scrutiny is the 1950s and 1960s, when Japan moved into small-car mass production and introduced most of the process techniques and manufacturing policies that characterized the Japanese automobile industry during the 1970s and 1980s. The central focus of this story is the rivalry between two firms that accounted for 50 to 85 percent of Japan's automobile production from the 1930s through the 1980s— Nissan and Toyota. Most important, these two companies adopted different techniques for manufacturing automobiles that, when combined gradually between the 1950s and the 1970s, resulted in the high levels of worker output that proved so difficult to imitate outside of Japan.

Nissan traditionally looked to the United States or Europe for guidance in product and production technology, and preferred to concentrate on the use of American-style automation or specialized machine tools in manufacturing. Toyota, on the other hand, evolved more independently while borrowing from Western firms eclectically and with greater emphasis on perfecting production management techniques and an "adaptable" manufacturing system appropriate for the domestic market prior to 1970: relatively low total volumes with increasing diversity in the types of vehicles in demand. Toyota's production system, bolstered by the selective introduction of automated equipment similar to what Nissan imported or developed, also turned out to be well suited to the increasingly higher volumes and more complicated product mixes of the 1970s and 1980s.

Many elements contributed to the development of Nissan, Toyota, and the other Japanese automakers, although interviews with engineers and other executives, and a first-hand view of their operations in Japan between 1980 and 1983, made it possible to identify several factors that appeared to be the most significant. Approximately half the material in this book deals with Nissan (Datsun) and its major suppliers, which were located in the Tokyo area and more accessible to study. Nissan was also the first Japanese company to introduce automobile product and production technology directly from the United States and Europe, and its employees were central figures in the formation and then dissolution of an industrial union that served Japan's automobile industry after World War II. The rest of the material focuses on Toyota and comparisons with other Japanese and American automakers.

The first two chapters examine the origins of Nissan and Toyota, their different methods of acquiring truck technology from the United States during the 1930s, and their transition, based largely on European technology, to small trucks and cars after World War II. Subsequent chapters are organized more by theme or function. The third deals with the character of postwar management-labor relations: the collapse of an industrial union during the mid-1950s and the creation of company unions as well as their effect on wage levels and managerial authority, which had a direct impact on manufacturing strategy, worker output, and operating profits. The last three chapters look at productivity, strategies for in-house manufacturing and components supply, and techniques for managing production and quality control.

Several subjects readers might expect to find in an account of a Japanese firm are absent or covered only in passing. The treatment of company finances, for example, is limited, since this seemed to be a topic in itself, related only tangentially to the subject of technology and management. Nor are there discussions of company songs or "badges," the "group orientation" of the Japanese and their high levels of education and discipline, or the role of "lifetime" employment and other personnel practices in fostering loyalty to and dependency on the company. While these and other factors no doubt contributed to the ability of Japanese automakers to compete in international markets, cultural inputs are difficult to measure, and other authors have published on these topics for years. The current need is for a systematic analysis of precisely how the Japanese formed the companies that made up Japan's largest export industry during the early 1980s, and how they managed the details of technology transfer and product development, labor relations, and the cultivation of what may very well be "revolutionary" manufacturing techniques.

This study thus attempts to rectify a major oversight—the absence of a comprehensive history of Nissan, Toyota, and the industry they have dominated for five decades in Japan. As background for the main chapters, the Introduction provides an historical overview of the Japanese automobile industry, including a discussion of the role government has played, and not played. Even though Japanese "business-government relations" is another topic that has inspired more than its share of literature, it makes little sense to applaud or even study the Japanese as managers of technology without realizing that government agencies protected domestic producers of automobiles until the late 1970s. Public officials had less influence on the automobile industry than on sectors such as iron and steel, shipbuilding, or electronics. But a single policy—protection against imports—turned companies that would surely have been business failures into highly profitable operations. This suggests an obvious but critical relationship: While government policy did not directly enhance the competitiveness of Japanese automakers abroad, a key factor in the success of Nissan, Toyota, and the entire Japanese automobile industry was protection at home and, simultaneously, a taste of international competition through tie-ups and gradual increases in exports.

ABBREVIATIONS USED IN THE TEXT

APM	action-plate method
cc	cubic centimeter
CPI	consumer price index
EDP	electronic data processing
EOQ	economic order quantity
FY	fiscal year
GATT	General Agreement on Trade and Tariffs
GHQ	General Headquarters of the Allied Forces
GM	General Motors
hp	horsepower
JAMA	Japan Automobile Manufacturers Association (Nihon Jidosha Kōgyō Kai)
JMA	Japan Management Association (Nihon Nōritsu Kyōkai)
JSA	Japan Standards Association (Nihon Kikaku Kyōkai)
JUSE	Japanese Union of Scientists and Engineers (Nihon Kagaku Gijutsu Renmei)
kg	kilogram
km	kilometer
MCI	Ministry of Commerce and Industry
MITI	Ministry of International Trade and Industry
mm	millimeter
mph	miles per hour
MRP	Materials Requirement Planning
NEC	Nippon Electric Corporation (Nippon Denki)
NHK	Japan National Broadcasting Corporation
OP	ordering point
QC	quality control
rpm	revolutions per minute
SQC	statistical quality control
TQC	total quality control
VAP	value-added productivity

INTRODUCTION: A HALF CENTURY OF GROWTH, PROTECTION, AND PROMOTION

In 1980, the first year Japan led the world in automobile output, Toyota made 3,200,000 vehicles and Nissan 2,600,000, eclipsing Ford of America (1,900,000 vehicles) to become the world's second and third biggest automakers, excluding overseas subsidiaries, behind General Motors of the United States (4,700,000). No less than five of the world's top dozen motor vehicle producers in 1983 were Japanese companies and all appeared, seemingly, only a decade or two after Japan began to make automobiles (Tables 1 and 2). This story, however, has yet to be explained.

Part of the explanation is simple: The Japanese automobile industry did not develop so quickly. Of the eleven firms that made motor vehicles in Japan during the early 1980s, all except Honda existed prior to World War II as manufacturers of cast-iron components, textile machinery, multi-purpose engines, motorcycles, 3-wheel vehicles, tanks, aircraft, and other precision machinery products. Nissan began producing trucks during the 1930s after importing designs, engineers, and equipment from the United States. Toyota, in contrast, copied components from Chevrolet, Ford, and Chrysler vehicles prior to World War II and then moved into small cars after 1945 by disassembling and analyzing several European models. Postwar Nissan, Isuzu, and Hino, again in contrast to Toyota, relied on Austin (BL), Rootes (Peugeot's Talbot subsidiary and the former manufacturer of the British Hillman), and Renault (France's largest automaker) to develop small cars comparable to European standards.

In these postwar years, Japanese engineers also learned to make automobiles in small lots, with strict inventory controls and the precise coordination of parts manufacturing and delivery, subassem-

1

Table 1: Major Automobile-Producing Countries, 1977-1983 (1,000,000 vehicles)

Country	1977	1978	1979	1980	1981	1982	1983
Japan	8.5	9.3	9.6	11.0	11.2	10.7	11.1
U.S.A.	12.7	12.9	11.5	8.0	7.9	7.0	9.2
W. Germany	4.1	4.2	4.2	3.9	3.9	4.1	4.2
France	3.5	3.5	3.6	3.4	3.0	3.1	3.3
Italy	1.6	1.7	1.6	1.6	1.4	1.5	1.6
Britain	1.7	1.6	1.5	1.3	1.2	1.2	1.3
World	40.9	42.3	41.5	38.4	37.5	36.3	39.7

Sources: Japan Automobile Manufacturers Association; Motor Vehicle Manufacturers Association of the U.S.

bly production, and final assembly. Japanese automakers began forming supply networks as well with a minimum of direct investment, established long-term programs to increase productivity and quality, subcontracted components and final assembly at unusually high levels to firms with lower wage scales, and invested consistently in machinery and equipment. In addition to these measures, Nissan, Toyota, and other companies reduced production costs further by dramatically increasing their manufacturing scales while restricting wage increases, hiring temporary workers, and persuading suppliers to lower prices on a regular basis throughout the late 1950s and 1960s.

The postwar transition from trucks to cars was also far easier to achieve than to start an industry from scratch, as the Japanese did in the 1930s. By the early 1980s, the Japanese automobile industry was already half a century old, with thirty years of trial and error preceding the large-scale exports of Datsun and Toyota cars to the United States and Europe that began during the late 1960s. This may not be common knowledge, but it is common sense: No manufacturing sector requiring such a broad base in precision machinery, specialty steels, thousands of metal, electrical, and other components, is likely to have come so far in merely one or two decades.

Table 2: World's Top Automakers, 1983 and 1984
(1000 vehicles)

Company (Country)	1983	1984
General Motors (U.S.A.)	5,098	5,676
Toyota (Japan)	3,272	3,429
Nissan (Japan)	2,483	2,482
Ford (U.S.A.)	2,476	3,287
Renault (France)	1,880	1,645
Volkswagen (W. Germany)	1,538	1,471
Peugeot-Citroen (France)	1,450	1,414
Fiat (Italy)	1,189	1,234
Mazda (Japan)	1,171	1,133
Chrysler (U.S.A.)	1,052	1,461
Honda (Japan)	1,032	989
Mitsubishi (Japan)	975	1,095

Sources: Nissan Motor Company, "Data File 1984," p. 29; Motor Vehicle Manufacturers Association of the U.S.; Ward's Automotive Yearbook; *and company sources.*

Note: Counting overseas subsidiaries, in 1983 General Motors produced 7,769,000 vehicles, Ford 4,934,000, and Chrysler 1,493,961. Worldwide figures for 1984 were 8,256,000 for GM, 5,584,651 for Ford, and 2,034,348 for Chrysler.

The Growth Record: Domestic Sales and Exports
Nor have the huge volumes attained in the 1970s and 1980s involved such drastic increases in production as is commonly believed. In terms of annual rises in vehicle output, the period of "rapid growth" in the Japanese automobile industry was already over by 1965 (Table 3). After producing 46,000 units in 1941 and passing this level in 1953, output rose an average of 40 percent a year between 1955 and 1964, 18 percent from 1965 through 1972, and only 7.5 percent

through 1980. Volumes were relatively low until the mid-1960s, but, in the decade following the Korean War, the automobile industry expanded as rapidly as any sector in the Japanese economy. Company executives invested in plant and equipment because they believed, from the examples of the United States and Europe, that demand for cars would rise along with national income. Indeed, production grew 10-fold between 1953 and 1960, when vehicle output reached nearly 500,000 units, and then topped 1,000,000 in 1963, 5,000,000 in 1970, and 11,000,000 in 1980. Not only did increasing sales during the 1960s and 1970s finally make it possible for Nissan, Toyota, and other Japanese automakers to benefit from "learning curves" and huge economies of scale: Protection against foreign imports kept domestic car prices at artificially high levels until the

Table 3: Japanese Automobile Production, Exports, and Growth Rates (vehicles, %)

Annual Statistics (Selected Years)

Year	Production	Domestic Sales	Exports	Export Rate(%)
1953	49,778	76,185	—	—
1954	70,073	70,648	—	—
1957	181,977	176,690	6,554	3.6
1960	481,551	407,963	38,809	8.1
1965	1,875,614	1,661,856	194,168	10.4
1970	5,289,157	4,097,361	1,086,776	20.5
1973	7,082,757	4,912,142	2,067,556	29.2
1980	11,042,884	5,015,628	5,966,961	54.0
1981	11,179,962	5,127,412	6,048,447	54.1
1982	10,731,794	5,261,553	5,590,513	52.1
1983	11,111,659	5,382,225	5,669,510	51.0
1984	11,464,920	5,436,757	6,109,184	53.3

Table 3 (continued)

Average Annual Growth Rates (Industry)

Period	Production(%)	Domestic Sales(%)	Exports(%)
1955-1964	40.3	37.1	—
1957-1964	—	—	72.2
1965-1972	18.2	15.0	39.1
1973-1980	7.5	2.4	15.7
1981	1.2	2.2	1.4
1982	− 4.0	2.6	− 7.6
1983	3.5	2.3	1.4
1984	3.2	1.0	7.8

Average Annual Growth Rates (Top Two Producers)

Period	Nissan(%)	Toyota(%)
1955-1964	35.1	37.3
1965-1972	24.3	22.6
1973-1980	4.8	6.1
1981	− 2.3	− 2.2
1982	− 6.8	− 2.4
1983	3.1	4.1
1984	0.0	4.8

Sources: Japan Automobile Manufacturers Association; Autmobile Industry Promotion Association (Jidōsha Kōgyō Shinkō Kai); Automotive News; Japan Economic Review; *Motor Vehicle Manufacturers Association of the U.S.*

late 1960s and helped to maintain profit margins and finance new investment in plant and equipment.

If the Japanese automobile industry is "young," it is young only as a high-volume export industry. Although Toyota and Nissan sold some vehicles overseas prior to 1945 and mounted small export drives between 1958 and 1965 to counter domestic recessions, quality control programs, instituted first in the 1950s to improve manufacturing processes and then vehicle designs, took until the end of the 1960s to raise the quality and performance of Japanese cars sufficiently to make large exports possible. On the other hand, since imports into Japan were expensive, Japanese customers bought 80 percent of domestic motor vehicle production as late as 1970. Only as growth in the home market slowed did Japanese automakers make greater efforts to send excess units abroad, with the result that exports approached or exceeded 50 percent of Japan's annual automobile output beginning in 1976.

Although sales overseas rose 72 percent a year between 1957 and 1964, again, the volumes were negligible. As with manufacturing trucks in the 1930s, however, these early efforts were useful: The Japanese thoroughly tested the American market, albeit through trial and error, and then designed suitable export models in stages after selling them at a profit in Japan. Japanese cars made in the 1950s already had durable frames and chassis since they were actually small trucks fitted with car bodies. But, to perform on American highways and appeal to housewives as second cars, these vehicles had to have bigger engines, improved transmissions, reduced maintenance requirements, better handling at high speeds, and more attractive interiors and exteriors. As Nissan, Toyota, and other Japanese automakers made the necessary modifications, exports grew 39 percent a year from 1965 through 1972. By 1974, Japan had replaced West Germany as the world's largest automobile exporter. The growth rate for exports dropped to a still high 16 percent annually during 1973-1980 and even reached the negative column in 1982. Yet it was still only this rise in overseas demand—with about half of export sales going to North America and 20 percent to Europe—that allowed the Japanese automobile industry to double production once again, since new vehicle sales in Japan between 1970 and 1980 increased by only 25 percent.

Protectionism and Technology Transfer
Although Japan clearly benefited from open automobile markets in the West prior to 1980, large imports from the United States and

Europe led both prewar and postwar Japanese governments to adopt highly protectionist policies while encouraging technology transfer into Japan. In two brief periods when domestic production was minimal and Japan had no major restrictions on vehicle imports—prior to 1936 and for several years after World War II—foreign manufacturers overwhelmed the local market. Even after the government took various measures to reduce imports, nearly one-third of Japan's car production between 1953 and 1959 consisted of European models assembled from knock-down sets or produced under license from parts made locally. The popularity of these vehicles confirmed the suspicions of government and business officials that imports from Europe could have sold well during the 1950s, and probably afterwards too, even if larger American vehicles with left-hand drive (right-hand drive is standard in Japan) might not have attracted the millions of new car buyers that appeared in Japan during the 1960s and 1970s.

The protectionist policies of successive Japanese governments made it possible for domestic firms to experiment in the automobile industry and to survive despite the existence of far larger and more efficient competitors in the United States and Europe that were anxious to export to Japan. The most important prewar legislation, passed in 1936, openly restricted imports of complete vehicles and knock-down sets that subsidiaries of Ford and General Motors, founded in 1925 and 1927, respectively, had assembled in Japan. The result was that, whereas Japan Ford, Japan GM, and other foreign companies had accounted for more than 95 percent of new vehicle registrations between 1926 and 1935, the production share of Nissan, Toyota, and Isuzu rose to nearly 57 percent by 1938 and to 100 percent in 1939, when Japan Ford and Japan GM ceased operating (Appendix A).

During the postwar Occupation (1945-1952), American vehicles again filled the Japanese market due to the low level of domestic production and the suspension of prewar restrictions on imports. Since sales of foreign vehicles drained Japan's small reserves of foreign currency, the Ministry of International Trade and Industry (MITI) restricted foreign exchange allocations and imposed a value-added tax of 40 percent on imported automobiles, reducing the level of imports from 44.6 percent in 1951 to 23.1 percent in 1954 and 8.9 percent in 1955 (Appendix B). Imports continued to decline throughout the decade, reaching 1 percent of new vehicle sales in 1960, and remained at this level for more than twenty years. At the same time, imports as a percentage of American automobile sales rose from 0.4

percent in 1951 to nearly 41 percent in 1984—with Japan producing 1 out of every 5 automobiles sold in the United States during 1980-1983 and as much as 67 percent of all American imports in 1980 (Appendix C).

After World War II, MITI also worried that, since Nissan, Toyota, Isuzu, and Hino were experienced only in truck manufacturing, they might never be able to compete directly with foreign car producers. The future was likely to bring ever higher imports while Japan missed the opportunity to develop what was an important export industry for many European countries. Formal tie-ups with foreign automakers appeared to be the fastest way to introduce new products, modernize manufacturing equipment, and complete the transition from trucks to cars. For this reason, in 1952 the Ministry encouraged domestic manufacturers to make arrangements with European automakers to assemble cars from imported knock-down sets for three or four years, and then switch gradually to components made in Japan. Within seven years or so, MITI hoped that Japanese companies would have assimilated this technology and become more competitive with foreign producers.[1]

While Nissan appeared to have an advantage over the other Japanese automakers because it had manufactured a few thousand Datsun cars and engaged in a tie-up with an American firm during the 1930s, the president of the company decided to take up MITI's suggestion and sign a contract with Austin in December 1952. Isuzu, established in 1937, and Hino, a heavy truck manufacturer separated from Isuzu in 1942, followed by concluding agreements with Rootes and Renault, respectively, in March 1953. Shin-Mitsubishi Heavy Industries, a prewar aircraft, tank, and ship producer reorganized in 1950 (later absorbed into Mitsubishi Heavy Industries, from which Mitsubishi Motors was separated in 1970), entered into a tie-up with an American firm, Willys-Overland (later merged with American Motors), to produce jeeps (Table 4). Toyota, as well as Fuji Seimitsu, a prewar aircraft manufacturer (later renamed Prince Motors and merged with Nissan in 1966), chose to design and manufacture small cars without foreign assistance.

The initial contract period for the tie-ups was seven years. Nissan completed its schedule of knock-down set assembly, local parts production, and assimilation of the Austin technology into the Datsun line within the contract term, although Isuzu and Hino were unfamiliar with passenger car technology and required extensions of several years to complete the switch to local production and to

Table 4: Japanese Automobile Tie-ups, 1952-1960

	Nissan	Isuzu	Hino	Shin-Mitsubishi
Foreign Company	Austin	Rootes	Renault	Willys-Overland
Country	Britain	Britain	France	U.S.A.
Agreement Signed	December 1952	March 1953	March 1953	September 1953
Product	Austin A40, A50	Hillman	Renault 4CV	Jeep
Restrictions	Exports prohibited	Exports prohibited	Exports prohibited[a]	Asian exports permitted
Domestic Production Completed	September 1956	October 1957	February 1958	June 1956
Contract End	March 1960	March 1960	March 1960	August 1958
Extensions	none	5 years	4 years	5 years
Tie-up Length	7 years	12 years	11 years	10 years

Source: Iwakoshi Tadahiro, Jidōsha kōgyō ron, p. 92.

Note: [a]Hino was permitted to bring up the issue of exports again at a later date.

9

10

Table 5: Vehicle Production Under Foreign Tie-ups, 1952-1964 (vehicles, %)

FY	Nissan Austin	Isuzu Hillman	Hino Renault	Mitsubishi Jeep	A (%)	B (%)
1952	—	—	30	204	0.6	0.6
1953	1,334	453	1,425	2,853	12.2	36.5
1954	1,540	2,127	2,420	2,934	12.9	42.1
1955	2,089	2,031	3,180	1,451	12.7	36.0
1956	2,718	2,132	3,640	1,893	9.3	26.5
1957	5,785	2,752	3,550	3,989	8.8	25.7
1958	3,935	3,327	4,364	5,437	9.1	23.0
1959	3,454	4,608	6,403	4,151	7.1	18.4
1960	—	8,711	7,796	7,832	5.1	10.0
1961	—	10,272	3,767	9,656	2.9	5.6
1962	—	8,946	886	8,770	1.9	3.7
1963	—	5,432	200	5,452	0.9	1.4
1964	—	998	—	700	0.1	0.2
Total	20,855	51,789	37,661	55,322		

Sources: Amagai Shōgo, Nihon jidōsha kōgyō no shiteki tenkai, *p. 136; and Japan Automobile Manufacturers Association.*

Notes: A = production under the tie-ups as a % of total 4-wheel vehicle output
B = cars produced under the tie-ups (excluding jeeps) as a % of total car output

design their own models. While the total number of vehicles produced through the tie-ups never exceeded 13 percent of Japan's automobile output in any one year, the European models accounted for 30 percent of car production during 1953-1959 and this increased the competition among all domestic automakers to upgrade their product technology (Table 5).

The Pre-1945 Base: Trucks and Other Ordnance Industries
It was not necessary to limit truck imports because Japan had already become a relatively efficient producer of these vehicles during World War II. In fact, by the early 1960s, Japan ranked second in the world in truck production, trailing only the United States, due to an unusually high percentage of output (including a small number of buses) devoted to these vehicles: 92 percent in 1941 and over 50 percent as late as 1967 (Table 6). While the main product of the pre-1945 industry had been standard-size trucks, the focus shifted to small trucks during the mid-1950s and then to small cars after 1960. Car output in Japan still did not exceed total truck production until 1968,

Table 6: Japanese Production by Vehicle Type, Selected Years (vehicles, %)

INDUSTRY:	Production	% Trucks	% Cars
1941	46,498	92.1[a]	3.9
1950	31,597	83.9	5.0
1955	68,932	63.2	29.4
1960	481,551	64.0	34.3
1965	1,875,614	61.9	37.1
1970	5,289,157	39.0	60.1
1975	6,941,591	33.7	65.8
1980	11,042,884	35.4	63.7
1982	10,731,794	35.3	64.1
1983	11,111,659	35.1	64.4

Table 6 (continued)

NISSAN:	Production	% Small Trucks	% Standard Trucks	% Small Cars	% Standard Cars
1941	19,688	4.6	86.6	8.1	—
1950	12,458	34.0	54.8	6.9	—
1955	21,767	34.7	32.1	30.3	—
1960	115,465	42.9	8.8	47.7	—
1965	345,165	45.1	4.8	48.8	0.4
1970	1,374,022	32.9	1.0	63.8	1.6
1975	2,077,447	25.0	0.9	69.8	4.0
1980	2,644,052	23.7	1.9	69.1	4.3
1982	2,407,734	18.6	5.3	66.7	8.8
1983	2,482,540	17.8	6.8	66.0	8.9

233 6987

TOYOTA:

1941	14,611	—	98.1	—	1.4
1950	11,706	31.7	62.4	4.0	—
1955	22,786	40.3	26.5	32.5	—
1960	154,770	53.4	19.0	27.2	—
1965	477,643	45.8	4.3	49.2	0.2
1970	1,609,190	30.1	2.5	64.6	1.8
1975	2,336,053	22.7	3.4	68.1	5.3
1980	3,293,344	19.8	9.2	62.1	7.8
1982	3,144,557	18.0	9.4	62.8	9.0
1983	3,272,335	16.5	10.1	65.2	7.6

Sources: Japan Automobile Manufacturers Association; Toyota Jidōsha Kabushiki Kaisha, Kōhō shiryō; Nissan Jidōsha Kabushiki Kaisha, "Nissan Jidōsha no gaiyō"; Nissan Jidōsha Kabushiki Kaisha, "Nissan Jidōsha Kabushiki Kaisha, Jidōsha sanjū nen shi; Toyota Jidōsha sanjū nen shi; Nissan Jidōsha Kabushiki Kaisha, Jidōsha kōgyō handobukku (1984).

Note: ªBus production is included in the industry truck total for 1941.

14

a record that is almost unique: Only the Soviet Union also developed a relatively large automobile industry by first manufacturing trucks for military and commercial use, and then increasing car production gradually.

In the case of Japan, the dominance of trucks for three decades reflected the late development of the car market, due primarily to low income levels and high retail prices. In retrospect, however, beginning with trucks posed certain advantages. When Nissan, Toyota, and Isuzu first entered the industry during the 1930s, personal income levels in Japan were too low to support large sales of domestically made cars. The army, on the other hand, demanded Japanese trucks and bought 60 percent of domestic production between 1937 and 1944 despite a variety of technical problems in these vehicles.[2]

The ready market that the military provided enabled the Japanese automakers to acquire valuable experience in technology transfer and mass production. Manufacturing plants also remained virtually intact after World War II, since they were not primary bombing targets, enabling Nissan, Toyota, and Isuzu to make several thousand trucks and other military vehicles for the U.S. Army during the Korean War. These orders helped each firm raise production up to the levels of the early 1940s and to acquire much needed funds for equipment investment and small-car development. Furthermore, until they had new car models ready by the late 1950s, Japanese automakers used truck frames, chassis, engines, and other components below car body shells as an inexpensive method of producing crude but relatively durable cars, suitable as taxis.

The development of the truck industry was also boosted by the massive transfer of domestic investment into heavy manufacturing industries prior to and during World War II. Whereas in 1937 Japanese companies had invested just 7 percent of their paid-up capital in machinery (including shipbuilding and machine tools), and 5 percent in metals, by 1945 these figures were 24 percent and 12 percent, respectively.[3] Much of this investment consisted of plant and equipment that would later benefit the automobile industry, as suggested in a 1954 government survey of automobile parts makers, which found that 40 percent of the 221 companies surveyed had entered this business after 1945.[4] In addition, several original-equipment manufacturers that had made aircraft during the war—the predecessors of Mitsubishi Motors, Fuji Heavy Industries, and Prince Motors—switched to automobiles after 1945 and brought their parts

suppliers with them, while two former precision machinery manufacturers—Toyo Kogyo (renamed Mazda in 1984) and Daihatsu—
also began to produce automobiles during the 1950s.

Government Promotion: A Mixed Record
In both the prewar and postwar periods, ironically, officials in the
Japanese government displayed a reluctance to promote the automobile industry due to the severity of foreign competition. Automakers were useful only for "strategic" reasons: either to supply the
military or to eliminate a major source of imports. Prior to World
War II, the army had to persuade MITI's predecessor, the Ministry
of Commerce and Industry (MCI), to help it establish and protect a
domestic industry. While MCI then served as the formal regulatory
agency for automobile producers during the 1930s, the army continued to determine policy—which consisted of restricting the activities of Japan Ford and Japan GM, reducing vehicle imports, and
indirectly subsidizing the operations of Nissan, Toyota, and Isuzu.
MITI adopted similar measures during the 1950s to help the postwar
automakers, but only after the Bank of Japan and the Ministry of
Transport argued that the industry was not worth protecting.

Government involvement in promoting the Japanese automobile
actually dates back to World War I, when the Japanese army became
interested in trucks and sponsored a law in 1918 to provide subsidies
to manufacturers and users of vehicles that military inspectors cer-
tified.[5] Japan had no recorded automobile output at this time, although individuals and companies had imported around 4500 vehicles,
nearly all cars, into the country. The new legislation authorized
three local firms—Tokyo Gas and Electric (est. 1910), Ishikawajima
Shipbuilding (est. 1889), and Kaishinsha (an automobile repair shop
and manufacturer founded in 1911)—to produce trucks. But the military subsidies failed to stimulate domestic production except for a
few experimental vehicles; it took a major earthquake in the Tokyo
area during 1923 to create significant demand for automobiles in
Japan. As the Tokyo municipal government imported thousands of
Ford Model T trucks to replace destroyed railways and trolley networks, and to transport materials for rebuilding the city, vehicle
registrations throughout the country rose from under 13,000 in 1923
to over 24,000 by the end of 1924. The central government facilitated
this increase by reducing duties instituted after World War I on the
importation of finished automobiles and components.

Ford received so many orders that it established a fully owned subsidiary in Japan during 1925 to assemble knock-down sets in the port city of Yokohama, neighboring Tokyo. General Motors followed with a Japanese subsidiary in 1927 and an assembly plant in Osaka. The national sales networks these companies organized then helped to raise the number of vehicle registrations in Japan to nearly 100,000 by 1931, although their success constituted a crisis for the local industry, since Japan made only 436 automobiles domestically in 1931, and this represented a decline of 5 percent over the previous year (see Appendix A). In fact, every Japanese firm that attempted to manufacture automobiles either closed down or was on the verge of bankruptcy during the late 1920s and early 1930s, while the wealthiest combines in the country—Mitsui, Mitsubishi, and Sumitomo—refused to enter the industry, despite repeated requests from the army and MCI.[6]

The general problem of high imports of manufactured goods prompted MCI to establish a committee in 1929 to investigate ways to stimulate the sale of domestic products. Based on a proposal by this committee, MCI organized a rationalization council for the automobile industry in 1931, composed of university professors; officials from MCI, the Ministries of the Army, Finance, and Home Affairs; and the presidents of the three automobile producers authorized under the 1918 military subsidies act. The council recommended that local producers merge and concentrate on manufacturing mid-size cars and trucks that would not compete directly with the larger American vehicles, and that the government raise tariffs on imports of complete vehicles and components. A merger did not take place at this time because executives from the firms involved in the council were unable to reach an agreement, although Ishikawajima Shipbuilding separated its automobile division in 1929 and this absorbed DAT Motors, the successor to Kaishinsha, in 1933. The new entity, named Automobile Industries, subsequently began producing standard-size and large trucks, mainly diesels, under the "Isuzu" logo, which the firm adopted as its company name in 1949. Nissan, incorporated in 1933, took over manufacturing rights to the small car and truck line that DAT Motors had designed but failed to manufacture in large volumes.[7]

The army's interest in the industry grew throughout the 1930s because the invasion of Manchuria in 1931 and subsequent expansion of military operations on the continent made trucks a necessity. Ford and Chevrolet models, requisitioned from private companies and citizens to transport troops, proved to be vastly superior to the few Japanese trucks that the army owned and had to repair constantly due to breakdowns on Manchuria's unpaved roads. To acquire an independent supply of trucks comparable in performance to American models, military officers began negotiations with MCI to promote the domestic industry. The talks stalled after the army suggested that Japan Ford and Japan GM be expelled from the country, and MCI argued that this would damage trade relations with the United States. The army persisted, however, until the cabinet adopted a set of measures in 1935 that military officers drafted and incorporated into the May 1936 automobile manufacturing enterprise law.[8]

While the 1936 legislation required companies producing more than 3000 vehicles per year to obtain a license from the government, only firms with more than 50 percent of their outstanding shares and positions on the board of directors owned or held by Japanese citizens were eligible to receive licenses. Those companies that obtained authorization received five-year exemptions from income taxes, local and business revenue taxes, and import duties on machinery, equipment, and materials purchased abroad. MCI also arranged exemptions to the commercial code to facilitate issues of new shares and bonds to raise capital, but reserved the right to approve or disapprove of the business plans of the licensed producers, to regulate any attempts to merge or dissolve, and to oversee all operations involving the production of miliary vehicles or equipment.

Japan Ford and Japan GM did not have to leave the country outright, but the Japanese government severely restricted their operations. First, MCI placed a ceiling on production that kept this around the level of 1934-1935. Second, and most important, the Ministry raised import duties in November 1936 on complete vehicles and components, including knock-down sets, and revised foreign exchange regulations to make it difficult for the American subsidiaries to pay for the parts they imported. Both firms left in 1939 after several attempts to merge either with Nissan or Toyota failed.[9]

The 1936 automobile manufacturing law had a major impact on the future structure of the industry. After the government granted a monopoly to three domestic producers, Nissan and Toyota accounted for as much as 85 percent of Japan's automobile production until the entrance of more than half a dozen other companies into the industry after World War II reduced their combined share to just over 50 percent by the early 1980s. Isuzu accounted for 15 percent of production prior to 1945 but then sank from third place among the Japanese automakers to rank ninth in 1983, with a production share of merely 3.5 percent—ahead of only Hino (0.5 percent) and Nissan Diesel (0.3 percent), which specialized in large trucks.

The 1936 legislation was also significant because it allowed the Japanese government to experiment with various promotional and protectionist measures. MCI eliminated complete vehicle imports, local assembly by foreign firms, and investment in the domestic industry from abroad, and provided tax exemptions while encouraging firms to acquire foreign technology and invest in new plant and equipment. The government did this, moreover, without instituting direct controls over automobile producers except during World War II and the postwar Occupation. MCI prohibited most car production in 1939, and this restriction remained in effect until a 1949 memorandum from the General Headquarters of the Allied Forces (GHQ) abolished it. In 1950, GHQ also eliminated controls established in 1939 on the prices and distribution of motor vehicles.

As a regulatory tool, MCI had relied on a control association set up for automobiles in 1941, one of eleven control associations for industries that the military felt were "strategic." Company executives staffed the association and used it to supervise production and to distribute materials, labor, and credit among themselves and their suppliers. Another control association organized dealerships in 1942. Both functioned like cartels, except that they implemented policies that the army determined and MCI enforced.[10]

GHQ abolished the control associations a few months after the Occupation began, and the Japanese did not resurrect them in the same form, although company executives formed several organizations to link managers throughout the industry. Most important was the Japan Automobile Manufacturers Association (Nihon Jidōsha Kōgyō Kai, abbreviated in English as JAMA), founded in 1948 as part of an attempt to persuade GHQ to modify its policies toward the automobile industry. Japanese bureaucrats used JAMA and similar organizations for parts manufacturers and for small vehicles to implement controls over production and the distribution of materials. After GHQ lifted these controls, the association evolved into a lobbying and public relations organ for the industry, usually headed by the president of Nissan or Toyota.[11] During the 1950s and 1960s, for example, JAMA and individual company executives pressed government officials to continue protectionist measures against imports and to provide low-cost loans. During the 1980s, the organization served in negotiations to restrain Japanese car exports but, since it had no formal authority, firms' limits actually depended on their agreeing to export quotas or any other constraints on their activities.[12]

Officials in the Japanese government and in GHQ concluded after World War II that the industry needed some type of regulation because there were severe shortages of materials. At the same time, companies needed to raise production levels to help them absorb the thousands of employees returning from the armed forces and from Japanese colonies. Although private demand was extremely low and inflation had destroyed the value of personal savings, there was a need for motor vehicles since fewer than half of the trucks registered in 1940, and only 18 percent of cars, were still operable at war's end. But, since GHQ solved this problem to its own advantage by selling 27,000 surplus military vehicles between 1946 and 1949, and deflationary measures adopted in 1949 depressed automobile demand further, company executives became unhappy with GHQ policy toward the industry. The American authorities had permitted truck production to resume in the fall of 1945, using whatever materials were available, although GHQ restricted car production to merely a few hundred units until 1949, because it did not consider cars essential.[13]

Only huge loans from government and private banks kept Nissan, Toyota, and Isuzu operating during the late 1940s. It was by no means certain that the industry would even survive in the face of foreign competition and sales of American military vehicles; consequently, officials at the Bank of Japan and the Ministry of Transport argued that Japan should use its limited resources to develop other industries. Even if Japan continued to manufacture trucks and buses, they wanted to eliminate restrictions on car imports and leave the passenger-car field to the Americans and Europeans.[14]

Postwar Japanese (and world) history would have been considerably different had this line of reasoning prevailed. MITI took the opposite position—that an automobile industry would stimulate other sectors of the economy, especially machinery and steel manufacturing, therefore it should be promoted and protected. Even before it was evident that the industry would not collapse, the Bank of Japan, the Japan Development Bank, and the Industrial Bank of Japan provided funds to keep Nissan, Toyota, and Isuzu out of bankruptcy. Arguments over the industry's potential then became moot during the Korean War as orders from the American army for $23,000,000 worth of trucks, military vehicles, and other equipment, combined with the dismissal of several thousand autoworkers during 1949-1950, restored these companies to profitability.

Once the recovery was underway by 1950-1951, government banks and private institutions provided additional funds to invest in new equipment and passenger-car development. Loans from the Japan Development Bank alone equaled 10 percent of new equipment investment for car production between 1951 and 1955, totaling 1.5 billion yen ($4,200,000), and 14 percent of fixed investment by automobile parts manufacturers from 1956 to 1965. MITI combined low-interest loans with tax privileges, such as special depreciation allowances for new machinery instituted for original-equipment manufacturers in 1951 and for parts suppliers in 1956. Beginning in 1956, MITI also exempted companies from import duties on machinery and tools purchased abroad, a measure used successfully in the 1930s, and allowed firms to deduct as income any revenues obtained from export sales. Japan had to abandon this latter practice when it joined the General Agreement on Tariffs and Trade (GATT) in 1964 as a full member, but the government subsequently permitted automakers to establish tax-free reserves for expenditures related to overseas marketing and to adopt depreciation schedules tied to export performance.[15]

While these and other measures clearly encouraged automobile production after World War II, MITI's role or influence in guiding the development of the industry can easily be exaggerated.[16] In 1948, for example, MCI (it adopted the name MITI the following year) published a five-year production plan for the industry, but this was far too ambitious and managers found it impossible to implement. MITI then drew up an equipment rationalization schedule for the industry in 1950 that might have served as a model for company planning except that the larger automakers already had equipment modernization programs underway. On the other hand, encouragement from the Ministry to increase production during the early 1950s and to invest in new equipment no doubt helped automobile manufacturers receive credit from government institutions or private-sector banks that felt reassured by MITI's determination to build up the industry.[17]

Another plan that MITI launched in 1955, to stimulate the development of a "people's car" by 1958, also had mixed results. The Ministry decided that Japan should manufacture a 4-passenger "minicar" with an engine displacement of no more than 500 cubic centimeters (cc), a cruising speed of 60km (37 miles), and a maximum speed of 100km (62 miles) per hour. It also recommended that the engine be able to go 30km on one liter (or 70 miles on one gallon) of gasoline, that the car operate for 100,000km (62,000 miles) without major repairs, and that companies keep the manufacturing cost under 150,000 yen ($417) per unit, assuming a production level of 24,000 vehicles annually. MITI then asked firms to submit prototypes in a sort of contest, with the winner to receive an official designation from the Ministry, exclusive manufacturing rights, and subsidies to improve the vehicle's performance.[18]

Company executives did not like the idea. The contest format was awkward, and no one was certain what benefits official approval from MITI would offer or how losing the contest would affect other firms. Managers also found it impossible to meet the suggested standards, particularly manufacturing costs and production levels. Japan had made fewer than 15,000 cars during 1954 and only 20,000 in 1955, yet MITI wanted one firm to produce 24,000 units of one model within three years. Company executives also feared that 3-wheel vehicles, of which Japan manufactured over 100,000 per year between 1953 and 1963, would provide steep competition for any such "people's car."

No one agreed to participate in a contest. Nevertheless, MITI's proposal provided standards for designing small cars; and most of the companies that tried to meet these specifications had possessed the technology to produce automobiles but had not yet found the incentive to enter the 4-wheel vehicle field. For example, Fuji Heavy Industries, founded in 1953 by a merger of several small firms previously with the Nakajima aircraft combine, introduced the Subaru 360cc minicar in 1958 after experimenting with motor scooters. Toyo Kogyo (Mazda), a cork producer established in 1920 that diversified into rock-drilling equipment, machine tools, and 3-wheel vehicles during the 1930s, was Japan's leading producer of 3-wheel vehicles in the 1950s but did not introduce 4-wheel mini-vehicles until 1958. Shin-Mitsubishi, which had produced motor scooters, 3-wheel vehicles, and American jeeps during the 1950s, began to manufacture a 500cc minicar in 1960. Daihatsu, an engine maker founded in 1907, diversified into 3-wheel vehicles during the 1930s and 4-wheel vehicles in 1958.[19]

But probably the major effect of MITI's minicar proposal was to accelerate the end of 3-wheel vehicle production in Japan. The prewar output record for these vehicles was 15,000 units, set in 1937 and equaled in 1948. Postwar production peaked at 280,000 units in 1960 and fell sharply thereafter to just 43,000 in 1965 and zero by 1975.[20] Three-wheel vehicles were popular only because car and truck prices in Japan were artificially high due to import restrictions and low domestic production; demand then shifted as Toyo Kogyo, Daihatsu, and Shin-Mitsubishi brought out 4-wheel mini-vehicles, and as Nissan, Toyota, Isuzu, Hino, and Prince built new factories between 1959 and 1962 and lowered their prices for slightly larger cars and trucks.

Rising economies of scale helped all the Japanese automakers reduce production costs by the early 1960s, although the entrance of 2- and 3-wheel vehicle manufacturers into the 4-wheel field created another problem, at least in the opinion of government and company officials—too many firms in an already crowded industry. MITI bureaucrats recognized that some competition encouraged technological development and cost reductions, but this seemed "excessive" because demand in Japan was far less than in the American or European markets.

In 1961, Japan ranked only seventh in the world as a 4-wheel vehicle producer, making just 1 automobile for every 10 made in the United States. Yet, by the mid-1960s, there were seven companies—Nissan, Toyota, Isuzu, Hino, Mitsubishi, Prince, and Toyo Kogyo—manufacturing both cars and trucks with engines in the 1000 to 2000cc (1- to 2-liter) class. Six firms—Toyo Kogyo, Daihatsu, Fuji Heavy Industries, Suzuki, Honda, and Mitsubishi—produced lighter vehicles below 1000cc. This situation prevented any one company from mass-producing sufficient numbers of one model to gain the economies of scale that made American cars or the Volkswagen Beetle so inexpensive. In Japan, the automobile industry was exceptionally crowded in comparison to Italy, where one firm (Fiat) accounted for 90 percent of a larger market, or compared to the United States and Germany, where single firms (General Motors and Volkswagen) accounted for half or more of total automobile production.[21]

Too much competition would not have mattered so much if MITI had felt confident that it could isolate Japan's automobile market from the rest of the world indefinitely. By 1960, however, there was already considerable pressure on the Japanese government from West Germany, France, Britain, and the International Monetary Fund to allow 4-wheel vehicle imports.[22] MITI responded in September by lifting restrictions on 257 items, beginning with 3-wheel trucks and tires, followed in 1961 by standard-size trucks and buses, in addition to 2-wheel vehicles, but this move conceded little, if anything, to trading partners. Japan was perhaps the world's most experienced producer of 3-wheel vehicles and, in any case, MITI did not consider these worth protecting. Japan was also a leading maker of motorcycles and motor scooters, and of the 800,000 4-wheel vehicles manufactured domestically in 1961, nearly 70 percent were trucks.

MITI considered further market liberalizations but tried as well to reduce competition in the industry, with limited success. In 1961, the Ministry asked car manufacturers to specialize in only one type of vehicle: minicars, sports cars and other specialty automobiles, or passenger cars with engine displacements above 500cc. This would have benefited Nissan and Toyota, since neither made mini-cars and specialty automobiles accounted for only a small percentage of sales. But it would have greatly restricted the future growth of Toyo Kogyo, Fuji Heavy Industries, Mitsubishi, and Daihatsu; they objected strenuously, and the Ministry had to shelve the idea. In 1963, MITI also failed to persuade Honda not to enter the 4-wheel vehicle field.[23]

As an alternative policy MITI attempted to promote mergers or tie-ups between domestic producers, but industry executives did not take these proposals very seriously either until a recession in 1965 seemed to indicate that rapid growth in the domestic market had come to a halt. While there was only one merger, between Nissan and Prince in 1966, MITI helped arrange several domestic tie-ups. Toyota became the largest shareholder in Hino during 1967 and in Daihatsu the following year, while Nissan became the major shareholder in Fuji Heavy Industries during 1968. Except for the merger between Nissan and Prince, however, these arrangements did not directly reduce competition or increase manufacturing scales because none of the newly affiliated firms offered the same product lines. Hino manufactured large trucks and Daihatsu made mini-vehicles, neither of which Toyota produced. Fuji Heavy Industries made mini-vehicles and aircraft, whereas Nissan did not. MITI officials had wanted to see mergers between some of the larger firms, but most companies preferred to retain their independence and deal with excess capacity by exporting.

The Closed Market
Although MITI and other ministries found it difficult to persuade managers to adopt all their suggestions, government officials never abandoned the most important form of assistance the domestic au-

tomakers received: direct or indirect protection from foreign competition until they had become internationally competitive in cost and quality. Even the September 1960 announcement that lifted import restrictions on several automotive products included a helpful redefinition of what constituted a "small" car in Japan. The Ministry of Transport had described this in 1949 as any vehicle with an engine displacement of up to 1500cc. The regulation was important because tariffs and commodity taxes, both for imported and domestic automobiles, varied with engine size, rising for larger classes. After 1960, the Ministry allowed a "small" vehicle to have an engine displacement of up to 2000cc, while MITI lowered the commodity tax on these cars from 30 to 15 percent and set import duties on all cars at a minimum of 34 percent.[24]

The result was that small Japanese cars remained protected from imports throughout the 1960s and much of the 1970s. Most of the automobiles Nissan and Toyota made had engines under 2000cc, while practically no American cars were this small and many European export models were above the limit. These measures, therefore, raised the prices of nearly all imported cars by a 34-percent duty and freed domestic automakers to develop models with engines up to 2000cc for the expanding Japanese market. These new regulations were especially significant because Nissan and Toyota had discovered during the late 1950s that, to sell cars in the American market, they had to equip vehicles with engines having displacements between 1500cc and 2000cc.

After Japanese firms had demonstrated the ability to export automobiles, MITI reopened the domestic market to foreign competition and investment—but only with great reluctance. It dropped import duties on standard-size cars slightly, to 28 percent in 1968 and to 17.5 percent in 1969, but did not lower the tariff on small cars until 1970 and then left it at a still high 20 percent. By this time, of course, Japanese automakers were no longer inefficient by world standards: Total production in Japan exceeded 5,000,000 units in 1970, of which 60 percent were cars and only 40 percent trucks and buses. Recognition of the industry's progress, and continued complaints from other nations, prompted MITI to lower duties on all car imports to 8 percent in 1972 and to eliminate them entirely in 1978. The Ministry also permitted foreign investment in 1970, for the first time since the 1930s. Chrysler immediately acquired a 15-percent interest in Mitsubishi Motors, while General Motors purchased 35 percent of Isuzu. In addition, Ford bought 24 percent of Toyo Kogyo during 1979, and General Motors acquired 5.3 percent of Suzuki's outstanding shares in 1981.[25]

But high tariffs and prohibitions on investment from abroad were only two of the measures the Japanese government used to restrict the market shares of foreign automakers. Commodity and weight taxes, levied on all automobiles after the early 1950s, penalized anyone buying a car with an engine displacement of over 2000cc. In 1983, for instance, the government taxed most cars with engines between 2000 and 6000cc (about 366 cubic inches) from 24,000 to 35,000 yen ($100 to $140), and cars with engines over 6000cc at least 52,000 yen ($215). The latter tax could be as much as 129,000 yen ($540) if the vehicle's length was under 3,048 millimeters (10 feet).[26]

Furthermore, until the Japanese government announced a revision of the system in March 1983, customs agents insisted on inspecting each imported vehicle and would not check one sample and grant a type certification, as the United States and European countries did, unless sales of a single model were of a volume comparable to domestic makes (a near impossibility under the old system). What is more, MITI allowed only agents registered in Japan to file import applications, rather than the manufacturers. Strict standards for vehicle safety and emissions also necessitated expensive alterations on most cars sold in Japan, doubling their prices after taxes and shipping costs, even though some of the regulations appeared to be arbitrary in the opinions of foreign automakers and governments.[27]

By the early 1980s, it had become the turn of Japan's trading partners to restrict automobile imports. New cars brought into the United States in 1984 faced a duty of only 2.7 percent (zero for Canada), although for trucks this was 25 percent. Until March 1985, the American government also regulated Japanese car imports by "voluntary" agreements, while the European Community taxed car imports at 10.4 percent and trucks from 11 to 22 percent.[28] The absence of tariffs in Japan since 1978, on the other hand, had no effect. Imports as a percentage of domestic automobile sales rose from 1 percent in 1977 to only 1.3 percent in 1979, before declining to an embarrassing 0.7 percent during 1981-1983—less than 40,000 vehicles in a market of 5,400,000 unit sales (see Appendix B). Neither did the spring 1983 revisions of import procedures result in a significant increase in car imports into Japan, although it was possible that American automakers might someday take better advantage of their Japanese partners to sell more automobiles in Japan or follow the example of Volkswagen, which arranged for Nissan to assemble one of its car models in a plant outside of Tokyo beginning in 1984.

But none of these developments will alter history. The Japanese government kept its domestic automobile market tightly closed precisely when sales were increasing rapidly each year and consumers had not yet determined their preferences. In the 1980s, unlike the 1950s and 1960s, Japanese cars were well made and inexpensive; it was unlikely that Japanese customers would switch, in large numbers, to imported automobiles that were more expensive and often inferior in quality. The only solution for Japan's competitors abroad, outside of continued restrictions on imports, was to upgrade product designs, reduce the costs of capital and labor, and improve techniques for managing personnel and production—innovations that the Japanese had taken half a century to introduce.

Chapter One

COMPANY ORIGINS AND TRUCK TECHNOLOGY TRANSFER

THE PREWAR LEGACY

American firms were clearly the world leaders in automobile technology and sales during the 1930s while Japan had no domestic industry to speak of and no apparent capability even to produce the steel and components that motor vehicles required. Yet a Japanese engineer and entrepreneur, Aikawa Yoshisuke (1880-1967), initiated the development of the Japanese car industry by establishing Nissan in 1933 to manufacture small vehicles that did not compete directly with the larger American imports. Within a few years he shifted to making trucks for the Japanese military, which enabled Nissan to set up "mass-production" facilities. Since the company was merely one subsidiary in a rapidly growing industrial group that Aikawa wanted to expand by entering new fields or areas that larger combines, such as Mitsui and Mitsubishi, had not yet entered, his rivals were Japan's old zaibatsu conglomerates, not General Motors or Ford.

Aikawa had previously worked in the United States and established relationships with several American engineers and businessmen. Since he also had relatively large financial resources at his disposal, he was able to choose a short cut to enter the automobile industry and then diversify his product lines. First, he acquired a fledgling Japanese producer of cars and trucks and merged it with a metal parts manufacturer that he had founded in 1911. To move into standard-size trucks during the mid-1930s, he hired American engineers and imported designs and an entire truck factory from the United States—creating a bias in Nissan toward American automated equipment and mass-production techniques that continued through the 1980s.

27

Toyota, with nowhere near the same financial resources during the 1930s, chose to rely more on general-purpose equipment and Japanese engineers or professors to design vehicles by studying foreign models selectively and then to set up production facilities after visiting foreign factories. Yet this experience eventually helped Toyota to introduce new models with advanced features more quickly than Nissan did and to manufacture them with equipment and techniques that proved to be more adaptable to the Japanese market. Nissan and the other Japanese automakers also struggled to modify American production technology to accommodate domestic needs, although Toyota was the most innovative in this area and perfected techniques that the entire industry came to imitate. At the same time, Nissan led in areas such as automation, computers, robotics, and statistical quality control; and only as both automakers learned from one another while competing domestically did the Japanese automobile industry evolve into its position as the world leader in production volume and manufacturing technology. However remote it may seem in the 1980s, the origins of this process—and of the strategies Nissan and Toyota followed for technology transfer and production management—date back to the Japanese truck industry of the 1930s.

THE NISSAN MOTOR COMPANY

The Nissan Combine
The name "Nissan" originated during the 1930s as an abbreviation used on the Tokyo stock market for the holding company that owned it, Nippon Sangyō (Japan Industries), which Aikawa had founded in 1928.[1] Although the history of this industrial group is little known outside Japan, at the end of World War II it included seventy-four firms; among the largest were Hitachi (paid-up capitalization of 435,500,000 yen), Nippon Mining (441,800,000), Nissan (75,000,000), and Nissan Chemical (52,600,000).[2] Japanese journalists and historians have referred to this combine as a "new zaibatsu" to distinguish it from older conglomerates such as Mitsui, Mitsubishi, and Sumitomo, which dated from the nineteenth century or earlier. Aikawa's achievement was especially impressive since, within merely one decade, he organized the largest single group of firms in metals, machinery, and chemicals within the Japanese empire, and accounted for 2.4 percent of domestic and overseas paid-up capital in 1937 (Table 7). A partnership with the government of Manchukuo (the name for the puppet regime that Japan installed in Manchuria

Table 7: Investments of the Four Largest Combines, 1937-1946 (1,000,000 yen, %)

	1937			1941			1946		
	A	B	C	A	B	C	A	B	C
Mitsui	670 (3.8%)	136 (3.7)	(8.6)	1,363 (4.7)	572 (6.3)	(10.7)	3,499 (10.5)	1,973 (13.0)	(12.5)
Mitsubishi	601 (3.4)	155 (4.3)	(4.5)	1,274 (4.3)	448 (4.9)	(6.5)	3,117 (9.3)	1,699 (11.2)	(13.2)
Aikawa[a]	434 (2.4)	179 (4.9)	(9.4)	2,066 (7.1)	999 (10.9)	(53.4)	1,792 (5.4)	1,055 (7.0)	(4.9)
Sumitomo	392 (2.2)	142 (3.9)	(1.4)	611 (2.1)	407 (4.5)	(6.1)	1,922 (5.8)	1,592 (10.5)	(13.3)
National Total	17,817 (100.0)	3,636 (100.0)	(0.9)	29,303 (100.0)	9,144 (100.0)	(5.0)	33,370 (100.0)	15,153 (100.0)	(4.1)

Source: Constructed from Mochikabu Kaisha Seiri Iin-kai, ed., Nihon zaibatsu to sono kaitai, II, 468-473.

Notes: A = Total domestic and overseas investments, defined as paid-up capital of subsidiaries and affiliates, with the parent firm or holding company controlling at least 10% of outstanding shares. Paid-up capital in holding companies is excluded.
B = Paid-up capital invested in machinery, metals, and chemicals.
C = Percentage of investments located in Japanese colonies (Manchuria, Korea, Taiwan, Southeast Asia). The national total is based on the investments controlled by the 10 largest combines in Japan.

[a]The name "Aikawa" was used in 1946 by the Holding Company Liquidation Commission to describe the combine consisting of companies controlled by Manchuria Investment Securities, K.K. Nissan, and other firms, such as Hitachi, that were part of the group headed by Aikawa Yoshisuke. His personal shareholdings, however, were minimal.

29

during 1932) increased this to 7.1 percent by 1941, surpassing both Mitsui (4.7 percent) and Mitsubishi (4.3 percent). But, since more than half of Aikawa's investments were either sold or lost in Manchuria during World War II, by 1945 the group had shrunk in size to rank behind Mitsui, Mitsubishi, and Sumitomo, before GHQ dissolved all holding companies during the Occupation.[3]

Aikawa, born in 1880, was the eldest son of a former samurai from what later became Yamaguchi prefecture. His father had little money, but his mother was the niece of Inoue Kaoru (1835-1915), one of Japan's most powerful politicians and an advisor to the Mitsui family. This proved to be an invaluable connection because it linked Aikawa to people of enormous wealth and political influence in Japan and abroad. Inoue also persuaded Aikawa to become an engineer and, after his nephew graduated from the mechanical engineering department of the University of Tokyo in 1903, he arranged for Aikawa to work as a factory laborer in Mitsui's machinery-manufacturing affiliate, Shibaura, the predecessor of Toshiba. Aikawa later switched to an iron casting shop for two years, before deciding to go to the United States to study the latest American casting techniques firsthand.[4]

In 1905, at Inoue's request, Mitsui Trading's office in New York City arranged for Aikawa to serve as an apprentice at the Gould Coupler Company of Depew, New York, near Buffalo, and to work briefly at the Erie Malleable Iron Company in Pennsylvania. At both firms Aikawa learned a technique called black-hearted iron casting, which had not yet been introduced into Japan. After returning to Tokyo in 1907, he convinced Inoue to help him found a new firm, based on this technology, to manufacture cast-iron tubing, couplings, and related products. Inoue, in turn, persuaded several relatives and associates, including the Mitsui, Kuhara, Fujita, and Kaijima families, to back his nephew financially.[5]

The Kaijimas, who owned a large coal mine and were related to Aikawa through the marriage of his younger sister, provided a site for a factory in the city of Tobata, in northern Kyūshū, the southernmost of Japan's four largest islands. They chose this location because of an arrangement made with a nearby government ironworks to obtain its surplus coke and pig iron. Aikawa was off again to the United States in 1908 to buy equipment, which he shipped back to Japan through Mitsui Trading in 1909. He formally incorporated Tobata Casting—the predecessor of both Nissan and Hitachi Metals—in 1910, with a paid-up capitalization of 300,000 yen ($150,000).[6]

While Tobata Casting got off to a slow start because there was no ready market or distribution system for the semi-finished goods that it produced, after World War I broke out Japan's inability to import cast-iron goods increased the orders to Tobata Casting enormously. By 1920 the firm had nearly 1000 employees and a capitalization of 2,000,000 yen ($1 million).[7] Aikawa then founded a holding company in 1922, Kyōritsu Enterprises, capitalized at 5,000,000 yen ($2,500,000), to acquire Tōa Electric Machinery, a telephone equipment manufacturer, and Yasugi Ironworks. Tōa Electric eventually became the nucleus of Hitachi's communications equipment division, while Yasugi merged with Tobata Casting before Hitachi absorbed Tobata in 1937 (this was separated again in 1956 as Hitachi Metals). Kyōritsu Enterprises did not have sufficient financial resources to take over additional firms, but managing a diversified concern provided Aikawa with the experience and confidence he would later find useful to expand his operations.[8] A new opportunity came in 1927 when Kuhara Mining, owned by his brother-in-law, Kuhara Fusanosuke (1869-1965), was on the verge of bankruptcy after being mismanaged following World War I.

Kuhara had started his firm in 1905 by purchasing a mine in the town of Hitachi, Ibaragi prefecture, a few miles northwest of Tokyo. By 1918, it was one of the biggest mining concerns in Japan, with a capitalization of 75,000,000 yen ($38,000,000) and a business that accounted for 50 percent of domestically produced silver, 40 percent of gold, and 30 percent of copper. But the price of copper and other metals fell sharply in the early 1920s while Kuhara made several poor investments, including a trading company that went bankrupt. To help him deal with these problems Kuhara brought in his brother-in-law as a company director in 1927 but then named Aikawa president the next year and left to join the cabinet of Prime Minister Tanaka Giichi as communications minister.[9] Despite a large number of debts, the mining company had huge reserves of gold and silver while its engineering and repair section, separately incorporated in 1920 as Hitachi, was beginning to develop into a leading electrical equipment and machinery manufacturer. With the support of the Fujita family, Aikawa obtained enough loans to keep the firm solvent as he reorganized Kuhara Mining's 15,000 stockholders into the Nippon Industries holding company and separated the mining division as Nippon Mining.[10]

While Mitsui, Mitsubishi, and other combines also contained holding companies, Nippon Industries was different in that it was not privately owned and its shares traded openly on the Tokyo stock market—allowing Aikawa to attract investment from the general public, sell stocks at high premiums, and expand into new capital-intensive industries such as electro-chemicals and automobiles.[11] Nippon Industries' stock holdings also grew enormously in value after the Japanese invasion of Manchuria in 1931 and the subsequent military build-up. In addition, huge government purchases of gold beginning in 1932, following a 1930 embargo on gold exports, sent the price of Nippon Mining's securities from an average of 22 yen per share in 1930 to 127 yen in 1934, and provided Aikawa with the money he needed to establish an automobile subsidiary.[12]

Aikawa's involvement in Manchuria was also related to his plans for the automobile business in that he promised the Japanese army to develop truck manufacturing, among other heavy industries, although his primary motivation was to escape corporate taxes in Japan.[13] He did this by transferring the holding company to Manchuria in December 1937 and registering it as a Manchurian enterprise, named Manchuria Heavy Industry Development Corporation (Manshū Jūkōgyō Kaihatsu Kabushiki Kaisha, abbreviated as Mangyō or Manchuria Development). Once in the colony, Aikawa encountered a host of problems that eventually persuaded him to retire from Manchuria Development when his term as president expired in 1942, although to maintain control over subsidiaries in Japan he founded Manchuria Investment Securities in 1941.[14] While stock sales reduced holdings in subsidiaries from the levels of the early 1930s, at war's end Aikawa's main holding company still owned 19 percent of Hitachi's outstanding shares (about half the number in 1937), and retained even higher ownership in Nippon Mining (38 percent) and Nissan (93 percent).[15]

After resigning from Manchuria Development in 1942, Aikawa continued to manage Manchuria Investment Securities, the Gisei Kai Foundation, which he established in 1942 as a conservative "think-tank" to plan for the postwar era, and K.K. Nissan, another holding company in Japan founded originally to maintain real estate in Tokyo.[16] He also served as an advisor to the Japanese cabinet from 1943 until the end of the war and in executive or advisory posts for subsidiaries in Japan. He was president of Nissan from 1933 to 1939 and then chairman (usually a nominal post in Japanese companies reserved for ex-presidents) during 1939-1941 and 1944-1945, although some firms resisted his efforts to control them. Aikawa was chairman of Hitachi as well from 1928 to 1941 and tried to involve this subsidiary more in automobiles and his other ventures, but the president, Odaira Namihei (1874-1951), who had worked in Hitachi from when it was a repair shop in 1905, proved difficult to influence and made further efforts to distance his company from Aikawa after taking over as chairman in 1941.[17]

Entrance into the Automobile Industry
Aikawa entered the automobile industry in 1933 by merging the automobile components department of Tobata Casting with a factory formerly owned by DAT Motors (originally called Kaishinsha), a small automobile importer, producer, and repair shop that dated back to 1911. Neither company had ties with the other until Tobata Casting purchased shares in DAT Motors during 1931, although the "DAT" logo was already nearly two decades old. DAT's founder, Hashimoto Masujirō, had named an in-house model line by taking the first letters of the surnames of his three major investors (Den Kenjirō, Aoyama Rokurō, and Takeuchi Meitarō). "Datson" came about when the firm introduced a new car in 1931 and wanted to suggest, in English, the "son of DAT." Nissan changed the latter part of the name to "sun" because of unfavorable connotations associated with "son" in Japanese, which can mean "damage" or "loss."[18]

Hashimoto designed the "DAT" during 1913-1914 by combining domestic and imported components, including a 2-cylinder, 10-horsepower engine (upgraded to 4 cylinders in 1916).[19] He completed only 6 units between 1913 and 1916, and none for the following two years as he converted the company into a car repair shop, placed it under the direction of a subordinate, and went to work for the Komatsu Ironworks, a manufacturer of machine tools and mining equipment. There Hashimoto learned better techniques for casting and forging, received a promotion to president, and visited the United States twice, where he bought 30 machines for manufacturing automobile parts. When the army offered subsidies to truck producers and users in March 1918, he decided to convert the DAT into a truck and to improve the casting of its engine by subcontracting this to Komatsu.

Hashimoto took until 1922 to perfect a truck design but used American nut and bolt sizes that military inspectors found unacceptable. He finally met the army's standards with a 1-ton truck in 1924 that allowed Kaishinsha (renamed DAT Motors in 1925) to receive a government subsidy, although Hashimoto was able to sell only around 2 units per month, since most Japanese preferred to buy Ford and Chevrolet models and there was little demand other than that which the subsidy system created. Low production forced him to cut his staff from 50 to 30 in 1924 and to merge in 1926 with another struggling automaker, Jitsuyō Motors, which the Kubota Ironworks had founded in 1919 to produce a motorized vehicle to replace the rickshaw.[20]

Kubota's chief designer was an American, William R. Gorham (1888-1949), who had studied electrical engineering at Heald Engineering College in San Francisco. Prior to arriving in Japan during 1918, he had manufactured airplane engines with his father, a sales agent for B.F. Goodrich in Asia, but they failed to get a contract from the U.S. government after World War I and closed down the business. Gorham had visited Japan previously and thought that he might find a market for his engines among the Japanese. While he was wrong about this and ended up establishing a shop outside Tokyo to produce 3-wheel vehicles, the Kubota family heard about the American, liked his models, and founded Jitsuyō Motors, capitalized at 1,000,000 yen ($500,000), to put them into production. Two of Gorham's friends from the United States also joined the company and took charge of layout and construction of a new plant in Osaka.

The Osaka factory, finished in 1920, employed 120 workers and had a capacity of 50 units per month and modern facilities for casting, tempering, machining, painting, grinding, vehicle assembly, and research. After a total output in 1921 of only 150 units, Gorham designed a 4-wheel model available as a car or a truck. But Jitsuyō Motors sold just 100 of these through 1923, mainly because Gorham had used an old-fashioned stick, rather than a wheel, for steering. The Kubota family complained that the trend in the automobile industry was changing and decided to switch to a round steering wheel in 1923. They also found a new designer, prompting Gorham and the other two Americans to accept Aikawa's offer to work full time for Tobata Casting.

Jitsuyō Motors still produced only 200 units of the new model between 1923 and 1926, bringing the company's total production since 1919 to around 450 units. Because the firm was losing money, army officials suggested that it merge with DAT Motors, which at least had the authorization to produce trucks and receive subsidies. The Kubota family gave in and the two automakers merged in 1926, although the new company made only 362 trucks during the next five years, all of which it sold to the army or to subsidized users. Gotō Takashi, later a managing director of Nissan, replaced Hashimoto in 1929 as chief designer and came out with an improved small car in 1931, the "Datson"—which Yamamoto Sōji (1888-1962), one of Aikawa's top assistants in Tobata Casting, saw and liked. Yamamoto, a former Chinese major at the Tokyo University of Foreign Languages who had joined the Kubota Ironworks in 1912, switched to Tobata Casting as a marketing specialist in 1926 but was interested in the automobile industry. Aikawa made him head of Tobata Casting's new automobile parts department in 1931 and told him to find a way to expand the business. After seeing Gotō's new model, Yamamoto persuaded Aikawa to buy a majority of DAT Motors' shares and went to the company himself as a director. Aikawa also transferred Gorham to DAT Motors to work with Gotō in the Osaka plant, although they only built 10 units of the new car during 1931-1932.[21]

Aikawa's interest in automobiles had been growing for more than a decade. While he had been in the United States in 1908, when Ford introduced the Model T, not until another trip to America in 1918 did he seriously consider manufacturing automobiles. After returning to Tokyo, he met Gorham to discuss the field but failed to convince the other stockholders in Tobata Casting to back a diversification into motor vehicles. Aikawa hired Gorham anyway in 1921 as a part-time consultant and in 1923 asked him to oversee the production of gasoline engines for boats and farm machinery. Gorham worked at this until 1931, when Aikawa decided to make automobile parts for the Japanese subsidiaries of Ford and General Motors.[22]

Aikawa's entrance into parts manufacturing came at the same time that the Japanese government was studying ways to promote the domestic automobile industry. In May 1931, a month before Tobata Casting acquired stock in DAT Motors, MCI formed a committee to encourage production and asked local firms to merge or cooperate in producing an automobile based on specifications it recommended. This led to the first serious attempts by Japanese companies to enter the industry. DAT Motors joined with the Ishikawajima Automobile Works and Tokyo Gas and Electric to develop a prototype, which they completed in March 1932. In March 1933, DAT Motors, minus its Osaka factory, which made the Datson, merged with Ishikawajima to form Automobile Industries, the predecessor of Isuzu. Tobata Casting subsequently took over the Osaka factory and manufacturing rights to the Datson line in exchange for the shares Aikawa bought in 1931. This was possible because Auto-

Figure 1: Formation of Nissan Motor

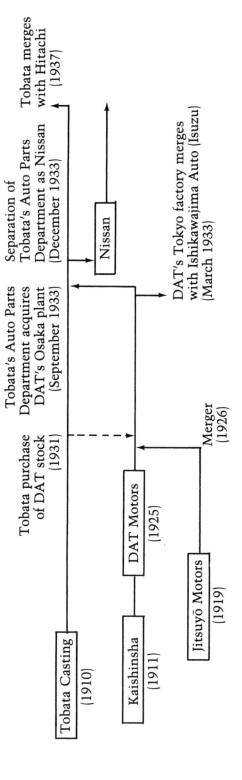

Source: Nissan Jidōsha sanjū nen shi.

mobile Industries only intended to produce standard-size and large trucks for the army. Then, in December, Aikawa separated the expanded automobile parts division of Tobata Casting and incorporated it as a new subsidiary, which he named Nissan Motor (Nissan) in 1934. He capitalized this at 10,000,000 yen ($4,000,000) and arranged for Nippon Industries to own 60 percent of the firm's outstanding shares and Tobata Casting the remainder[23] (Figure 1).

Since the majority of executives and stockholders in Tobata Casting still opposed the idea of producing automobiles because they did not believe there would be a market for vehicles made in Japan, Aikawa used Nippon Industries to buy out Tobata Casting's entire investment in June 1934.[24] Thereafter, the group's holding companies, and Hitachi, owned the automobile subsidiary (Table 8). Just before he went to Manchuria in 1937, Aikawa even tried to make Nissan a subsidiary of Hitachi but president Odaira and other Hitachi executives refused to go along with this, primarily because they were wary of Aikawa and suspected that he might involve them further in the Manchurian development scheme.[25]

The reluctance of Tobata Casting's directors and owners to support Aikawa's move into automobiles is not difficult to understand. Most Japanese businessmen and financiers hesitated to challenge Ford and General Motors, while DAT Motors had never been able to mass-produce automobiles and had always been close to bankruptcy. On the other hand, in 1932 DAT Motors was the most experienced automobile producer in Japan, even if on an extremely small scale, and the acquisition provided Aikawa with engineers, automobile designs, and manufacturing facilities.[26] In addition, even though Japan Ford and Japan GM dominated the industry, prospects for domestic producers were getting better. Not only was the government promoting local companies and considering protectionist measures, but Mitsui, Mitsubishi, and Sumitomo had declined, repeatedly, to enter the field, providing an opening for smaller companies, including Toyoda Automatic Loom. Aikawa was also willing to face considerable risk because the 10,000,000 yen ($4,000,000) that he invested in Nissan came entirely from premiums Nippon Industries earned by selling Nippon Mining stock. He considered this "interest-free capital" and intended to use it to diversify into automobiles and other new industries that seemed important to the nation and capable of providing a future source of earnings for the holding company.[27]

Aikawa expected to succeed because the Datsun was a small car

Table 8: Nissan Motor—Major Shareholders, 1934-1946

Year	Shareholders (%)
1934 (April)	Nippon Industries (59), Tobata Casting (39), Other (2)
(October)	Nippon Industries (99), Other (1)
1937 (October)	Nippon Industries (92), Dai-Ichi Mutual Life (8)
1938 (April)	Manchuria Development (48), Hitachi (43), Dai-Ichi Mutual Life (8), Other (1)
(October)	Manchuria Development (49), Hitachi (43), Dai-Ichi Mutual Life (8)
1941 (September)	K.K. Nissan (45), Manchuria Development (24), Manchuria Investment (23), Dai-Ichi Mutual Life (8)
1942 (March)	K.K. Nissan (45), Manchuria Development (2), Manchuria Investment (45), Dai-Ichi Mutual Life (8)
(September)	K.K. Nissan (45), Manchuria Development (0.1), Manchuria Investment (46.9), Gisei Kai (8)
1943 (March)	Manchuria Investment (47), K.K. Nissan (45), Gisei Kai (8)
1946 (August)	same as above

Source: Eigyō hōkokusho.

and American companies did not manufacture small vehicles; he even predicted initial sales of 5000 units per year and that these would grow to 10,000 or 15,000 units annually within five or six years. Despite anticipating losses from start-up costs and the need to set aside 20,000,000 yen ($8,000,000) from premiums to keep the automobile subsidiary operating, he also began building a new factory in Yokohama. In the meantime, he accepted parts orders from Japan Ford and Japan GM.[28] Aikawa was convinced that subcontracting would be a valuable experience because, if parts were not up to standards, the American subsidiaries would not buy them. Between November 1933 and October 1935, his company produced 521,000 yen (about $170,000) worth of components for Japan Ford (65 percent of the total), Japan GM (16 percent), as well as Harley Davidson and other firms. These consisted mainly of brake drums, wheel hubs, spring brackets, axle shafts, and u-bolts.[29] Aikawa continued DAT Motors' practice of importing some parts from the United States, but his goal was to to learn enough from subcontracting to make complete vehicles independently within five years.[30]

Another part of Aikawa's strategy to acquire technology and reduce financial risks was to explore a joint venture with an American firm. His first merger negotiations, conducted with Japan GM, went on for several years but ended after the government passed the 1936 automobile industry law.[31] Aikawa then began cooperating with Japan Ford in 1937 when Nissan was unable to provide an additional 2800 trucks that the army needed and had to get special permission from MCI for the American firm to assemble these. Although Japan Ford made another 5000 trucks for Aikawa in 1939 which he shipped to Manchuria, the American company was also talking with Toyota about a merger.[32] The army brought Aikawa into these discussions during 1939 as well, because Nissan was having trouble starting an automobile industry in Manchuria and making trucks that would stand up to American models. But Aikawa had plans to leave for Germany late in 1939 to ask Hitler for assistance in developing Manchuria, so he stepped down as president of Nissan, moved up to chairman, and appointed Murakami Masasuke (1878-1949) as his successor.

Murakami, a mechanical engineer trained at Kyoto University, was one of Aikawa's most senior subordinates. He had joined Tobata Casting in 1918 as a managing director and served as president during 1933-1937 before moving to Nissan as a director when Hitachi absorbed Tobata Casting. The new president surprised Aikawa by sending him a petition, signed by the other company directors, opposing the idea of a merger and stating their wish to remain independent. A confrontation had to wait until Aikawa returned, although by then war had broken out in Europe and the joint venture had to be scrapped because Ford decided to close its Japanese subsidiary.[33] With the permission of the Japanese government, however, Nissan hired many of Japan Ford's employees and confiscated most of the assembly machinery in its Yokohama plant and shipped it to Manchuria Motors, which Aikawa had founded during 1939.[34]

Direct Technology Transfer

Even without a merger, Aikawa acquired American technology during 1933-1938 by importing machinery, vehicle and engine designs, and hiring American engineers to set up production facilities. First, Tobata Casting concluded a contract in February 1933 with Mitsubishi Trading to import 200 machines and machine tools, including the latest American stamping and forging equipment. Nissan then spent the entire fall of 1933 and the first few months of 1934 constructing a plant in Yokohama that opened for Datsun production in April 1934. This plant used new machinery and some older equipment brought up from the Osaka factory, which Aikawa had converted into a casting shop for Datsun parts.[35]

American engineers directed all of Nissan's operations. Even before he formed the company, Aikawa had sent Gorham and another mechanical engineer, Albert Little, to the United States to recruit additional personnel. They hired 3 men to work full time during 1933-1935, including a well-known forging expert, George Motherwell, who later took a job with Opel in Germany. While Aikawa did not want to continue paying high salaries to the Americans and instructed his Japanese staff to take over as soon as possible, he decided during 1936-1938 to bring in more foreign engineers to set up production for standard-size trucks.[36]

The men Gorham and Little hired arrived in August 1933 and immediately went to work improving Nissan's machine processing, stamping, and forging shops. They not only taught the Japanese how to operate the equipment properly and to apply modern techniques for process control and standardization, but they also used upset forging and taper rolling machines, said to be the first in Japan, to produce several components that DAT Motors had imported. Since Nissan required more employees to operate the new equipment, productivity remained at merely 2 vehicles per year for each worker, although Aikawa also had to hire personnel because he adopted the American strategy of manufacturing as many materials and parts in house to achieve greater control over quality and standardization.

Nissan made considerable advances in the manufacturing of body shells and frames. Whereas DAT Motors had bought shells from Japanese suppliers and fitted them onto old-fashioned wooden frames, the Americans convinced Nissan to switch to steel frames and set up in-house body fabrication using the most advanced stamping-press equipment and techniques known in the United States. The 70-meter conveyor set up in Yokohama also allowed Nissan to become the first Japanese company to produce parts and finished automobiles on a machine-paced assembly line.[37] One problem was that the low quality of domestic steel materials made machine processing and heat treatment difficult, forcing Aikawa to import steel from the United States and Germany until Nissan completed a steel factory. But this provided as well a reason for the Americans to give the Japanese much-needed lessons on specialty steels, blast furnaces, die materials, Keller die-cutters, and continuous processing of steel materials from furnaces through upset forging and rolling.

Gorham, of all the foreign engineers, contributed the most to making Nissan an automobile manufacturer that used equipment and techniques comparable to those in American firms. As the welding instructor, he showed the Japanese how to connect rods, close wheel rims, and make gas tanks from thin sheet steel. He also took charge of layout and construction for the entire Yokohama plant after Aikawa sent him to study Ford's plant in Dearborn, Michigan, for several months during 1933-1934. Once Nissan finished the initial work on the Yokohama plant and was making almost all the Datsun parts in house, Aikawa brought Gorham back to Tobata Casting.[38]

Late in 1935, Aikawa decided that he wanted to manufacture standard-size trucks for the army, in addition to the Datsun line.[39] Rather than labor to produce these with the engineers and machinery at hand, he opted to buy more technology and assistance. In December he sent two of his best technical experts to the United States and Europe to look for manufacturing equipment and a vehicle design suitable for either a car or truck. One of these men, Nissan Director Asahara Genshichi (1891-1970), held a PhD in applied chemistry from the University of Tokyo and had joined Tobata Casting in 1931. The other, Managing Director Kubota Tokujirō (1891-), had attended the Osaka Higher Industrial School (later Osaka University) and was the nephew of the owner of the Kubota Ironworks. Kubota had served as president of DAT Motors during 1925-1931 and stayed with the Osaka factory when Tobata Casting took it over.[40]

Asahara had been handling the merger negotiations with Japan GM and was able to use this connection to visit plants that General Motors owned in the United States and Germany. He and Kubota also received introductions to several other automobile manufacturers but they made no progress in finding a suitable design, so Kubota went from their last stop in Germany to the United States, where he planned to continue looking. Asahara, who had gone to London on business for Nippon Industries, then received a cable from Aikawa telling him to go to Detroit, meet Kubota, and start negotiations with the Graham-Paige Company, the fourteenth largest automaker in the United States. After setting a company production record in 1929 of 62,600 units, Graham-Paige had run into financial problems by building too many factories. While it had already sold one truck line to Chrysler, which placed this under the Dodge nameplate, the company still had engine and truck designs for sale.[41]

Aikawa found out about Graham-Paige in February 1936 when the Minister of Finance and a personal friend, Ishiwatari Sōtarō, introduced him to the president of the Libbey-Owens-Ford Glass Co., the largest automobile glass manufacturer in the United States. Graham-Paige was not only one of its customers but the president, Joseph Graham, was a major shareholder in the glass company. The Libbey-Owens-Ford executives were in Japan to observe a Sumitomo affiliate, Nippon Plate Glass, which had imported a manufacturing process from the American firm and shown higher worker productivity, and happened to be discussing government regulations regarding royalty payments when Ishiwatari asked if they would help Nissan find a tie-up partner. The president suggested Graham-Paige, offered to meet with Aikawa, and arranged an appointment in April between Joseph Graham and Aikawa's representatives, Asahara and Kubota.[42]

Graham-Paige had an entire factory on West Warren Avenue in Detroit lying idle. Graham offered to sell all its equipment to Nissan along with designs for a 1.5-ton truck and a 6-cylinder engine. Asahara and Kubota immediately took the blueprints but wired Aikawa for instructions regarding the machinery. He replied that they should buy if Graham would sell at 10 percent above scrap value, provided that the machines seemed to be no more than two years old. Graham agreed, and they set the price at $180,000. In addition to manufacturing equipment, jigs, and tools for parts production, he gave Nissan a stamping press for free and arranged for a 30-year-old Nissan employee, Harashina Kyōichi, a mechanical engineer trained at the University of Tokyo, to spend several months at Graham-Paige to study its manufacturing operations.[43] For an extra $6000, Graham-Paige also built a wooden prototype of the truck while Asahara and Kubota were traveling back to Japan. This turned out to be a "cab-over" model, apparently copied from General Motors, which placed the truck cab over the engine rather than behind it. The advantage of this design was that it allowed more cargo space and a shorter turning radius than conventional trucks with cabs sitting behind the engines. Graham-Paige finished the prototype in July 1936 and shipped it directly to Yokohama.

The first blueprints from Graham-Paige arrived in May, a month after Asahara and Kubota signed the contract. Nissan then attempted to cast the engine block and cylinder heads at the Osaka factory, but unsatisfactory results convinced Aikawa to build a new casting shop on one of two sites that Nippon Industries owned in Yokohama. He contacted Kubota while he was still in the United States to buy equipment. Graham subsequently introduced Kubota to the Ferro Machine Casting Company of Cleveland, Ohio, which had built casting factories for Graham-Paige and Ford. The Ford plant was especially advanced since it cast parts such as crankshafts that most companies, including Nissan, produced through cruder forging methods. Toyota was also putting pressure on Nissan to improve its casting technology because Toyoda Kiichirō had sent an engineer to study Ford a few months earlier and had already started casting crankshafts.

Kubota signed a contract with Ferro in October that called for the American firm to send casting machinery to Yokohama, set it up, and teach Nissan engineers how to operate it. Then he returned to Japan by plane, along with several American engineers, and began work before the end of the month. They completed an initial phase of construction in January 1937 and in March began casting Datsun crankshafts and other parts. In addition, Kubota reached two other agreements while he was in the United States. One was with Spicer, a parts subcontractor for Graham-Paige that agreed to provide assembly blueprints and specifications for front and rear axles, a transmission, and propeller shafts for the Graham-Paige truck. Nissan paid only a small fee and no royalties. Another was with a Graham-Paige subcontractor for designs to make aluminum piston casts. Nissan paid a royalty of 10 cents per piston through the first 300 and then ceased payments.

Nissan also inherited Tobata Casting's 1933 contract with Mitsubishi Trading. Aikawa had usually dealt with Mitsui Trading while Inoue Kaoru was alive, but he switched to Mitsubishi after it became the Japanese sales agent for several American machine tool manufacturers. Mitsubishi then purchased and shipped $30,000,000 worth of machinery and tools between 1933 and 1938, for which Nissan

Table 9: Nissan Motor Assets and Liabilities, 1934-1946 (1000 yen)

Year	Land	Buildings	Machinery/ Equipment	Tools/ Fixtures	Total Fixed Assets	Total Assets	Paid-up Capital	Total Liabilities
1934	761	441	2,382	38	3,621	6,113	5,015	1,098
1936	1,008	1,553	7,327	1,663	11,554	14,871	10,642	4,229
1938	3,158	2,847	13,283	6,188	30,357	48,016	11,600	36,416
1940	3,158	3,420	16,213	4,860	33,503	74,031	34,859	39,172
1942	6,055	3,950	16,240	6,034	48,748	92,079	44,961	47,118
1944	13,042	9,704	16,889	6,153	79,085	158,474	86,215	72,259
1945	14,045	24,021	24,807	5,694	97,194	266,984	88,952	178,032
1946	15,349	28,298	32,221	8,025	108,945	538,325	77,485	460,840

Sources: Eigyō hōkokusho *and* Nissan jidōsha sanjū nen shi.

Note: *Total fixed assets do not always equal the sum of the columns on the left because some construction projects in process are included only under total assets.*

44

paid a commission of 1.5 percent, making Aikawa Mitsubishi Trading's largest customer during the 1930s outside of its own group. In addition to the Graham-Paige equipment and Ferro's casting machinery, during 1936-1938 alone Mitsubishi imported for Nissan several drill presses from the Avery Drilling Company in Cincinnati, Ohio, 15 automatic lathes for making screws from the Gridley Machine Company in New Britain, Connecticut, 3 forging machines from the National Machinery Company in Ohio, and equipment to expand truck production and manufacture artillery shells.[44] Nissan's fixed assets nearly tripled between 1936 and 1938 as a result of these purchases and land transferred from Nippon Industries, while the loans that Aikawa arranged caused the automaker's total liabilities to rise 9-fold in two years—a rate of increase more rapid than during the later years of World War II (Table 9).

Approximately 15 engineers came from Graham-Paige to help Nissan, in addition to 5 from Ferro and Spicer. Several of these men stayed two and three years because of various problems that developed.[45] The new equipment, and components imported from Graham-Paige and the other American firms, arrived late, while Japanese engineers had no experience operating the specialized American machine tools. Another difficulty was the lack of standardization in specifications and quality between parts that Nissan made in house and bought locally or imported. Aikawa had to abandon ambitious production plans for 1937 after Nissan completed only 1356 of the cab-over trucks, including 500 made from parts Graham-Paige sent.[46] But Nissan made over 8000 standard-size trucks the following year, along with more than 8000 Datsun models, establishing the company as Japan's first "mass producer" of automobiles (Table 10).

It was particularly frustrating to translate the American blueprints into metric. "I had a heck of a time," recalled Kawazoe Sōichi, who took charge of this, since he had been educated at the University of Dayton and the Massachusetts Institute of Technology. Another problem was that 80 percent of the machinery and tools Nissan acquired to manufacture the cab-over were used; by the time they arrived in Japan it was necessary to do considerable repair work. Nissan also bought 13 new Gleason gear-cutters; American engineers came to show the Japanese how to use them, but the mathematics was too complicated for the regular machine-operators. Two Japanese engineers with particularly good backgrounds in mathematics had to learn how to use the machines first and then teach the other workers.[47]

Table 10: Nissan Production, 1934-1945 (vehicles, employees, %)

	Cars	Standard Trucks[a]	Small Trucks	% Trucks	Total Production	Average Employees	Units Employees
1934	650	0	290	30.9	940	1,218	0.8
1935	2,631	0	1,169	30.8	3,800	1,914	2.0
1936	2,562	0	3,601	58.4	6,163	2,874	2.1
1937	4,068	1,384	4,775	60.2	10,227	5,804	1.8
1938	4,151	8,249	4,191	75.0	16,591	9,057	1.8
1939	1,370	13,786	2,625	92.3	17,781	9,173	1.9
1940	1,162	13,991	772	92.7	15,925	7,706	2.1
1941	1,587	17,194	907	91.9	19,688	7,570	2.6
1942	871	15,974	589	95.0	17,434	7,744	2.3
1943	566	9,958	229	94.7	10,753	?	—
1944	9	7,074	0	99.9	7,083	?	—
1945	0	2,001	0	100.0	2,001	?	—
Total	19,627	89,611	19,148	84.7%	128,386		

Sources: Nissan Jidōsha sanjū nen shi *and* Nijūichi seiki e no michi: Nissan Jidōsha gojū nen shi.

Note: [a]*Includes buses, which accounted for 2.4% of Nissan's production between 1934 and 1945.*

Design Modifications

Design flaws in the Graham-Paige truck also preoccupied Nissan between 1937 and 1940. The truck performed terribly on Manchuria's rough, dirt roads and had to be modified, but Nissan engineers were not sure what to do, so in 1937 Kubota hired a professor at Osaka University, Maeda Riichi (1896-), to examine the truck. Maeda had studied automotive design in London and Detroit and at the Massachusetts Institute of Technology during 1929-1931. After he agreed to come to Yokohama, Kubota set up a department of research, which he headed personally, and made Maeda chief of the testing section.[48]

The most serious defect in the cab-over, dubbed the model 80, was the design of the frame. The wheelbase (the distance between the front and rear axles) was too short, and the front of the vehicle was too heavy. To make matters worse, the front tread (the distance between the two front wheels) was wider than the rear tread. On paved roads the truck rode smoothly and had the advantage of a short turning radius and overall length, and a relatively large cargo area. But on bad roads the vehicle vibrated so much when accelerating that the suspension system tended to break, along with the rear axle, which was too weak for heavy loads or rough terrain. Even on muddy or soft dirt roads the rear wheels rubbed against the grooves in the road that the front tires dug, making the vibrations worse, while the cab sat over the engine and was so high that army drivers found the truck hard to steer. Nor was the air filter capable of keeping road dust from entering the engine and damaging the pistons, rings, and bearings, though Maeda solved this problem by having Nissan's design department copy an air cleaner made especially for American farm trucks.[49]

The engine, fortunately, was a sturdy side-valve design displacing 3670cc, with an output of 85 horsepower at 3400 revolutions per minute (rpm). It had 7 bearings, 2 more than in most 6-cylinder engines made in the United States, because Graham-Paige had wanted to use the block for heavy-duty diesel engines.[50] With only minor modifications of the compression ratio Nissan used this engine for the next twenty years, until an American consultant who had designed engines for Willys-Overland, Donald D. Stone, widened the cylinder bore and relocated the valves overhead, a more efficient arrangement that American and European automakers (as well as Toyota) had adopted in the mid-1930s.[51] This modification produced higher compression inside the combustion chambers and more

Table 11: Nissan Standard-Size Trucks, 1937-1966

Year	Model	Max. Load/Speed (kg /km-hr.)	Dimensions (mm)				Tread (mm)		Weight (kg)	Turning Radius(m)	4-Speed Trans.	Engine	
			Length	Width	Height	Wheelbase	Front	Rear				Model	cc
1937	TS80	2000/?	4669	1905	?	2641	1664	1651	?	5.8	slide	AT	3670
	TL80	"	5512	2035		3251	"	1600		6.9	"	"	"
1941	180	4000/?	5895	2000	2140	4000	1500	1600	2368	8.0	"	"	"
1950	180	"/75	6473	2180	2150	"	1544	1670	2860	"	"	NT85	"
1952	380	" / "	6858	"	2160	"	1530	"	2970	7.8	"	NA	"
1953	480	4500/79	"	2240	2200	"	1568	1672	3290	"	"	NB	"
1956	580	5000/85	7008	"	2250	"	1560	1678	3460	"	"	NC	3956
1959	680	"/97	7085	2275	2310 2415	4200	1602	"	3625	8.2	synchro-mesh	P	"
1969	780	6000/95	7250	2365		4150	1625	1700	4005	8.1	"	"	"

Source: Nissan Jidōsha sanjū nen shi *and* Nissan Jidōsha shashi.

48

horsepower, allowing Nissan to continue placing the engine in its standard-size trucks until management discontinued the model line in 1973 (Table 11). In 1939, however, the cab-over was the chief reason why Aikawa was interested in a tie-up with Japan Ford: He wanted to obtain a quick replacement. After negotiations broke down, Aikawa had no choice but to order Asahara to replace the model 80.

Nissan engineers started work on a new design toward the end of 1939, completed a prototype in mid-1940, and began producing the new version, which Maeda designated the model 180, in January 1941. The 180 was ready so soon because Nissan was able to use the old engine and mountings, along with most other components, and only had to design the cab and frame from scratch. Lengthening the wheelbase and making the front tread 100mm narrower than the rear tread corrected the earlier problem in the frame. Nissan also strengthened the suspension to handle a 40-percent increase in load capacity and eliminated the cab-over design entirely by placing the cab behind the engine, in the conventional style. While this increased the turning radius, the longer body compensated for the decrease in cargo space. The army liked the new model, and Nissan made it, with no modifications, until 1950. The basic frame remained the same until 1959.[52]

Despite these problems and forecasting five years of losses for the automobile subsidiary, Aikawa misjudged prospects for its short-term earnings, since Nissan was profitable early on and did not show a deficit until the last few months of World War II. Between 1935 and 1944, the company averaged a pre-tax profit rate of 9.3 percent on paid-up capital and 7.5 percent on sales. The expense of shifting to trucks reduced earnings drastically after 1936, and Hitachi and Nippon Mining, in comparison, had earnings twice as high as Nissan's during the 1930s. Yet Nissan (and Toyota) disproved the fears of old zaibatsu executives and demonstrated that it was possible to manufacture automobiles profitably in Japan—at least within a controlled market (Table 12).

The Military Connection: Pros and Cons
While contacts in the military helped Aikawa to sell all the trucks he could produce, after 1938 the army prevented Nissan from manufacturing Datsun cars and interfered with the management of group firms in Japan and Manchuria. Clashes with military officials even resulted in the resignations of two close associates whom Aikawa had chosen to head Nissan: Murakami Masasuke and Asahara Gen-

Table 12: Nissan and Toyota—Financial Performance, 1934-1945 (1000 yen, %)

	Nissan					Toyota				
FY	Paid-Up Capital	Sales	Pre-Tax Profits	Profits Capital (%)	Profits Sales (%)	Paid-Up Capital	Sales	Pre-Tax Profits	Profits Capital (%)	Profits Sales (%)
1934	10,079	2,443	96	1.0	3.9					
1935	10,562	6,192	811	7.7	13.1					
1936	11,000	8,577	1,060	9.6	12.4					
1937	11,475	28,403	1,229	10.7	4.3	9,000	7,794	−224	—	—
1938	33,341	69,300	3,665	11.0	5.3	10,500	23,428	827	7.9	3.5
1939	34,558	83,676	3,736	10.8	4.5	18,750	58,750	2,971	15.8	5.1
1940	35,542	72,847	3,305	9.3	4.5	27,750	66,818	1,859	6.7	2.8
1941	44,458	117,763	4,228	9.5	3.6	30,000	91,308	5,460	18.2	6.0
1942	58,354	95,235	4,820	8.3	5.1	33,750	93,612	5,629	16.7	6.0
1943	78,348	66,658	5,786	7.4	8.7	58,145	82,968	10,078	17.3	12.1
1944	88,007	60,363	7,952	9.0	13.2	71,290	129,572	16,099	22.6	12.4
1945	72,445	56,116	−13,886	—	—	71,290	79,067	631	0.9	0.8

Sources: Nissan Jidōsha sanjū nen shi and Toyota Jidōsha sanjū nen shi.

shichi. Furthermore, because Nissan had become a large subsidiary in a major combine by the end of the war, GHQ purged everyone on the board of directors during the Occupation. So many top executives came and went at Nissan under Aikawa's direction or during the Occupation that no less than 7 men served as president between 1933 and 1951, giving Nissan a reputation for unstable management and adding to the shortage of skilled managers after the war (Table 13).

Murakami, who had worked for Aikawa since 1918, became president of Nissan in 1939 and quit three years later in a dispute regarding the chairmanship of the automobile industry control association. Military officials had chosen Suzuki Shigeyasu, president of Isuzu (Diesel Industries), over Murakami because he had been a lieutenant general and they wanted an army man to supervise

Table 13: Nissan Top Executives, 1933-1985

Term	President	Term	Chairman
1933-1939	Aikawa Yoshisuke		
1939-1942	Murakami Masasuke	1939-1941	Aikawa Yoshisuke
1942-1944	Asahara Genshichi		
1944-1945	Kudō Haruto	1944-1945	Aikawa Yoshisuke
1945	Murayama Takeshi		
1945-1947	Yamamoto Sōji		
1947-1951	Minoura Taiichi		
1951-1957	Asahara Genshichi		
1957-1973	Kawamata Katsuji	1957-1962	Asahara Genshichi
1973-1977	Iwakoshi Tadahiro	1973-1985	Kawamata Katsuji
1977-1985	Ishihara Takashi		
1985-	Kume Yutaka	1985-	Ishihara Takashi

Sources: Nissan Jidōsha shashi *and* yūka shōken hōkokusho.

the industry. Most private executives supported Murakami since he was president of the largest automaker, but Suzuki refused to step aside and the army stuck by its appointment. Murakami felt he had been mistreated and, citing poor health, he resigned as president of Nissan in February 1942.[53]

Asahara succeeded Murakami after serving as a director and then executive director of Nissan since 1933. He is a central character in the company history not only because he was closely involved in the tie-up with Graham-Paige but because he returned to Nissan during 1951-1957 as president and guided the firm through another tie-up with Austin. But, unlike Aikawa, who was more interested in building empires than automobiles, Asahara was a scientist and an academic. After graduating from the chemistry department of the University of Tokyo in 1915, he stayed on as a graduate student and lecturer, receiving a PhD in 1925. From 1917 to 1922, he studied applied chemistry in the United States and Britain, mainly at Cornell University, while maintaining an affiliation with the Riken Institute of Physical and Chemical Research until 1931 as a metallurgy specialist.

Aikawa heard about Asahara when he was a graduate student working on steel properties. Since he thought the research might prove valuable to Tobata Casting someday, he gave Asahara money to continue his education on the condition that, if he left academia, he consider a job with Aikawa's company. Asahara was not particularly interested in business but by 1931 he was married, with four children, and finding it difficult to support a family on the Institute's meager stipend. He finally agreed to join Tobata Casting and switched to Nissan in 1933.[54] Aikawa then made Asahara a director of the holding company, Hitachi, and several other subsidiaries, using him to evaluate and oversee the larger manufacturing enterprises in the combine.[55] While Aikawa remained as the president of Nissan from 1933 to 1939, he placed Asahara in charge of technical matters and made him manager of the Yokohama plant during the 1930s.[56]

Asahara's resignation in 1944 followed a confrontation with the prime minister, General Tōjō Hideki, concerning the system of army supervisors for military suppliers. Nissan, which had become an official supplier in December 1943 after the army asked Aikawa to produce aircraft engines, made only 1600 between 1943 and 1945, but a controversy erupted when an officer assigned to the Yokohama plant did not like the way Nissan manufactured pistons and refused to give his approval. The plant manager, Harashina Kyōichi, tried to negotiate the matter; he got nowhere and contacted President Asahara. Asahara told Aikawa, who was serving as a cabinet advisor and had direct access to Tōjō. Aikawa then convinced the prime minister to order the supervisor to pass the engines and to change the system so that suppliers would have some say in choosing their supervisors.[57]

While MCI's wartime replacement, the Ministry of Munitions, did not oppose this ruling, other top officials in the army persuaded Tōjō to reverse his decision and the system continued as before. To make matters worse, the army officially censored Asahara for Nissan's poor performance. Asahara wanted to protest but Aikawa advised him not to oppose the prime minister as well as the army and to resign quietly, which he did in September 1944. Aikawa then returned to the post of Nissan chairman and appointed an advisor to the company, Kudō Haruto, who had served briefly in 1934 as a director, to replace Asahara as president.

Asahara was disappointed at losing his job, yet both he and Aikawa had become bored with manufacturing trucks for the military. Aikawa appeared to lose interest after the government stopped him from making Datsun cars, while Asahara, during the 1940s, even considered joining Toyota to start another automobile company.[58] Relations between the two men remained cordial after Asahara left, although they deteriorated during the 1950s when Aikawa pressured Asahara and the top executives of Hitachi, Nippon Mining, and other former subsidiaries to sell company assets and contribute to his political campaign fund for the Diet and to his lobbying effort for small and medium-size firms. Asahara insisted that this would be a misuse of company assets and refused.[59]

Postwar Continuity: Group Ties and Company Personnel
While Aikawa's combine decreased in size after 1941, even before GHQ dissolved it during the Occupation, all the companies formerly in the group reorganized during the 1950s—nominally. In 1956, twelve firms, led by Nissan and Hitachi, agreed to form an association to provide sports and recreational facilities for their employees, and to coordinate advertising and procurement. The president of Hitachi directed the organization until Kawamata Katsuji, then the president of Nissan, took over in 1971 (Table 14). During the early 1980s, 125 member firms represented nearly 300,000 employees, although the group demonstrated little coordination compared to companies formerly in the Mitsui, Mitsubishi, and Sumitomo zaibatsu, and func-

Table 14: Old Nissan Group, 1982

Main Company	Employees	Subsidiaries		Total Employees
		Firms	Employees	
Nissan Motor	62,130	13	17,043	79,173
Nissan Diesel	8,000	2	1,040	9,040
Hitachi	72,277	32	47,471	119,748
Hitachi Shipbuilding	17,019	6	3,845	20,864
Hitachi Metals	8,800	3	905	9,705
Hitachi Cable	5,125	4	924	6,049
Hitachi Chemical	4,287	9	4,681	8,968
Hitachi Construction	4,300	—	—	4,300
Hitachi Sales	3,700	2	210	3,910
Nippon Mining	5,875	13	5,190	11,065
Nissan Chemical	1,736	11	1,232	2,968
Nissan Fire & Marine	3,106	4	849	3,955
Nippon Suisan	4,640	2	531	5,171
Nippon Oils & Fats	3,119	3	467	3,586
Nippon Reizō	2,900	5	886	3,786
Nissan Construction	1,625	—	—	1,625
Totals	208,639	109	85,274	293,913

Source: Nissan Konwa Kai kaihō *21: 33-66 (August 1982).*

tioned primarily as a social organization, with annual meetings of company presidents supplemented by monthly branch gatherings and committee meetings held at 55 local chapters.[60]

Ties between Nissan and Hitachi, though strained at times during the 1930s and 1940s, also continued after the war through mutual procurement and technical cooperation regarding electrical and electronic components for automobiles, automated manufacturing equipment, and computer hardware and software. The two firms were linked as well through the Industrial Bank, which had close ties with MITI and the Ministry of Finance, and had provided funds during and after World War II to numerous firms that were not part of industrial groups having their own financial institutions, including Nissan, Hitachi, Nippon Mining, and Nissan Chemical. In addition, the Industrial Bank ranked as a major shareholder in eleven firms belonging to the old Nissan combine, led by Nissan and Hitachi.[61] (Table 15).

Aikawa's various activities in Japan and Manchuria landed him in prison for twenty-one months after World War II on suspicion of war crimes. Although GHQ acquitted and released him in September 1947, the American authorities barred Aikawa from holding a public or corporate office. GHQ also dissolved the Gisei Kai foundation for its right-wing associations, but he subsequently formed another group to lobby on behalf of small and medium-size businesses, and served in the upper house of the Diet before retiring after an election defeat in 1959.[62] Aikawa retained a modest fortune after World War II and kept himself occupied with Diet politics, financing small businesses and road construction, and serving Prime Minister Kishi Nobusuke, a former employee in Manchuria, as a special ambassador, before dying in 1967 at the age of 86.[63]

In his later years, Aikawa is said to have been proud of the firms he established but frustrated that he was unable to regain control of them after 1945.[64] As a youth, he had looked up to Inoue Kaoru and, as a young man, he had admired the founders of American conglomerates such as U.S. Steel. The books that most influenced his life were written by Andrew Carnegie and his contemporaries about business empires, wealth, and the theory of natural selection.[65] Aikawa became interested in automobiles because it was a new industry that the "old zaibatsu" did not dominate and which seemed capable of providing a stable, future source of revenue for his holding company; but the "new zaibatsu" he created was primarily a collection of independent companies with different traditions and man-

Table 15: Industrial Bank Holdings in Former Nissan-Group Firms, 1984 (percentage of shares held, shareholder ranking)

Company	Percentage	Rank
Nissan Motor	6.1	1
Hitachi	2.6	3
Nissan Chemical	4.8	3
Nissan Diesel	2.7	5
Nissan Fire & Marine	5.0	6
Nissan Auto Body	4.8	2
Nippon Mining	4.8	1
Nippon Suisan	4.7	2
Hitachi Metals	1.9	3
Nihon Radiator	2.0	7
Hitachi Cable	1.3	7

Source: Tōyō Keizai, Kaisha shikihō *(June 1984).*

agements. He gained control through stock acquisitions and placing trusted subordinates in strategic executive positions "as if he were playing a chess game."[66] The result looked impressive on paper, as did the membership list of the former group in the 1980s, but it had little cohesiveness even prior to World War II.

Executives in Hitachi, Nissan, and other firms came to resent Aikawa's schemes and treatment of them, and they used the opportunity brought about by the removal of Nippon Industries to Manchuria to assert their independence. There was little that Aikawa could do about this, even after he returned to Japan in 1942; he simply had too many subsidiaries to manage. He followed Nissan more carefully than other subsidiaries, but had to leave the firm during the Occupation. By the time the American authorities ended the purge of businessmen in 1951, he was 71; Nissan's new chief executives also preferred to sever their contacts with Aikawa and other members of his immediate family.[67] For these reasons, Nissan never acquired the character of a "family-owned" firm that Tobata Casting had once possessed or that managers of Nissan's main domestic rival—Toyota—utilized so effectively from the 1930s through the 1980s.

Yet Aikawa remains a key figure in the history of the Japanese automobile industry. He pioneered the direct transfer of truck technology from the United States to Japan and created the first domestic automaker capable of mass-producing vehicles that compared favorably with American models. The company he left behind then grew rapidly after World War II under the guidance of executives and engineers that Aikawa, and his subordinates, had chosen. Even in 1965, nearly 90 percent of the members on Nissan's board of directors had joined the company before 1945. This figure was still 50 percent in 1971 and 20 percent as late as 1981, including Nissan President Ishihara Takashi (Table 16).

Table 16: Year of Company Entry for Nissan Executives, 1955-1984

Year	Total Number of Executives	Year of Company Entry	
		1934-1940	1941-1945
1955	11 (100%)	9 (82%)	0
1960	17	14 (82%)	0
1965	24	21 (88%)	0
1971	32	16 (50%)	0
1975	39	11 (28%)	4 (10%)
1981	46	5 (11%)	4 (9%)
1984	45	3 (7%)	2 (4%)

Source: Yūka shōken hōkokusho.

Note: Executives include directors and higher officers.

THE TOYOTA MOTOR COMPANY

The Toyoda Concern

Toyoda Sakichi (1867-1930), a carpenter's son who became a famous loom inventor and entrepreneur, did not found Toyota but provided his eldest son, Kiichirō (1894-1952), with the idea and the money. Sakichi established his first company in 1918, Toyoda Spinning and Weaving, capitalized at 5,000,000 yen ($2,500,000) and based on a factory he had built a few years earlier to produce high-quality thread for the automatic loom that he was developing. When this machine was ready for production in 1926, Sakichi separated the loom manufacturing department as Toyoda Automatic Loom and capitalized it at 1,000,000 yen ($460,000). This soon became the main firm in the Toyoda concern. Sakichi then sold the patent rights for the automatic loom to the Platt Brothers of Great Britain for 100,000 pounds, worth about 1,000,000 yen in Japan, and gave the entire sum to Kiichirō to experiment with motor vehicles.

While Sakichi had become interested in cars during a trip to the United States in 1910 that lasted four months, his specialty was cotton thread and loom-machinery production; not until Ford and General Motors established subsidiaries in Japan during the 1920s did it occur to him to have Kiichirō study automobiles. Kiichirō, a mechanical engineer trained at the University of Tokyo, had worked for his father since graduating from college in 1920. Although his thesis dealt with pneumatic pumps, he soon became a specialist in casting technology and machine-parts manufacturing for Toyoda Spinning and Weaving. When Sakichi established Toyoda Automatic Loom in 1926, Kiichirō became a managing director in charge of loom production, and then headed the negotiations with the Platt Brothers—which gave him an opportunity to spend several months during 1929-1930 visiting automobile plants in Great Britain.[68]

Kiichirō was reluctant to take up automobile manufacturing, and probably would not have, except that his father repeated this request before he died in 1930.[69] Japan Ford and Japan GM so completely dominated the market that not even the largest combines in Japan were willing to risk an investment in the automobile industry. Sakichi was unable to compete with these zaibatsu financially but he had personal reasons for wanting his son to move into the field. He had been unable to make Kiichirō president of Toyoda Automatic Loom or the heir to his personal fortune, even though Kiichirō was his eldest male child, because in 1915 Sakichi had adopted Kodama Risaburō (1884-1952), the husband of his eldest daughter and the younger brother of the head of Mitsui Trading's branch in Nagoya, Kodama Kazuo, to strengthen his ties with the Mitsui group. Sakichi became indebted to Kazuo when Mitsui Trading financed his move during 1914 into cotton spinning using a machine he had invented. Since Risaburō was older and, technically, the new "eldest" son, Sakichi made him president of Toyoda Automatic Loom and asked Kiichirō to serve as his subordinate.[70]

Entrance into the Automobile Industry
Risaburō opposed an investment in automobiles as being too risky, given the amount of capital expenditure required, American competition, and the small size of the domestic market. Kiichirō still had enough authority to establish an automobile department within Toyoda Automatic Loom during 1933, although he had to plead before the board of directors in August 1933 for more money after spending the 1,000,000 yen Sakichi gave him, and another 4,000,000 ($1,000,000) as well, without moving beyond the experimental stage. At first Risaburō refused to provide any more funds, but his wife, Kiichirō's elder sister, persuaded him to honor Sakichi's wish that Kiichirō move into the automobile business. He then agreed to lower dividends and triple Toyoda Automatic Loom's capitalization to 3,000,000 yen in 1934 and to double it again to 6,000,000 in 1935, with 4,000,000 yen of the new funds going to the automobile and steel manufacturing departments.[71]

Once the Japanese government passed the 1936 automobile industry law, Risaburō saw that the venture could be profitable and decided to cooperate fully with his brother-in-law. Subsequently they separated the automobile department from Toyoda Automatic Loom; Risaburō took the post of Toyota president and moved up to chairman in 1941 when Kiichirō became the chief executive.[72] The new company's name came from a contest held in 1936 to find a suitable logo to replace "Toyoda," which means "abundant rice field." From 27,000 suggestions, Kiichirō and other members of the automobile department chose "Toyota," an alternate reading of the two ideographs that make up the family name, for its clarity in sound and potential advertising appeal.[73]

The independent establishment of Toyota was financially motivated. Early in 1937, Toyoda Automatic Loom began constructing an automobile plant with a planned monthly capacity of 1500 vehicles. Although Kiichirō expected this to cost 30,000,000 yen before it was done, Toyoda Automatic Loom's capitalization was merely

6,000,000 yen. The factory seemed beyond its fund-raising capabilities, so Risaburō and Kiichirō agreed to incorporate the automobile department to attract additional investors, which it did. The restrictions on foreign producers as well as potential military demand helped them to raise 9,000,000 yen to capitalize Toyota in 1937. Several banks arranged another 25,000,000 yen in loans, and the Mitsui group provided about half of all outside funds through stock purchases and bank credit.[74]

Kiichirō could have abandoned the automobile industry after his father died or when he ran out of money in 1933. No doubt he felt loyalty toward his father, and this encouraged him to continue. But entering a new and important field was also much more challenging than supervising loom production in what had become his brother-in-law's company.[75] Though Kiichirō was not a brilliant inventor or an entrepreneur like his father, he was a highly competent engineer who enjoyed solving technical problems. He was also a talented manager and chose excellent assistants. Nor was he reluctant to delegate authority or defer to others more expert than he in specialized areas of design, manufacturing, marketing, or finance.

Kiichirō predicted in 1936 that Toyota would make, within a few years, automobiles that were "cheaper and better than foreign imports."[76] He was wrong about this, since Toyota needed until the mid-1950s to make trucks comparable to those that Nissan or American manufacturers made, and another decade or more to produce cars that would compete favorably with European models. He also did not foresee that the Japanese government would prohibit passenger-car production in 1939, a ruling that both he and Aikawa Yoshisuke opposed, and which delayed their progress in car development. Kiichirō had just completed work on a mid-size car and sold 400 to the army for use in Manchuria when MCI announced the restriction. Like Aikawa, however, he had realized several years earlier that the largest market in Japan was for standard-size trucks and that he would have to produce these to survive as an automobile manufacturer. Kiichirō hardly got started as a car producer prior to 1945, since Toyota's annual car output peaked in 1937 at merely 577 units, compared to more than 3000 trucks (Table 17).

Indirect Technology Transfer
The importance of the prewar period for Toyota was not car production but product development through indirect technology transfer—some have called this "reverse engineering"—and the experience

Table 17: Toyota Production and Industry Share, 1935-1945 (vehicles, employees, %)

Year	Trucks	Cars	Buses	Total	Employees	Units Employees	Production Share(%) Toyota	Nissan	Other
1935	20	0	0	20	—	—	0.4	74.7	24.9
1936	910	100	132	1,142	—	—	9.4	50.6	40.0
1937	3,023	577	413	4,013	3,000	1.3	22.2	56.6	21.2
1938	3,719	539	357	4,615	4,000	1.2	18.9	68.0	13.1
1939	10,913	107	961	11,981	5,200	2.3	34.7	51.5	13.8
1940	13,574	268	945	14,787	5,200	2.8	32.1	34.6	33.3
1941	14,331	208	72	14,611	5,200	2.8	31.4	42.3	26.3
1942	16,261	41	0	16,302	6,500	2.5	43.8	46.9	9.3
1943	9,774	53	0	9,827	7,500	1.3	38.0	41.6	20.4
1944	12,701	19	0	12,720	6,000	2.1	58.5	32.5	9.0
1945	3,275	0	0	3,275	4,000	0.8	48.7	29.8	21.5
Total	88,501	1,912	2,880	93,293					
%	94.8	2.0	3.1	100.0					

Sources: Toyota Jidōsha sanjū nen shi *and* Nissan Jidōsha sanjū nen shi.

Notes: Employee totals are rounded estimates.
Production share percentages are for domestically produced four-wheel vehicles.

modifying designs and manufacturing trucks gave to company engineers. During the trip to Britain in 1929-1930, Kiichirō had concluded that he did not have to tie up with a foreign manufacturer or acquire an existing firm to enter the automobile industry. He had a shortage of money but plenty of confidence that he would be able to duplicate American vehicles in stages, test manufacture components at Toyoda Automatic Loom, and solve any problems that arose with the assistance of Japanese experts. He also intended to study American production technology and then adapt it to lower output volumes, and make as many components in house as possible, due to the scarcity and low quality of parts and machine tool manufacturers in Japan. Unlike Aikawa, however, Kiichirō was unafraid of competing directly with the American subsidiaries and planned to manufacture a standard-size car that combined the superior features of Ford, Chevrolet, and Chrysler. He then hoped to produce and sell vehicles cheaper than his foreign competitors, who had to ship knock-down sets to Japan and assemble them locally.[77]

There were several reasons why Kiichirō chose not to rely on a foreign automaker. First, by 1930, knowledge of automobile design and manufacturing was no longer limited to a few experts in the United States and Europe. While it was still an advanced technology, Kiichirō knew several Japanese engineers and university professors who were studying automobiles and believed it would be relatively easy to purchase and copy foreign vehicles without violating patent laws. Second, Toyoda Automatic Loom had accumulated experience in precision-machinery design and manufacturing, metals casting, forging, painting, and assembly—skills needed in automobile production. Third, Kiichirō had visited automobile factories abroad, had a good idea of how they operated, and intended to send more engineers to study plant layouts. Fourth, he knew that it was possible to purchase equipment abroad and duplicate machines in Japan.[78]

Neither was Kiichirō in a hurry. He accepted that it would require several years to prepare for mass production without foreign assistance. Aikawa, on the other hand, wanted to move into the industry quickly and so he bought an existing manufacturer, DAT Motors, and then hired American firms and engineers to expand from small vehicles to standard-size trucks. Two years after Nissan was founded in 1933, it made over 1000 vehicles and, five years later, over 12,000. Given the scale of manufacturing that had taken place in Japan until then, these levels were impressive, although Kiichirō was not far behind. Since he built his first engine in 1931, he took a few years longer to produce at volumes comparable to Nissan. But, dated from 1933, when Kiichirō established the automobile department in Toyoda Automatic Loom, he needed only three years to make 1000 vehicles and six to approach an annual production level of 12,000 units.

He began by copying a 2-cylinder, 60cc engine that Smith Motors in the United States made for 2-wheel and 3-wheel vehicles. A former classmate, Kumabe Kazuo, with whom Kiichirō had written his graduation thesis, assisted him. Kumabe had gone on to graduate school and became a professor at the University of Tokyo, where he gave courses on automotive engineering and sat on the 1931 council that MCI set up to promote the domestic automobile industry.[79] They took until the summer of 1933 to mount the engine on a frame and finish 10 motorcycles. Kiichirō then began to recruit other Japanese experts to help them. He also had a company director who was in Britain to monitor the Platt contract, Ōshima Risaburō, purchase machine tools in Germany and the United States. In addition, during January 1934, Kiichirō sent Toyoda Automatic Loom's specialist on engine casting, Suda Takatoshi, to the United States to study factory layout, parts manufacturing, and materials. Suda visited Ford, General Motors, Chrysler, Packard, Nash, and Graham-Paige before returning to Japan in July 1934, two months after Ōshima arrived with machine tools. The previous December, another close friend of Kiichirō, Yamada Ryōnosuke, a professor at the Tokyo Institute of Technology, had come down to Aichi prefecture to oversee construction of a pilot factory in the town of Kariya, which they completed in March 1934.[80]

Kiichirō hired other Japanese specialists for machine tools and steel manufacturing, vehicle design, factory layout, production management, and marketing. Fukuda Benzō, a chief engineer at Daidō Steel, set up the machine tool and steel manufacturing departments. A machine tool shop was important because Kiichirō wanted to save money and develop in-house skills by importing only one of each machine and then having his own engineers or local subcontractors make facsimiles of the originals.[81] A specialty steel factory was essential, since the lack of manufacturers in Japan was probably the most serious obstacle faced by Japanese firms attempting to compete with the American assemblers. After some initial difficulties, in 1935 he opened a steel manufacturing department within Toyoda Automatic Loom that grew large enough to be separated in 1940 as an independent firm, the present Aichi Steel.[82] The machine tool factory, completed in May 1937, served as the basis for Toyoda Machine Works, incorporated in 1941.

Ikenaga Higuma, a design engineer who had worked for Tokyo Gas and Electric as well as for Hakuyōsha, a small automobile producer that went bankrupt during the late 1920s, joined Kiichirō in 1934 to draft vehicle specifications. Two experts on styling and painting, Wada Mitsuzō and Kishida Hidetō, along with another of Kiichirō's classmates, Itō Seigo, who had supervised the production of 3-wheel vehicles for Nippon Air Brake, assisted Ikenaga. Naruse Masao, a professor who had spent ten years studying gear-manufacturing techniques, came in after an expensive gear-cutting machine arrived from the United States and no one else was able to operate it properly.

Mishima Tokushichi, a sheet-metal expert, helped make high-quality sheet steel thin enough for car bodies and panels. Two other PhDs who worked on steel materials, Nukiyama Daizō and Nukiyama Shirō, assisted Mishima. Saitō Naoichi, an engineer trained at Tōhoku University, came to work with Suda on factory layout. In September 1935, they began designing a new plant in Koromo (renamed Toyota City in 1959) that opened fourteen months later. For marketing, Kiichirō hired Kamiya Shōtaro and two of his assistants from Japan GM, and engaged Kobayashi Hideo from the Ministry of Transport and Ita Kaoru from MCI as consultants. Many of these individuals—Ōshima, Suda, Ikenaga, Itō, Kamiya, Kumabe, Saitō—continued to work at Toyota (or Toyota Motor Sales after 1950), serving in executive positions on the board of directors.[83]

Kiichirō handled most of the initial engine work himself, assisted by Professor Kumabe. During 1931 they bought and tested foreign engine components while surveying local firms that might be able to copy the parts. Then, in 1932, Kiichirō purchased a Chevrolet engine after deciding that this would be easier to produce than a Ford engine, and in October 1933 had the automobile department of Toyoda Automatic Loom acquire a new Chevrolet car and begin disassembling it to analyze the pieces. The department also placed orders with Japan GM for various replacement components, although in November Kiichirō and Suda visited parts makers between Osaka and Tokyo to line up potential suppliers.

Toyoda Automatic Loom used sketches of the 1933 Chevrolet to make its first engine (model A) in September 1934. This had 6 cylinders and displaced 3389cc. Casting of the cylinder block and pistons did not go well, so Kiichirō put Suda in charge of this since he had learned a new oil core casting technique while visiting Ford. Kiichirō, Ōshima, and Suda also ordered malleable cast-iron parts from Tobata Casting, as well as iron and steel components from Hachiman Steel and Sumitomo Metals. They obtained some of the other components from suppliers in the Nagoya area but had to import the body, frame, and chassis from the United States.[84]

Ikenaga began working on a car body design early in 1934 and used a 1934 Chrysler DeSoto the automobile department acquired in April 1934 as a model because he felt this had the best body lines. Ford appeared to have the strongest frame and rear axle, so he used these components but took the front axle from a Chevrolet and added a free-floating suspension system for the axles to make sure the car would not fall over if an axle or axle shaft broke on a bumpy road. In addition, he selected a 141-inch wheelbase, in between the most common lengths for standard-size American cars, usually either 157 or 131 inches, so that he could use the same frame and chassis to make both a mid-size car and truck with a body equivalent to vehicles with a 157-inch wheelbase, merely by sliding the engine forward. He made some design changes in components to avoid violating patent laws and chose certain parts that patent laws no longer covered. The result was a hybrid car, finished in May 1935, that had a Chrysler body and Ford and Chevrolet parts.[85]

While Suda had an early version of the model-A engine ready in September 1934, the vehicle was not yet finished, so Kiichirō placed this in a Chevrolet for testing. The engine put out between 48 and 50 horsepower at 3000 rpm, about 10 horsepower less than the original Chevrolet equipment. Fifty horsepower was adequate for a mid-size car but not for a standard-size truck. Suda eventually discovered that the problem was in the cylinder heads, which he redesigned while widening the overhead valves to allow the combustion chambers to consume gasoline more efficiently. The modified engine delivered 62 horsepower with only a minor increase in fuel consumption—Toyota's first improvement over Chevrolet.[86]

Toyoda Automatic Loom obtained chassis components and other parts that were difficult to manufacture, such as gears, directly from General Motors, but fabricated the cylinder head and blocks, housing, and transmission case in house. While Kiichirō had trouble buying the proper suspension parts and decided to make these, he managed to order electrical parts, spark plugs, and hydraulic brakes, tires, batteries, radiators, wheels, springs, pistons, gaskets, and related components from Japanese firms that produced imitations of

American equipment. There were still problems resulting from inferior steel materials as late as 1941, and too many defects in procured components, particularly in the electrical system, caused breakdowns that made the 1935 car a practical failure. The experience convinced Kiichirō to manufacture more parts and materials in house. Until production equipment was ready in 1936, he imported the electrical components that failed in the first vehicle, but the factory that he eventually established became Nippon Denso in 1949.

After the machinery and tools that Ōshima and Suda ordered arrived during 1934, Kiichirō made the prototype tested in May 1935. While the manufacturing did not go particularly well, he went ahead with plans to build an assembly plant in Kariya that opened in May 1936 with 50-meter conveyors on 3 lines, 1 for cars and 2 for trucks. The main factory in Koromo began operating in 1938 with a monthly capacity of 1500 vehicles.

Kiichirō and Suda, the chief engineer for the Koromo plant, also decided to buy universal machine tools or easily adaptable specialized machinery rather than single-function machine tools and large stamping or forging presses, even though Nissan had imported single-function machines and American engineers considered specialized, mass-production equipment to be more economical and to require less skilled labor. They had several reasons for not following their competitors. First of all, Kiichirō and Suda knew that their vehicles contained many defects and would have to be constantly improved, and that specialized, single-function machine tools and heavy dies made it difficult and expensive to modify designs. Furthermore, since Kiichirō did not believe that he would be able to produce cars and trucks at anywhere near the volumes of American manufacturers, for machines such as body stamping presses he preferred smaller equipment than used in the United States or at Nissan. The type of machine he wanted was not even readily available in the United States, so he had Komatsu, a local machinery manufacturer, produce a small-scale press to his specifications.[87]

Toyoda Automatic Loom completed only 3 of the 1935 car models, due in part to difficulties encountered in design and manufacturing. But, like Aikawa, Kiichirō had already begun to see the limitations of the Japanese car market and had realized that the military would be his best customer. Two months before Ikenaga completed a car design, Kiichirō purchased a Ford truck; in March 1935, he and his assistants began copying the frame, axles, and body. They had the first Toyota truck, the G-1, ready by August, equipped with the modified A engine.[88] This proved to be the basis for 8 new truck models introduced between 1937 and 1956 (Table 18). Problems with weak springs, gear breakage, and transmissions inspired most of these model changes, and the longest that Toyota manufactured a single truck model was 4 years, the BM (1947-1951). Yet the modifications that Toyota engineers had to make on a regular basis provided experience in design and problem solving that Nissan engineers did not have at the end of World War II.

Engine Technology: A Comparison

Toyota and Nissan both got excellent service from the 6-cylinder engines they copied or acquired during the 1930s (Table 19). Toyota placed the same 3389cc engine in all its standard-size trucks from 1938 through 1951, while Nissan used its 3670cc Graham-Paige engine from 1937 until 1956, with only minor modifications. The Toyota engines prior to 1951 were slightly smaller and less powerful than the unit Nissan made, although the Toyota (or rather, the Chevrolet) engine had a more advanced design, incorporating overhead valves.

Valves supply fuel to cylinders and remove waste gases. Placing them over the cylinders made it easier to modify the shape of the engine's combustion chambers (which encase the pistons and cylinders) so that the latter were able to withstand greater temperatures and pressures, and burn fuel more efficiently. Combined with high-octane antiknock gasoline, these modifications allowed an engine to have a substantially higher compression ratio (the minimum and maximum volumes of the compression chambers). This improved efficiency, measured by the conversion of heat to mechanical energy, and resulted in higher torque (pulling power) and horsepower without increasing the engine's displacement.

The advantage of overhead valves became more apparent in the 1950s, when competition between Nissan and Toyota to upgrade their engine technology intensified. Toyota conducted research during the war indicating that a wider cylinder bore, in combination with overhead valves, would significantly raise the power of the A engine.[89] Toyota engineers tested this idea in an experimental model, completed in 1948, that had bores enlarged from 84.1mm to 90mm and a piston-stroke length left unchanged.[90] The wider bore increased

Table 18: Toyota Standard-Size Trucks, 1935-1964

Year	Model	Dimensions (mm)				Weight (kg)	Maximum Load (kg)	Engine	
		Length	Width	Height	Wheelbase			Model	Size (cc)
1935	G1	5950	2191	2219	3594	2470	1500	A	3389
1937	GA	"	"	"	"	"	"	"	"
1939	GB	6412	2190	2220	3609	2600	2000	B	3386
1942	KB	6458	"	2235	4000	2720	4000	"	"
1944	KC	"	"	"	"	2680	"	"	"
1947	BM	"	"	"	"	"	"	"	"
1951	BX, FX	6610	"	2190	"	2970	"	B, F	"
1954	FA5	7040	2230	2250	4150	3360	5000	F	3878
1956	FA60	7145	2270	2276	"	3475	"	"	"
1958	FA70	7135	2330	2265	"	3550	"	"	"
1964	FA100	7270	2400	2400	4100	3815	"	"	"

Source: Toyota Jidōsha sanjū nen shi.

Note: Toyota introduced minor model changes in 1960 (FA80) and 1962 (FA90).

Table 19: 6-Cylinder Engines for Nissan and Toyota Trucks, 1935-1973

Engine Model	Period	Valves	Cylinder (mm) Bore × Stroke	Displacement	Horsepower/rpm	Compression Ratio (n:1)	Max. Torque (kg · m/rpm)
Toyota A	1935-1938	overhead	84 × 102	3389cc	62/3000	5.42	19.4/1600
Nissan A	1937-1941	side	82.5 × 114.3	3670	85/3400	6.5	23 /1200
Toyota B	1938-1951	overhead	84.1 × 101.6	3386	75/3200	6.0	21 /1600
Nissan NG85	1941-1950	side	(same as A)	(same as A)	80/3300	5.7	(same as A)
Toyota F	1951-1964	overhead	90 × 101.6	3878	95/3000	6.4	24 /1600
Nissan NT85	1950-1953	side	(same as A)	(same as A)	85/3600	6.2	24 /1600
Nissan NB	1953-1956	side	(same as A)	(same as A)	95/3600	6.8	24 /1600
Nissan NC	1956-1959	side	85.7 × 114.3	3956	105/3400	6.8	27 /1600
Nissan P	1959-1964	overhead	"	"	125/3400	7.0	29 /1600
Toyota F*	1964-1969	overhead	(same as F)	(same as F)	130/3600	7.7	30 /2200
Nissan PF	1964-1973	overhead	(same as NC)	(same as NC)	130/3600	7.6	30 .1600

Sources: Toyota Jidōsha sanjū nen shi; Nissan Jidōsha sanjū nen shi; Nissan Jidōsha shashi; Toyota no ayumi.

the displacement of the engine from 3386cc to 3878cc, roughly 0.5 liters, but horsepower jumped from 75 at 3200 rpm to 95 at only 3000 rpm.

In 1951, introduced as Toyota's F engine, this forced Nissan to improve its side-valve, 6-cylinder engine, which proved more difficult. Nissan engineers took until 1953 to get the NB unit to produce 95 horsepower; the side-valve arrangement also required a higher speed (3600 rpm) to achieve this, compared to the Toyota engine (3000 rpm). Not until 1956 did Nissan incorporate the concept of a wider cylinder bore, which produced more power without changing the piston stroke, although, once modified, Nissan's new engine (NC) put out 105 horsepower at 3400 rpm and delivered more torque than the slightly smaller F engine.

This comparison between Nissan and Toyota engines is especially significant because it is the first instance where Toyota matched American technology, which Nissan had purchased, without relying on foreign assistance. The design that Nissan bought from Graham-Paige, while more than adequate, did not incorporate the most advanced valve technology in the industry. Copied from a Chevrolet, the Toyota engine did. Changing specialized manufacturing equipment and dies was cumbersome and expensive, so Nissan engineers did not make any major changes in their engine until 1959. They managed to increase horsepower gradually by raising the level of compression inside the engine and by widening the cylinder bore, but this did not train them to design overhead valves or any other type of engine. In fact, all the engines Nissan offered between 1933 and 1960 it either inherited from DAT Motors or imported from Graham-Paige and Austin; and it took an American consultant to redesign the Graham-Paige engine with overhead valves for Nissan's 1959 standard-size truck.

The Toyota Strategy: Eclectic Borrowing and In-House R&D
By the time Kiichirō stepped down as president of Toyota in 1950 he had established several policies that postwar managers continued with even more success than he had enjoyed. One was to avoid tie-ups with foreign firms, if possible, and to copy the best technology available from different sources. Kiichirō chose this approach not only because his funds were limited but also because he was sincerely interested in building automobiles rather than buying them. Aikawa, in contrast, was too busy managing an industrial combine to consider the negative long-term effects of depending so heavily

on American engineers, although many factors, including in-house production costs and techniques, the efficiency of suppliers, and marketing, contributed to the performance of automobile manufacturers and to the success of new models.

Kiichirō also differed from Aikawa in that he personally made sure Toyota did not overlook applied research and development after realizing, during the 1930s, that he could not duplicate or modify foreign technology without adequate facilities and a relatively large staff of technical experts. Kiichirō's recruitment efforts insured that the finest engineers and professors in Japan played a role in designing and manufacturing the first Toyota vehicles. To retain their services he also established a research institute for automobiles in Tokyo during 1936 and invested 2,000,000 yen in facilities, a sum equal to a third of the total capitalization of Toyoda Automatic Loom, and provided a budget of 300,000 yen per year. In 1940, Kiichirō reorganized this as the Toyoda Institute of Physical and Chemical Research to carry on applied and basic research on automobiles and other technologies.[91]

In addition, when Kiichirō founded Toyota he created a research department within the company and headed it personally while serving as an executive vice-president. Even though the department was busy testing foreign and domestic vehicles, Kiichirō had it conduct experiments with new designs and materials. Postwar management expanded the research department as soon as Toyota recovered financially and built a modern technical center in 1954, modeled after facilities at Ford and General Motors. Although on a much smaller scale than the American centers, this required two years to construct and came equipped with laboratories for design, photography, and physical and chemical experiments.[92]

No Japanese automaker during the 1950s or 1960s was able to approach the efforts that giant firms such as General Motors and Ford made in automotive research. The important comparison, however, is with other domestic firms. While Nissan set up a research department in 1937, this merely tested the cab-over truck and other models Nissan made or acquired. Top executives then abandoned the department during World War II, and not until 1958-1960 did they invest in research facilities that approximated those available at Toyota.[93]

But even Kiichirō, like Aikawa and Asahara, gradually lost interest in manufacturing trucks for the army. In 1937, he had Toyota's research department begin studying aircraft design; the next year he made experimental propellers at the Koromo plant for airplanes and helicopters. By 1942, Kiichirō had an aircraft department and was copying a Beechcraft when the army offered him a contract to manufacture aircraft components. He then separated the department as another subsidiary, Tōkai Aircraft, capitalized at 12,500,000 yen. Toyota held a 60-percent investment in the company while Kawasaki Aircraft contributed 40 percent and most of the engineers and designs.[94]

Kiichirō became interested again in producing passenger cars after World War II but developed health problems stemming from a bout with alcoholism and high blood pressure. He resigned from Toyota in 1950 as part of the solution to a lengthy strike. Although the board of directors planned to reinstate him as president and named him a company advisor in 1951, Kiichirō's condition worsened, and he died two years later of a cerebral hemorrhage at the age of 57.[95]

Chapter Two

THE POSTWAR TRANSITION: TRUCKS TO CARS

REORGANIZATION AND RECOVERY

In the years after 1945, transition and survival were related questions for Nissan and Toyota as well as for the entire future of automobile manufacturing in Japan. They could no longer make standard-size trucks for the Japanese army; if they were to continue as automakers in a peacetime economy they would have to manufacture small cars and trucks for private firms and individuals. Manufacturing facilities throughout the industry were largely intact, but production was greatly reduced from pre-1945 levels due to GHQ restrictions and shortages of materials, operating capital, and credit for installment sales. Not only did extreme inflation make it impossible for companies to reduce costs or to estimate future expenses, but the return of conscripted workers swelled employment rolls, while the formation of unions, officially sanctioned by GHQ, made it difficult to reduce wages or fire unneeded employees.

Productivity was remarkably low. In 1947, Nissan produced only 4421 vehicles, down from 19,688 in 1941, yet the number of workers had risen from 7550 to 8500; vehicles per employee per year thus fell from 2.6 to 0.5. The situation was the same at Toyota, where productivity dropped from 2.8 units during the early 1940s to 0.65 in 1947. Only a combination of huge loans, the dismissal of thousands of employees, and special orders from the U.S. Army during the Korean War, saved the Japanese automobile industry from bankruptcy and enabled it to surpass the 1941 production record of 46,498 units in 1953 (Table 20).

GHQ also designed policies to "democratize" the Japanese economy by ending the system of holding companies and combines and redistributing shares to the general public. In addition, during 1947 the American authorities purged approximately 1500 top company executives, ranging from auditors to chairmen, in 405 firms affiliated mainly with the ten major combines (Mitsui, Mitsubishi, Sumitomo, Nissan-Aikawa, Yasuda, Ōkura, Furukawa, Asano, Nakajima, and Nomura).[1] GHQ used at least two criteria to determine which firms to purge: the level of industrial concentration of the group to which companies belonged; and the capitalization of individual firms. In most cases, it did not order the dismissal of executives in companies with nominal capitalizations under 100,000,000 yen.[2] Aikawa had nominally capitalized Nissan at 120,000,000 yen during the latter years of the war; only 75,000,000 yen of this was paid up, but the firm lost all of its top executives. Toyota was affiliated with the Mitsui group, but not as a direct subsidiary.[3] Moreover, Kiichirō had nominally capitalized the firm at 97,000,000 yen, just under the cutoff point. Even though its paid-up capital stood at 71,290,000 yen, only slightly less than Nissan's, Toyota retained all of its executives.

Changes occurred in Toyota management after the war but not as a result of GHQ policy. Toyoda Kiichirō resigned as president in 1950 to take responsibility for the firing of 2146 employees, a third of Toyota's work force. Ishida Taizō (1888-1979), the president of Toyoda Automatic Loom and a close associate, replaced him. This appointment was temporary at first but, after Kiichirō died in 1952, Ishida stayed to carry out Kiichirō's program to develop a small car and to improve Toyota's manufacturing techniques. Ishida continued as president until 1961 and then remained as chairman until 1971. The other key executive in Toyota, Kamiya Shōtarō (1898-1981), who had been in charge of marketing automobiles for Kiichirō since 1935, became the head of Toyota Motor Sales in 1950 and did not step down as president until 1975.

The capital difficulties Toyota faced during the late 1940s resulted in closer ties with the Mitsui Bank. Nakagawa Fukio (1899-1967), who had joined the bank in 1914 after graduating from the Kobe Higher Commercial School (later Kobe University), came to Toyota in 1950 to monitor the company's financial reorganization.[4] From executive director he rose to executive vice-president in 1953 and succeeded Ishida as president in 1961. During the 1950s, Mitsui and several other banks also became the largest shareholders in Toyota, replacing Toyoda Automatic Loom and Toyoda Industries. Mitsui continued to be the largest shareholder in the company, with 5.1 percent in 1983, followed by the Tōkai and Sanwa Banks (5.0), and

Table 20: Postwar Automobile Production, 1946-1954

(vehicles)

Year	NISSAN			TOYOTA			INDUSTRY		
	Trucks	Cars	Total	Trucks	Cars	Total	Trucks	Cars	Total
Pre-1945 peak	17,963	1,587	19,688	16,261	41	16,302	44,870	1,628	46,498
1946	6,406	0	6,406	5,821	0	5,821	14,914	0	14,921
1947	4,366	55	4,421	3,868	54	3,922	11,106	110	11,320
1948	8,150	246	8,467	6,682	21	6,703	19,211	381	20,367
1949	10,630	647	11,730	10,385	235	10,824	25,560	1,070	28,700
1950	11,072	865	12,458	11,014	463	11,706	26,501	1,594	31,597
1951	12,186	1,705	14,381	12,451	1,470	14,228	30,817	3,611	38,490
1952	10,911	2,376	13,962	11,788	1,857	14,106	29,960	4,837	38,966
1953	11,000	3,049	14,593	12,422	3,572	16,496	36,147	8,789	49,778
1954	14,690	4,650	19,823	18,122	4,235	22,713	49,852	14,472	70,073

Sources: Nissan Jidōsha sanjū nen shi, Toyota Jidōsha sanjū nen shi, *and the Japan Automobile Manufacturers Association.*

Notes: The pre-1945 peaks were in 1941 for Nissan and the industry as a whole, and in 1942 for Toyota. Totals include bus production. The 1941 industry total also includes a small number of buses.

75

Toyoda Automatic Loom (4.3). But stockholders in Japan had less impact on company management than their American counterparts; and, while banks were often major shareholders, their influence usually came from the holding of long-term or short-term loans. Except for 1949-1950, Japanese banks interfered little in Toyota's affairs due to management's policy of not borrowing long term. Management finally eliminated these loans altogether in 1977, after two decades of gradual reductions; in contrast, Nissan continued to rely more heavily on loans from the late 1940s through the early 1980s.[5]

Nakagawa was the first and only president appointed from outside the Toyota group. After he died in 1967, this post reverted to the senior member of the Toyoda family, Toyoda Eiji (1913-), who was Kiichirō's cousin (Table 2). The Mitsui Bank did not send anyone to replace Nakagawa, although, beginning in 1959, Toyota served as a "depository" for the bank's ex-presidents, who became Toyota auditors while moving from president to chairman of the bank. While auditor was a part-time position carrying no responsibilities except to verify annual reports and present them at stockholders' meetings, Toyota's reception of ex-presidents reinforced the tradition of close ties between Toyota and the Mitsui Bank that dated back to World War I and Toyoda Sakichi.[6] The only executives from outside the Toyota group to reach the board of directors after Nakagawa's death were the vice-chairman in 1984, Yamamoto Shigenobu, who joined Toyota as a managing director in 1970 after a career in MITI; and Executive Vice-President Ōno Hiroyasu, who entered Toyota in 1969 after heading the Bank of Japan's branch in Kumamoto.[7]

Postwar Nissan, on the other hand, experienced numerous changes in ownership and management, and had to endure considerably more interference from banks. After GHQ dissolved Nissan's principal shareholders (Manchuria Investment Securities, K.K. Nissan, and the Gisei Kai) and reissued its stocks for public sale, banks and insurance companies became the major owners of Nissan, as in the case of Toyota. But the Industrial Bank, Nissan's largest postwar creditor, also began buying Nissan's stock in the 1950s and became a principal shareholder. The bank held the largest number of outstanding shares in 1984, 6.1 percent, followed by Dai-Ichi Mutual Life (5.4), the Swiss Credit Bank (5.3), and the Fuji Bank (4.8), Nissan's primary source of short-term loans.[8]

Not only did low sales and high expenses increase Nissan's indebtedness to the Industrial Bank to nearly 82,000,000 yen by 1948, but the company also owed 317,000,000 yen to the Reconstruction

Table 21: Top Executives: Toyota and Toyota Motor Sales, 1937-1985

Term	President	Term	Chairman
Toyota (Pre-Merger)			
1937-1941	Toyoda Risaburō		
1941-1950	Toyoda Kiichirō		
1950-1961	Ishida Taizō		
1961-1967	Nakagawa Fukio	1961-1971	Ishida Taizō
1967-1982	Toyoda Eiji	1972-1978	Saitō Naoichi
		1978-1982	Hanai Masaya
Toyota Motor Sales			
1950-1975	Kamiya Shōtarō		
1975-1979	Katō Seishi	1975-1979	Kamiya Shōtarō
1979-1981	Yamamoto Sadazō	1979-1982	Katō Seishi
1981-1982	Toyoda Shōichirō		
Toyota (Post-Merger)			
1982-	Toyoda Shōichirō	1982-	Toyoda Eiji

Sources: Toyota Jidōsha Kabushiki Kaisha, Kōho shiryō *(1982), and* yūka shōken hōkokusho.

Finance Bank (a former division of the Industrial Bank), 44,000,000 to the Fuji Bank, and 15,000,000 to other institutions. To assist in Nissan's reorganization, GHQ appointed the Industrial Bank and the Fuji Bank to manage the automaker's extensive liabilities.[9] While Nissan gradually reduced this debt in proportion to its capitalization and sales, the Industrial Bank retained considerable say in investment decisions, and matters such as the selection of new presidents, until Nissan became one of Japan's largest corporations during the 1970s.

Nissan's finances were especially difficult to restructure after World War II because GHQ purged all the company's senior executives between 1945 and 1947. Murayama Takeshi, who assumed the presidency in August 1945, left on the 1st of October along with Chairman Aikawa and 13 other members of the board of directors. Yamamoto Sōji took over as president after the next stockholders' meeting and selected 8 new company directors, including William Gorham. Nissan resumed production at this time but, during April 1947, Yamamoto, Gorham, and 3 other executives had to resign as well. Since there was practically no one else left, Yamamoto chose the head of Nissan's general affairs department, Minoura Taiichi (1891-), to carry on as president.

Minoura, a 1917 graduate of the law faculty at the University of Tokyo, had been employed as a reporter before going to work for Nippon Oils & Fats, a chemical subsidiary in the Aikawa group. While he was a company director when he switched to Nissan in 1944, Minoura had merely three years of experience in the automobile industry. Since he also found politics more interesting than management and did not feel qualified to untangle the company's intricate finances by himself, the new president asked the Industrial Bank to send him an accountant.[10] The individual that came from the bank in July 1947, Kawamata Katsuji (1905-), even though he was new as well to the automobile industry, quickly became the most influential executive in the company as he rose from managing director to president (1957-1973). In addition, Kawamata became a permanent director of the Japan Federation of Employers Associations (Nikkeiren) in 1962 and vice-chairman of the Federation of Economic Organizations (Keidanren) in 1972, the two most important business organizations in Japan, and still remained in Nissan as an unusually powerful chairman until retiring in mid-1985.

The major reason why Kawamata joined Nissan was that he had not been satisfied with his career in the bank. After graduating in 1929 from the prewar predecessor of Hitotsubashi University, he had gone to work for the Industrial Bank as a company analyst and then served during World War II as an army accountant. He returned to the bank in 1946 but was sent to manage the Hiroshima branch—an unenviable post during the Occupation and outside the upper-management track at the bank's head office in Tokyo. When one of his superiors suggested that he join Nissan, he quickly agreed, even though he had barely heard of the near bankrupt automaker.[11]

Upon arriving at Nissan, Kawamata immediately took charge of financial matters; since Nissan had always relied on its holding companies to arrange loans or to provide financing, no one in the company was familiar with banks or capital markets.[12] But it was not only his role as an accounting expert that enabled him to eclipse President Minoura in authority so quickly. Because Kawamata monitored Nissan's balance sheet he was also drawn into intense wage negotiations conducted during the summer of 1947 with a union formed the previous year. To reflect these mounting responsibilities, and to deal more effectively with labor leaders, he pressed Minoura for a promotion to executive director in 1948, making him second in command, behind only the president.

Two subsequent events involving the union helped Kawamata rise to the company presidency. First, in September 1949, when Nissan management dismissed 1760 workers, Minoura collapsed during a series of critical negotiations and showed himself to be incapable of running the company under pressure. Kawamata took over and made sure that the dismissals stuck, adding substantially to his reputation as a forceful executive. Second, during a potentially disastrous strike lasting several months in 1953, Kawamata encouraged the creation of a second, pro-management union, which broke the strike and contributed to the collapse of the industrial union that had united autoworkers throughout Japan since 1947. The leaders of Nissan's second union then provided critical support for Kawamata when he wanted to succeed Asahara Genshichi as president in 1957—even though several other top executives had far longer records of service in the company.[13]

In addition to accepting loans and firing workers, Nissan management took other measures to avoid bankruptcy while sales were low, such as doing extensive repairs for the U.S. Army. Between April 1947 and December 1949, Nissan received 1480 vehicles that needed engine and chassis rebuilding, body repairs, repainting, and miscellaneous other work. Nissan had to operate under the close supervision of American officers, but this provided income and valuable experience: Nissan engineers had the opportunity to analyze relatively new cars, trucks, and jeeps, while managers observed the operations management techniques that the U.S. Army had perfected.[14]

Nissan cut the number of its workers from 9000 in 1947 to 6900 in 1950, despite severe union protests, while the Industrial Bank, and the Fuji and Kyōwa Banks, provided 80,000,000 yen in loans to help management settle with workers and to assist parts suppliers and dealers during several strikes that the union called.[15] Production levels then recovered during 1950-1951 as Nissan made 4325 trucks and other vehicles for the U.S. Army, and 710 for the Japanese police reserves—a total equal to nearly half of the 11,730 units Nissan made in 1949. Toyota received special orders for 5629 vehicles and Isuzu for 1256, but Nissan also manufactured 200,000,000 yen ($555,600) worth of gasoline tanks for airplanes and other equipment since its 2000-ton sheet metal stamping press, acquired from Graham-Paige, was well suited to fabricating such components.[16]

From a pre-tax profit rate of 0.1 percent on sales between April 1946 and December 1950, Nissan's earnings rose to 9.1 percent of sales by March 1952. During the same one and a half years, Toyota's profit margins on sales rose from zero to 9.6 percent. Both firms were then able to attract new capital by offering dividends to shareholders[17] (Table 22). Profitability was not due entirely to the Korean War orders. The dismissal of thousands of employees during 1949-1950 had created a shortage of workers; rather than hire back union members Nissan and Toyota kept down the number of expensive, regular employees by granting more overtime, hiring temporary or seasonal workers, and subcontracting jobs to small firms with lower wage scales. These measures proved so successful in maintaining earnings that the automakers continued them.[18]

But Nissan still had to choose a more permanent chief executive to replace Minoura, who announced in 1951, at the same time that GHQ lifted the ban against former business leaders, that he would like to resign and run for political office as a member of the Liberal Party.[19] This was a critical time to leave, because investment funds were finally available and top executives had agreed that they would have to improve the prewar Datsun to survive as an automaker. Nissan needed a strategy and a leader, but GHQ's "democratization" measures had worked only too well: Aikawa Yoshisuke no longer dominated the company, and this made it possible for several interested parties—the Industrial Bank, new postwar executives, the union—to influence management and the process of selecting a new president.

As the outgoing top executive, Minoura's opinion regarding a successor mattered much more than it would have before 1945. But he did not have the authority to chose the next president alone, and the other senior members in the firm, especially Kawamata, who doubled as the Industrial Bank's representative, expected to be in on the decision. Mioura felt obligated as well to discuss the matter

Table 22: Nissan and Toyota—Financial Performance, 1945-1952 (1000 yen, %)

Period (Month/Year)	Pre-Tax Profits	Net Sales	Profits / Sales(%)	Dividend (%)
NISSAN				
10/1945-3/1946	− 154	44,158	—	—
4/1946-8/1946	5,547	115,793	4.8	—
8/1946-12/1950	19,575	13,364,828	0.1	—
1/1951-3/1951	114,104	1,754,827	6.5	20
4/1951-9/1951	439,535	6,326,035	6.9	30
10/1951-3/1952	457,626	5,040,477	9.1	30
TOYOTA				
10/1945-3/1946	221	37,204	0.6	—
4/1946-8/1946	6,464	118,825	5.4	—
8/1946-11/1949	10,979	7,665,887	0.1	—
11/1949-3/1950	− 76,524	2,070,537	—	—
4/1950-9/1950	0	2,129,266	—	—
10/1950-3/1951	249,300	4,348,120	5.7	20
4/1951-9/1951	483,775	5,775,146	8.4	30
10/1951-5/1952	677,202	7,059,454	9.6	30

Sources: Nissan Jidōsha sanjū nen shi, Toyota Jidōsha sanjū nen shi, *and* Tōyō keizai, *30 July 1955, p. 57 (dividend rates).*

with Nissan's main banks and stockholders (the Industrial Bank fell into both categories), and with union leaders, who were becoming increasingly powerful because executives at Nissan and the Industrial Bank were anxious to avoid a repetition of the strikes that workers had organized nearly every year since they formed the union in 1946.

When Yamamoto Sōji heard, in 1951, that Minoura planned to resign, he declared his availability and appealed to the Industrial Bank for support. In some respects he was a logical candidate. Yamamoto was the last Nissan president in office when the purge went into effect and, since he had entered Tobata Casting in 1926, no one still working in the company had more seniority. He had also served as a managing director at Nissan from 1933 to 1936, president of Nissan Motor Sales from 1937 to 1941, and president of Nissan during 1945-1947. In 1948, GHQ allowed Yamamoto to establish a firm, Fuji Motors, to repair army vehicles, but he fully expected to return to Nissan when the purge ended. Minoura was in a difficult position because Yamamoto had chosen him in 1947 as a temporary successor, he knew that his former boss was waiting to come back, and yet he preferred another candidate, Asahara Genshichi.[20]

Asahara had joined Tobata Casting five years after Yamamoto and served Nissan as a director or executive director from 1933 to 1942, and then as president before quitting in 1944. Although GHQ cited him under the purge, he remained close to the industry by assisting the American authorities as an advisor for the automobile and transport industries. GHQ did not permit Asahara to have any contacts with his old firm, however, and he spent much of his time at home doing research on coal properties. But, in 1951, at age 60 and still one of Japan's top authorities on automobile technology, he was anxious to go back to work. Asahara notified Minoura, a personal friend, and the directors of the Industrial Bank, that he, too, was available.[21]

Kawamata recommended that Asahara be brought back as president. He later claimed there was no one more familiar with the company or who seemed to be a better choice, and that he believed Asahara would have returned to Nissan after 1945 had it not been for the purge.[22] Kawamata had every reason to prefer Asahara. Yamamoto was an expert in finance and marketing, and a domineering manager who disliked delegating authority; Kawamata had a similar personality but he had been with Nissan only four years. Yamamoto was sure to challenge the executive director's authority over finances and labor relations. Asahara, on the other hand, had little interest in accounting or union negotiations—he wanted only to build a better Datsun.[23]

The union leaders also preferred Asahara. Or, rather, they did not want Yamamoto, who had been highly insensitive to workers' salary demands while he was president and, what was worse, had tried to control the union's activities. His close association with Aikawa and the Manchurian venture, including several years as president of Manchuria Motors, also tainted Yamamoto's candidacy; the union leaders leaned rather far to the political left and were highly critical of businessmen who had cooperated with Japanese militarists. On the other hand, Asahara had not been drawn into Manchurian affairs so deeply. He had stayed mainly with Nissan during the war and, when he resigned in 1944, it was because he supported one of his managers in a dispute with Tōjō and the army's supervisory system for military suppliers. Since the Industrial Bank was especially sensitive to the views of the union officials, their opinions had extra weight. With Minoura, Kawamata, the union, nearly all of Nissan's employees, and even the retired Aikawa behind him, Asahara became president of Nissan for the second time in October 1951.[24]

NISSAN-AUSTIN VERSUS TOYOTA

When Asahara returned, Nissan was by far the most experienced car manufacturer in Japan. Between 1934 and 1950, the company produced 21,539 cars, 12.5 percent of total output during these years, while Toyota made only 2685 cars during the same period—2 percent of its entire production until the Korean War. Yet Nissan had difficulty maintaining its edge over Toyota, for several reasons. One was that 85 percent of the cars it made prior to 1951 came out before 1942, and the Datsun design dated back to the mid-1930s. In contrast, Toyota waited until 1947 to introduce a line of small cars and trucks, and used foreign automobiles made during the late 1940s as models. The Toyota vehicles thus contained more recent technology. It was also possible to develop small car and truck lines simultaneously because all the cars that Nissan and Toyota made before the late 1950s utilized the same frames, chassis, engines, and many other components as the corresponding truck models. This factor may even have given Toyota an advantage over Nissan in costs because Toyota quickly became Japan's top producer of small trucks during the 1950s. Yet the Datsun was the only Japanese car that originated prior to World War II. And, like many other machinery and electrical goods made in Japan, its history demonstrates how a Japanese company combined foreign and domestic technology to turn an initially mediocre product into a valuable export commodity.

The Datsun Line
The first Datsun truck (model 1121) made after World War II, introduced in 1946, was essentially the same as the 1938 version except for a slight widening of the body (Table 23). The first postwar car (DA) came out in 1947 as a modest revision of the 1936 model, with the rear tread and body widened to improve stability and handling. These modifications partially utilized experimental designs that Nissan engineers had finished in 1942, based on a 1937 Opel Kadett, but did not manufacture due to government restrictions.[25]

For more than twenty years, the Datsun car continued to be no more than a small truck fitted with a car body. The frame, chassis, transmission, and engine were identical to the complementary truck model until 1955. Nissan also made few changes in the engine prior to the late 1950s. Altering the diameter of the cylinder bore improved performance slightly but, essentially, Nissan fitted the same engine in all Datsun models between 1933 and 1956, until Austin made a new unit available in 1957.

Nissan's design department just prior to the Korean War contained approximately 15 engineers in two sections: one for chassis and one for engines. The individuals primarily responsible for the Datsun car line were Hara Teiichi (1916-), in charge of body design, and Takahashi Hiroshi (1915-), who headed a group that worked on the engine. Both men would be promoted to company directors in 1963; Hara rose eventually to executive director and Takahashi to executive vice-president. But, when they received the task of upgrading the Datsun after World War II, neither had accumulated much experience with cars. This was another reason why president Asahara decided in 1952 that a tie-up with Austin was the best and fastest way to upgrade Nissan's car technology.

Hara, who graduated from the mechanical engineering department of the University of Tokyo and entered Nissan in 1939, had taken college courses on automotive engineering given by Kumabe Kazuo, Toyoda Kiichirō's classmate and assistant (and a Toyota managing director during 1946-1950). After working on transmissions for six months at Nissan, Hara was drafted into the army, where he designed tanks from the fall of 1939 until returning to Nissan in the summer of 1944 to work on aircraft engine design at the Yoshiwara plant. Hara was still there when Yoshiwara began preparing to manufacture the Datsun line in 1946.[26] Since no one left in Nissan knew how to design a car body, Hara undertook the job and began by collecting and redrawing old Datsun blueprints, then sending them to the company's design department in Yokohama. He also roadtested the 1938 Datsun and found it unstable because the front and rear treads were too narrow and the body too high. The steering mechanism was poorly designed as well, and the suspension system tended to break down on rough roads.

To help redesign the car, in 1946 Nissan recruited a large number of engineers from the aircraft industry (which the American authorities dismantled as part of the Occupation). But it still took nearly two decades to produce a vehicle that performed adequately on American highways. The 1951 DS-4 was an improvement over the prewar Datsun models since it had a lower, longer, and wider body, but this and the next full model change in 1955, the 110 (which began the Datsun series that continued through the 1980s), rode and handled like trucks. Both had parallel springs instead of independent suspension, and were too high and narrow, although these deficiencies were not really the fault of Hara's group; top management did not even tell him to start working on an authentic car design until 1954 because Nissan's main business was still trucks.

Takahashi had studied aircraft engine design at Osaka University before joining Nissan in 1938. But, since Aikawa had just acquired an engine from Graham-Paige for standard-size trucks, while the Datsun came with a smaller engine inherited from DAT Motors, Takahashi did not have much engine design work to do until the army ordered Nissan to produce aircraft engines in 1943. He went to the Yoshiwara plant, worked with Hara, and then began studying the Datsun engine directly after the war.

Nissan was already behind Toyota in small-engine technology when both firms introduced their first postwar car models in 1947. The new Toyopet line offered a 995cc engine that was considerably more powerful than the 722cc Datsun engine. Takahashi managed to raise the output of the Datsun engine by the relatively simple method of widening the cylinder bore from 55 to 60mm, which increased displacement to 860cc and horsepower from 15 to 21 at 3600 rpm. While the modifications gave Nissan managers sufficient

Table 23: Datsun Models, 1924-1955 (mm, unless noted)

Year	Model	Max. Load/Speed	Length	Width	Height	Wheelbase	Tread Front	Tread Rear	Weight	Engine Model/cc
Trucks										
1924	DAT 41	? 24km-hr	4484	1212	1757	2134	1219	1219	900kg	— —
1929	DAT 61	? "	2710	1175	"	2819	965	965	"	L/495
1932	Datsun	500kg/ 65	"	"	"	1880	"	"	"	"
1938	17T	" "	3020	1197	1550	2005	1038	1049	620	7/722
1946	1121	" "	3023	1250	"	"	"	"	"	"
1947	2225	600 "	3147	1458	"	"	"	1180	"	"
1949	3135	500 /67	3117	1398	1580	"	"	"	655	"
1950	4146	" /72	3295	"	"	"	"	"	690	D10/860
1951	5147	600 /70	3398	"	"	2150	1048	"	750	"
1953	6147	" /72	3406	"	1590	"	"	"	755	B/860
1955	120	750 /75	3742	1466	1555	2220	1186	"	865	"
Cars										
1931	Datson	2 pass./65	2667	1118	?	1880	965	965	400	L/495

Year	Model									
1932	Datsun	4	"	"	?	"	"	"	"	"
1936	15	"	3129	1190	1600	2005	1038	1049	630	7/722
1947	DA	"	3160	1330	1570	"	"	1180	"	"
1949	DB	"	3515	1420	1560	"	"	"	800	"
1950	DS2	72	3500	1400	1550	"	"	"	770	D10/860
1951	DS4	"	3750	1450	1535	2150	1048	"	900	"
1954	DS6	78	3825	1462	1518	"	"	"	920	B/860
1955	110	85	"	1466	1540	2220	1186	"	890	"

Engines (4-cylinder)

Year	Model	Vehicles	Compression Ratio (n:1)	Size	Valves	Bore × Stroke	Max. hp/rpm	Max. Torque (kg. m/rpm)
1931	L	Datson, Datsun	—	495cc	side	54 × 54	10/3700	—
1933	L	Datsun	—	748	"	56 × 76	12/3000	—
1935	7	Datsun, DA, DS	5.0	722	"	55 × "	15/3600	3.8/2000
1950	D10	DS2-5, DB2-5	5.2	860	"	60 × "	21/ "	4.9/2400
1954	B	110	6.5	"	"	" × "	25/4000	5.1/ "
1958	B1	A120, A20	"	"	"	" × "	27/4200	5.3/ "

Source: Nissan Jidōsha sanjū nen shi.

confidence to expand Datsun production equipment, the engine block was already twenty years old by the early 1950s and would have to be replaced soon.[27]

The Infusion of British Technology

Takahashi's group did not attempt to make an entirely new engine, just as Hara did not start working on an authentic car design until 1954. One reason was that Nissan oriented its research and product development efforts toward solving specific problems rather than trying to generate new designs.[28] To be fair to Nissan management, however, current wisdom in the Japanese automobile industry, and in government ministries, held that firms should not try to produce cars by themselves. This is why MITI encouraged Nissan, Isuzu, Hino, Mitsubishi, and Toyota to join up with foreign automakers to close the gap in car technology.[29]

Whether or not firms concluded formal tie-ups, every Japanese automaker studied European cars during the late 1940s and 1950s because these were far more suitable than American vehicles for Japan's narrow roads and the shortages of materials and fuel. Nissan engineers were actually dissecting the Morris Minor in 1952 when Austin's general manager for the Far East asked if Nissan would be willing to assemble a model in Japan. Renault, Rootes (Hillman), and Willys-Overland (Jeep) were also interested in having Japanese firms produce their vehicles because MITI had just decided to restrict the importation of complete cars and to continue the prohibition on foreign investment, which left tie-ups as the best way for European or American automakers to enter the Japanese market. For their part, Japanese firms viewed these arrangements as technological shortcuts—to save time, if not money, in developing small cars up to European standards.[30]

Asahara welcomed a tie-up. During the 1930s, Graham-Paige had made it possible for Nissan to produce standard-size trucks of reasonably good quality within a couple of years; he was easily convinced again that Austin could help improve the Datsun much faster than Nissan could do on its own.[31] Like Aikawa, Asahara considered technology a "product" to be bought as needed, and he disagreed with Kiichirō's method of copying from other firms without acquiring patent rights. Nissan studied foreign vehicles and, at times, borrowed design concepts, such as the air filter from an American farm truck that Maeda placed in the cab-over to make it run better in Manchuria. But Asahara would not rely on this method to produce a new car. He was a cautious individual and the Austin tie-up provided a guarantee. While independent development might or might not succeed, with the British company he knew exactly what type of technology he was getting and what type of product Nissan would be able to offer by the end of the 1950s.[32]

Asahara wanted an engine larger than the one in the Datsun but smaller than the Graham-Paige 6-cylinder unit. In addition, he was looking for modern body technology. Nissan was manufacturing the Datsun with a separate frame and chassis, whereas cars in Europe offered the more advanced "monocoque" construction, pioneered by Citroen in 1934, which combined the frame and chassis into one solid unit. Monocoque vehicles were cheaper to produce, sturdier, and gave a much smoother ride than was possible with the design used by Nissan (and Toyota until 1955).[33]

Yet not everyone in Nissan agreed with Asahara that a tie-up was necessary. Some engineers felt competent enough to produce a new model without foreign assistance.[34] Asahara's most serious opposition, however, came from Executive Director Kawamata, who believed that Nissan should concentrate on improving the Datsun and try to mass-produce this as Volkswagen was doing with the Beetle, rather than move into an unfamiliar and larger car that did not seem as well suited to the Japanese market. Kawamata also worried that a tie-up would prevent Nissan engineers from learning how to plan, design, and manufacture cars on their own. Nor was he satisfied with the contract Austin was offering because there was no option to purchase manufacturing rights. This meant not only that Nissan would have to prepare to assemble and then produce the Austin with local parts, and pay royalties, but simultaneously it had to design a new Datsun and a replacement for the slightly larger Austin.[35]

But Asahara was president in 1952 and, contrary to popular myths about the style of Japanese management, neither he nor his predecessors and successors were inclined to run the company by "consensus." To substantiate his position he commissioned a study of 1288 Austin cars registered in Japan, most of which had been imported during the 1930s, and collected reports on the car from the United States and Europe. These materials indicated that the Austin was an excellent vehicle with an especially good engine.[36] Asahara then decided to go ahead with the tie-up and announced this decision at a board meeting, even though he knew that Kawamata and several engineers opposed it. There was no debate over the matter since it did not seem that anyone would be able to change Asahara's mind.[37]

The president notified Austin (which was in the process of merging with Nuffield to form the British Motor Corporation) that he
would like to discuss the tie-up in more detail. Austin sent a vice-
president to Japan in October 1952 to conduct further negotiations,
which Asahara handled personally, and offered Nissan a contract
proposal in mid-November; Asahara wanted to pursue the discussions in England and led a team of engineers to Austin's head offices.
They concluded an agreement on December 4th and stayed another
month to observe Austin's facilities. In Japan, meanwhile, Nissan
submitted an application for MITI to approve the tie-up on December
5th and received permission on the 23rd.[38]

The contract contained seven clauses and resembled those signed
by Isuzu and Rootes, Hino and Renault, as well as Shin-Mitsubishi
and Willys-Overland. First, Nissan agreed to import 2000 units annually of the Austin A40 in knock-down sets that it would assemble
in Japan and sell under the Austin trademark. Nissan and Nisshin
Motors, Austin's sales representative in Japan, would market the
vehicles. Second, Nissan was to shift gradually to locally made parts
and make the entire Austin in Japan within three years. Third, Austin agreed to provide technical assistance for assembly and local
parts manufacturing, and to give Nissan specifications for designs,
materials, components, jigs and tools. Fourth, the British company
allowed Nissan to use any patents that it held. Fifth, both firms
were to exchange technical personnel as necessary. Sixth, Nissan
would pay royalties beginning in the second year of operations. For
the second year they fixed the payments at 2 percent of the factory
retail price (excluding taxes) of the Austin in Japan or a minimum
of 10,000 pounds. From the third year the royalty was 3.5 percent
per vehicle, or a minimum of 30,000 pounds. Finally, Nissan and
Austin limited the contract period to seven years.[39]

Asahara set up an Austin department in February 1953 and gave
it two tasks: operate the assembly shop, and oversee the transition
to local production. The department began by constructing an assembly shop at the Tsurumi factory in Yokohama, which it finished
by September. The first Austin cars Nissan assembled from knock-
down sets came off the line in November, under the direct supervision of British engineers. In December, Nissan began utilizing local
components such as tires, batteries, glass, trim, and foam rubber for
seats. As of January 1954, more than 220 parts were Japanese. Even
with a model change, by August 1955, Nissan was making over half
the car locally and experimenting with the manufacture of the en-

gine and transmission. Nissan was assembling most of the car from Japanese components before the end of 1955, although it did not officially take over complete production of the Austin until September 1956.[40]

Assembling the Austin was not a problem. The blueprints sent from Britain were easy to understand and foreign currency allocations that the Japanese government imposed limited production to a maximum of 200 vehicles per month until Nissan switched to Japanese components.[41] The difficult part of the tie-up was to localize parts production, although Austin helped by sending engineers and inspectors to Japan, as provided for in the contract. Nissan also dispatched several of its technical experts to Britain for stays ranging from a month and a half to three months at a time.[42]

The car that Nissan finally built in Japan, the 1955 Austin A50, seated 5 passengers and had a 1489cc (1.5 liter) engine. This was slightly larger than the model assembled from knock-down sets, the A40, which seated 4 and had a 1197cc engine. Since both were larger and more expensive than the 860cc Datsun, they supplemented rather than replaced Nissan's subcompact. When the tie-up ended in fiscal 1959 (March 1960), Nissan then introduced its own compact, the Cedric, modeled in part after the A50 and also produced in the Tsurumi plant.

The most Austin cars Nissan made in any one year was 5785 in fiscal 1957. This represented approximately 31 percent of all the cars it produced and 10 percent of total output for that year (Table 24). From nearly 44 percent (1334 units) of Nissan's car production in 1953, however, the Austin declined to around 13 percent (3454 units) in 1959, reflecting the improvement and increased sales of the Datsun line. The total cost to Nissan in royalties came to about 600,000,000 yen ($1,700,000) between 1954 and 1959.[43] Equipment investment to localize production of the Austin, on the other hand, cost nine times this figure or 3.3 billion yen ($9,200,000) during 1954-1955, more than twice Nissan's paid-up capitalization of 1.4 billion yen as of October 1953.[44]

Sasaki Sadamichi (1911-), a mechanical engineer from Kyoto University who had entered Nissan in 1937, directed the Austin department during the mid-1950s. He delegated authority for Austin assembly to the assistant general manager and concentrated on preparations to manufacture the car in Japan. Not only did Sasaki make sure that Nissan met the localization schedule; at the same time, he prepared himself to set up new car plants for Nissan in the future

Table 24: The Nissan-Austin Tie-up, 1953-1959
(vehicles, %)

Year	Nissan-Austin Production	% of Nissan's Car Production	% of Nissan's Total Production
1953	1,334	43.8	9.1
1954	1,540	33.1	7.8
1955	2,089	31.7	9.6
1956	2,718	21.0	8.1
1957	5,785	30.8	9.8
1958	3,935	23.3	7.2
1959	3,454	12.9	4.4
Total	20,855	23.3	7.4

Sources: Amagai Shōgo, Nihon jidōsha kōgyō no shiteki tenkai, *p. 136, and* Nissan Jidōsha sanjū nen shi.

by visiting Austin and other automakers in Europe and the United States. He moved to the Yoshiwara factory in 1957 to head the Datsun manufacturing department and then, in 1959, became chief of the construction and preparations office for the Datsun car factory that Nissan was planning to build in Oppama, Kanagawa prefecture (a few miles southeast of Yokohama and Tokyo). After he was promoted by President Kawamata to company director in 1960, Sasaki helped supervise the construction of an entire series of new factories throughout the 1960s and 1970s, until he became president of a Nissan affiliate, Fuji Heavy Industries, in 1978.[45]

Nissan left a record of the Austin tie-up in the company's in-house technical journal, *Nissan gijutsu* (Nissan engineering), which devoted a special issue to the subject in November 1956. The first article, written by two engineers from the design department, reported on parts specifications and tests on the Austin A50 and how well the components Nissan made fared in comparison to the originals.[46] Most of the Japanese parts compared favorably with the British components. The data were especially useful because Nissan coordinated the switch to local parts with the introduction of its own new models, using technology acquired in the tie-up. One of the engineers who wrote on the testing of these parts, Fujita Shōtarō, was also the chief designer of the 1960 Cedric as well as the Nissan Junior, a mid-size truck introduced late in 1956 and equipped with the Austin engine.[47]

Nissan manufactured about half the Austin parts with no major problems. The Yoshiwara factory began making small cast components in 1954, while the Yokohama plant started producing cylinder blocks and heads, brake drums, fly wheels, exhaust manifolds, and crank bearing caps during 1955. Nissan sent samples to Austin in March and received approval in August.[48] Even when difficulties arose, Asahara would not extend the localization schedule; he even had Nissan complete the switch to Japanese parts before the planned date, whereas Hino and Isuzu had to receive extensions from their tie-up partners. More important, Asahara refused to allow his engineers to get by with inferior components or procedures and insisted that they copy the originals exactly to see whether or not Nissan could duplicate the British car.[49]

One example of how Asahara managed the tie-up involved the manufacturing of differential gears. No matter how hard Nissan tried, the Japanese parts made more noise in operation than Austin's original equipment, so Executive Director Harashina decided that Nissan was not ready to meet the British standards and placed an order for 2000 more crown gear and pinion sets with Austin. Asahara found out about this, canceled the order, called in Harashina as well as Sasaki, and pointed out, not without some anger, that the whole point of the tie-up was to learn how to make these parts, not how to buy them. He then asked Austin to send an engineer to Japan to find out what Nissan was doing wrong. Austin was obligated to help under the 1952 contract, and it was to the British company's advantage to have Nissan produce as many cars as possible because it received a royalty on each sale. The Austin engineer who came to Japan, a man named Tomlins, discovered that Nissan did not have the gear-cutting machinery set correctly. Neither Harashina nor Sasaki had noticed this because they did not actually try to make a set of the gears themselves—a mistake they did not repeat.[50]

Jigs and tools presented another problem because Nissan needed the same equipment that Austin had but intended to manufacture at only one-tenth the scale. The Japanese had to find some compromise between acquiring what they needed and keeping the cost of local production down so that their Austin model did not become too expensive. The British firm met its obligations by providing a full complement of equipment specifications and process schedules, but Nissan still encountered difficulties. For example, it was a major challenge to reproduce the Austin body exactly because the quality of sheet steel in Japan was low, and Nissan lacked experience in making car bodies and stamping dies.

Prior to the tie-up, Shin-Mitsubishi had made car shells for the Datsun, as well as for Toyota and Isuzu car models. All the bodies Nissan made in house had to be finished by hand before going to the final assembly line. Asahara refused to accept this crude technique for the Austin and insisted that Nissan learn how to make the Austin body as the British fabricated it, since foreign automakers had found in-house body manufacturing was essential for changing models quickly and cheaply. Some of Nissan's engineers argued that it would be easiest to subcontract Austin bodies to Shin-Mitsubishi, along with the Datsun. Asahara prevailed, but it took well over a year to make an acceptable shell.

Nissan first had to copy Austin's stamping punches and dies; this went slowly because Nissan's die-making technology was not on a par with the British. The Japanese engineers had to upgrade their entire die shop, which they did after visiting several automakers, including Austin, to find the best and cheapest way to make quality dies. Engineers from the Austin department, as well as from engineering, machine tool design, tool manufacturing, and stamping, cooperated in the project, while an Austin inspector made two special trips to Japan to assist. Asahara and Austin finally approved the most difficult components to duplicate—roof panels, dashboards, front fenders, and front suspension cross members—after Nissan made scale models of dies for each component and then adjusted the actual die molds.[51] In the process, Nissan improved its equipment and skills sufficiently to terminate the contract with Shin-Mitsubishi in 1955.[52]

Since Nissan subcontracted as much as 70 percent of the Austin (by value), suppliers played an enormously important role in the success of the tie-up. Some of these firms contributed articles to Nissan's technical journal describing their roles. Hitachi, for example, reported on its development of a carburetor for the Austin A50. It had made this component for Nissan trucks since the 1930s, but the standard-size carburetor was too big for the Austin, even though engineers tried to fit it in. Hitachi designers worked with members of Nissan's engine design and testing sections to cut down the larger unit. Nippon Hatsujo (Japan Springs) made springs in cooperation with Nissan's chassis design section and improved the heat-treatment method. Tokyo Kiki Industries, with the assistance of Nissan's chassis design section, provided shock absorbers; the original Austin equipment was ill suited to Japanese roads, so both firms studied a variety of shock absorbers before coming up with a hybrid design that did not violate another firm's patent rights.[53]

The most advanced manufacturing technology that Nissan introduced as a result of the Austin tie-up was transfer machinery (automatic production and conveyance equipment) to manufacture cylinder blocks and heads. This was not new in the United States or Europe; Ford had installed transfer machines during the early 1930s to bore holes in engines. Other firms followed, although Japanese companies were slow to copy this equipment because it was costly and their manufacturing scales were too low to justify the expense. During 1955-1956, several Japanese appliance firms installed transfer machines to make electric motors, while Toyota received a grant from MITI in 1954 to introduce equipment in June 1956 that automatically drilled holes in truck engine blocks and moved them on to subsequent machining stations. But these were small, almost experimental machines, whereas Austin made it possible for Nissan to acquire equipment that integrated several machining operations into a single production sequence to approximate the level of automation at the larger automakers in Europe.[54]

Although Nissan began studying Austin's transfer machines early in 1953, it did not decide to copy them until April 1955. During these two years the engineering department debated whether to buy similar machines or to arrange individual machine tools in line sequence. Nissan, again, was under pressure from Toyota, which had already installed a transfer machine, even though one of its key engineers preferred machine tools in line sequence, modified with limit switches and special jigs, to approximate automated equipment at less cost. Neither did Nissan's sales volumes require mass-production machinery such as Austin was offering, although the arguments in favor of transfer machines won out when an internal study indicated that the new equipment would cost only 20 percent more than single-function machine tools arranged in sequence, reduce personnel needed for machining operations and conveyance, and cut the amount of floor space required for the machine shop. Nissan engineers also expected the transfer machines to raise productivity and insure greater uniformity in quality.[55]

Since it was too expensive to import, Nissan had to find a manufacturer in Japan capable of reproducing Austin's machinery, even though company engineers disliked the way Japanese firms made machine tools and did not believe they were capable of combining hydraulic and electrical components well enough to produce specialized machines for automobile manufacturing. Japanese tool makers had little experience with automobiles since Nissan had imported most of its equipment from the United States, and Toyota either did the same or made equipment in its own machine tool shop or through Toyoda Machine Works. Nissan engineers eventually decided to supervise the building of the transfer machines directly and to use data from manufacturing tests to perfect the equipment before installing it permanently.

In June 1955, Nissan placed orders for four transfer machines with Hitachi Seiki and Toshiba, and asked each firm to make two of the machines—three for engine blocks, and one for cylinder heads. Nissan engineers then held approximately twenty meetings over the next several months with the machine-tool suppliers before Hitachi Seiki completed the first unit in February 1956. The other three arrived by April—much to the surprise of observers from Austin, who had not expected the Japanese to copy their machines so easily. Japanese firms made all the parts, except for some hydraulic pumps and micro-limit switches, for a total cost to Nissan of 200,000,000 yen ($550,000). Nissan then conducted no less than 600 tests in the Yoshiwara factory before moving the transfer machines to Yokohama in August; several years later, this became Nissan's main engine plant.[56]

The Austin equipment linked a series of 15 stations for milling, boring, planing, drilling, reaming, and hole finishing with other operations that checked hole depth or removed shavings. Nissan set the line speed to transfer materials to the next station every 3 minutes but, once the machines were operating smoothly, it reduced this to 1 minute. Separate control panels for different machines even allowed workers to stop part of the transfer machine in operation, rather than the entire unit, adding a flexibility that American or European factories usually did not possess. The machines initially produced 1.5-liter engines for the Austin A50 and the Nissan Junior truck; by November, Nissan was using them to make 1-liter engines for the Datsun as well. This was possible because the Datsun engine borrowed the block and heads from the Austin; the lower displacement came from a shorter piston stroke.

Productivity rose immediately because Nissan now required only one-fourth to one-tenth of the workers previously employed in engine manufacturing operations. In fact, the machines were so efficient that management ordered two more sets for the Yoshiwara factory in 1958 to manufacture Datsun transmission cases.[57] Not until the mid-1960s did Toyota approach a similar level of automation in its machining operations and, by this time, Nissan was farther ahead in the use of computers and other specialized manufacturing equipment.

Pluses and Minuses of the Austin Tie-up
While the Austin tie-up improved Nissan's design and production technology, it did not provide the long-term advantage over Toyota that Asahara had anticipated. The 1959 Datsun 310 and the 1960 Cedric enabled Nissan to regain its lead over Toyota in the domestic car market during 1960-1962, after falling behind in 1953, 1955, and 1957-1959. But, once it became necessary to introduce new models independently—such as when a model change for the 310 came due in 1963—Nissan again fell behind Toyota in car sales, this time permanently. Between 1963 and 1984, Toyota accounted for 35 percent of all cars made in Japan, compared to Nissan's 29 percent (Table 25). The efforts of Toyota Motor Sales helped Toyota maintain a larger share of this market. The Austin tie-up, however, like the Graham-Paige tie-up, had both good and bad points, and it appears Toyota avoided some of the disadvantages of relying on foreign assistance by designing new products on its own.

Acquisition of the 1489cc Austin engine, which went into the Nissan Junior truck and the Datsun line, was a major plus. The Austin body also provided a model for the 1959 Datsun. In addition, making the Austin in Japan prepared Nissan to introduce monocoque unit-body construction in the 1959 Datsun along with independent suspension and a synchromesh transmission offered between 1955 and 1957. Nissan would not have been added these features so early without the tie-up, although the chief designer of the Datsun 310, Hara Teiichi, admitted that Nissan could have acquired all these technologies merely by analyzing foreign vehicles or by studying information that was publicly available, which is what Toyota did. Furthermore, Hara's group had to redesign the Austin's chassis and

Table 25: Japanese Car Production, 1950-1984
(vehicles, %)

Year	Industry	Nissan%	Toyota%	Others%
1950	1,594	54.3	29.0	16.7
1951	3,611	47.2	40.7	12.1
1952	4,837	49.1	38.4	12.5
1953	8,789	34.7	40.6	24.7
1954	14,472	32.1	29.3	38.6
1955	20,268	32.5	36.5	31.0
1956	32,056	40.4	37.4	22.2
1957	47,121	39.9	42.2	17.9
1958	50,643	33.3	41.9	24.8
1959	78,598	34.0	38.5	27.5
1960	165,094	33.3	25.5	41.2
1961	249,508	30.7	29.6	39.7
1962	268,784	33.1	27.7	39.2
1963	407,830	29.1	31.6	39.3
1964	579,660	29.1	31.4	39.5
1965	696,176	24.4	33.9	41.7
1966	877,656	26.4	36.0	37.6
1967	1,375,755	25.6	34.7	39.7
1968	2,055,821	27.8	32.1	40.1
1969	2,611,499	26.7	36.9	36.4
1970	3,178,708	28.3	33.6	38.1
1971	3,717,858	29.6	37.7	32.7

Table 25 (continued)

Year	Industry	Nissan%	Toyota%	Others%
1972	4,022,289	33.6	37.0	29.4
1973	4,470,550	33.3	36.5	30.2
1974	3,931,842	31.9	37.8	30.3
1975	4,567,854	33.6	37.5	28.9
1976	5,027,792	32.0	34.4	33.6
1977	5,431,045	29.8	34.7	35.5
1978	5,975,968	29.0	34.1	36.9
1979	6,175,771	28.2	34.2	37.6
1980	7,038,108	27.6	32.7	39.7
1981	6,974,131	26.7	32.2	41.1
1982	6,881,586	26.4	32.8	40.8
1983	7,151,888	26.0	33.3	40.7
1984	7,073,173	26.1	34.1	39.8

Sources: Japan Automobile Manufacturers Association, "Nissan Jidōsha no gaiyō," Toyota Jidōsha Kabushiki Kaisha, Kōhō handobukku; Nissan Jidōsha sanjū nen shi; Automotive News; Motor Vehicle Manufacturers Association of the U.S.

suspension system after Japanese taxi drivers, the main buyers of the car, reported numerous broken axles and other problems after just two and three months of use.[58]

Nissan made improvements while switching to local parts, and the whole process provided company engineers with additional experience in durability testing and product development. But the way Asahara managed the tie-up also wasted time and placed unnecessary restrictions on company engineers. Not only did Nissan spend three years assembling the Austin from knock-down sets and preparing to manufacture the car locally only to find that it was not so well suited to Japan and had to be modified, but company engineers felt inhibited because Asahara wanted them to follow the Austin blueprints to the letter. Moreover, once Nissan had signed the contract, it was awkward to reject Austin parts in favor of components from another manufacturer. In contrast, Toyota operated without any of these restrictions and was able to offer monocoque construction in the 1957 Toyota Corona, two years before Nissan made this available in the Datsun.[59]

Another problem was that outside firms supplied from 30 to 40 percent of the Austin's parts to the British automaker using patents that Austin did not own. While these components were replaceable, Nissan and its suppliers had to find substitutes or acquire the patent rights separately. Sometimes Nissan engineers resorted to the same methods Toyota used—copying parts from foreign cars and changing them slightly to avoid patent violations. The objective of the tie-up, however, had been to avoid this. Nissan, meanwhile, still paid royalties on every Austin it made, regardless of where the parts came from or whether it changed the designs. In addition, finding the right materials at affordable prices was another problem Asahara did not fully consider before he began the tie-up, which made it impossible to duplicate all the Austin's parts exactly. Some materials, such as the nickel steel Austin used for its crankshaft and camshaft, were not even available in Japan, so Nissan had to substitute molybdenum steel.[60]

Nissan improved its painting technology by adopting Austin's enamel, which required baking at 150 degrees centigrade, instead of a lacquer paint that dried naturally but placed a constraint on the production flow since the lacquer took longer to dry. The new paint still had to be modified, however, because it did not dry as well as it was supposed to; and Nissan engineers visited Austin's painting facilities only to find that their own techniques were adequate, even if their paint was not. Neither did Nissan gain any real advantage in painting through the tie-up because Toyota also began using enamel during the mid-1950s at approximately the same time.[61]

Studying Austin's factories and production equipment helped Sasaki and other engineers design Nissan's new plants of the 1960s, although the tie-up consumed time during the 1950s that Nissan might have devoted to improving existing production facilities or to building newer ones more quickly. Toyota, in comparison, opened postwar Japan's first new automobile factory in 1959—three years before Nissan built a comparable facility to mass-produce the Datsun. Toyota engineers designed their factory independently, whereas

Nissan management relied on American assistance to prepare the final layout.[62]

After the tie-up ended, Nissan engineers realized they had not acquired any technology from Austin that was unavailable through "indirect" methods—copying from foreign firms, or studying literature that was publicly available. They felt, nevertheless, that the experience was useful because it forced Nissan to raise the level of its product and production technology more quickly than management was planning before 1952. While no Japanese firm manufactured at sufficient volumes to compete with foreign automakers until the mid-1960s, the arrangement with Austin showed Nissan engineers and top executives what a quality European car was like and how it was manufactured, and convinced Nissan engineers that they could no longer fit a car body on top of a truck frame and chassis and hope to survive in an open market or in competition abroad. The tie-up also saved money when it came to developing the 1957 and 1959 Datsun models, the Nissan Junior truck, and the 1960 Cedric. In addition, Nissan acquired specifications for advanced transfer machines and greatly improved its capabilities for making car bodies and cast parts.[63]

But the first major step Nissan took toward producing an original and exportable small car was to introduce the 1959 Datsun 310. While previous models relied heavily on prewar blueprints and techniques, the 310 combined components technology from the Austin, work on the engine by Donald Stone, and a body design (which closely resembled the Austin) from Hara's team. The design department began long-term planning for the car around 1953 but did not decide on the final specifications until it conducted tests and consumer surveys on the 1955 and 1957 Datsun models. A survey done in Japan during the fall of 1955 set basic performance standards: a top speed of 105km (65 miles) per hour and sufficient power to climb a 6-degree incline at 60km (37 miles) per hour.[64]

The engine in the 1955 Datsun 110 was merely an enlarged version of the 1933 unit. Takahashi had increased the displacement from 748cc to 860cc by widening the cylinder bore from 55 to 60mm, but the 110's maximum speed of 85km (53 miles) per hour was barely suitable for city driving in Japan. Meanwhile, Toyota had offered a 995cc engine since the later 1940s and in 1954 installed a 1453cc engine with a top speed of 100km (62 miles) per hour in the Toyopet Crown. Nissan engineers were unable to widen the bore any further on the 860cc engine; while they considered lengthening the stroke, this would have made the engine sluggish and inefficient. Since Takahashi's group did not have an alternative design, in May 1955 management hired Donald Stone to design and test an engine for the 1957 Datsun.[65]

Stone considered developing a totally new engine but then decided to use the Austin unit that Nissan was preparing to manufacture. At 1.5 liters it was almost twice the size of the 1955 Datsun engine, so he cut it down by reducing the height of the cylinder block, modifying the crankshaft, and shortening the piston stroke from 89 to 59mm (Table 26). Since he did not change the diameter and pitch of the cylinders, Nissan was able to use the Austin production equipment to make what engineers called the "Stone engine."

Not only did a shorter piston stroke cut displacement from 1489cc to 988cc and result in a top speed of 95km (59 miles) per hour, but the Austin engine had 3 bearings and overhead valves, making it sturdier and more efficient than the 2-bearing side-valve Datsun engine. Nissan also improved its ability to deliver horsepower and torque by gradually raising the combustion ratio for the 1961 and 1966 models. The latter version then became standard equipment in Nissan's most popular car, the Datsun Sunny (exported as the 210 and the Sentra), introduced in 1966. The company still used it in Pulsar models (a sportier version of the Sunny) during the early 1970s, before switching to newer engines with larger displacements.[66]

After Stone placed the 1-liter engine in the 1957 Datsun, Hara took the car to California for testing, only to discover that the engine was not powerful enough for American highways. The top speed of 59mph was too slow; moreover, constant running at maximum capacity seriously strained the engine and caused it to burn oil and overheat. Like earlier Datsun models, the 210 also vibrated excessively at around 50mph and the shimmy worsened with prolonged driving, due primarily to the separate frame and chassis construction and to a poor suspension system. While the car was adequate for Japan, Hara realized that an export model had to offer a larger engine and a more advanced chassis.[67]

First, Hara decided to raise the displacement to around 1200cc by lengthening the piston stroke from 59 to 71mm, which was still shorter than the 89mm stroke in the Austin A50 engine. The modification resulted in a displacement of 1189cc and a rise in horsepower from 34 to 43 at 4800rpm. Nissan did not offer the 1.2-liter engine as standard equipment in Japan but placed it in a special export model, the 1959 Datsun P310. Hara eliminated the shimmy problem in 1959 by adopting monocoque body construction, independent suspension, and new shock absorbers and stabilizers. Since the vehicle no longer had to double as a pickup truck, Nissan designers also made the Datsun 310 and subsequent models in the series wider, lower, and lighter, to give them handling characteristics more like European cars (Table 27).

Redesigning the A50 for Japanese roads proved to be a useful engineering exercise because it helped Nissan strengthen the Datsun for export and develop the compact-size Cedric (Datsun 280-C). Nissan actually produced two different versions of the Austin: the B130, the original vehicle assembled from knock-down sets; and the B131, the modified version made from Japanese components. The B131 had a stronger chassis, a slightly broader wheelbase, and a wider and higher body. Nissan also improved the performance of the engine, without changing the displacement, by raising the compression inside the combustion chambers to produce more torque and increase horsepower from 50 to 57 at 4400rpm, giving the Japanese version a top speed of 128km (79 miles) per hour with 6 passengers, compared to 109km (68 miles) per hour with 5 passengers for the standard Austin.

While the Cedric replaced the Austin, it was not a copy because Nissan did not have manufacturing rights to the A50.[68] The Cedric body was flatter and longer, despite a difference of only 10mm in the wheelbase. Yet the structural resemblance between the two cars was not accidental, since the chief designer of the Cedric, Fujita Shōtarō, had analyzed the Austin A50 and tested the parts Nissan made for the car in Japan.[69] He completed a first prototype in October 1957 while other engineers were still testing the 1488cc engine, and had a second ready in February 1958. Nissan waited until April 1960 to introduce the Cedric so that it did not compete with the Austin, which Nissan continued to produce through December 1959 and sell until the tie-up formally ended the following March. During these intervening months, Nissan converted the Tsurumi factory to produce the Cedric.[70]

During the late 1950s, Nissan also developed a powerful 1.5-liter engine for the Cedric and Nissan Junior, following Stone's concept of a wide cylinder bore and short piston stroke. By enlarging the cylinder bore in the Austin engine from 73mm to 80mm, and reducing the stroke length from 89mm to 74mm, compression and torque rose while total displacement fell by 1cc and horsepower

Table 26: Datsun Models, 1957-1968 (mm, unless noted)

Year	Model	Max. Load/Speed	Length	Width	Height	Wheelbase	Tread Front	Rear	Weight	Engine Model/cc
Cars										
1957	210	4 pass./95km-hr	3869	1466	1535	2220	1170	1180	925kg	C/988
1959	310	5 /105	"	1496	1480	2280	1209	1194	860	"
1964	410	" /110	3990	1490	1415	2380	1206	1198	880	C1/"
1966	Sunny	" /135	3800	1445	1345	2280	—	—	625	A10/"
1968	510	" /145	4120	1560	1400	2420	—	—	905	L13/1296
Trucks										
1957	220	850kg/90km-hr	3742	1466	1625	2220	1170	1180	915	C/988
1961	320	1000 /105	4125	1515	1610	2470	"	1187	955	E1/1189
1965	520	" /120	4245	1575	1545	2530	1250	1267	960	J/1299

Engines (4-cylinder)

Year	Model Vehicles	Compression Ratio (n:1)	Size	Valves	Bore × Stroke	Max. hp/rpm	Max. Torque (kg. m/rpm)
1957 C	210, 310	7.0	988cc	overhead	73 × 59	34/4400	6.6/2400
1961 C1	311, 312	8.0	"	"	" × "	45/4800	7.2/4000
1959 E	P310	7.5	1189	"	" × 71	43/4800	8.4/2400
1961 E1	P311, P312, P410	8.2	"	"	" × "	55/4800	8.8/3600
1965 J	P411, 520	"	1299	"	" × 77.6	62/5000	10.0/2800
1966 A10	Sunny 1000B10	8.5	988	"	" × 59	56/6000	7.7/3600
1968 L13	510	"	1296	"	83 × 59.9	72/6000	10.5/3600

Sources: Nissan Jidōsha sanjū nen shi *and* Nissan Jidōsha shashi.

Table 27: Nissan Compact-Size Vehicles, 1954-1966 (mm, unless noted)

Year Model	Max. Load/Speed	Length	Width	Height	Wheelbase	Tread Front	Tread Rear	Weight	Engine Model/cc
Cars									
1954 Austin A40	4 pass./109km-hr	4050	1600	1630	2350	1220	1270	1020kg	1G/1197
1956 Austin A50/B130 5	/ "	4090	1580	1550	2510	"	1240	1050	1H/1489
1957 Austin A50/B131 6	/128	4120	"	1570	2520	"	"	"	"
1960 Cedric 30	" /130	4410	1680	1520	2530	1330	1373	1170	G/1488
1966 Cedric 130	" /140	4680	1690	1455	2690	1375	1375	1290	H20/1982
Trucks									
1957 Junior B40	1750kg/90km-hr	4290	1675	1820	2490	1380	1400	1475	1H/1489
1960 Junior B140	" /95	4590	"	1830	2610	"	"	1450	G/1488

1962 Junior 40	2000	/110	4660	1690	1730	2800	"	"	1500	H/1883
1966 Junior 41	"	/120	4665	"	1745	"	1384	1404	1485	H20/1982

Engines (4-cylinder)

Year	Model	Vehicles	Size	Valves	Bore × Stroke	Max. hp/rpm	Max. Torque (kg. m/rpm)	Compression Ratio (n:1)
1954	1G	A40	1197cc	overhead	65.5 × 88.9	42/4500	8.6/2200	7.2
1956	1H	A50/B130, Junior B40	1489	"	73 × 89	50/4400	10.2/2100	"
1957	1H	A50/B131, Junior B42	"	"	" × "	57/ "	11.0/2400	7.4
1960	G	Junior B140, Cedric 30	1488	"	80 × 74	71/5000	11.5/3200	8.0
1963	G	Datsun Z/SP310	"	"	" × "	80/5600	12.0/4000	9.0
1966	H20	Junior 41, Cedric 130	1982	"	87.2 × 83	92/4800	16.0/3600	8.2

Sources: Nissan Jidōsha sanjū nen shi *and* Nissan Jidōsha shashi.

improved dramatically—from 57 at 4400rpm to 71 at 5000rpm. The Cedric was heavier, so its top speed of 130km (81 miles) per hour was only 2km per hour faster than the Austin, but Nissan designers would soon fit a version of this engine into a Datsun sports car. They had offered a sports model in 1952 and again in 1959 but the famous "Z" series (Fairlady) began in 1963—by combining a Datsun 310 chassis with a souped up, high-compression Cedric engine that produced 80 horsepower, rather than 71. In addition, Nissan put a V-8 engine into the 1963 Cedric and marketed it as a luxury car, then enlarged it three years later and renamed it the "Nissan President," an executive's limousine manufactured in small numbers for the Japanese market.[71]

Development of a Product Strategy
The entire experience of competing to introduce new models during the 1950s made it necessary for Nissan and Toyota to develop a policy toward model changes. Between 1951 and the early 1980s, both firms introduced major modifications no more than once every four years (Tables 28 and 29). Nissan on occasion made slight improvements in successive years, such as when Hara modified the Datsun 110 body and won the automobile industry design award given out by the *Mainichi* newspaper in 1956.[72] Toyota often waited

Table 28: Nissan Full Model Changes—Cars, 1959-1984

Series	Model Years	Frequency
Bluebird[a]	1959, 1963, 1967, 1971, 1976, 1979, 1983	4 years
Cedric[b]	1960, 1965, 1971, 1975, 1979, 1983	5
Sunny[c]	1966, 1970, 1973, 1977, 1981	4
Laurel	1968, 1972, 1977, 1980	"
Skyline	1968, 1972, 1977, 1981	"
Gloria	1967, 1971, 1975, 1979, 1983	"

Source: "Nissan Jidōsha no gaiyo" (1984).

Note: [a]Exported as the Maxima; [b]as the 280C; [c]as the 210 or Sentra.

Table 29: Toyota Full Model Changes—Cars, 1955-1984

Series	Model Years	Frequency
Crown	1955, 1962, 1967, 1971, 1974, 1979, 1983	5 years
Corona	1957, 1960, 1964, 1970, 1973, 1978, 1982	4
Publica/ Starlet	1961, 1969, 1973, 1978, 1984	6
Corolla	1966, 1970, 1974, 1979, 1983	4
Mark II	1968, 1972, 1976, 1980, 1984	"
Celica	1970, 1977, 1981	5.5

Sources: Toyota Jidōsha Kabushiki Kaisha, Kōhō shiryō, *"Toyota 1983: Jidōsha sangyō no gaikyō," Toyota 1984: Jidōsha sangyō no gaikyō," and* Toyota no ayumi.

five years or more between model changes—in marked contrast to American manufacturers such as General Motors, which used to put out new models annually. Entirely new designs actually came out every two or three years in the United States until model changes became less frequent during the late 1970s, although, from the 1930s through the mid-1970s, American automakers competed on the basis of expensive annual changes in body styling that added nothing in the way of technical improvements.[73]

Annual model changes were a marketing luxury that Nissan and Toyota wisely avoided. They were relatively poor financially, inexperienced at car design, and operating within a protected market, although it was unlikely that cosmetic modifications would have appealed to Japanese consumers during the 1950s or early 1960s, since the main reason for low car sales was high prices. The quality and performance of Japanese models were also below the standards of European cars available in Japan through tie-ups, and this pressured both Nissan and Toyota to develop models that would be competitive at home and potentially exportable. Since the best way to accomplish this was through a gradual process of incremental improvements, with or without a tie-up, both firms began to follow similar schedules for new-model development (Table 30). Nissan and Toyota usually started basic planning around six years before actual production of a new model, made full-scale prototypes four years in advance, then allowed a year for primary production preparations—an overall program that made it possible to incorporate the results of extensive testing and retesting of vehicles and production equipment before settling on final designs.[74]

Table 30: New-Model Development

Stage	Lead Time	Characteristics
I. Long-term product planning	Variable	Market research, R&D input
II. Basic planning	6 years	General specifications determined; survey of competitors' products; estimates of time and costs for new model
III. Design planning	5 years	Body styling, using clay models; details determined, with cost estimates
IV. Prototype design	4 years	Full-size clay model and a prototype constructed; chassis designed, built, and tested; completed model built and tested
V. Production model design	3-2 years	Design made, using test data; second test model built and new blueprints drawn up; outside suppliers requested to make sample parts; study of cost reductions; sales preparations begun; initial preparations of dies, jigs, and tools

Table 30 (continued)

Stage	Lead Time	Characteristics
VI. Primary production planning	1 year	Main preparation of dies, jigs, and tools; design plans revised and blueprints made; accurate production cost estimates made; outside parts makers chosen; value analysis done on all designs to reduce costs
VII. Secondary production preparations		Testing of equipment and tools, with changes made as necessary; thorough testing of the new model, and blueprints revised again; planning for manufacturing, training of workers and setting of standard times; intensive preparation of dealers for servicing

Source: Iwakoshi, pp. 231-234.

Yet Nissan's sales performance after the Austin tie-up was disappointing to managers, mainly because the model change for the 1959 Bluebird, the 1963 Datsun 410, while not inferior technologically, sold poorly. The 410 was not entirely Japanese; top management had still lacked confidence in company designers and hired an Italian firm, Pininfarina, to do the body styling. But the Italians did not study the Japanese market and added a rear fin that may have been popular in Europe and the United States but that did not appeal to Japanese consumers.[75]

Low demand for the 410 contributed to a drop in Nissan's share of car production from the 31 percent averaged during 1959-1964 to 24 percent in 1965—nearly 10 percent less than Toyota (see Table 25). Aided by the Austin tie-up, however, Nissan reduced Toyota's lead in total production of cars and trucks from an average of 9 percent a year between 1955 and 1959 to about 5 percent. This continued to be the margin separating the two firms into the early

Table 31: Production Shares, 1950-1984 (%, vehicles)

Period	Nissan %	Toyota %	Subtotal %	Others %	Industry Volume
1950-1954	34.0	35.1	69.1	30.9	50,000
1955-1959	30.6	39.8	70.4	29.6	150,000
1960-1964	21.4	26.2	47.6	52.4	1,000,000
1965-1969	22.1	27.2	49.3	50.7	3,000,000
1970-1974	27.9	32.4	60.3	39.7	6,000,000
1975-1979	27.2	32.0	59.2	40.8	8,000,000
1980-1984	22.6	29.5	52.1	47.9	11,000,000

Sources: See Table 20 and Appendix D.

1980s, although Toyota was increasing its lead over Nissan during 1983-1984 and probably would have been ahead by a few percent more during the late 1960s and 1970s if Nissan had not merged with Prince in 1966 and taken over two of its compact car lines (Table 31 and Appendix D).

TOYOTA AND TOYOTA MOTOR SALES

Nissan and Toyota accounted for 8 or 9 of the 10 best selling cars every year between 1973 and 1983 in the highly competitive Japanese market. Toyota usually provided 6, led by the Corolla and Corona, and Nissan 3, led by the Nissan Sunny (also called the 210 and the Sentra) (Table 32). In terms of price and basic technology, there was little difference between the products these two firms offered. And, although the Sunny outsold the Corolla worldwide in 1983, 556,340 units to 555,706, Toyota models gradually developed a slightly better reputation for handling precision, engine smoothness, and seating comfort.[76] Toyota Motor Sales, formed in 1950 and merged with Toyota in 1982, also tried to make sure that Toyota models had the lowest prices and the largest advertising campaigns in the industry. Toyota's small but consistent advantage over Nissan in production share was due to a combination of skills in product development, marketing, and manufacturing. This performance was all the more extraordinary, given that Toyota never received direct assistance from a foreign automobile manufacturer, although top executives had negotiated with General Motors in 1936 and then four times with Ford between 1938 and 1960 regarding joint ventures or tie-up arrangements.

Tie-up Negotiations: Attempts and Failures
The 1936 discussions took place between Toyoda Automatic Loom and General Motors' subsidiary in Japan, which initiated the talks in an effort to retain a base in the country after the 1936 automobile industry law required that domestic automakers be at least 50-percent owned and managed by Japanese nationals. Toyoda Kiichirō rejected the idea because he was still manufacturing automobiles experimentally and was not prepared to commit himself or Toyoda Automatic Loom to a joint venture. In addition, Kiichirō, as well as Kamiya Shōtarō, who had joined Toyoda Automatic Loom in 1935 after working for Japan GM, preferred to deal with Ford, for two reasons. Ford allowed foreign partners to export complete vehicles back to the United States, whereas General Motors did not; and General Motors did not permit engines or other major subassemblies to be manufactured outside of the United States, while Ford did. It seemed obvious to both men that an agreement with Ford would provide greater access to American automobile technology.[77]

While negotiations with Japan Ford began in 1938 and resulted in a tentative agreement between the American subsidiary and Toyota for the joint production of standard-size trucks, there was no consensus in the Japanese government regarding whether such a tie-up should be permitted or which ministry should oversee it. After the talks had gone on for a few months the Ministry of the Army halted them by preventing Kamiya, who was handling the negotiations for Toyota, from going to the United States to work out the final details of the contract with Ford's home office. The army then announced that it would permit a tie-up only if Nissan were allowed to join.

At the time, Nissan was manufacturing a large number of trucks for the army and had committed itself to setting up automobile production in Manchuria. Since the truck design bought from Graham-Paige was flawed, there was pressure on Nissan to put out a new model. Army officials believed that Ford might provide a new truck design and promoted a second round of negotiations involving

Table 32: Ten Best Selling Car Models in Japan, 1973-1983

Rank	1	2	3	4	5	6	7	8	9	10
1983	Toyota Corolla	Nissan Sunny	Mazda Familia	Toyota Corona	Nissan Bluebird	Toyota Carina	Toyota Sprinter	Toyota Mark II	Toyota Crown	Nissan Skyline
1982	"	"	"	Nissan Bluebird	Toyota Corona	"	Honda City	Nissan Skyline	Toyota Mark II	Toyota Crown
1981	"	Nissan Bluebird	"	Nissan Sunny	Toyota Mark II	"	Nissan Skyline	Toyota Crown	Toyota Sprinter	Toyota Corona
1980	"	"	Nissan Sunny	Toyota Crown	Toyota Carina	Nissan Skyline	Mazda Familia	Toyota Corona	"	Toyota Mark II
1979	"	Nissan Sunny	Toyota Corona	Nissan Skyline	"	Nissan Bluebird	Toyota Crown	Toyota Mark II	"	Nissan Laurel

Year									
1978	"	Nissan Skyline	Toyota Mark II	Mitsubishi Garon	Toyota Carina	Toyota Corona	Nissan Bluebird	Toyota Crown	Toyota Sprinter
1977	Toyota Mark II	Nissan Sunny	Mitsubishi Garon	Datsun Bluebird	Nissan Skyline	"	Toyota Sprinter	Toyota Carina	Nissan Laurel
1976	Toyota Corona	"	Nissan Skyline	"	Toyota Sprinter	Honda Civic	Toyota Carina	Mitsubishi Garon	Toyota Crown
1975	Nissan Sunny	Toyota Corona	Honda Civic	Nissan Skyline	Toyota Carina	Toyota Sprinter	Nissan Bluebird	Toyota Crown	Nissan Laurel
1974	"	"	"	"	"	"	"	Toyota Mark II	Toyota Crown
1973	"	Nissan Skyline	Toyota Carina	Toyota Corona	Nissan Bluebird	Toyota Mark II	Nissan Violet	Toyota Sprinter	"

Sources: "Toyota 1983: Jidōsha sangyō no gaikyō," p. 25, and "Toyota 1984: Jidōsha sangyō no gaikyō," p. 25.

115

the three firms; they reached a tentative agreement late in 1939 that called for a joint venture, with Nissan and Toyota dividing a 60-percent interest and Japan Ford investing the remaining 40 percent. Yet Nissan's president, Aikawa Yoshisuke, left for Germany without convincing his successor, Murakami Masasuke, or other key subordinates, to support the proposal. Murakami managed to delay the joint venture long enough for war to break out in Europe and relations between the United States and Japan to worsen, forcing Japan Ford to close down.[78]

Toyota started negotiations with Ford again in June 1950. This time, management was interested in Ford's small car, the Consul, built for the European market. Yet the Korean War broke out on June 25th, prompting the U.S. Department of Defense to set emergency restrictions on overseas investment and the dispatching of technicians abroad. This ended the discussions, although a group of Toyota executives, headed by Toyoda Eiji, remained in the United States for the rest of the year to observe Ford's factories and office facilities. They applied much of what they learned to Toyota's plants and office management systems. In fact, the success of the programs they introduced beginning in 1951 encouraged the Japanese executives to believe that the company did not need a tie-up, especially since Toyota's 1953 car prices were already lower than those of the European imports being assembled in Japan, and work on the Toyopet Crown, for the 1955 model year, was going well.

Kamiya, the first president of Toyota Motor Sales, also had specific reasons for opposing a tie-up after World War II. Along with Ishida Taizō, Toyota's president, and engineers in top management such as Toyoda Eiji, he was satisfied with the progress of the Toyopet series introduced in 1947 and worried that Toyota would not be able to export cars built with imported parts under license (such restrictions affected Nissan, Hino, Isuzu, and Shin-Mitsubishi). Kamiya in particular wanted to avoid potential limits on production due to government quotas on allocations of foreign currency, since these would curtail Toyota's ability to import knock-down sets or components. In addition, he was wary of MITI bureaucrats and feared that they might place other restrictions on the company's operations if Toyota were involved with a foreign automaker.

Toyota nonetheless held a fourth round of negotiations with Ford in 1960. On this occasion, Kamiya sought a joint venture that would produce the Publica subcompact and market it overseas. He even wanted the new firm to merge with Toyota Motor Sales, but Ford executives saw no obvious benefits for their company in the deal and decided to continue producing small cars through their British subsidiary.[79] Rather than seek another partner, Toyota proceeded with its program of independent car development, although there were tie-ups within the Toyota group for specific technologies, such as ductile iron casting techniques, electrical and electronic components, and automatic transmissions.

Independent Product Development

In the competition with Nissan, nothing was more important than the experience Toyota engineers accumulated designing their own vehicles and accommodating design changes in manufacturing. Toyota trucks of the 1930s and early 1940s were so prone to breaking down that the army hesitated to buy them, but this forced Toyota to improve its products. By the mid-1950s, not even Nissan engineers could find any differences in quality or performance between Nissan and Toyota vehicles. Toyota actually had an advantage in that it used more universal machine tools, which made it easier to modify outdated or faulty designs and to introduce new features. Nissan, in contrast, not only had trouble developing new engines and chassis because company engineers lacked design experience, but the manufacturing equipment Nissan acquired during the 1930s and 1950s made it difficult and expensive to change specifications.[80]

Another advantage Toyota had came as a result of Kiichirō's realization, even before he incorporated Toyota as a separate firm, that he needed a formal structure to coordinate product development. In Toyoda Automatic Loom's automobile department he thus set up a staff office for "supervision and improvement" to solve problems in manufacturing or product designs, manage relations with dealers, gather technical information or feedback from customers, settle claims, and advise parts suppliers. After 1937, this became part of Toyota's staff organization, although, during the war, management moved the office to the manufacturing and then the research departments, before maintaining it from 1943 to 1945 as an independent committee. Kiichirō reestablished the office during the late 1940s, and it continued to play an important role in product development and quality control after the mid-1960s as a section in Toyota's quality assurance department.[81]

Toyota was also ready by 1947 to introduce a model to compete with the Datsun because Kiichirō had made certain that car research and experimental design continued throughout the war. Toyota's first subcompact (EA), designed in 1938, was actually a copy of a German DKW (Audi) with a 585cc engine (Table 33). When govern-

Table 33: Toyota Models, 1936-1966 (mm, unless noted)

Year	Model	Length	Width	Height	Wheelbase	Weight	Maximum Load	Engine Model/cc
Cars								
1936	AA	4737	1734	1737	2851	1500kg		A/3389
1938	EA	3220	1300	1250	2610	650		E/585
1940	AE	4500	1730	1635	2500	1220		C/2258
1943	AC	4884	1734	1746	2850	1550		B/3386
1947	Toyopet SA	3800	1590	1530	2400	1170		S/995
1951	Toyopet SF	4280	"	1600	2500	1250		"
1954	Crown RS	4285	1680	1525	2530	1210		R/1453
1957	Corona ST10	3912	1470	1518	2400	960		S/995
1960	Corona PT20	3990	1490	1440	"	940		P/997
1961	Publica UP10	3520	1415	1380	2130	580		U/697
1965	Corona RT40	4110	1550	1420	2420	945		2R/1490
1966	Publica UP20	3620	1415	1380	2130	620		2UB/790
1966	Corolla KE10	3845	1485	1380	2285	710		K/1077
Trucks								

Year	Model						
1947	Toyopet SB	3950	1590	1725	2400	1125	1000kg	S/995
1952	Toyopet SG	4195	1594	1735	2500	1170	"	"
1953	Toyopet RK	4265	1675	"	"	1220	1250	R/1453
1954	Toyo-Ace SKB	4237	"	1850	"	1130	1000	S/995
1956	Toyopet RK23	4290	"	1700	2530	1360	1500	R/1453
1958	Toyopet RK30	4275	"	"	"	1370	"	"
1959	Toyo-Ace Pk20	4260	1690	1895	2500	1165	1000	P/997

Engines (4-cylinder)

Year	Model	Size	Valves	Bore × Stroke	Compression Ratio (n:1)	Max. hp/rpm	Max. Torque (kg. m/rpm)
1937	C	2258cc	overhead	84.1 × 101.6	6.4	48/2800	15.5/1400
1947	S	995	side	65 × 75	6.5	27/4000	5.9/2400
1953	R	1453	overhead	77 × 78	6.8	48/4000	10 /2400
1959	P	997	"	69.9 × 65	7.5	45/5000	7 /3200
1961	U	697	"	78 × 73	7.2	28/4300	5.4/2800
1965	2R	1490	"	" × 78	8.0	70/5000	11.5/2600
	2UB	790	"	83 × 73	9.0	45/5400	6.8/3800
1966	K	1077	"	75 × 61	"	60/6000	8.5/3800

Source: Toyota Jidōsha sanjū nen shi.

ment restrictions prevented Kiichirō from manufacturing the car, he decided in 1939 to move his designers to Shanghai, where he had purchased a repair shop two years earlier and converted it to assemble knock-down sets. Engineers in China then completed two standard-size cars in 1940 and 1943, but made only a few for government and military officials.[82]

Directly after World War II, Kiichirō recruited more design engineers from the aircraft industry and put them to work with his regular staff studying various European cars, particularly British and German models. Based on designs sketched out during the war and then modified in 1945-1946, Toyota came out with the first "Toyopet" (SA) in 1947. The body shell looked like a Volkswagen with a slightly elongated front, although everything else about the car was the same as the Toyopet truck. While the 995cc side-valve engine was not as efficient as the better European engines, its top speed of 87km (54 miles) per hour with 4 passengers was considerably faster than the postwar Datsun, which had a 722cc engine and a maximum speed of merely 65km (40 miles) per hour. Not surprisingly, the Toyopet car and truck models sold better and bolstered Toyota's reputation in the industry. The next model changes in 1951 and 1952 were even more popular and enabled Toyota to pass Nissan in total sales.[83]

In 1950, Toyota engineers also began work on the first Japanese car that would not use a truck frame and chassis—the Toyopet Crown RS, introduced in 1954. This offered the first car body that Toyota manufactured in house. There was still considerable overlapping with truck technology since the engine, a 1453cc unit with overhead valves, came from the 1953 Toyopet truck. But the Crown, and a slightly less expensive version, the Master, received excellent appraisals for performance and a price that Toyota Motor Sales set below the European cars assembled by Nissan, Isuzu, and Hino. While all had engines in the 1.5-liter class, Toyota introduced the Master at 884,860 yen ($2458) and the Crown at 969,860 ($2694), compared to 1,170,000 yen ($3250) for Nissan's Austin A50.[84]

Toyota's new cars were still too large and expensive to stimulate mass sales in Japan, but they proved it was possible to compete with Japanese automakers that had opted for tie-ups. Due to its low price and durable construction, for example, the Crown became the choice of two out of three taxi drivers, who made up as much as 90 percent of car demand in Japan during the early 1950s. Toyota then improved the Crown gradually, without a full model change until 1962. When

Toyota introduced the new model, industry analysts found it comparable in quality and performance to Nissan's Cedric.[85] Furthermore, the next car that Toyota designed, the 1957 Corona, set another precedent in the Japanese automobile industry by offering monocoque construction. Toyota engineers had studied this feature in foreign models made during the late 1930s and after the war; this prepared them to experiment in 1953 by making a standard-size bus with the monocoque design. While Nissan learned how to copy this type of construction when it made the Austin, it was not ready to introduce this into the Datsun line until 1959.[86]

Toyota was less successful when it tried to gain a head start over Nissan in the subcompact field by introducing the 698cc Publica in 1961. This sold originally for 389,000 yen ($1081), even though various studies of car prices in the United States and Europe had indicated that, to sell in large volumes, an automobile should be no more than 1.4 times higher in price than the average family income. Since Japanese families earned an average of only 150,000 yen ($417) per year in 1961, the Publica cost 2.6 times this figure. Toyota Motor Sales was aware that the car was too expensive, but Kamiya hoped to boost production through exports and then cut costs and prices gradually. The joint venture with Ford failed to materialize, however, and low domestic sales forced Toyota to concentrate on developing other car lines such as the Corolla. Publica sales thus languished during the 1960s, and the line did not undergo a model change until 1969. Toyota replaced this in 1973 with the Starlet.

Nissan executives, as usual, were more cautious. They limited their product strategy to improving the basic Datsun series and did not attempt to make a smaller or cheaper car until the 1966 Sunny, which turned out to be Nissan's top-selling model. Toyota engineers and marketing experts, meanwhile, were busy studying what had gone wrong with the Publica and designing another car specifically for export—the Corolla, by far the most successful series in Toyota history[87] (Table 34).

Domestic Marketing Strategies
Much of the credit for Toyota's sales record after 1950 goes to Kamiya Shōtarō (1898-1980), president of Toyota Motor Sales from 1950 to 1975. After graduating from the Nagoya Higher Commercial School (later Nagoya University) in 1917, he went to work for Mitsui Trading's offices in Seattle and finally London, where he purchased steel from 1919 to 1924. Kamiya left Mitsui in 1925 to start his own

TABLE 34: Toyota Car Models—Cumulative and 1983 Production (vehicles, %)

Series	Year Introduced	Cumulative Production	1983 Production	% of 1983 Car Production
Corolla	1966	10,538,828	625,633	26
Corona	1957	5,409,207	190,077	8
Mark II	1968	3,054,474	206,162	9
Crown	1955	2,678,305	130,630	5
Celica	1970	2,539,739	183,502	8
Carina	1970	2,113,364	150,749	6
Sprinter	1968	1,537,152	119,737	5
Starlet	1973	1,105,706	118,606	5
Tercel	1978	898,758	163,904	7

Source: "Toyota 1984: Jidōsha sangyō no gaikyō," p. 17.

trading company but returned to Japan in 1927 after this venture failed and took a job with Japan GM in Tokyo, where the firm located its central office for Japanese marketing operations. (The head office and assembly plant were in Osaka.) By 1930, at age 32, he was the top manager in Tokyo.[88]

Kamiya became dissatisfied with Japan GM primarily because he worried that the military would prohibit foreign automakers from remaining in Japan. Just before the army actually drafted such legislation he decided to join a Japanese automobile company. He considered Nissan but preferred Toyoda Automatic Loom, which was close to his home in Nagoya. An acquaintance from his time in Mitsui's Seattle office provided an introduction to Toyoda Kiichirō, and they met in 1935. Kiichirō had not yet found someone to take charge of marketing; he was impressed with Kamiya's credentials and immediately offered him a job and complete authority over this area. Kamiya accepted, despite a cut in salary from 600 yen ($200) to 120 yen ($40) per month. He also brought to Toyoda Automatic Loom his assistant at Japan GM, Katō Seishi (1909-), who would succeed Kamiya as president of Toyota Motor Sales in 1975; and he convinced the owner of a Chevrolet dealership in Nagoya, Hinode Motors, to become the first Toyota dealer.

During the 1930s, Kamiya tested most of the basic strategies that he would use to sell Toyota cars after World War II, but first he had to recruit dealers from Japan GM because Kiichirō did not have enough money to establish his own sales agencies. Since Kamiya knew people from all over the country through the General Motors subsidiary, which had set up dealerships in every prefecture, he was able to persuade many dealers to accept Toyota franchises. After World War II, Toyota Motor Sales continued to recruit dealers and capital from around Japan rather than fund and manage dealerships directly.

The 1936 automobile industry law encouraged Chevrolet and Ford dealers to shift to Japanese automakers; Kamiya also took advantage of the fact that many were unhappy with the way the American subsidiaries treated them. Japan GM, for example, usually dropped dealers who were in financial trouble, rather than provide assistance. Since Kamiya had heard many of these complaints, when he started building a sales network for Toyota he made sure to promise dealers that Toyota Motor Sales would treat them as "equal partners" and help anyone who had difficulty financing orders.

Another task facing Kamiya when he joined Toyoda Automatic Loom was to set a price for Kiichirō's truck. The vehicle was far from perfected and broke down frequently, even on the way to the showroom in Nagoya for its debut. To sell the truck, Kamiya decided to do two things: price it below the competing American models, and guarantee servicing after the sale. He fixed the price at 2900 yen ($967), 200 yen ($67) less than comparable Ford and Chevrolet trucks. While this meant selling at below cost, he hoped that, once Toyota established a market position, rising sales and manufacturing scales would lower production expenses. The 1936 legislation made it unnecessary to test this theory, but setting prices below those of the competition, and even below cost temporarily, became one of Toyota's primary marketing strategies after 1945, in Japan and abroad. In addition, Kamiya promoted sales of an untested product by establishing a training program for dealers and servicemen. Toyota Motor Sales expanded this system after 1950 so that every franchise was able to make and guarantee repairs.

After Kiichirō made Kamiya a managing director of Toyota in 1945, he began planning to detach the sales department. GHQ restrictions on Toyota's assets prevented him from carrying this out until 1949, when Toyota ran up a huge inventory of unsold vehicles and an operating deficit of 200,000,000 yen. The Bank of Japan then organized a consortium of 24 banks, led by the Teikoku (Mitsui) and Tōkai Banks, which provided funds on three conditions: that Toyota incorporate the sales department to separate operating capital from other funds, limit production to orders from the sales company, and discharge surplus employees. Since Kamiya had already drafted plans to create a marketing subsidiary, he was able to do this within a few months. GHQ prohibited Toyota from investing directly in the new company, although Kamiya managed to transfer 358 employees from the sales department and continued using the Toyota trademark and his former office facilities.

Toyota was also better prepared than Nissan to organize a national sales network during the 1950s, due to Kamiya's special efforts to recruit new dealers during and immediately after World War II. The control association for automobile distribution, set up in 1942, had eliminated the need for Nissan to have a sales company or a marketing network because the army purchased all its production. Toyota trucks, on the other hand, were not as well made. Since the military bought only what it needed to supplement its other purchases, the government allowed Toyota to sell some of its production to the private sector, helping the company to maintain contacts with dealers.[89] The Japanese government also chose Kamiya to be a managing director of the control association, putting him in touch with Nissan dealers, who had little or nothing to sell. Before the association dissolved in June 1946, he created an opportunity to use these contacts to Toyota's advantage.

In May, Kamiya organized a meeting for prospective dealers at Toyota's head offices and invited all the Nissan (and Isuzu) dealers. Then he tried to persuade them to accept Toyota franchises while they were still under the formal direction of the control association and not obligated to return to Nissan (or Isuzu). Kiichirō was chairman of the meeting and spoke of the plans Toyota had to introduce new cars and to grow along with the entire Japanese automobile industry, while Kamiya talked about their commitment to treating dealers as equals. The strategy worked: Only 47 of the 106 dealers Nissan had before the war rejoined the firm after GHQ dissolved the control association.[90] Kamiya also founded an organization for dealerships and appointed a former Nissan dealer as the first chairman to assure the new recruits that they were welcome.

Nissan thus resumed operations after World War II with a handicap in marketing that it never fully overcame. To rebuild a sales network by recruiting franchised dealers, as Toyota did, required time and contacts around the country, so management decided to fund dealerships directly. Using this strategy, Nissan matched the number of Toyota outlets during the early 1950s, although Toyota Motor Sales still had an advantage because Kamiya used local people to manage and own dealerships. In Japan, selling an automobile usually involved more personal contact between the sales personnel and customers than was common in the United States; Nissan salesmen sent out from Tokyo had a difficult time competing with Toyota dealers who were natives of the areas in which they worked.[91]

Aside from the franchise system, Toyota Motor Sales employed several other methods to outsell its competitors. During the 1930s, both Nissan and Toyota had copied the marketing networks set up by Japan GM and Japan Ford, which consisted of one main dealership (usually with several outlets) in each prefecture. After the war, they attempted to reconstruct these and expand the number of outlets, although in 1956 Kamiya decided to allow more than one dealership in a single prefecture. He did not trust the majority of Toyota dealers, who had sold mostly trucks in the past, to promote car sales, and wanted to organize specialized dealers to handle new car models like the Corona. From this time on, Toyota Motor Sales set up new dealerships for each new model line and did not allow any dealer to carry a full complement of Toyota vehicles.

Not only did the number of Toyota dealers double between 1956 and 1957; Kamiya eliminated another problem as well: In the past, salesmen often neglected to push one line if another was selling better. Specialization, however, limited the number of products a dealer had to offer, and this forced salesmen to promote even slow-selling models. Honda had pioneered this marketing strategy in Japan during 1952 by establishing separate sales agents for its different motorcycle lines. Nissan did not catch on until Toyota had improved its market share from 32 percent in 1954 to 44 percent in 1957, although, with the introduction of the Datsun 310 in 1959, Nissan abandoned the practice of having one large dealership per prefecture and began establishing dealerships for each new car line[92] (Table 35).

Kamiya also lived up to his promise to treat dealers as "equal" partners. When he reorganized Toyota's network during 1952-1953 to place franchises under the supervision of the sales company, he borrowed directly from General Motors' manual to write up profes-

Table 35: Dealerships, 1956-1959 (number of dealerships, 1,000,000 yen)

Company	1956	1957	1958	1959	Total Capital	Capital per Dealer
Toyota	50	109	108	108	2,757	25.5
Nissan	49	59	63	89	2,733	30.7
Isuzu	50	40	43	43	1,135	26.4
Hino	33	37	42	52	741	14.3
Prince	—	39	40	41	483	11.8

Source: Okumura Shōji, "Jidōsha kōgyō no hatten dankai to kōzō," in Arisawa Hiromi, ed., Gendai Nihon Sangyō kōza, V, 358.

sional guidelines for sales training, promotion techniques, and pricing. But he reassured dealers that Toyota Motor Sales was a specialized subsidiary formed to work with them and to provide assistance. He also urged them to hire college graduates, started a training program for these recruits that became the Toyota Sales College in 1958, located at the Chūbu Nippon Driving School in Nagoya, which Toyota Motor Sales owned, and established the Toyopet Repair Company in 1954 as well as other repair schools throughout Japan to train servicemen.[93]

One of Toyota Motor Sales' most successful strategies to increase car demand was to invest in driver education. Kamiya first experimented with this approach in 1957 by spending 400,000,000 yen ($1,100,000) to buy the bankrupt Chūbu Nippon Driving School, the largest institution of its kind in Asia. Since the capitalization of Toyota Motor Sales was then only 1 billion yen ($2,800,000), Kamiya encountered considerable resistance from other company directors. Nevertheless, he was convinced that driver education, using Toyota cars, would increase sales as more and more Japanese obtained automobile licenses. The school proved to be enormously successful, prompting Kamiya to invest in several others around the country, often in conjunction with local dealerships. The schools usually guaranteed to provide a student with lessons at a predetermined fee until he or she passed the driver's test. Toyota dealers, meanwhile, offered installment plans with small down payments to the students.[94]

Toyota Motor Sales was also the first company in the Japanese automobile industry to make extensive use of installment plans. Kiichirō had founded a firm called Toyoda Finance in 1939, modeled after the credit subsidiaries of Ford and General Motors in the United States, but it ceased operating in 1940 due to wartime regulations. In the late 1940s, Toyota and Nissan tried again to introduce credit systems, although both had difficulty finding banks to cooperate. After the establishment of Toyota Motor Sales in 1950, however, Kamiya convinced Tōkai, Mitsui, and other banks to support an extension of installment sales, using the vehicles sold to customers as collateral, and recruited Tokio Marine and Fire Insurance to insure debts if vehicles were stolen or damaged in accidents before a customer completed the car payments. General Motors, Ford, and Chrysler had started both these practices but they had not been adopted in Japan.

The production and marketing system Kamiya and Ishida set up in 1950 continued until Toyota Motor Sales merged with Toyota in 1982. Toyota sold all its output to Toyota Motor Sales at wholesale prices for notes payable within 60 days. Toyota Motor Sales resold these vehicles to dealers in return for promissory notes payable within 50 days, signed by the individual customer. The sales company then sent these notes to its banks for credit, which the banks used to redeem the notes given to Toyota in payment for vehicles received. Customers, meanwhile, paid directly to the banks, offsetting the loans extended to Toyota Motor Sales.

The major benefits of this arrangement were that the sold vehicles served as collateral, and funds used for sales were clearly separated from Toyota's operating capital. Toyota Motor Sales was able to concentrate on marketing, and Toyota on manufacturing and equipment investment, even in times of tight credit. In contrast, while Nissan usually matched Toyota's spending on machinery, it did not have a separate system for financing sales and, during the Austin tie-up, fell short of funds for its dealers, contributing to the decline in Nissan's market share during the 1950s.[95]

Another feature of the system was that Toyota limited its production to the demand that Toyota Motor Sales created, based on firm orders from franchised dealers. Bankers insisted on this arrangement to restrict the size of Toyota's inventories after the financial crisis of 1949-1950. Nissan, which had no such restraint on production levels, since it owned dealers directly and did not have a sales company after 1949, tended to store excess inventories on dealers' lots when sales were slow. This practice could be risky if management did not plan accurately or responsibly, yet it provided a potential advantage: Nissan could manufacture in larger lots and cut prices due to savings from economies of scale. Managers did this if the projected savings were greater than the additional expenses generated by carrying more inventories of components and completed vehicles before dealers actually paid for them.[96]

Kamiya became concerned about Nissan's potential advantage in 1953, when he wanted to cut the price of the new Toyopet models but was unable to convince dealers to take on extra inventory. Without substantial orders in advance from Toyota Motor Sales it would be difficult for Toyota to reduce costs. Company bankers were watching to make sure there were no violations of the 1950 agreement; nonetheless, Kamiya found a way out by setting up just one dealership, Tokyo Toyopet, that Toyota Motor Sales would directly own and manage. This would place large orders for Toyopets and function as a buffer to hold finished-car inventories until price cuts led to an increase in sales. Kamiya could not reveal his true purpose and announced, instead, that he was founding Tokyo Toyopet to improve the distribution network in Tokyo as quickly as possible for the new Toyopet models.

Tokyo alone accounted for 30 percent of Japan's entire demand for automobiles; the reception of a new car in this city could determine its success or failure. While company bankers accepted this reasoning, regular dealers were upset, although Kamiya told them that Tokyo Toyopet was an exception and that he would maintain the franchise system. Kamiya also claimed that the new dealership would benefit them by trying out new marketing ideas, which it did. Tokyo Toyopet hired 100 college graduates as salesmen, designed a sophisticated training program, and instituted a standardized price list—practices subsequently adopted throughout the Toyota sales network.[97]

Before settling on the final design and price of the new Toyopet, Toyota Motor Sales also surveyed taxi drivers to find out what type of vehicle they preferred. They wanted something reliable and inexpensive, which Toyota engineers set out to design. As orders came in from Tokyo Toyopet, Toyota Motor Sales reduced the price of the standard Toyopet model from 1,200,000 yen ($3333) in August 1952 to 950,000 yen ($2638) in January 1953, around 200,000 yen

($556) less than the Austin, Renault, and Hillman models available in Japan. The popularity of the Toyopet series convinced Toyota management that their decision not to become involved with a foreign manufacturer had been correct.[98]

Kamiya used the same approach to market the first Toyota truck in 1935 and the 1953 Toyopet: He determined what price would outsell his competitors and then left it up to production engineers and planners to find ways to cut manufacturing costs. Toyota management still employed this strategy to set prices in the early 1980s, although, during the 1950s and 1960s, domestic sales increased rapidly enough after initial price reductions to offset the cuts through greater scales of production and procurement. After 1970, Toyota Motor Sales relied on increases in exports to lower production costs and offset price cuts.[99] But, even with protection against imports, rapidly growing demand intensified the competition between Nissan and Toyota for new customers, causing car prices at both firms to drop every year, without adjusting for inflation, from the early 1950s through 1973, when they began to rise gradually.[100]

Profit margins remained high during the late 1950s and 1960s because demand rose faster than domestic automakers could build factory capacity or recruit suppliers. Price cuts were possible because companies lowered their manufacturing costs through economies of scale, new equipment, higher levels of subcontracting to firms with lower wage levels, and other techniques that led to rises in productivity. In marketing, however, Toyota Motor Sales had another advantage over Nissan in that no one expected Kamiya to operate at much of a profit; his job was to distribute vehicles and finance sales. During the 1950s, therefore, Toyota Motor Sales was able to cut prices while managing profit rates on total revenues of only 1 or 2 percent (before taxes), far less than Nissan or Toyota and its other major subsidiaries.[101]

Both before and after World War II, Nissan stressed manufacturing technology over marketing. It also had lower sales and profits than Toyota from the 1950s through the early 1980s, although one reason was that costs in the Tokyo-Yokohama area were higher than in the countryside, where Toyota located its manufacturing facilities. Kawamata realized this when he entered Nissan in 1947 and gradually increased the company's emphasis on cost accounting to raise earnings. After he became president of the company in 1957, Kawamata usually would not authorize price cuts before Nissan achieved savings in production costs unless it was absolutely necessary to compete with Toyota. Marketing also received little attention under Asahara Genshichi; as a technical expert, he openly favored a concentration of resources in automation and product engineering—a predilection that Nissan engineers who worked under him continued to display through the early 1980s.[102]

Even though Kamiya did not sit on Toyota's board of directors after 1950, his influence, and the existence of Toyota Motor Sales, made it impossible for Toyota to neglect marketing. He also made sure that Toyota Motor Sales cooperated closely with Toyota in all areas of operations. Consultations between the two companies were largely informal, until they established a joint executive council system during 1962-1963 that provided for executive meetings, usually once a month, to discuss production planning, exports, domestic marketing, servicing, finances, advertising, parts procurement, and product development.[103] They also exchanged personnel occasionally, but this did not become a formal practice until a few years before the 1982 merger.[104]

While it was primarily a marketing organ, one of the most important functions of Toyota Motor Sales was to assist Toyota in product development. Based on the assumption that new model planning began with market research, in 1956 Kamiya created a unified department for planning and research to coordinate market strategies developed by researchers at Toyota Motor Sales with product planning by Toyota's design engineers. After the 1982 merger, this became the Tokyo research department of the new Toyota Motor Corporation. Much of the information Toyota Motor Sales gathered came from monthly or semi-annual surveys, usually conducted through dealers, which asked customers their preferences for styling, model types, colors, prices, and other features. Toyota also used these surveys to estimate potential demand for new models.

The planning and research department usually advised Toyota to combine known consumer preferences when developing new models rather than present radically new concepts, but in production planning it often made ambitious recommendations. Toyota management even credited the department with having done the initial studies that led to the construction of a new car plant in 1959. The department also had a central role in determining the designs and prices for the Publica and the Corolla, and encouraged a vigorous export policy during the middle and late 1960s after predicting, correctly, that growth in domestic sales would slow down considerably during the 1970s.[105]

Entrance into Overseas Markets

Japanese automobile exports actually began prior to World War II. In fact, sales abroad accounted for 20 percent of Nissan's output between 1939 and 1944, totaling 30,000 units, and 6 percent of Toyota's production (about 6000 units), although these were mainly standard-size trucks sent to Manchuria, Korea, Taiwan, and other areas under Japanese military control. Between 1946 and 1957, Nissan and Toyota exported only about 2 percent of annual production, consisting again mainly of standard-size trucks sold to Okinawa, Taiwan, Korea, and Southeast Asia.[106] Selling trucks to divisions of the Japanese army or to less developed Asian nations did not prepare Nissan and Toyota to export cars to the United States and Western Europe. Yet it did accustom both firms to sending at least some of their output abroad and established relationships with dealers and vehicle assemblers in foreign countries. More important, even when the industry was on the verge of collapse during the late 1940s, Kamiya and Asahara assumed that, as automobile manufacturers, they would someday export cars.

Both firms still had a serious problem with costs until the late 1960s, due mainly to low volumes of production and to concomitant high prices for components and materials, especially sheet steel. In 1957, only 26 percent of the vehicles made in Japan, totaling a mere 47,000 units, were cars; not until 1968 did Japan's production of cars exceed that of trucks. In 1957, the Volkswagen Beetle and Renault's basic model each sold for less than the equivalent of 400,000 yen ($1111) in West Germany and France, while the Austin cost about 500,000 yen ($1389) in Britain. The Toyota Corona, in contrast, listed for 610,000 yen ($1694) in Japan and the Datsun 210 for 650,000 yen ($1806). Neither Japanese car was competitive, but in the domestic market a 40-percent value-added tax, in addition to shipping costs for importers, kept the prices of European cars high and restricted their market shares to about 1 percent of total sales.[107]

By the late 1960s, however, the Japanese had lowered production costs and retail prices to international levels. Even in 1967, the standard Corolla cost 485,000 yen ($1347) in Japan, compared to the equivalent of 495,000 yen ($1375) for the Volkswagen Beetle in West Germany. The Datsun Sunny, priced at 410,000 yen ($1139), was less expensive than a comparable car such as the Austin Mini-Deluxe, which cost about 482,000 yen ($1339) in Britain, while other Datsun and Toyota models cost about the same or less than European models in the same class (Table 36).

Table 36: International Car Price Comparisons, May 1967

Country/Model	Engine	Price in 1000 yen	Price in U.S. $
Britain			
Ford Cortina Deluxe	1297cc	622	1728
Vauxhall Viva Deluxe	1159	536	1489
Austin Mini-Deluxe	998	482	1339
Germany			
Volkswagen 1300	1285	495	1375
Ford 12M	1288	591	1642
Opel Kadett L	1072	603	1675
France			
Simca 1000GL	944	470	1306
Simca 1301GL	1290	631	1753
Italy			
Fiat 124	1197	645	1792
Japan			
Datsun Sunny Standard	988	410	1139
Sunny Deluxe	"	460	1278
Datsun 510 Standard	1296	560	1556
510 Deluxe	"	640	1778
Toyota Publica Standard	790	414	1150
Toyota Corolla Standard	1077	485	1347
Corolla Deluxe	"	543	1508

Sources: Iwakoshi and Toyota Jidōsha sanjū nen shi.

Notes: Prices are adjusted to include the 15% commodity tax in Japan. Currency converted at the official exchange rate of $1.00 = 360 yen.

Aided by low prices and improving quality, Japan's car exports rose from under 400,000 units in 1967 to 1,000,000 in 1970 and to around 6,000,000 during the early 1980s (Appendix E). The shift in American preferences from large to smaller vehicles helped, but the export performance of the Japanese automobile industry would not have been possible without better designs and cost reductions after failed efforts to sell cars in the United States during the late 1950s and early 1960s. Toyota Motor Sales took the lead in trying to export and lost money in the attempt, although the experience was valuable for Toyota as well as for Nissan, which tried to avoid Toyota's mistakes in the United States.

In 1949, Kamiya became director of a new association for the promotion of automobile exports. This encouraged him to think in terms of marketing abroad, although he did not seriously begin planning a car export drive until he visited the United States in 1955 and noted the rising popularity of European imports, especially the Volkswagen. The German company served, in fact, as a model for the export programs of both Toyota and Nissan; they studied Volkswagen's marketing strategies, dealer relations, and decision to establish a fully owned sales subsidiary.[108]

Toyota Motor Sales sold only 301 cars abroad in 1957, but this was enough to convince Kamiya to invest $1,000,000 to set up an American subsidiary in California during October. He was in a hurry because he feared that American automakers would introduce their own small cars (which they did in 1960) and thus make a late entry into the market impossible. As the first president of Toyota Motor Sales, U.S.A., Kamiya sent two Toyopet Crown samples to the January 1958 imported-car show held in Los Angeles. After hearing of his plans, Nissan countered by entering a 1957 Datsun 210, although both Japanese cars performed badly in road tests on American highways by overheating, burning oil, and vibrating excessively, since their engines were too small and neither had a chassis designed to withstand prolonged high-speed driving.[109] Kamiya essentially closed down his sales subsidiary until 1964, but, by this time, Toyota had improved the Crown and the Corona and started work on the Corolla, making sure to incorporate the results of American consumer surveys and on-site testing.

Nissan was more cautious and waited to establish a sales company in the American market until it had a car specifically designed for export.[110] During 1957-1958, Nissan also avoided a direct investment in the United States by engaging two Japanese trading companies, Marubeni and Mitsubishi, to sell the Datsun 210 to independent American dealers. Using feedback from dealers and tests done in the United States, Nissan designers upgraded the 1959 Datsun 310 and equipped it with an extra-large engine, borrowed from the Austin. Only then was President Kawamata ready to establish a sales subsidiary, which he located in California during 1960 and capitalized at $1,000,000. Nissan's president from 1977 to 1985, Ishihara Takashi (1912-), who joined the firm in 1937 after graduating from the law faculty of Tōhoku University, directed exports during the 1950s and became the first president of the American subsidiary, although he remained in Japan for most of his five-year term while two vice-presidents, Katayama Yutaka (west coast) and Kawazoe Sōichi (east coast), ran the company.[111]

In addition to studying Volkswagen, conducting road tests in the United States, and collecting reports from local dealers, Nissan and Toyota hired American consultants and advertising firms to assist in their marketing efforts and attempts to improve designs. Nissan also participated in a three-month tour of the United States that the Japan Productivity Center sponsored during 1958 for 27 Japanese companies interested in exporting. During this trip, the Japanese participants came to the conclusion that American firms were better equipped to determine the preferences of American consumers than the research departments of Japanese companies. Nissan hired A.C. Nielsen and an industrial designer, Dave Chapman, Inc., to supplement studies that Marubeni and Mitsubishi provided. Toyota representatives did not attend the tour, presumably because management was already committed to the American market, although Kamiya agreed with its conclusions and engaged an American advertising firm, Compton.[112]

Nissan and Toyota used these surveys to coordinate product design with marketing strategies. The data helped them determine, for instance, that Americans would usually be interested in Japanese subcompacts as second cars, mainly for housewives; therefore, they should ignore luxury features and concentrate on cars that were convenient to use, inexpensive, and needed little maintenance. American consultants also suggested that the Japanese develop automatic transmissions and station wagons capable of pulling a boat or a trailer at a speed of 60mph for families to use on trips. One study even predicted that American cars would become bigger and less fuel-efficient while urban areas grew more crowded—thus assuring the Japanese that demand for small cars in the United States would increase.[113]

The 1982 Merger
For the thirty-two years of its existence, Toyota Motor Sales performed several functions that a manufacturer could not have done alone. While Toyota concentrated on product engineering and man-

ufacturing, Toyota Motor Sales built the largest dealer network in Japan and used its marketing skills to provide additional information to Toyota on consumer preferences (Table 37). This arrangement allowed a select group of executives and personnel to specialize in marketing far more than was possible for Japanese automakers without sales subsidiaries—all except Toyota, Hino, and Mitsubishi. Nissan and other companies imitated Toyota Motor Sales' marketing practices and thereby limited Kamiya's effectiveness.[114] In general, however, Nissan preferred to concentrate on assimilating British technology and improving its manufacturing operations after eliminating its sales subsidiary in 1949 because it was in debt, seemed

Table 37: Dealer Network Comparison, December 1983

Company	Dealerships	Outlets	Employees	Employees/Outlet
Toyota	318	3,665	115,793	31.6
Nissan	258	3,265	81,677	25.0
Mazda	170	1,406	N.A.	N.A.
Mitsubishi	328	1,329	32,854	24.7
Honda[a]	513	N.A.	N.A.	N.A.
Isuzu	111	621	18,999	30.6
Daihatsu	70	548	13,436	24.5
Subaru	64	410	8,715	21.3
Hino	56	235	8,310	35.4
Suzuki[a]	135	513	N.A.	N.A.
Nissan Diesel	42	202	6,278	31.1

Source: Nissan Jidōsha Kabushiki Kaisha, Jidōsha kōgyō handobukku *(1984), pp. 119.*

Notes: aIncludes total for 2-wheel vehicle dealerships.
N.A. = Not Available.

to be ineffective or redundant, and was a potential post to which the unwanted Yamamoto Sōji might return.[115]

While sales expanded rapidly each year, and the leading Japanese automakers competed fiercely for new customers, Toyota Motor Sales was both an asset and a luxury. By the late 1970s, however, growth had slowed and no major automaker was willing to tolerate duplication in management or operations. This was, at least, the public explanation Toyota gave for the 1982 merger: It eliminated having two sets of executives and redundancies in market research, and simplified the process of information gathering and analysis. Absorbing Toyota Motor Sales as an in-house division also rationalized vehicle distribution, ending the practice whereby Toyota sold its output to Toyota Motor Sales, which then resold the vehicles to dealers. Furthermore, the merger made it easier for Toyota to manufacture overseas or enter into joint ventures. Toyota Motor Sales used to handle sales abroad, but Toyota's directors considered this arrangement undesirable if they were to begin producing cars outside of Japan. These "merits" outweighed several potential drawbacks or problems: the loss of Toyota Motor Sales as a distinct organ for market analysis; personnel difficulties caused by joining the two firms; and opposition from Toyota dealers.

The first year of the merger confirmed management's belief, and the fears of executives in other firms, that it would not hurt Toyota but strengthen the company. In the fiscal year ending June 1983, the new Toyota Motor Corporation set records for earnings by a Japanese company and for sales by a manufacturing firm. Although these results combined the balance sheets of two previously independent firms and did not indicate a significant expansion of Toyota's overall business, the merger clearly streamlined Toyota and provoked questions as to why it had not occurred years ago. Toyoda Eiji, president of Toyota from 1967 to 1982, had, in fact, argued during the 1960s that a sales subsidiary was no longer necessary, but Kamiya refused to allow the dissolution of his company. Not until 1979, at age 81, did Kamiya retire as chairman of Toyota Motor Sales. After he died the following year, Toyota finalized a date for the merger.[116]

a. The First Datsun (1932)   b. Toyota G1 (1935)   c. Nissan 180 (1941)

a. Toyopet SA (1947) b. Toyopet SB (1947) c. Toyota Crown RS (1955)

a. Austin A50 (1956)   b. Datsun 310 (1959)   c. Toyota Corona ST10 (1957)

a. Datsun Sunny (1966)   b. Nissan Fairlady Z (1984)   c. Toyota Corolla (1984)

Windshield Handling Robot (Nissan Zama Factory)

Car Assembly Line with Kanban (Toyota Motomachi Factory)

Aikawa Yoshisuke
(Nissan founder and
president, 1933-1939)

Asahara Genshichi
(Nissan president, 1942-
1944, 1951-1957)

Kawamata Katsuji
(Nissan president, 1957-
1973)

Ishihara Takashi (Nissan
president, 1977-1985)

Toyoda Kiichirō (Toyota
founder and president,
1941-1950)

Kamiya Shōtarō (Toyota
Motor Sales founder and
president, 1950-1975)

Ōno Taiichi (Kanban-
system inventor, Toyota
vice-president, 1975-1978)

Toyoda Eiji (Toyota
president, 1967-1982)

Toyoda Shōichirō
(Toyota president, 1985-)

Chapter Three

THE HUMAN DRAMA: MANAGEMENT AND LABOR

Between the mid-1950s and the early 1980s the Japanese automobile industry benefited from well-educated, disciplined employees who cooperated more with management and accepted lower wages than workers in the United States. While salaries in Japan rose substantially after the mid-1960s, workers at Nissan and Toyota during 1980-1983 still cost their employers about 30 percent less in annual wages and benefits than American autoworkers. The discrepancy was even larger at the subsidiaries and other subcontractors that accounted for 70 percent of the manufacturing cost of each car Nissan and Toyota produced during the early 1980s.[1] Certain features of the employment system as it developed in postwar Japan, such as guarantees to male employees at large firms of a job until retirement and remuneration based primarily on seniority, with semi-annual bonuses affected by the company's performance, encouraged Japanese workers to support rather than to confront management, and to tolerate low monthly salaries for most of their careers. But probably the most important characteristic that contributed to differences in management-labor relations between postwar Japan and the United States was that Japanese workers organized unions not by industry or trades but by company; and these company or enterprise unions contained white-collar as well as blue-collar employees.

THE POSTWAR UNION MOVEMENT

Prior to World War II, American labor leaders concluded that unions joining only the non-management employees of a single firm tended to have weaker bargaining positions than trade unions or federations embracing all the workers in an entire industry. American unions

137

limited to factory workers were also more likely to challenge management positions than those combining blue-collar and white-collar workers. These convictions led to the formation of the United Automobile Workers of America during the 1930s. In Japan after the mid-1950s, however, not only did most unions lack effective industry-wide affiliations, but many union officials were white-collar college graduates headed for managerial posts as they gained seniority in their firms. It was not surprising, consequently, that often they sympathized with managers and rarely pressed for wage demands, benefits, or rigid job classifications that might become a burden to their companies in the future. While there was no simple, convincing explanation why blue-collar industrial unions did not take hold in Japan, the question was fundamental to any interpretation of how Japan developed industries characterized by low production costs, flexible job routines, and high worker productivity.

Yet unionization, despite being relatively new to Japan after World War II, became extremely popular in a remarkably short period of time. After GHQ authorized the establishment of unions in December 1945 as part of its democratization program for Japanese industry, unionized workers rose from zero to 56 percent by 1949, twice the international average. This declined in later years to a still high level of 34 percent.[2] Workers unionized rapidly for a combination of reasons: GHQ's mandate, the entrance of many prewar labor activists who had been silent or suppressed before 1945 into the postwar union movement, and the existence of industry patriotic associations formed during the wartime mobilization begun in 1939 to ration materials and to oversee industrial safety and employee welfare. But not only unions based on companies became popular after World War II; by 1953, eighteen of Japan's largest industries had also organized labor federations.

The industrial union that served the automobile industry began in 1947 and was called the All-Japan Automobile Industry Labor Union (Zen Nihon Jidōsha Sangyō Rōdō Kumiai, abbreviated as Zenji). This dissolved in 1954, following an initially unified strike in 1953 at Nissan, Toyota, and Isuzu. While Toyota and Isuzu workers settled with management after several months of short strikes and negotiations, the Nissan union continued in a deadlock until a group of white-collar workers formed a second union. Unlike the original Nissan union, this refused to join or support Zenji, which then collapsed after the strike fund ran out and management began offering wages to employees to join the new union. Yet the circumstances that led to Zenji's demise did not suggest that this and other industrial unions were destined, as a matter of cultural necessity, to fail in Japan. Industrial unions might well have survived had managers and white-collar workers headed for managerial posts not united during the 1950s to break up labor federations and replace them with pro-management, company unions.

The unionization movement in Japan became highly emotional and factionalized during the postwar Occupation as political parties and labor leaders competed for union support, while the economy suffered from inflation and then deflation, eventually forcing managers to fire thousands of workers. When several unions joined together in 1946 to form the All-Japan Congress of Industrial Unions (Zen-Nihon Sangyō-betsu Rōdō Kumiai Kaigi, abbreviated as Sanbetsu), members of the Japan Communist Party quickly dominated its leadership. A rival organization founded in the same year, the Japan Confederation of Labor (Nihon Rōdō Kumiai Sōdōmei, abbreviated as Sōdōmei, the namesake of a prewar labor federation disbanded in 1940), split into right and left factions. GHQ felt sympathetic toward leftist unions to the extent that they counterbalanced ultraconservative elements still present in Japan. But it would not support a Communist labor movement and banned a planned general strike in February 1947, then issued an order during the summer of 1948 prohibiting government employees from striking. The American authorities also acquiesced in the 1949 removal of workers and media figures who were purported members or supporters of the Japan Communist Party.

As an alternative to Sanbetsu, GHQ backed the formation of a new federation in 1950, the General Council of Trade Unions of Japan (Nihon Rōdō Kumiai Sōhyō Gikai, abbreviated as Sōhyō). While this organization acquired additional support from Sōdōmei's left wing and from the corresponding faction in the Socialist Party, the All-Japan Confederation of Labor (Zen-Nihon Rōdō Sōdōmei, abbreviated as Dōmei) replaced Sōdōmei in 1964 after the right wing of the Socialist Party broke away to form the Democratic Socialist Party (Minshatō). Between the early 1950s and the 1980s, the Japanese labor movement thus consisted of two main divisions: Sōhyō on the left, and Sōdōmei or Dōmei on the moderate right. With 4,700,000 members in 1983, Sōhyō continued to be the largest labor federation in Japan, although government or public employees, chiefly workers from the national railways, the postal service, municipalities, government ministries, and teachers, formed the majority of its remaining unions. Dōmei had around 2,200,000 members, mostly from company unions, including those at Nissan and Mitsubishi Heavy Industries. The membership in unaffiliated unions, including Toyota and most of the other Japanese automakers, was roughly equal to the combined total of Sōhyō and Dōmei in the early 1980s.

The split within Sōhyō during the first half of the 1950s had a major impact on management-labor relations throughout Japan.[3] The left wing, which originally had broken away from Sōdōmei, dominated the organization from 1951 to 1955 under the direction of Takano Minoru (1901-1974). In 1951, Sōhyō first endorsed political stands opposing Japan's rearmament and the presence of American military bases, and called for Japanese neutrality and a comprehensive peace settlement involving China and the Soviet Union. In 1952, when Zenji voted to join it, Sōhyō supported strikes to pressure the government to change its policies, and demanded large wage increases and guarantees against further discharges of employees. Several major strikes subsequently erupted during 1952-1954 in several industries and numerous individual companies. As at Nissan in 1953, the usual outcome of these strikes was for unions in manufacturing industries to end their affiliations with Sōhyō. This trend contributed to the rise of enterprise unions that were not part of national organizations of workers in the same industry and increased the ability of managers to reduce wages and numbers of permanent employees. In exchange for their cooperation, some of the larger unions that left Sōhyō also received what amounted to "lifetime" employment for permanent male workers and the institution of seniority wage systems, in addition to other benefits.

The exit of company unions from Sōhyō also made it possible for the right wing of the organization to take over the executive committee in 1955. The new leaders opposed the use of strikes to struggle for political ends and focused instead on economic gains such as wage hikes and reductions in working hours. While they still encouraged workers in the same industry to take unified stands when bargaining with management, Sōhyō's moderate leadership accepted the principle of company unions and the practice of launching symbolic strikes each spring, of an hour or perhaps a day, as part of an annual bargaining process for the next year's contract.

Managers at Nissan, and labor officials, differed in their interpretations of these events and the 1953 strike. Leaders of the first union, and of Zenji, viewed 1953 as a defeat for organized labor. Founders of the second union, and company executives, saw their victory in

1953 as insuring the future competitiveness of Nissan and the entire Japanese automobile industry. Nissan's Kawamata Katsuji aptly summarized management's view in 1964 when he wrote that employees "who loved the company" and wanted to cooperate with management, based on feelings of "mutual trust," established the second union and "extinguished the red flag from Nissan in 1953." Their action allowed managers to begin more effective long-term planning and investment, confident that striking workers or an uncooperative union would not interfere: "In 1952-1953, Japan's economy turned toward recovery, allowing the automobile industry to introduce new technology and to replace old equipment. This favorable turn, combined with the stabilization of management-labor relations, created the prosperity of Nissan today."[4]

The first volume of Nissan's company history, published in 1964, elaborated on this version of the postwar union movement while arguing that the "average" Nissan employee desired cooperation and "mutual trust" in relations with management. American authorities encouraged the formation of labor unions but employees were unfamiliar with them and this made it possible for a small group of labor activists and Communists to gain control. Workers then rebelled against this leadership and "reorganized" the Nissan union. In this interpretation, which reflects a view of Japanese management-labor relations commonly held outside of and within Japan, Nissan workers, of their own "free will," chose to support management and to oppose those employees who did not, for the mutual benefit of the company and themselves:

> There were several strikes prior to 1953 and the formation of a new union. The average employee, however, did not fail to carry out the ultimate objective of building up the Japanese automobile industry through cooperation between management and labor. Employees, from the time of the company's establishment, displayed this effort and a positive attitude became rooted in their traditional spirit. Workers continued this effort after the war in the revival process when they created a union. Even though it later became a labor union and the Nissan chapter of Zenji, the foundations of their essential spirit remained.
>
> Unstable political and economic conditions, and the unfamiliarity of a democratic labor movement, influenced the course of the first Nissan union. Due to the mistaken guidance of some of its leaders, the union temporarily became involved in an ideological labor movement when extremely radical unions sprang up throughout the country. But as union activities became more radical and deviated from normal management-labor relations, increasing

numbers of employees started to reflect on these developments. Although it became entangled in this vortex of undisciplined labor activity, the Nissan spirit that had been cultivated for so many years reappeared in the hearts of the average employees. Union members realized that the improvement of their economic situations depended on the progress of company operations, and that this would come as a result of cooperation and mutual trust between management and labor. These conclusions spread as the first Nissan union became more radical. Elements critical of its activities joined together and reorganized the original union.[5]

The problem with this version of events is the underlying assumption that a company union, rather than shop committees or an industrial or trade union, was the more natural object of loyalty for Japanese workers. Nissan's company history also fails to mention that managers relied on a group of white-collar employees to form the second union, and later promoted these men into high executive positions at Nissan and affiliated companies. Kawamata, an executive director in 1953, led the opposition to the first union and management's support for the second union; he also used the backing of the new labor leaders to assist him in 1957 to become president of the company.

Management-labor relations in Nissan took on an unusual character (for a Japanese company) after 1957 as Kawamata's ploy to control labor "backfired." The bargain Kawamata made with the second union placed considerable restraints on his authority, and on his successors; the expectations of the new union leaders for consultations and career advances made the job of Nissan president especially difficult when these officials felt ignored, or that they were not being promoted quickly enough into top management. Furthermore, the influence of the second union in company decision making, even during the early 1980s, was a major reason why Nissan had difficulty committing itself to building a car plant in Great Britain and why it had been unable to duplicate the line assembly speeds or cycle time rationalizations and other methods to increase worker productivity that helped make Toyota so profitable.[6]

Although Nissan executives denied it for decades, they were, to a large degree, responsible for the 1953 strike and the end of the industrial union. They not only expected a dispute to occur, but planned it—once they found employees willing to establish a second union. Nissan's company history also neglected to mention this, or that management had the backing of the Japan Federation of Employers Associations (Nikkeiren), the Industrial Bank and the Fuji Bank, and executives at Toyota and Isuzu. Nor did it point out that the policies Zenji adopted during 1950-1952 were a reaction to the firing of thousands of Japanese autoworkers in 1949-1950 and the huge profits that Nissan, Toyota, and Isuzu earned as a result of the Korean War.

Nissan's official history, and Kawamata's reconstruction, indicated that the 1953 strike resulted from Communist domination of the union and the presentation of outrageous monetary and political demands. Other evidence presented in this chapter suggests that the dispute centered on the effectiveness of the Nissan union's organization, especially its authority over areas of shop administration such as overtime scheduling, and the concern of managers at other firms in Japan that their unions would adopt shop committees, which Nissan workers had copied from automobile manufacturers in the United States and Europe.

Only on the most immediate level was the 1953 strike a contest between Nissan executives and the first union, or an internal dispute between radicals and pro-management company employees. In a larger sense, it was a contest between organized labor, with the goal of joining workers in the same industry, and Japanese managers, supported by young white-collar workers headed for managerial posts, who sought to reduce the power of labor federations created after World War II. Each side had its formal institutions: Sōhyō represented labor, while Nikkeiren took up the cause of management.

Private businessmen founded Nikkeiren in Tokyo during April 1948 to lobby GHQ and the Japanese government, and to assist firms facing union challenges. This was one month after Zenji adopted unified wage demands and automobile industry executives withdrew from a joint management-labor council formed to solve problems in the industry by regular negotiations. Nikkeiren then absorbed organizations of businessmen set up in various industries, including the automobile industry, established local chapters throughout Japan, and used its financial, legal, and personal resources to oppose the labor movement. While Zenji lasted until 1954, when the struggle with management was over, so too was Japan's first experiment with a labor federation modeled after the United Automobile Workers of America.

THE RISE AND FALL OF AN INDUSTRIAL UNION

Formation of Company Unions and the Industrial Organization
Employee organizations at Nissan and Toyota prior to 1945 consisted of health-insurance unions formed during 1937-1938 and patriotic associations established in 1939 (Toyota) and 1941 (Nissan).

Neither company set up a labor union until after GHQ issued a directive in December 1945 that legalized trade unions. At Nissan, nearly 4800 workers organized in February 1946 and then presented to management, during the next six months, a series of demands calling for a formal labor contract, the elimination of differences in pay scales between blue-collar and white-collar workers, and the creation of a management-labor council for mutual consultations. Management approved the contract and established the council in August to bring together representatives from the union and management to debate wage proposals, working conditions, dismissals, production policies, factory safety, and employee welfare.[7]

Labor representatives from Nissan, Toyota, and Isuzu also met during the spring of 1946 and decided to join Sanbetsu as independent unions. They were not ready to form an industrial union and preferred to remain apart from Sōdōmei, where it appeared that too many of the prewar "bosses" had returned to dominate the organization. Union leaders in the automobile companies were optimistic that Sanbetsu would become a broad labor federation joining workers in several industries, although its executive committee soon came under the control of Communist Party members, prompting representatives from the Toyota union to insist on withdrawing and forming a separate federation for the automobile industry. The head of Nissan's union, Nakamura Hideya (1911-), a 1936 graduate of the law faculty of Kyoto University, preferred to remain in Sanbetsu, but Nissan workers convinced him to form a union with Toyota. This turned out to be Zenji. Isuzu joined a year after Nissan and Toyota because the executive committee of its union still contained a large number of Communists who wished to remain in Sanbetsu.[8] Delegates from 108 unions, representing nearly 45,000 workers, then attended Zenji's inaugural conference in April 1947. Nissan had the largest branch in eastern Japan (centered on Tokyo and Yokohama), while Toyota and Daihatsu had the main branch unions in central and western Japan.

Nissan employees also elected a new union head in April 1947, Masuda Tetsuo (1913-1964), who subsequently became the dominant official in Zenji and made the Nissan branch the most activist union in the labor federation. As a 1938 graduate of the prestigious law faculty at the University of Tokyo, Masuda normally would have risen to the highest ranks of the company. After only six years in Nissan, and at age 31, he was already chief of the correspondence section when the army drafted him in 1944. Since the army stationed

Masuda in Japan, he was able to return to Nissan directly after the war ended. When GHQ authorized the establishment of unions in December 1945, he quickly became involved in organizing workers, although he had not been a labor activist during the 1930s.[9] After Masuda lost an election to Nakamura Hideya in 1946 for head of the company union, he transferred to the Yoshiwara plant as chief of the production section and became the head of a branch union set up at this factory. He took over as director of the Nissan company union in 1948 and served two one-year terms, before Zenji's membership elected him chairman of the industrial union in 1950. Masuda served three successive one-year terms and returned to Nissan in the spring of 1953 to head the Nissan Zenji chapter.[10]

Zenji faced several problems during the first years of its existence. In addition to the inexperience of autoworkers with an industrial union, many members criticized the Japan Communist Party and Sanbetsu, which some of Zenji's officials still supported. Another problem was that the union organizers and officials consisted mainly of lower management staff or section chiefs, such as Masuda, yet section chiefs as union officials had both positive and negative elements. On the one hand, their familiarity with management's difficulties made it easier to agree with company executives on the industry's problems and possible solutions. But, since the union leaders were also their staff superiors, most workers were reluctant to challenge the policies of the executive committee, with the result that Zenji officials, especially Masuda, tended to decide on policies with little consultation of the union membership or concern for contradictory opinions.

Masuda and the other union leaders, at least according to Kumagaya Tokuichi, an Isuzu employee and member of Zenji's executive committee during the late 1940s, preferred not to adopt positions that managers considered "radical." Yet the smaller unions in Zenji, where workers received the lowest wages and had almost no guarantees of employment, severely criticized the executive committee and claimed that the union officials, nearly all of whom were section chiefs at Nissan, Toyota, or Isuzu, identified too closely with management positions and subordinated the interests of the workers to vague promises of increasing or "reviving" production.[11] In March 1948, at Zenji's second annual convention, the executive committee bowed to the wishes of these smaller unions to present unified demands to management for a minimum wage and higher base pay. Nissan and other unions then organized several short strikes to pressure company officials to grant these requests. In response, executives throughout the automobile industry refused to continue participating in the joint conferences founded in 1946.[12] This was the first major breach in management-labor relations in the Japanese automobile industry; disputes thereafter occurred annually between 1949 and 1953.[13]

Divisions between Management and Labor
The most serious issues dividing managers and union officials during 1948-1950 centered on the need for companies to hold down wage costs and to reduce employee rolls, due to huge operating deficits and extremely low output levels. At Nissan, many of the problems centered on attempts to revise the company's wage system. Management had, in 1936, introduced the Halsey system from the United States to determine pay for factory workers based on hourly premiums rather than piece rates. Workers who exceeded standard output received premiums as high as one-third of their hourly wages. Between 1936 and 1940, management extended this system to all manufacturing departments while office staff received monthly salaries. Nissan continued to use the Halsey method after World War II, with the addition of a minimum guarantee and cost allowances to adjust premiums, but the adjustments proved to be disadvantageous to workers and nearly impossible to calculate due to inflation.

In March 1947, the Nissan union negotiated an end to this system and to the practice of having different pay scales for blue-collar and white-collar workers, agreeing to substitute a "market-basket" formula with a sliding base adjusted to rises in basic commodity prices. This caused the average wage to rise from 278 yen per month in March 1946 to 600 yen in May 1947 and to 830 yen in July; since Nissan was falling short 10,000,000 yen a month in operating capital, company executives unilaterally decided to abandon the sliding wage in August and to fix 830 yen as the monthly base for all employees. When production levels increased in 1948, and extreme inflation continued, the union went on strike until the company instituted a sliding wage scale based on a three-month average of commodity prices.[14]

In 1949, GHQ instituted strict deflationary measures that depressed the entire Japanese economy in an attempt to reduce inflation. While this succeeded, one side effect was that automobile demand remained low, despite the need for Nissan, Toyota, and Isuzu to increase production. The subsequent rise in wages and in inventories of unsold vehicles precipitated financial crises at each firm. In October, Nissan management announced a general wage cut of 10 percent and a return to the Halsey method of computation, with premiums of one-third the hourly rate for exceeding standard output. When union leaders protested that this would lead to a decrease in wages because there were no plans to raise production, management responded by firing 1826 workers—one fifth of all Nissan employees. Two months of intermittent strikes and worker demonstrations followed until union leaders accepted management's action on November 30th. A similar process of wage reductions, worker discharges, union protests, and settlement by negotiation, took place at Isuzu, where 1271 workers lost their jobs in September 1949.[15]

Employee dismissals throughout the automobile industry reduced Zenji's ranks from over 43,000 in 1949 to around 30,000 in 1950. Approximately 100 unions remained in the federation, representing small and large companies, although 60 percent of the members worked at Nissan, Toyota, or Isuzu. The firings, moreover, convinced Masuda and other union leaders that management was not interested in bringing the industry back to full employment, and that their priority had to be the protection of remaining jobs. Masuda thus called for the unions at Nissan, Toyota, and Isuzu to present unified demands, set up shop committees, and mount a joint strike if the dismissals continued. On this platform, workers elected him chairman of Zenji in April 1950.

The threat did not work. Toyota fired 2000 employees in the summer of 1950, despite heated protests by the company union and Zenji. Masuda also failed to organize shop committees except at his own firm, Nissan. He and other top officials then concluded that Zenji needed the backing of a national labor federation not limited to the automobile industry, so they began considering an alliance with Sōhyō. But, since special orders received during the Korean War had brought automobile factories back to capacity for the first time since the early 1940s, the dismissal of so many workers just prior to June 1950 gave labor an advantage in the next round of negotiations: Companies were short-handed, and this allowed Zenji to extract generous wage boosts for its members during 1951.

Sōhyō, meanwhile, had become increasingly active during the Korean War, encouraging unions to strike to oppose the Japanese government's attempts to limit unionization and the rights of workers, and to protest the passage of legislation intended to reduce Communist activities. After the left wing of Sōhyō took over its executive committee at a national convention in July 1952, several industries, led by coal and electric power, launched major strikes. These did not deter the majority of Japanese autoworkers, however, and Zenji's membership ratified the proposal to join Sōhyō in October 1952.[16]

Masuda Tetsuo was not a member of the Japan Communist Party. According to a former management official at Nissan, he even opposed the Communist faction that existed within the Nissan union. Neither did Masuda get along well with Nakamura, the first head of the Nissan union, who was more sympathetic to Sanbetsu and the Communist platform. Yet it was not his politics so much as success in gaining wage hikes and organizing workers that made Masuda a primary target of Nissan executives and Nikkeiren directors.[17] Nissan management was especially concerned because Masuda's term as Zenji chairman ended in March 1953 and he was expected to return to head the Nissan union's negotiations for a new labor contract.[18]

Tensions between Masuda and Nissan executives had been increasing since 1949. Masuda had fought with President Yamamoto Sōji in 1947, since Yamamoto had tried to control the new union. After he left the company under the purge, Masuda felt that management pursued negotiations honestly and fairly; then Kawamata pressured him to accept the dismissal of one-fifth of Nissan's employees in 1949, while the Industrial Bank provided loans to make certain that the company continued to operate, even with strikes by the union, and had funds to settle with the fired workers. The 1949 incident persuaded Masuda not only that he needed backing from a broader national organization, but that he had to find an effective way to pressure management. For this reason, to increase the authority of the union in factory administration, he began to set up committees in each shop modeled after worker committees existing at Ford in the United States, Renault in France, and automakers in West Germany.[19]

Each shop consisted of 50 to 100 workers; groups of 10 employees elected 1 delegate to each shop committee. These committees included management representatives, usually factory section heads, who were also members of the union until July 1953. While the committees normally held meetings during working hours with management's permission, when disputes arose, chairmen frequently convened unauthorized meetings and excluded staff representatives if they disagreed with the positions of the union leadership.

Management first tried to control this practice in 1951, when the Nissan union demanded a return to the sliding base. Company executives refused but agreed to compensate workers with a generous wage increase. At the same time, however, they declared that Nissan would not pay employees for time spent in unapproved union meetings during working hours. Although managers did not enforce this rule until 1953, the decision reflected their desire to restrict the power of the shop committees, which had grown as shop-committee chairmen assumed the authority to grant or refuse overtime requests from management. Masuda realized that the committees presented difficulties to lower management staff when superiors ordered production increases, but he also knew that the authority of the chairmen greatly strengthened the union's bargaining position.[20]

The 1953 Strike
When the 1953 wage negotiations began in May, labor officials at Nissan, Toyota, and Isuzu relied on a unified platform that Sōhyō recommended. Masuda drew up the specific proposal, which asked for a sliding wage scale based on seniority and a guarantee to new employees of a monthly base wage of 10,000 yen ($28). This would rise 1000 yen ($3) for each year of service, so that an employee with 6 years seniority would receive a base wage of 16,000 yen ($44) per month, while someone with 19 years would get 34,800 yen ($97). The highest a monthly base could rise to was 36,000 yen ($100) after 20 years of employment. No official in Zenji or the member unions thought that managers at Nissan, or at Toyota and Isuzu, would accept Masuda's terms. They were to be a starting point for negotiations.[21]

On June 4th, Nissan executives flatly rejected the union platform and claimed that they would raise the monthly base from the April average of 29,775 yen to as much as 53,000 yen for some workers—more than double the industry average of 24,368 per month. Management also decided to deduct pay for time spent in unauthorized meetings, and refused to accept requests for a return to the retirement bonus system abandoned in 1949, prior consultations before transferring employees, increases in cultural and recreational funds, or the addition of temporary workers to the union as regular members. In response, shop-committee chairmen held more meetings while promoting a work slowdown. The Nissan, Toyota, and Isuzu unions convened a joint strike committee on June 14th and then held strikes ranging from one hour to one day before Toyota reached a settlement on August 4th and Isuzu on August 5th.[22]

The dispute at Nissan became especially heated after management insisted on June 18th that section heads leave the union and that shop committee meetings be subject to the approval of factory and department managers, or section chiefs. This issue had been brewing since white-collar and blue-collar workers founded the union in 1946. Labor contracts during 1947-1948 had exempted section heads in personnel, general affairs, and accounting from membership, but agreement on the issue ended in 1949. Although management tried in 1951 to exclude all section chiefs, it dropped the matter temporarily when union officials refused.[23]

On 23 June 1953, Nissan executives disregarded union protests and convened a general meeting of section heads; they voted to leave the union. Committee chairmen reacted to this, and to deductions in pay envelops received on the 25th for attending unauthorized union meetings, by stopping work on the 26th and holding "kangaroo courts" to condemn department and section heads. Nissan managers responded by threatening to close down company factories and by preparing to do this as soon as the union ordered a strike. Employees went back to work except for one hour on July 3rd and half a day on the 11th. Management then declared a "holiday" on July 13th and 14th "to provide union members with an opportunity to reflect and search for a reasonable solution." But, when negotiations failed to progress, the union ordered unlimited strikes on July 16th in several factory sections, bringing production to a halt.[24]

By this time, according to the company history, Nissan managers had come to the conclusion that the shop-committee system was causing a "gradual paralysis of staff functions." Executives further complained that union meetings, and contract negotiations in general, had taken on too much of a political character, since union leaders criticized the rearmament of Japan, national defense policies, and the government's attempt to regulate strikes and labor activities. Union policies, at least in the view of Nissan's official historians, made a settlement impossible: "Some of the union leaders began to advocate the idea that, even if the company were destroyed, at least the workers would remain. In response, management took the position that, to insure the survival of the company, it was necessary to reestablish managerial authority and to normalize union activities."[25]

Masuda was aware that, since the company had given in to high union demands the previous year, it probably would not do so again. As he realized later, however, wages and other union requests were secondary issues in the strike. Nissan executives, led by Kawamata, had decided not to compromise in 1953. They wanted to reduce Masuda's influence and, if possible, eliminate the first union and its shop committees. The strategy they followed was to isolate the Nissan union from Toyota and Isuzu with the cooperation of executives at these two firms and Nikkeiren officials; shut down Nissan's factories and keep them closed until a second union forced a settlement; receive credit from company banks to support employees not on strike, suppliers and dealers, and those workers who formed the second union; fire the first union's leaders and have them arrested. Nissan executives knew that some workers at Toyota and Isuzu were pressuring their union officials to settle with management. When these firms reached agreements early in August, the lockout of Nissan workers began.[26]

According to Okumura Shōji, assistant general manager of Nissan's planning department in 1953, management was most concerned about permission for overtime. The union did not oppose plans to increase production, and workers gladly received overtime and extra income. But labor officials attempted to win large increases after 1950 in base wages and premiums; shop committee chairmen found that overtime permission was an effective lever to use against management. This created a crisis in spring 1953 because Nissan had just completed plans to raise production levels and to assemble the Austin in Japan, while the union increased its wage demands and threatened to cut overtime. Nissan's attempt to rationalize scattered production facilities was another problem because the company needed to move employees around freely, but shop committees prevented the transfer of workers without prior consultations.[27]

Matsuzaki Shirō, head of the tool department in Nissan's Yokohama plant during 1953, also recalled that the shop-committee system, rather than wage demands, was the central issue in the strike. Yet he felt it was not simply overtime permission or employee transfers but the general tendency of workers to ignore staff superiors and obey committee chairmen that "made it impossible to run the company."[28] Other contemporary accounts of the strike confirmed that committee chairmen held meetings without authorization from management, refused to provide lists of who attended, and then insisted that the company pay workers for time spent in these meetings, in accordance with government labor laws. When supervisors threatened to dock workers for going to these meetings, chairmen responded by meeting more frequently.[29]

As the first major step toward a full-scale lockout, Nissan management closed part of the Tsurumi plant on July 21st. Four days later, Nissan received and ignored a court order prohibiting pay deductions for time workers spent in union meetings. Employees in the securities section of the general affairs department subsequently went on an unlimited strike. The decision of white-collar workers in this section to support the union was particularly damaging to management because Nissan was in the process of carrying out a capitalization increase to finance Austin assembly and an expansion of production equipment. Then, on August 4th, the union ordered all sections not on strike to stop working for the first hour of each day; this prompted managers to close all factories and spend 2,500,000 yen ($7,000) to erect barricades. Section and department chiefs, led by Managing Director Harashina Kyōichi, head of the Yokohama plant, stationed themselves inside the blockaded areas overnight to protect the machinery.[30] "Management," in the words of Okumura, "simply disappeared. Company executives set up an undercover office and moved frequently. When the union tried to resume the negotiations, it had no one to negotiate with."[31]

Some employees attempted to enter the factories, go back to work, and hold meetings, but the company expelled them on August 7th after having the Yokohama district attorney arrest Masuda and 6 other members of the executive committee on the charge of "promoting violence and injury." On the 14th, Shizuoka prefectural authorities arrested 3 more union leaders from the Yoshiwara plant. Six days later, management fired Masuda and the other members of the union's executive committee; by December, Nissan had discharged 88 more workers and disciplined another 53 for violating company work regulations.[32] Nissan's board of directors did not discuss or approve the lockout decision. Nor did Asahara Genshichi order it. Since taking over as president in October 1951, he had preferred to negotiate with the union rather than face a strike, even though other managers criticized him for allowing wages to rise so high. Executive Director Kawamata ordered the lockout on his own authority and used Director Iwakoshi Tadahiro, head of Nissan's personnel department from 1947 to 1952, to negotiate with the white-collar employees who agreed to form a second union.[33]

Masuda knew that Kawamata was responsible for the hard-line stance because, as late as July 1953, even though Asahara criticized the union for excessive wage demands and ordering strikes on the shop floor, the president was still willing to continue the discussions. But, once Masuda declared a full-scale strike, Asahara seems to have accepted Kawamata's strategy of locking out the workers, arresting the union officials, and dealing with the second union. Masuda also interpreted management's refusal to pay employees for time spent in union meetings as a straightforward attempt to control union activities and to counter its opposition to production plans that called for excessive overtime and the use of temporary workers. Yet he felt betrayed that management rejected the union's proposals outright, refused to compromise on any item, and then ordered a lockout and recognized another union because "this destroyed the first union's shop system and wage increases, and created conditions that supported management policy and the staff system."[34]

While Kawamata admitted that he "took the lead" in authorizing the lockout and approving the second union, he maintained that most company executives favored this policy.[35] Since he was in charge of finances, Kawamata felt it was his duty to take a stand against large annual wage increases and to put an end to the shop committees' usurpation of staff authority in the factories, which he believed could have destroyed the company.[36] Nissan was not headed for financial ruin in 1953; in the two years prior to the strike, the company had enjoyed record profits and paid out large dividends, despite the generous wage increases Asahara granted. Yet Kawamata had barely managed to keep the firm solvent during the later 1940s, and this experience was too recent to forget. He wanted restraints on wages and absolute control over production scheduling.

As a former official of the Industrial Bank, Kawamata also believed he had a special responsibility to insure that Nissan solved its labor problems and that the Japanese economy recovered from the postwar depression. He admitted that businessmen throughout Japan had agreed on these objectives when they established Nikkeiren in 1948 to lend one another "mutual support." The Nissan union became a target only because its officials acted as if they did not care whether the company survived or collapsed, as long as the union remained: "They attempted to surmount the managerial class, move on to political activities, and overthrow the social structure," wrote Kawamata in 1964, "all of which reflected, needless to say, a revolutionary ideology."[37] But company executives did not merely worry that the union would become even more intransigent after Masuda returned from Zenji headquarters; nearly half a year before the spring 1953 wage negotiations were to start, they decided to try to break the existing union and the entire Zenji organization.[38]

In the opinion of Okumura, who wrote a book on automobile manufacturing in 1954 and an essay on the industry's development in 1960, the breakdown in management-labor relations and the collapse of the industrial union was a gradual process that did not result from overly radical, political, or "revolutionary" tendencies on the part of the union leadership. He maintained that officials at Nikkeiren, and at the Federation of Economic Organizations (Keidanren), began watching the activities of the Nissan union during the Korean War. Prior to 1950, managers and labor leaders had cooperated because both saw GHQ restrictions on materials allocation and car production, and the sale of used army vehicles, as obstacles to the industry's recovery and expansion. The return of workers from the Japanese military made it all the more imperative that management and labor work together to increase output. Company executives were especially willing to negotiate since GHQ, which had legalized and encouraged unions, seemed more likely to modify its policies in response to labor demonstrations than to the protests of Japanese businessmen or bureaucrats.

This cooperation did not last. Inflation made unions raise their wage demands and the employee dismissals during 1949-1950 turned union leaders against management. Then Zenji came out against the Korean War, creating problems not only for GHQ but also for managers who relied on special orders to increase production. When Nissan accepted contracts to make napalm bomb shells and other ordnance for the U.S. Army, in addition to trucks and weapon carriers, the union protested. Toyota and Isuzu employees said nothing, however, so company executives and conservative newspapers branded Nissan workers "radical."

Zenji's national reputation, according to Okumura, continued to grow during 1951-1952 after automakers granted large salary increases and the Nissan union led in the movement to join Sōhyō. Media publicity brought increasing national attention to Nissan in particular and made businessmen around the country worry that other unions would demand equally high wages and shop committees, reducing company profits and the ability of firms to invest. After the wage hikes of 1952, Nikkeiren and Keidanren decided to end the cycle of annual disputes and salary increases by supporting the replacement of radical unions with pro-management, company unions. In this sense, Okumura was convinced, the 1953 strike occurred because Nissan management desired it. Nissan executives promoted the second union and felt they could win in a long struggle with the first union, since they had the backing of the leading business organizations in the country and the company's main banks.[39]

Nikkeiren officials, led by Director Maeda Hajime (1895-), openly warned Japanese businessmen through national publications during 1953 that Nissan's shop-committee system, and the holding of union meetings without authorization, would not only continue at Nissan but spread to other firms. In July 1953, Maeda took the further step of publicly urging Nissan executives not to submit to union demands and declared that Nikkeiren would give its full support to management. Nikkeiren then provided legal assistance when Nissan closed its factories, fired the union leaders, and had them arrested. More important, Nikkeiren arranged for firms in Kanagawa prefecture to give jobs to Nissan subcontractors during the strike and obtained promises from executives at Toyota and Isuzu not to exploit the situation by increasing production in an attempt to take over part of Nissan's market share.[40]

The Industrial Bank and the Fuji Bank assisted by contributing 540,000,000 yen ($1,500,000) in special loans to Nissan while management shut down production operations.[41] This sum exceeded Nissan's total pre-tax earnings between October 1952 and September 1953. Executives channeled some of this money, admitted Okumura, to subcontractors and subsidiaries on the condition that they donate a certain percentage to the workers plotting to form a second union. Company Director Iwakoshi also provided funds to these employees for various purposes, such as to print circulars protesting the policies of the first union.[42]

Masuda, in an account of the Nissan strike published in June 1954, offered his theory why Nissan management and Nikkeiren officials decided to challenge the union in 1953. Production levels in the automobile industry remained depressed after World War II, raising inventories while inflation kept prices high, yet Nissan, Toyota, and Isuzu had to increase output to pay for the new equipment they wanted to introduce. They might have cut prices to stimulate demand once their financial positions improved, but too many producers in a limited market made it difficult for the industry as a whole to reduce excess capacity. Nor could firms lower prices by making more automobiles because the market would not absorb them. The automakers had to reduce their costs at low volumes of production; to do this, managers pressured workers to accept longer hours and lower wages. While Nissan's union frustrated company executives because it controlled overtime scheduling and opposed the use of inexpensive temporary workers, still, in Masuda's opinion, the 1953 confrontation could have been avoided if Nikkeiren, the Industrial Bank, and executives in other firms had not supported Nissan managers and encouraged them to oppose the first union and Zenji.[43]

The Second Nissan Union
Nissan's company history justified management's actions in 1953 by insisting that workers had become unhappy with the policies of the first union, and noted that several employees had openly opposed Masuda during the strikes in 1949. Although "the strong controls of the union restricted the development of this critical element," at Zenji's national convention in the summer of 1952, and at the Nissan chapter's convention, workers again criticized the union officials and continued to challenge them during 1953. When a no-confidence motion intended to depose Masuda and the other union leaders failed on August 7th, 506 workers gathered at the Asakusa Kōkaidō hall in Tokyo on August 30th to organize another union, which they named the "Nissan Motor Labor Union" (Nissan Jidōsha Rōdō Kumiai). Several slogans that the second union adopted emphasized its support for management and opposition to the "Communist" leaders of the first union:[44]

— Those who love the union love the company.
— A cheerful union, a cheerful life.
— A truly free and democratic union does not produce dictators.
— Avoid shifting the burden to workers in a thorough rationalization of company operations.
— Fight for wages that promote the desire to work.
— Strengthen the management council and utilize capable individuals.
— Guarantee a wage based on productivity increases.
— Destroy the "kept union" that is tied to the Japan Communist Party.

Nissan management recognized the new union immediately and began negotiating with its leaders on September 1st for a new labor contract. Both sides agreed that factories and offices should remain closed temporarily, although management offered to pay employees part of their salaries until the factories reopened. These events caught Masuda and the other leaders in the first union unprepared; they agreed, on September 3rd, to strict terms that management set down to reopen negotiations. But when 200 members of the new union tried to go back to work at the Yoshiwara plant on September 8th, workers in the first union prevented them from leaving the premises and forced them to stay overnight. After similar incidents occurred at other factories, Nissan management again closed down all facilities until it reached a settlement with the first union on September 23rd.[45]

While Nissan's company history glossed over the issue of the no-confidence vote, this demonstrated how strong the support continued to be for Masuda and the first union's policies, even after the lockout. A study of the strike published in 1956 by the parent company of a leading Japanese magazine, *Chūō kōron,* revealed that the union called for the referendum after management fired Masuda and the other union leaders to decide whether or not to go on with the strike. Of the 6091 workers who voted (83 percent of all union members), 5230 or 86 percent wanted to continue. Only 650 (11 percent) opposed this, while 211 ballots (3 percent) were invalid. In addition, the 1956 study concluded that the main reason Nissan employees switched to the second union was financial: They had gone several months without pay, depleting the union's strike fund, while Nissan management paid employees 60 percent of regular wages to sign up with the new union. This amounted, in effect, to a bribe to quit the Zenji chapter. Masuda was left with no option but to accept management's restrictions on union activities and to release the company from any obligation to pay workers for time spent in unapproved meetings.[46]

The new union had 3072 members on October 5th and 5063 at the end of 1953. By this time, a mere 2186 workers remained in the Zenji chapter; a year later there were only 300. The first union also had to file for bankruptcy because of payments made to employees during the strike. Zenji depleted its coffers as well by providing assistance to Nissan workers and had to dissolve in December 1954. The first union continued until Masuda, who had spent time in jail and was no longer a Nissan employee, asked the second union in September 1956 to accept the 70 workers still under his direction. He did this only after courts in the city of Yokohama and in Kanagawa prefecture rejected his attempt, and the attempts of 17 other

former union officials, to sue the company. Nissan settled all pend-
ing litigation out of court in November 1956.[47] Management had
won.

Despite the repeated assertions in Nissan's company history, most
of the 506 workers who joined the second union on August 30th
were not "average" blue-collar workers: They were college graduates
and engineers, some of whom accused Masuda and other executives
in the first union of being not merely "Communists" but, what was
worse, intellectuals.[48] Yet, even though he was a graduate of the
most elite faculty of the most elite university in the country, and a
former section head, Masuda still had the overwhelming majority
of Nissan workers support him throughout the 1953 strike.

The leader of the white-collar employees siding with management, Miyake Masaru, was a 1949 graduate of Kawamata's alma
mater, Hitotsubashi University. Masuda knew him because they
had first argued during 1949, just after Miyake entered Nissan and
the union's executive committee ordered a strike to protest the large-
scale firing of factory workers. It was not so much the dissension
within the union that bothered Masuda; he was more disturbed by
the "collusion" between managers and college graduates who joined
Nissan during the Occupation, and the clandestine role of Kawamata
and other executives in helping these employees create another union.
The very idea of a "company union" with no industrial ties or distinct identity ran contrary to his belief that only a clear separation
between management and labor could protect the rights of workers:
"If company policies and the interests of the union are identical,
then there is no need for a labor union."[49]

The second union did not admit to "collusion" but revealed in a
white paper published in June 1954 that it originated as a small
"study group" founded at the time of the employee firings in 1949.
The membership, composed mainly of college graduates who had
recently entered the firm, wanted to work, not to strike, and organized the study group after failing to persuade Masuda not to order
a walkout. The group had 40 members initially but had grown to
around 200 by 1953 as workers joined who disapproved of the affiliation with Sōhyō.[50]

Kawamata claimed that he heard of the study group only in 1952,
although Matsuzaki admitted that, by the winter of 1952, Nissan
managers had already begun to join these employees in "studying"
how to break the union.[51] In addition to encouragement from Nik-

keiren, an organization called the Institute for World Democracy (Sekai Minshū Kenkyūjo) assisted Nissan managers and dissident employees. Nabeyama Sadachika, Tanaka Seigen, and Kazama Jō-kichi, 3 former members of the Japan Communist Party who had renounced this allegiance prior to World War II, established the Institute during the Occupation in an attempt to reduce the influence of political leftists in Japanese industry. They received funding from various conservative businessmen, including Mizuno Shigeo, a former president of the *Sankei* daily newspaper.[52]

Nabeyama, who thought the Nissan union was particularly dangerous, mounted a mail campaign in 1953 to encourage management not to give in to Zenji.[53] He and other associates also recruited workers in their twenties to "educate" them in anti-Communist principles and the use of second unions to break strikes or radical labor organizations. The head of Nissan's union in 1985, Shioji Ichirō, was among those who attended the Institute and "studied" directly under Nabeyama. Shioji then entered Nissan in spring 1953, just prior to the start of wage negotiations, and helped to oppose Masuda and organize the second union.[54]

While it frustrated Masuda that white-collar workers collaborated with management, perhaps this was predictable since these employees had managerial ambitions. Miyake, the first executive secretary of the new union, chairman during 1954-1956, and then head from 1955 to 1962 of Jidōsha Rōren, the extended union for Nissan and its closest affiliates, went on to manage Nissan's personnel and domestic marketing departments. Another original member of the study group, Kasahara Kōzō, was the first head of the second union before taking over as chief of the No. 1 testing department. Other leaders of the new union during the 1950s and early 1960s who rose to management positions included Aisō Genjirō, executive secretary from 1955 to 1957, union chairman during 1957-1958, and vice chairman of Jidōsha Rōren from 1957 to 1962; Kawanabe Seiichi, union chairman during 1959-1960 and vice-chairman of Jidōsha Rōren from 1962 to 1963; Matsumoto Kimio, union chairman during 1960-1961 and vice-chairman of Jidōsha Rōren from 1962 to 1963; and Masuda Katsuki, vice-chairman of the union during 1960-1961 and vice-chairman of Jidōsha Rōren from 1962 to 1963.[55]

Furthermore, 10 members of Nissan's board of directors in 1979 were formerly in Miyake's study group, while 5 others became presidents of Nissan affiliates. Supporters of the study group and the second union among the ranks of top executives and middle managers also benefited from the second union's support. Not only did Kawamata remain as president from 1957 to 1973, but Iwakoshi succeeded him during 1973-1977. Furthermore, during their terms in office, Kawamata and Iwakoshi promoted at least 9 individuals who supported the study group to positions ranging from Nissan executive director to vice-president, and president or chairman of Fuji Heavy Industries, Nissan Auto Body, and Nihon Radiator.[56]

The 1953 strike involved a short-term financial sacrifice for the company since it lasted five months, including three when production stopped completely, and cost Nissan upwards of 400,000,000 yen ($1,100,000). Yet this sum was a bargain for management because a mutual agreement with the new union leaders regulated meetings during working hours and modified the shop-committee system to restore the authority of section chiefs. Even though the company fell short of funds in 1954 due to a drop in sales during the strike, bank loans made it possible for Nissan to carry out its investment plans for the Austin tie-up and new equipment after the second union granted substantial wage concessions.[57]

Collapse of the Industrial Union
The financial loss to Japanese autoworkers after the strike was indeed remarkable. By 1953, Zenji's demands had brought the average monthly wage in the automobile industry above major manufacturing sectors such as shipbuilding or iron and steel (Table 38). Yet, in 1955, with a new labor contract that permitted lower premiums and reductions in base wages, monthly income fell behind both of these industries. Nissan employees had also been among the best paid manufacturing workers in Japan at the time of the strike and received wages that were 25 percent higher than the automobile industry average, which Toyota and Isuzu workers received[58] (Table 39). With the establishment of the second union, the average monthly wage at Nissan fell 16 percent in one year and did not reach the 1953 level again until 1964—without adjusting for inflation.[59]

Kumagaya believed that Zenji collapsed because the executive committee came to rely too heavily on Chairman Masuda, who insisted on a unified front and a centralized organization. This isolated Zenji's leadership from the more conservative union members, although Kumagaya also felt that all Zenji officials failed to educate workers to look beyond company loyalties and rivalries, and to develop a higher political or class consciousness. Most of all, they

Table 38: Average Monthly Wages in Manufacturing Industries, 1951-1958 (yen)

Year	Iron and Steel	Shipbuilding	Automobiles	Rolling Stock
1951	17,010	N.A.	15,088	13,403
1952	18,654	18,393	18,218	16,408
1953	20,501	21,027	21,600	19,164
1954	21,886	21,654	22,600	20,764
1955	22,944	24,649	20,568	20,487
1956	26,536	28,242	23,042	24,005
1957	27,223	31,127	22,498	26,056
1958	29,522	31,017	23,568	25,600

Source: *Rōdō Sho (Ministry of Labor), "Mai-tsuki kinrō tōkei chōsa" (Survey of monthly labor statistics), cited in Kodaira Katsumi, Jidōsha.*

underestimated management's ability to organize an effective opposition.[60]

This last oversight was critical because Masuda alienated company executives and workers such as Miyake and Shioji with his leftist political views and unbending opposition toward anything suggesting the remilitarization of Japan. Masuda not only criticized Nissan's acceptance of orders from the U.S. Army and the Japanese police reserves during the Korean War, but he also named the official organ of the Nissan union "Peace" and used this vehicle to remind workers of the 1949-1950 employee firings and to list the locations of all American military bases in Japan. The issue marking Zenji's 7th anniversary in 1953 also pointed out that half of Hino's workers were temporary and engaged in the repair of U.S. Army vehicles, criticized Japan's cooperation with the United States during the Korean War as foreshadowing a return to Japanese colonialism and militarism, and attacked Nikkeiren and the Industrial Bank for opposing Nissan's wage increases.[61]

162

Table 39: Average Monthly Wages and Employees' Ages—Nissan and Toyota, 1950-1983 (yen, average age)

FY	Nissan		Toyota	
	Wages	Employees' Ages	Wages	Employees' Ages
1950	18,582	—	14,985	31.5
1953	29,358	34.6	21,538	32.4
1954	24,698	35.3	23,672	33.2
1955	24,705	36.1	23,170	35.3
1956	25,653	36.7	25,020	35.8
1957	22,463	37.2	24,105	34.3
1958	24,638	37.3	23,807	33.3
1959	24,054	36.9	21,331	31.4
1960	23,694	36.5	19,957	28.5
1961	25,251	36.0	24,564	27.6
1962	26,397	35.0	25,245	27.3
1963	27,001	32.4	28,085	26.7
1964	29,983	29.1	32,086	25.6
1965-1969	42,209	29.7	48,865	26.3
1970-1974	89,530	31.4	102,625	28.5
1975-1979	179,731	33.8	200,007	31.2
1980	231,917	35.1	258,791	32.3
1981	247,520	34.6	267,315	32.4
1982	254,915	34.6	283,038	32.2
1983	283,457	35.2	301,247	32.6

Source: Yūka shōken hōkokusho.

With all Masuda's faults as a union strategist, however, Kumagaya was convinced that his goals were laudable because they reflected the desire to promote Japan's development from a "low-wage, agricultural nation" to an industrialized state that treated and paid workers in a manner comparable to the Western democracies. Since neither Masuda nor Kumagaya believed that management could be trusted to do this, the union had to take the lead, and Zenji's chairman imported the shop-committee system to pressure management.[62]

Masuda and other union officials expressed many of these same convictions and regrets in "self-criticisms" written voluntarily in December 1954 that specifically blamed Zenji's collapse on their failure to maintain a united front with Toyota and Isuzu workers.[63] To Kumagaya as well, this was the basic reason why Zenji did not succeed: The leadership did not try hard enough to accommodate dissident workers, despite the pressure Toyota's "reconstruction group" and Isuzu's "head office group" put on local union officials to settle with management. Masuda would not compromise with these workers, or with Miyake and his friends, perhaps because he knew that many of them had managerial ambitions. But, in Kumagaya's opinion, had he been able to satisfy them, or had Toyota and Isuzu continued to support the Nissan Zenji chapter a bit longer in 1953, the industrial union probably would have withstood management's challenge.[64]

The bankruptcy of the first union, and of Zenji, remained unresolved. The Nissan chapter ran up debts to Zenji of 106,000,000 yen ($294,000) during the strike; most of these funds came from Sōhyō, which also gave the Nissan chapter 160,000,000 yen ($444,444) when management declared a lockout.[65] Masuda hoped to repay the loans once his members returned to work but, as they joined the second union, contributions to the repayment fund dwindled. Although Toyota and Isuzu workers were supposed to contribute to Zenji's strike fund, negotiations dragged on throughout 1954 until, in December, Zenji's directors decided to dissolve the federation. This released Toyota and Isuzu from their obligations and left the Japanese automobile industry with nothing but company unions.

The leaders of the second union, in addition to accepting managerial posts after leaving their positions in the union, expanded their authority beyond Nissan by founding the Federation of Labor Unions in the Japanese Automobile Industry (Nihon Jidōsha Sangyō Rōdō Kumiai Rengo Kai, abbreviated as Jidōsha Rōren) in January 1955 to join the employees of the larger subsidiaries and dealers in the Nissan group: 22 separate unions, representing 9209 workers. In 1956, the union at Minsei Diesel (later Nissan Diesel) also joined Jidōsha Rōren, while the employees at Shin-Nikkoku Industries (later Nissan Auto Body) followed in 1957. The unions at Nissan Auto Body, Nissan Diesel, and Atsugi Auto Parts then merged with the Nissan company union in 1961[66] (Table 40).

Masuda Tetsuo's fate was much more modest. After dissolving the first union he took a job in an auto body shop that later went bankrupt, then worked in a plating factory, and then for a trading firm that dealt with China and which also failed. He suffered from high blood pressure and died of a stroke while at work in 1964, at age 51. On the recommendation of Takano Minoru, the former head of Sōhyō, the labor federation buried Masuda in a common tomb for "victims of the liberation movement."[67]

Table 40: Nissan Employees and Jidōsha Rōren, 1954-1963

	Nissan Employees	Jidōsha Rōren
1954	7,700	—
1955	7,000	9,200
1956	6,700	11,400
1957	7,700	13,100
1958	7,800	19,600
1959	7,800	20,400
1960	9,400	26,400
1961	12,000	40,200
1962	14,200	53,325
1963	16,100	77,300

Source: Nissan Jidōsha sanjū nen shi, *p. 481, and data section.*

Note: Figures are rounded to the nearest hundred. Employee totals are for March of the year indicated.

RELATIONS AFTER THE 1953 STRIKE

The founders of the second union criticized Masuda for holding "undemocratic" elections—making workers vote for union officials on open ballots in front of shop-committee chairmen.[68] Yet they never changed the election system either; instead, Miyake and his colleagues substituted new candidates. After the early 1960s, they also chose to rely on a national labor federation and a political party for outside support, although they switched to Dōmei and the Democratic Socialists. In addition, Miyake offered huge savings to management in wage reductions, and promised to cooperate in implementing productivity increase programs and other measures to insure the future prosperity of the firm. Permanent male employees, in return, received job guarantees until retirement. The bargain worked, except that journalists, scholars, and company employees criticized the second union and management for Nissan's "peculiar" system: unopposed union candidates and open ballot elections; domination for decades by a small group of labor officials who often moved up to managerial posts; and the tendency of the union's executive committee to set policies with little concern for the opinions of Nissan workers.[69]

Management-Labor Collaboration
Management and the second union also collaborated after 1953 to remove employees who had been sympathetic to the first union. Even department and section heads faced demotion or transfer to lesser jobs if they did not leave the company. According to Okumura, who resigned in 1957 to open a patent examiner's office, approximately 1000 workers quit in the two years following the strike and the dissolution of the first union[70] (see Table 40). Part of the reason for this was that the labor contract signed in 1955 required Nissan employees to join Jidōsha Rōren, and gave the union tacit authority to fire workers by dropping them from its rolls. While Nissan had to allow exceptions to this "union-shop" system after it merged with Prince Motors in 1966, in general, after 1955, management and the second union used this device to prevent potentially disruptive workers from entering or continuing at the company. Even during the early 1980s, applicants had to declare whether or not they were members of the Japan Communist Party or the Sōka Gakkai, a large Buddhist organization affiliated with the Kōmeitō Party that supported ethical reform in government and other measures which the Liberal Democrats and Social Democrats opposed. Nissan either

denied members and sympathizers of these organizations employment or encouraged them to resign if they were already working.[71]

The second union operated with temporary officials during September 1953 then held a formal election in October to choose a union chairman (Kasahara Kōzō), a vice-chairman (Takeuchi Takeshi), an executive secretary (Miyake Masaru), directors for seven union departments (public relations, organization, education, labor affairs, correspondence, accounting, and general affairs), and heads for the branch unions at Yoshiwara, Atsugi, Tsurumi, Shinbashi, Tokyo, and Osaka. The new executives agreed with management to restrict union activities during working hours to regular meetings that the office of the company president authorized. The labor contract they signed also pledged that the union would not demand wages for time spent in unauthorized meetings, and that applications shop committee chairmen submitted for meetings would specify the nature of the activity, members to attend, and their time and place.[72] The schedule of union meetings approved for March to September 1954 served as a model for future years (Table 41).

While the second union did not eliminate the shop committees, it subordinated them to company sections and moved the real authority of the union back to the management council system. Managers and labor leaders had participated in these joint meetings from 1946 to 1948, when company officials withdrew after Zenji intro-

Table 41: Authorized Union Meetings, 1954

Meeting	Frequency	Length
Annual convention	once per year	one day
General assembly	twice per year	"
Representatives council	once per month	4 hours
Branch assembly	twice per year	2 hours
Shop-committee chairmen conference	once per week	"
Branch committees	"	"
Branch executive committees	"	"

Source: Nissan sōgi hakusho, *p. 10.*

duced unified wage demands. But the revisions of November and December 1953 used company sections as a basis for choosing representatives to the lower-level councils, and gave the central council and four subcommittees authority to bargain with management and to set union policy (Figure 2).

Under the new system, each company section chose one representative to councils serving factories and staff offices. These councils selected members for an executive secretariat, which divided itself into subcommittees for production, engineering, control, and employee welfare. The three officials forming the union's executive committee were permanent representatives of the subcommittees and the executive secretariat. An agreement with Nissan management also required the company president, and top executives from managing director and above, to attend the meetings of the subcommittees and the central council. The production subcommittee was responsible for specific problems in manufacturing, while engineering handled long-term production planning and personnel requirements. Control dealt with staff administration and company policy, and employee welfare with shop conditions, safety, housing, scholarships, and worker training. The subcommittees, the executive secretariat, and lower-level councils met monthly, and the central council met every few months. Nissan later expanded the system to bring department and section heads, their immediate staff assistants, and all members of the board of directors into these meetings.[73]

Probably the most important change that came with the new union was an immediate reduction in the base wage (53 percent of a worker's monthly income) and the introduction in 1955 of higher standards, which took five years to draw up and implement, for calculating premiums (13 percent of monthly income). Like the previous master table, this measured worker productivity by groups, but it raised standards for all manufacturing processes to reflect Nissan's increased production levels and the introduction of high-performance equipment.[74] Average monthly income in Nissan subsequently dropped from 29,358 yen ($81.55) in 1953 to 24,698 yen ($68.60) in 1954, and to 22,463 yen ($62.40) in 1957 (see Table 39). Not only was the 1953 base unequaled until 1964, in nominal values, but wages fell nearly 3 percent a year between 1954 and 1959, and rose merely 4.6 percent annually during 1960-1964. At Toyota, wages increased only 0.1 percent per year between 1954 and 1959, although they rose 9 percent annually during 1960-1964 (Table 42). Total annual compensation (wages and benefits) per Nissan employee, in

Figure 2: Nissan's Management Council System, 1954

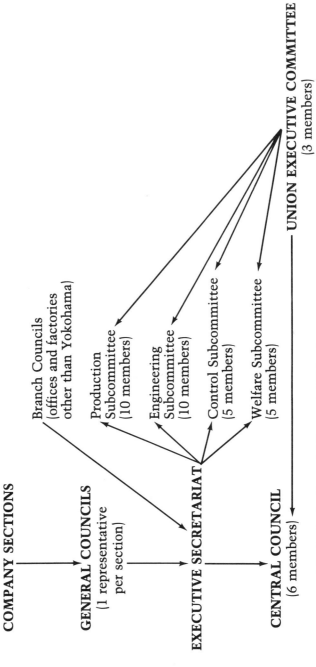

Source: *Nissan Jidōsha Rōdō Kumiai, Nissan sōgi hakusho.*

Table 42: Average Annual Wage Increases, 1954-1983

(%)

FY	Nissan	Toyota
1954-1959	−2.9	0.1
1960-1964	4.6	9.0
1965-1969	13.1	14.8
1970-1974	17.5	16.3
1975-1979	12.3	13.0
1980-1983	6.6	5.1

Source: See Table 39.

constant values, also fell by more than 10 percent in the decade following the 1953 strike and did not rise substantially above the 1951-1954 average until the 1970s, despite major gains in productivity after 1955.[75]

With the expansion of production and large wage hikes after 1965, however, Japanese autoworkers increased their pay scales relative to other major manufacturing sectors. In the spring of 1983, average monthly income at firms with 8000 or more employees was 6 percent higher in the automobile industry than in shipbuilding, and roughly equal to electronics and electrical equipment. Although most automakers were still between 5 and 11 percent behind companies in the iron and steel, precision machinery, and industrial machinery sectors, Nissan paid wages that were 5 percent above the automobile industry average compared to 17 percent above the average for Toyota and 21 percent below for Isuzu (Table 43).

In periods of both declining and rising wages, the second union at Nissan received nearly 100 percent of its formal wage requests because of the way labor officials formulated them. The top executives in the union determined proposals for one-year labor contracts after exchanging information with employees who worked in Nissan's accounting and personnel sections; the union's inclusion of white-collar office staff facilitated this communication. Then the union discussed the contract informally with higher management representatives, before announcing demands publicly. Rapidly rising

Table 43: Average Monthly Wages at Major Firms, Spring 1983 (1000 yen)

Industry	Firms	Income	Scale
Automobiles	9	242	1.00
Electronics/electrical	15	243	1.00
Shipbuilding	5	227	0.94
Precision machinery	2	254	1.05
Iron and steel	8	268	1.11
Industrial machinery	3	260	1.07
Non-automotive manufacturing	33	249	1.03
Automobile Industry			
Toyota		283	1.17
Toyo Kogyo (Mazda)		268	1.11
Hino		262	1.08
Daihatsu		260	1.07
Nissan		255	1.05
Suzuki		236	0.98
Honda		218	0.90
Fuji Heavy Industries		202	0.83
Isuzu		191	0.79

Source: *Tōyō Keizai,* Kaisha shikihō.

Note: *Major firms defined as companies with 8000 or more employees.*

profits and sales led to agreements during 1965-1974 that increased monthly income 15 percent a year. Sharp drops in earnings between 1974 and 1978 caused management to restrict its final offers to around 70 percent of what the union asked for, although monthly income still rose more than 12 percent annually during the second half of the 1970s, before dropping to 5 percent between 1980 and 1982.[76] There was also a large wage increase at Nissan in 1983, almost double Toyota's, despite lower operating profits and employee productivity.[77]

Close relations between Nissan executives and the second union were largely the product of a weakened distinction between management and labor—a phenomenon that occurred in most large Japanese firms since company unions combined blue-collar workers with white-collar employees headed for managerial positions. At Nissan after 1953, the union's labor affairs department and the company's personnel department coordinated their activities to the point where, to an outside observer, they seemed almost indistinguishable. In addition, since most heads of the personnel department, who were usually company directors responsible for labor relations, had gone through the ranks of executive positions in the union, they retained considerable influence over the younger union leaders.[78]

The second union and Nissan management also attempted to publicize and strengthen their philosophy of cooperation rather than confrontation by establishing a foundation in 1959 called the Association for Research on Modern Management-Labor Relations (Kindaiteki Rōshi Kankei Kenkyū Kyōkai, abbreviated as Kindai Rō-ken). This held lectures and funded studies promoting cooperative relations with management, published a journal, and mediated labor disputes. The founders included Miyake Masaru, head of the Nissan union and Jidōsha Rōren in 1959; Iwakoshi Tadahiro, then a Nissan managing director; Minoura Taiichi, Nissan's president during 1947-1951 and chairman of management organizations for the automobile industry and Kanagawa prefecture; and Hayashi Nobuo, head of a local labor organization and a professor at Yokohama City University. By the late 1970s, the association had 1125 individual and corporate members, and a head office located in Tokyo.[79]

Not all observers of management-labor relations at Nissan after the 1953 strike found them satisfactory. One article published during 1964 in a journal devoted to labor issues maintained that the exchange of information between managers and the second union subverted the entire concept of collective bargaining and independent wage proposals, resulting in substantial losses for Nissan workers during the later 1950s and early 1960s. Yet the author also found that most employees were reluctant to oppose the union because they intended to stay with Nissan for their entire careers. Company staff, along with shop-committee chairmen, closely monitored their statements and voting records, while upper management rarely promoted workers to section heads or foremen if they declined to cooperate with union officials.[80]

The second union was able to influence staff promotions in Nissan through a recommendation system that evaluated a candidate's activities in the union and standing in the hierarchy of union officials. While management usually approved only about half the recommendations that the executive committee submitted for positions such as shop foreman, the company treated a negative appraisal from the union as a veto.[81] Presidents before Ishihara Takashi were even reluctant to move middle managers to top executive posts if the union opposed the promotions, based on the reasoning that the ability to get along with the union helped an individual to be an effective executive at Nissan, and also reflected potential managerial talent.[82]

One incident that grew out of this system of close relations between management and the union occurred in the spring of 1963. Miyake had left his post as head of Jidōsha Rōren in September 1962 to become manager of Nissan's domestic marketing department and then the personnel department. The former union head wanted an immediate appointment to company director, but President Kawamata refused and asked him to wait. To pressure Kawamata, Miyake then had the union stop one of Nissan's production lines—a "secret strike," as Managing Director Maeda Riichi described it.[83]

Kawamata had fully intended to promote the ex-union leader. "We were grateful to Miyake," Matsuzaki recalled—for founding the second union and supporting management during the 1950s. "The Kawamata-Miyake combination went extremely well, even too well. Kawamata used Miyake too often, and the latter began to think of himself as a sort of 'emperor.' Miyake wanted to be more than just a department head and took the attitude that, since he had chosen many of the department heads, he deserved to be higher in rank. He became conceited." But nobody went from union chairman to director in one step. Kawamata wanted Miyake to spend a few years as a department head to learn more about management operations first hand. When he heard of the strike, however, the president became furious and vowed never to promote any individual who put his self-interest so far above the company. Miyake stayed at Nissan until 1966, when he resigned to become president of a car dealership affiliated with the Seibu department store chain.[84]

Miyake had expected Kawamata to repay him for two "debts" incurred after he established the second union. The first dated back to 1955. During the strike, Asahara had begun to feel that Kawamata was usurping his authority as president; afterwards, he complained that the executive director was taking advantage of his relationship with the leaders of the second union to dominate company policy. Asahara then attempted to remove Kawamata from Nissan by appealing to the head of the Industrial Bank, Nakayama Sōhei, to send the executive director to a subsidiary, Minsei (Nissan) Diesel, as president. Nakayama apparently agreed to ask Kawamata to move but word of this got to both Kawamata and Miyake, and the union head ordered a strike at the Yokohama factory in May 1955 as a warning to leave Kawamata where he was. Neither Asahara nor the Industrial Bank wanted to face a renewal of problems with the union, so they dropped the idea of transferring Kawamata.[85]

The second incident took place when Kawamata wanted to succeed Asahara in 1957. Asahara had decided several years earlier not to remain as president too long; he also turned 65 in 1956, had endured criticism from other executives and the press for having fallen behind Toyota in sales, and found Kawamata and the second union difficult to deal with. He wanted to move up to chairman, a position of semi-retirement in most Japanese firms, and preferred Harashina Kyōichi as a successor. Harashina, a mechanical engineer trained at the University of Tokyo, had worked for Tobata Casting and Nissan since 1930 and risen from director in 1944 to managing director in 1948. Asahara then made him an executive director in 1956 to rank along with Kawamata.[86]

In comparison to Harashina, Kawamata was unpopular among Nissan employees, particularly those who had been with the firm since the 1930s. These workers, and the engineers in particular, did not like the idea of a representative from the Industrial Bank taking over as president. Yet, as in 1951, the outgoing chief executive did not have sufficient authority to choose a new president on his own. The directors of the Industrial Bank favored Kawamata but might not have opposed Asahara's choice except that the union chairman made it known he would only support Kawamata. The union's vote was apparently decisive, although Kawamata insisted that he was entitled to become president because he had served as executive director—second in command to the president—for nine years, far longer than Harashina, despite the latter's seniority in the company. Kawamata thus took over for Asahara in 1957, while a disgruntled Harashina left in 1960 to become president of Nissan Diesel, where he remained until retiring as chairman in 1982 at age 76.

Nissan's Other Chairman

After Kawamata promoted Miyake to department manager in 1962 he needed another partner in the union and found this in Shioji Ichirō (1927-), who took over for Miyake as head of the Nissan union and Jidōsha Rōren. Since he was still the dominant figure in Nissan's union during the 1980s, Japanese journalists had come to refer to him as "Emperor Shioji" and "the other chairman" in Nissan, besides Kawamata.[87] Not only was Shioji one of the best known union leaders in Japan but he was also a director of the Japan Productivity Center and a vice-chairman of Dōmei (since 1964); vice-chairman of the International Metalworkers Federation—Japan Council (since 1967); and the chairman of Jidōsha Sōren, a nominal umbrella organization for unions in the automobile industry that Shioji founded in 1972.[88] He also had close affiliations with the Democratic Socialist Party, preferred to be known as a dedicated anti-Communist, and advocated the philosophy that labor must cooperate with management because the success or failure of the company had a direct impact on his authority: "If one's company does not grow in a healthy manner, then the influence of the union leaders in that firm weakens... Since my company is Nissan, if it does not grow as expected, then I lose the support of the workers and the basis of my own influence."[89]

The eldest son of a former owner of a dairy products company in Tokyo, Shioji entered the Imperial Navy's engineering college in 1943 but did not graduate due to the war. For several years after 1945 he worked on a transport ship bringing back Japanese colonists from China, as a dance instructor, and as a radio repairman; then in 1949 he entered Nippon Oils & Fats, and enrolled in the night division of Meiji University's law faculty.[90] While working at the chemical company, Shioji also became an active opponent of its union leaders and began attending the Institute for World Democracy (Sekai Minshū Kenkyūjo) to "study," under Nabeyama Sadachika, critiques of Marxism and how to break leftist unions or strikes by organizing second unions.[91]

When he graduated from Meiji University in March 1953, Shioji quit Nippon Oils & Fats (which had been a subsidiary in the old Nissan group), and tried to enter Nissan. It was against company practice to hire a night college graduate who had worked for another firm, but he went to Nissan's personnel office on three successive days to request permission to take the company's entrance exam. The head of the personnel department, Inomata Ryōji (later a vice-president of Nissan Diesel), finally allowed Shioji to take the exam and granted him an interview with Iwakoshi, since he was the company director in charge of personnel and labor relations. Shioji impressed both men with his anti-union background; Iwakoshi personally decided to admit him to the company on the assumption that Shioji would aid management efforts already underway to oppose the first union.[92] He initially assigned Shioji to the accounting section in the Yokohama factory, which was the center of the union's activities; there Shioji met Masuda and members of the "study group" that would soon found the second union. Shioji recalled both encounters in a 1978 interview:

> When I entered Nissan, I believed that I wanted to become president. Really, that's what I thought... But, with the 1953 strike, many things came to the surface. The Communist Party controlled the union leadership and they used Marxist slogans to lie. I just couldn't stand the sight of them trying to move people through lies. Then the union summoned the twenty-four college graduates who had entered the company to give us what appears to have been the union indoctrination, mainly by the union head, Masuda Tetsuo. Later, at a general union meeting, someone accused one of the new graduates of being a Nikkeiren spy and looked at me, because earlier I had complained at the union office. After I met Mr. Masuda we argued for about an hour. Word of this got to the democratization group, and they asked me to join them. This group was trying to democratize the Zenji Nissan chapter and, since they asked me to help, I became one of the first leaders of the new union movement. But this happened only because I opposed the activities of the red union.[93]

After they organized a second union, Shioji became the head of its accounting section.[94] At the same time, he transferred to Nissan's personnel department to work directly under Inomata, training new workers and insuring that they did not join Masuda's union. Shioji's job with young recruits then gave him the idea to establish a youth division within the union. Miyake approved, beginning with the 1955 entrants. As Nissan added hundreds and then thousands of workers in subsequent years, Shioji became the most powerful official in the union. Nissan's company history noted the creation of this youth division and Shioji's role in its establishment:[95]

> The efforts of young employees in the history of the Nissan labor union, and in the recovery and development of the company after the hundred-day strike, have been particularly significant. Many workers who desired a union that was truly beneficial to the members stood up to the violent pressures from the Zenji Nissan chapter during the 1953 dispute; among them were young employees whose hearts burned with a sense of justice. When the formation of the Nissan union revived the dispute, young volunteers, who had foresight and courage, on their own initiative decided to form a group to work for Nissan's revival and to train themselves to assume the responsibilities of the future.
>
> Of their own free will, passions burned to unite these energies. This enthusiasm and self-sacrificing spirit moved the younger union members to establish the Nissan Labor Union Youth Division on 1 March 1955, with more than 500 volunteers in the Yokohama branch. The current chairman of Jidōsha Rōren, Shioji Ichirō, served as the first director. At their inaugural convention, the youth division adopted the slogan "We Make It, We Do It, Our Youth Division."
>
> As these words indicate, young employees formed the youth division of their own free will. It functioned as an independent organization and developed rapidly, with the goals of cultivating originality and skills through cultural, athletic, and educational activities aimed at individual improvement. The Nissan Labor Union Youth Division subsequently established organizations in each branch union and quickly expanded its structure, membership, and activities. Although young workers form the majority of the division, they aim not merely to "carry the burden of tomorrow" for the organization and the company. The youth division encourages them to realize that they also 'carry the burden of today.'[96]

However one may judge this youth division, or the curious hyperbole and repetition used to describe it, clearly, Shioji was an ambitious and able organizer of men.[97] For this talent, and for his ideology, Miyake designated him as a successor, and the union's election system helped to ratify this year after year once Shioji became a full-time union official in 1959. In 1960 he also studied abroad at the invitation of the U.S. Department of State, attending the Harvard Business School and spending five months at the headquarters of the United Automobile Workers in Detroit. During this trip he decided not to move up into management but to pursue a career in the union "to modernize Japan's labor movement."[98]

But not until the merger with Prince in 1966 did Shioji become as close and as useful to Kawamata as Miyake had been during the 1950s.[99] Although Prince had a market share of only a few percent and was not especially profitable, Kawamata and Iwakoshi wanted the merger because it would eliminate a competitor with similar product lines and add to Nissan's technological skills. As a former aircraft manufacturer, Prince still had some of the best engineers in the automobile industry, as well as small divisions for textile-machinery and rocket-engine manufacturing. MITI and the Industrial Bank also offered to arrange cheap loans to finance the acquisition.

The only problem was the Prince union and its 7300 members, who were firm supporters of Sōhyō and maintained an affiliation through the National Trade Union of Metal and Engineering Workers (Zen-koku Kinzoku Rōdō Kumiai). Union officials argued that the merger was part of the government's attempt to eliminate the union and further concentrate production in the automobile industry, and that the merger would lead to wage reductions and employee firings. Shioji exacerbated the situation by announcing that he would support these measures if necessary in a company "reorganization." This set off a bitter media struggle between Sōhyō and Dōmei.

After conducting seven months of fruitless negotiations with the Prince union during 1965, Shioji decided to appeal directly to Prince workers through a leaflet campaign. The leaders of the Prince union countered with their own leaflets but resigned after a vote of no confidence, although by this time there was little doubt that the merger was going through. Prince elected new officials in the spring of 1966, who formed a second union independent of Sōhyō, and the two companies merged on schedule in August. The second Prince union then joined Jidōsha Rōren in October and merged with the central Nissan union in June 1967. While scores of workers remained loyal to the old Prince union, their numbers gradually dwindled to around 70 by the early 1980s.[100]

The chairmen of Nissan's group union since the mid-1950s—Miyake and Shioji—were able to influence management at least in part because Kawamata found them useful. Miyake not only helped to solve the 1953 strike by creating the second union, but he supported Kawamata to stay in the company and to become president in 1957. Shioji played a critical role in facilitating the merger with Prince, which Kawamata and other Nissan executives badly wanted, while his control over the Nissan union enhanced his standing with management. Shioji also founded Jidōsha Sōren during 1971 in an attempt to create an industrial union devoted to working with management. In the process he hoped to strengthen his position as a national labor leader, although Shioji was unable to convince Toyota and the other member unions to merge or to adopt unified platforms. This lack of support for Shioji all but eliminated any significance that Jidōsha Sōren might have had.

The decline in the Nissan union's ability to receive all its wage demands during the second half of the 1970s reflected lower profits but also a noticeable deterioration in Shioji's relations with Nissan management, especially after Ishihara Takashi took over as president. Ishihara, who had worked in Nissan since 1937, never became close to Kawamata or the other executives that dealt directly with the second union. Asahara named him a company director in 1954, although Kawamata placed him in charge of exports and sent him temporarily to the United States in 1960 and to Mexico in 1961 to set up sales subsidiaries. These were not important assignments at the time, since Nissan's exports were so low; some Nissan employees even felt that Ishihara had been exiled.[101] Export sales increased substantially under Ishihara's direction, however, and this convinced Kawamata to promote him to managing director in 1963 and then to place him in charge of domestic sales two years later. Ishihara strongly supported Nissan's introduction of the Datsun Sunny, even though Kawamata was reluctant to invest in a car in the 1-liter class since Toyota's Publica had sold so poorly. After the Sunny became Nissan's best-selling model, many executives favored Ishihara to succeed Kawamata in 1973 as president. But, since Kawamata wanted to reward his long-time deputy, Iwakoshi, with this post, Ishihara had to settle for an appointment to executive vice-president until, at 65, he replaced Iwakoshi in 1977.

Problems with Shioji began when the new president removed several top executives who had worked closely with the labor leader and made it clear that he wanted the board of directors to operate more independently of the union. Ishihara also favored an ambitious program of constructing manufacturing facilities abroad to counter political opposition to Japanese car exports. Shioji, in turn, opposed major projects such as the location of a car factory in Great Britain, and even ordered a limited strike in February 1982 to remind Ishihara of his authority in the union and that they had several areas of disagreement, including the president's directive to increase productivity and his supposed disregard for worker safety.

In reality, Shioji used these issues to protest Ishihara's determination to distance himself from the union chief and reclaim the authority, lost under Kawamata and Iwakoshi, to make decisions even if Shioji disagreed. Chairman Kawamata sided with Shioji for several years in his opposition to the Britain project but, convinced that Nissan had to move some production overseas for political reasons, he consented in October 1983 to support a scaled-down version of the original plan.[102] While Shioji lost this argument, he won an important victory in March 1983 when Ishihara signed the first agreement in the Japanese automobile industry that prohibited the introduction of robots and automated equipment if these would result in the elimination of jobs for human workers. This appeared to represent a reversal of the union's longstanding preference for encouraging productivity increases through automation rather than through production management techniques, although Nissan managers were more likely to restrict new hiring than to abandon their commitment to robotics and other automated systems.

By late 1984, however, Shioji, who held a life-time appointment as head of the Nissan union, was having trouble maintaining his hold on company employees and his authority in general. During October 1984, for the first time in the union's history, the 3000 white-collar workers in the Tokyo branch unanimously approved a motion criticizing Shioji's behavior and system of control, which had already lasted 23 years.[103] In addition, Ishihara managed to convince Kawamata to retire as chairman in June 1985, allowing Ishihara to move up to chairman and his personal choice as a successor, Kume Yutaka (1921-), to take over as president. Kume, a 1944 graduate of the University of Tokyo's engineering department, entered Nissan in 1946 and rose quickly through the ranks of top management during Ishihara's presidency—from director in 1973 to executive director in 1982 and executive vice-president in 1983.[104]

Toyota: A Different Setting and History
While the first and second Nissan unions were atypical in the Japanese automobile industry in the amount of influence they had over management decision making, in comparison to the United Automobile Workers of America the second union fit into the Japanese pattern of company unions that tended to cooperate with managers far more than they confronted them. Yet, in any firm where labor officials supported programs to lower wages or suppress activist workers, and where they readily moved into management if they chose to, it was difficult to determine who was leading or using whom. Some labor leaders in Nissan, Toyota, and other firms

throughout Japan took advantage of the system to further their careers in management. At the same time, company unions achieved gains in wages and benefits, although these were less than American autoworkers received, despite extraordinarily high levels of productivity in Japan, and were limited mainly to the largest firms in the industry. But restrictions on wages, especially at subcontractors, were only one of the advantages of company unions. Others included cooperation in the introduction of automated equipment and programs to increase productivity or to improve quality control.

Toyota provided the best example of what managers were able to achieve with a work force that made little effort to challenge the company in areas such as shop administration or production scheduling. Two factors, however, contributed to the differences in management-labor relations at Nissan and Toyota: geography, and the inclination of employees to view Toyota as a family enterprise.

Many people unfamiliar with Japan tend to view its automobile industry as monolithic and the country as small and homogeneous in all respects. In reality, Japanese companies even in the same industry often differ from one another as much as any two firms in the United States or Europe, and in ways that greatly affect their relative performances. And while Japan is much smaller in geographic size than the United States, whether a company operates in an urban area or the countryside has a major impact on the approaches managers take toward production control, subcontracting, or labor relations.

For all its international success during the 1970s and 1980s, many Japanese still regarded Toyota as a "rural" company since it located factories and main offices in the countryside of Aichi prefecture, a couple hundred miles southwest of the Tokyo-Yokohama metropolis where Nissan had its head offices and most of its factories. When Kiichirō founded Toyota in 1937, the area was nothing but farmland, and, even in 1950, Toyota City (named Koromo until 1959) had just 30,000 people; nearly everyone either farmed or worked for Toyota or one of its suppliers. By the early 1980s, the city had grown to a population of around 300,000, yet 95 percent of its industrial freight and 70 percent of the residents still depended on Toyota, directly or indirectly.[105]

Beginning in the 1930s, Toyota actively recruited workers from Aichi or nearby prefectures because Kiichirō wanted to hire the same unskilled, malleable farm boys, with strong backs and communal loyalties, who had helped to make his father's companies so successful.[106] Since there were not many alternatives for employment in that part of Japan, workers and residents tended to be grateful to the Toyoda family and Toyota group companies for their economic contributions to the area. After management fired a third of Toyota's workers in 1950, employees lucky enough to remain were usually more concerned with keeping their positions than with their "rights" as workers, or with the fate of the industrial union and its executive committee in Tokyo. It is surprising that Toyota workers supported Masuda and Zenji to the extent they did, although workers throughout the industry benefited from the large wage hikes Zenji won during and after the Korean War.

While Toyota went through two months of intermittent strikes in 1950 before workers accepted management's decision to discharge employees and cut wages, union leaders were far less sympathetic with Communist or socialist aims than their counterparts at Nissan or Isuzu. The Toyota union suggested the idea of an industrial union in 1947 primarily to break away from Sanbetsu, which had become dominated by Communist Party members. They did not protest the military orders accepted during the Korean War, while Nissan's union did. Nor did Toyota workers organize shop committees. As Zenji became more involved with national politics, the Toyota union concentrated on achieving guarantees of employment and wage increases for permanent employees, and cooperated with management on measures to reduce costs and increase productivity.[107] Yet another factor which eased management-labor relations at Toyota was that the company had avoided much of the bitterness between management and the union that emerged at Nissan during 1948-1953. Masuda took the 1949 firings as a personal defeat and a blow to organized labor; Kawamata saw them as a personal victory and a success for managers throughout the country. It became increasingly difficult for the two men to compromise, and eventually Kawamata decided that Nissan needed another union. No comparable struggle occurred at Toyota after 1950.

As a proportion of total employees, Toyota fired more workers in 1950 than Nissan did in 1949. But managers at each firm dealt with the disputes in different ways. Kiichirō agonized over the dismissals and procrastinated as long as he could because he felt a special loyalty toward the workers he had hired to found the company. Not only did he worry but he decided, in effect, to fire himself.[108] After his resignation, the union settled with management. Throughout this dispute, and in 1953, Toyota executives made no attempt to break off negotiations and found a second union to end their labor problems. At least in the opinion of Okumura, who studied Toyota's operations after leaving Nissan in 1957, union officials appreciated the commitment of Kiichirō and other managers to negotiate without trying to subvert their authority, and this helped both sides reach an agreement in August 1953.[109]

This is not to say that Toyota made no efforts to control its labor force. Executives encouraged union leaders to cooperate by moving them regularly into managerial posts, as at Nissan; they also fired the most activist members of the union in 1950, while granting other workers "lifetime" employment in exchange for their loyalty. Management then treated permanent workers as an elite group, with higher salaries and more benefits than temporary employees; this tended to reduce opposition from union members as well as from the large number of temporary workers seeking promotions to regular status.[110]

Toyota used other devices as well to diffuse or contain potential discontent. Executives began a suggestion system in 1951, copied from Ford, that brought nearly all employees into the management process, although managers also put pressure on workers to participate.[111] More important, around 1960 Toyota adopted an aptitude evaluation and individual report system that became an effective tool for personnel administration. Management staff compiled the aptitude evaluation to judge an employee's suitability for a particular job or promotion by soliciting formal opinions from supervisors and co-workers. Employees then had to file an individual report at the end of each year that stated their objectives for the coming year, how well they met those of the past year, and whether or not their current positions were suitable. The company sent these reports, along with comments on the behavior and attitudes of the workers, to their families. In Japan, especially in a rural area where people were highly sensitive to public criticism, managers found that involving the family made employees conform more readily to company policy.[112]

Another characteristic that made relations between management and labor somewhat easier at Toyota than at Nissan was the role of the Toyoda family. Toyota was never privately owned and, in 1984, it had over 61,000 shareholders. Chairman Eiji and President Shōichirō together held less than 1 percent of its outstanding shares; banks were the principal owners.[113] Yet the prestige of the Toyoda family was still enormous within the company and its affiliates.

Their reputation, combined with Toyota's rural location and a large number of employees recruited from the local area, encouraged workers to feel a special sense of loyalty and community not present to the same extent at more urban companies such as Nissan. Family members continued to hold executive positions in Toyota, not because of ownership, but because of the history and traditions of the firm.

In contrast, loyalty to a family was never a factor at Nissan. Aikawa Yoshisuke was not a popular president, and postwar executives made sure that he left no heirs in the company. Although the lines between them were not always distinct, after 1945, two main divisions competed to control Nissan management: Kawamata and others who reflected the influence of the Industrial Bank and close ties to the second union; and older employees, mostly engineers, who joined Nissan in the 1930s and supported Asahara during the 1950s. Asahara was the only president in Nissan's history to attract loyalty from a large number of employees, but his postwar presidency was short and he struggled to maintain his authority after 1953.

The continuance of three generations of managers from one family was not unheard of in postwar Japan, although many large family enterprises founded prior to World War II became publicly owned after 1945 and switched to outside, professional managers. Toyota actually represented a compromise: Financial ownership by the family was never complete, and members descended from or related to Sakichi, beginning with Kiichirō, studied engineering and management in college. Kiichirō's successors as president, Ishida Taizō and Nakagawa Fukio, as well as Kamiya Shōtarō in Toyota Motor Sales, accepted the special role of the Toyoda family and helped to prepare Kiichirō's cousin Eiji, and the sons of Risaburō and Kiichirō, to become professional managers.[114]

Eiji, the son of Sakichi's younger brother, graduated in 1936 from the mechanical engineering department of the University of Tokyo. He entered Toyoda Automatic Loom after college, went with Kiichirō to Toyota in 1937, rose to director by 1945 and then to executive vice-president by 1960. After succeeding Nakagawa in 1967, Eiji stayed on as president until the merger with Toyota Motor Sales in 1982, when he moved up to chairman. He also served as a director of Toyota Motor Sales, U.S.A., the Toyota Central Research Laboratories, Aichi Steel, Toyoda Machine Works, Aisin Seiki, and Toyoda Automatic Loom.

Shōichirō, Kiichirō's eldest son and a mechanical engineer like

Figure 3: The Toyoda Family: Members in Top Executive Posts, 1983

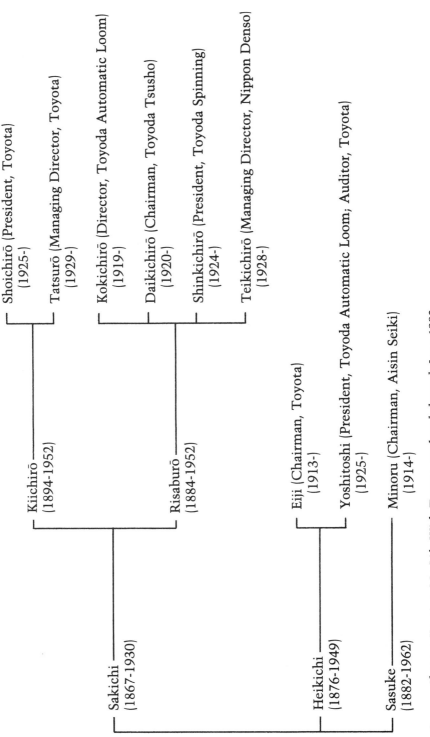

Source: Shotaro Kamiya, My Life With Toyota, updated through June 1983.

his father, attended Nagoya University, which, after 1945, sent many of its engineering graduates to Toyota. He joined his father's company in 1947; five years later Ishida promoted him to director, at age 27. Shōichirō trained carefully and took twenty years to reach executive vice-president, while gaining an excellent reputation as a quality control engineer and production manager. He also served as a director of Nippon Denso, Toyota Motor Sales, U.S.A., and, to prepare for the merger, as president of Toyota Motor Sales during 1981-1982.[115]

Nor were family members in the Toyota group limited to Eiji and Shōichirō (Figure 3). Another son of Kiichirō, Tatsurō (1929-), entered Toyota Motor Sales in 1953 and became a director of Toyota in 1980 and manager of the Takaoka plant in 1981, before being named president in 1984 of New United Motor Manufacturing, Toyota's joint venture with General Motors in Freemont, California. Risaburō had four sons: During the early 1980s, one was a director of Toyoda Automatic Loom, which assembled vehicles for Toyota, another was a managing director of Nippon Denso, and two served as the president and chairman of Toyoda Tsusho and Toyoda Spinning and Weaving. Eiji's younger brother was president of Toyoda Automatic Loom and a Toyota auditor, while his two sons worked at Aisin Machinery and Toyoda Spinning and Weaving. His brother-in-law, Imai Shinzō, was president of a transport subsidiary and had two sons working for Toyota and Nippon Denso. The husband of Kiichirō's eldest daughter, Nishida Akira, was chairman of Toyota's concrete-manufacturing subsidiary. Another younger brother of Sakichi, Sasuke (1882-1962), had two sons who were the chairman of Aisin Seiki and an executive director of Toyoda Gōsei, a rubber manufacturing subsidiary, and three sons-in-law who included a consultant to Aisin Seiki, the president of Toyota Auto Body, and a managing director of Toyoda Spinning and Weaving.[116]

The performance of the Toyota group after 1950 suggested that a rural, "family" atmosphere was not a disadvantage. While there may have been some resentment among top managers not connected to the Toyoda family who felt they were passed over to make way for less talented family members, everyone who entered Toyota knew of this possibility. Public complaints about the choice of managers in the parent company were rare, although these did surface on occasion with regard to subsidiaries such as Toyota Motor Sales. But most employees expected members of the Toyoda family, if they had the experience, talent, and willingness to serve, to hold the top executive posts in the company.[117]

Chapter Four

MANUFACTURING: STRATEGY, IMPLEMENTATION, PERFORMANCE

THE PRODUCTIVITY-COST DIFFERENTIAL

By the early 1980s, the Japanese automobile industry had become famous throughout the world for the quality of its products as well as for the productivity of its labor force. Several studies concluded that Japanese automakers were able to manufacture and ship a small car to the United States for about $1500 less than it cost American firms to produce a comparable vehicle. Since shipping from Japan was about $400 per car, the Japanese cost advantage was approximately $1900.[1] The actual figure depended on the type of car, the yen-dollar exchange rate, and the particular companies being compared. In the case of Toyota, the most efficient Japanese automaker, its 1984 cost advantage was at least equal to the $1800 price differential between a Tercel sold in Japan and the United States with similar equipment.[2] The main source of the Japanese advantage lay in higher physical output per worker as well as a lower cost of labor, although differences between the structures of the automobile industries and leading firms in the United States and Japan contributed to misunderstandings about just how much more "productive" Japanese autoworkers were, as well as when and how the "differential" appeared. Dealing with this problem required an analysis of both methodology and the historical, or statistical, record.

Vertical Integration

For example, a comparison of data on the world's largest automobile companies that Nissan publishes annually reveals a startling but highly exaggerated edge for the Japanese in vehicle productivity—cars and trucks produced per employee per year. Between 1960 and 1983, General Motors (worldwide) averaged from 8 to 11 units per

186

worker, compared to 10 to 15 at Ford in the United States, and 11 to 16 at Chrysler. The U.S. firms showed improvements between 1980 and 1983, but they as well as every other non-Japanese auto-maker appeared to be far behind Japan's top 5 producers, which averaged more than 44 units per worker in 1983, led by Toyota with 58 (Table 44).

Common sense suggests that it would be truly miraculous if Japanese autoworkers were 4 or 5 times more productive than Americans or Europeans. And the truth is that they are not. While Japanese companies, as well as newspapers and other observers in Japan and the United States, have cited statistics such as these, simply dividing a firm's nominal production by total employees produced skewed results favoring the Japanese due to their much lower levels of vertical integration between components production and final assembly. In fact, Japan's 10 major automakers were more like a collection of manufacturing and assembly plants for bodies, engines, transmissions, and other key components than they were comprehensive automobile producers.

From the mid-1970s through the early 1980s, Nissan and Toyota accounted for only 30 percent of the manufacturing costs for each car sold under their nameplates; they paid the rest to outside contractors, including subsidiaries (defined in Japanese corporate reports as companies in which the parent firm owned 20 percent or more of outstanding shares), loosely affiliated companies (in which parent

Table 44: Vehicles per Employee Productivity, 1960-1983

1960-1982 FY Vehicles per Employee

	1960	1965	1970	1975	1980	1982
GM (worldwide)	8	10	8	10	10	10
Ford (U.S.)	14	14	12	12	10	12
Chrysler (worldwide)	11[a]	12	11	11	13	16
Nissan	12	13	30	41	47	41
Toyota	15	19	38	50	61	56

Table 44 (continued)

1983 FY

Company	Vehicles	Employees	Vehicles Employee
GM (U.S.)	5,098,338	463,000	11
Ford (U.S.)	2,476,458	163,400	15
Chrysler (U.S.)	1,051,955	65,832	16
VW (W. Germany)	1,538,206	148,100	10
Toyota (Toyota Group)	3,376,224	58,706 (132,085)	58 (26)
Nissan (Nissan Group)	2,518,491	59,335 (105,094)	42 (24)
Mazda	1,171,350	27,395	43
Honda	1,032,440	27,969	37
Mitsubishi	974,705	24,000	41

Sources: Nissan Jidōsha Chōsa-bu, Jidōsha kōgyō handobukku *(1984); Tōyō Keizai,* Kaisha shikihō; *annual reports;* yūka shōken hōkokusho. *See Tables 47, 70, and 71 for data on the Nissan and Toyota groups.*

Notes: Employee totals for this and other tables include the employees at Toyota Motor Sales prior to the 1982 merger, unless noted.

[a]Refers to Chrysler's U.S. employees.

firms had less than a 20-percent equity interest), and non-affiliated suppliers[3] (Table 45). Dividing in-house manufacturing and other operating costs by sales minus operating profits (to exclude the effects of fluctuations in profitability, different rates of taxation, interest costs or revenues, or other extraordinary income or losses) provides a cost-based definition of integration that makes it possible to compare the Japanese and U.S. automakers directly, using publicly available data. According to this measure, the level of integration was only 26 percent at Nissan during 1979-1983 and 28 percent at

Table 45: Vertical Integration at Nissan and Toyota,
1955-1983 (% of manufacturing costs accounted for in house)

	Standard-Size Trucks		Small Cars and Trucks	
FY Period	Nissan	Toyota	Nissan	Toyota
1955-1959	49	38	—	—
1960-1964	—	28	39	—
1965-1969	—	—	36	42
1970-1974	—	—	35	34
1975-1979	—	—	29	30
1980-1983	—	—	30	30

Source: Yūka shōken hōkokusho.

Note: Manufacturing costs equal materials plus labor plus depreciation and miscellaneous expenses. Although the percentage of costs subcontracted has not changed at Nissan and Toyota since 1976, remaining at 70%, according to Nissan's accounting department, this number is calculated annually and revised whenever it changes more than a percentage point or so (Kawarada interview, 17 December 1984).

Toyota, compared to 43 percent at General Motors and 36 percent at Ford in 1979 (the last year for which these figures were available), and 32 percent at Chrysler during 1979-1983 (Table 46).

It is clear that higher levels of outside manufacturing exaggerate the nominal productivity of workers in original-equipment manufacturers such as Nissan and Toyota, especially since automakers based in the United States had many more subsidiaries in which they controlled an equity interest greater than 50 percent. The American corporate reports treated these firms as consolidated subsidiaries and included their employee totals. Nissan in 1984 had only 2 subsidiaries with more than 1000 employees in which its equity interest was higher than 50 percent; Toyota had none that fit this category. If workers in publicly listed subsidiaries were added, regardless of equity, to their personnel rolls, productivity for the Nissan and Toyota groups during 1983 would fall to 24 and 26 units

Table 46: Company and Group Integration, U.S.-Japan, 1965-1983 (%)

FY	Nissan In-House	Nissan Group	Toyota In-House	Toyota Group	GM In-House	Ford In-House	Chrysler In-House
1965	32	54	41	74	50	36	36
1970	29	52	35	66	49	39	36
1975	22	50	30	73	45	36	36ª
1979	26	70	29	74	43	36	32
1980	26	73	29	76	—	—	34
1981	26	71	28	75	—	—	31
1982	26	75	26	70	—	—	34
1983	26	78	26	73	—	—	28

Sources: Yūka shōken hōkokusho *and annual reports.*

Notes: ªEstimate, assuming that the level of payments to suppliers (as a percentage of sales) in 1975 equaled the average for 1974 (64.1%) and 1976 (64.3%), since Chrysler did not publish this figure in 1975.

per worker, respectively; this figure should actually be lower, because Hino, Daihatsu, and Fuji Heavy Industries assembled cars and trucks for Nissan and Toyota but were not formal subsidiaries.[4]

Adding manufacturing and other costs paid to subsidiaries to in-house costs also provides a way to measure integration within the Nissan and Toyota "groups"—parent firms plus companies in which the automakers had an equity interest of at least 20 percent. As a percentage of the total cost of sales, vertical integration in the Toyota group was 73 percent between 1965 and 1983, and 52 percent in the Nissan group from 1965 to 1975, before rising (as Nissan invested more heavily in suppliers) to 78 percent by 1983.[5] These levels indicate that the Nissan and Toyota groups were far more integrated than Ford, Chrysler, or General Motors, the most highly integrated American automaker (see Table 46).

Table 46 (continued)

In-house vertical integration is defined as internal manufacturing and other operating costs divided by sales minus operating profits. Group vertical integration is defined as internal operating costs plus operating costs paid to affiliates (20%-equity minimum) divided by sales minus operating profits.

Since the Japanese and U.S. firms do not publish comparable data, I employed the following methodology and assumptions to construct the table above. For Nissan and Toyota (including Toyota Motor Sales), I multiplied the percentage of manufacturing costs for small cars not subcontracted (see Table 45) by total manufacturing costs listed in the yūka shōken hōkokusho (Japanese 10-K reports), added other operating expenses incurred in house (executive and other non-manufacturing employee compensation, retirement and severance payments, and depreciation), and divided by sales minus operating profits. For group integration, I added operating costs paid to affiliates, listed in the notes to the balance sheets in the Japanese reports, to in-house costs. For the U.S. firms, I subtracted payments to suppliers from sales minus operating profits and divided by sales minus operating profits. GM and Ford stopped publishing data on payments to suppliers after 1979, so I could not calculate their levels of integration for 1980-1983.

The Japanese figures are estimates, therefore, assuming that the percentages Nissan and Toyota published regarding subcontracting are accurate, and that total subcontracting was roughly equal to that for small cars.

Although low levels of in-house integration helped the Japanese automakers improve productivity through specialization in a few functions, such as final assembly and the manufacturing of key subassemblies or other parts, the Japanese automobile industry in the aggregate still had an advantage in productivity over the American automobile industry. As expected, however, this appeared to be less than between individual automakers. Japan's 10 major automobile manufacturers had 193,000 employees in 1983, while another 1,080,000 Japanese, many working at small, less efficient subcontractors, made automotive components. They brought the productivity of the industry down to about 8.7 vehicles per worker, approximately 50 percent more than employees in the American automobile industry, where 1,350,000 workers in 1981 (the latest year when complete data were available) each averaged 5.9 vehicles.[6]

Much of the apparent productivity increase at Nissan and Toyota after 1960 came from declining levels of vertical integration—from 50 percent during the 1950s to 30 percent or less, depending upon how it is measured, by the 1980s. While it was difficult to count the actual number of firms in their subcontracting networks, since so many of these were small enterprises controlled through a "pyramid" of primary, secondary, and tertiary suppliers, according to a recent estimate Nissan and Toyota each controlled roughly 200 small subsidiaries and primary subcontractors, who in turn employed 5000 secondary subcontractors, and perhaps 30,000 tertiary subcontractors. About 90 percent of the secondary and tertiary subcontractors had less than 500 employees each and most had far fewer, while about 80 percent of the primary subcontractors were larger.[7]

Subcontracting to subsidiaries or other firms reached these high levels in the Japanese automobile industry after demand expanded rapidly beginning around 1955. Managers decided that it was cheaper, safer, and faster to recruit suppliers rather than to hire more employees or invest directly in additional equipment for making components. Subcontracting lowered fixed costs, required less operating capital, and made it possible to cut production levels simply by reducing outside procurement, passing on the risks of over-capacity to subsidiaries and other suppliers. Nissan and Toyota even began, after the late 1960s, to subcontract between 30 and 40 percent of final assembly.[8] This exaggerated the apparent productivity of their workers even further, since final assembly was typically less automated than processes such as transmission or engine manufacturing.

Between the early 1970s and 1980s, only around 60 percent of the vehicles produced under the Toyota logo came from Toyota assembly plants: Toyota Auto Body, Kantō Auto Works, Toyoda Automatic Loom, Hino, and Daihatsu assembled the other 40 percent. Toyota management gave assembly work to Hino and Daihatsu, after investing in these firms during 1967-1968, primarily to utilize their excess capacity.[9] Similarly, only about 70 percent of Nissan vehicles came from its factories during this same period: Nissan Auto Body, Nissan Diesel, Aichi Machine, and Fuji Heavy Industries produced the rest. As in the case of Toyota, Nissan began to subcontract final assembly to Fuji Heavy Industries in 1970 because Subaru sales were sluggish and this firm also had too much factory capacity.[10]

Subcontracting not only made Japanese autoworkers at the top firms appear to be more productive; this strategy lowered costs by reducing labor, capital, and inventory requirements. The savings in personnel costs are particularly obvious, since most suppliers had lower wage scales than Nissan or Toyota; these scales usually declined according to a firm's size, measured by total employment. Monthly income in transport-equipment manufacturers with 100 to 499 workers in 1981 was only 82 percent that of firms with 500 or more employees, and only 67 percent at firms with 30 to 99 employees.[11] Even the largest subsidiaries of Nissan and Toyota paid lower wages than the parent firms; average monthly income in 25 subsidiaries during fiscal 1983 was 79 percent of the wages at Nissan and Toyota. Hino and Daihatsu were from 4 to 9 percent behind Toyota, while workers at Fuji Heavy Industries received merely 73 percent of the monthly wages Nissan paid (Table 47).

Product Mix
Differences in product mix and variation within model lines also affected productivity, since about 93 percent of all Japanese cars made in the early 1980s were subcompacts and compacts with far more limitations on available combinations of equipment or colors than in the United States. During 1983, 52 percent of Ford's U.S. car production and 65 percent of Chrysler's were small vehicles; small-car production was only 25 percent at General Motors. U.S. assembly plants also had to accommodate more than 200 possible combinations of body models and division nameplates, optional equipment in different price categories, and colors (up to 14), while the average Japanese automaker offered merely 36 possible combinations.[12] An American consulting firm even calculated that the 1982 Ford Thunderbird offered 69,120 possible option combinations, the Chevy Citation 38,016, and the Plymouth Horizon 6656, compared to 32 for the Honda Accord, 384 for the Toyota Tercel, and 768 for the Corolla.[13]

Options tend to increase with car size as customers move from budget to luxury models; these variations in final assembly, even more than vehicle size, reduce productivity and raise costs by requiring extra labor, placing manufacturers that produce many large vehicles at a disadvantage. Although options often brought higher profit margins, by 1984, American automakers were reducing options and other product variations to simplify production, as well as designing new model lines better suited to highly automated manufacturing systems and the final assembly of modules rather than individual components—techniques which were more com-

194

Table 47: Average Monthly Wages per Employee (Excluding Bonuses)—Nissan and Toyota Groups, 1983

(yen, number of employees)

Company	Wages	Scale	Employees
Nissan Group			
Nissan	283,457	100	59,335
Fuji Heavy Industries	207,794	73	13,928
Nissan Diesel	183,070	65	6,685
Nissan Auto Body	270,391	95	7,200
Nihon Radiator	231,243	82	4,839
Aichi Machine	249,006	88	4,403
Atsugi Auto Parts	237,261	84	4,314
Kantō Seiki	215,251	76	3,041
Ichikō Industries	268,229	95	3,074
Daikin Works	289,485	102	1,597
Ikeda Bussan	197,557	70	1,572
Fuji Kikō	225,698	80	1,503
Jidōsha Denki	150,972	53	1,545
Kasai Industries	246,485	87	1,128
Fuji Ironworks	166,543	59	1,103
Tochigi-Fuji Industries	236,446	83	770
Tokyo Sokuhan	255,138	90	585
15 Subsidiaries Average	228,185	81	43,359

Table 47 (continued)

Company	Wages	Scale	Employees
Toyota Group			
Toyota	301,247	100	58,706
Daihatsu	274,239	91	10,482
Hino	287,698	96	8,462
Nippon Denso	232,935	77	29,210
Aisin Seiki	217,404	72	7,971
Toyota Auto Body	202,718	67	6,576
Toyoda Automatic Loom	269,423	89	6,400
Kantō Auto Works	271,354	90	5,727
Toyoda Gōsei	251,180	83	4,630
Aichi Steel	289,310	96	3,463
Toyoda Machine Works	195,239	65	3,552
Koito Works	195,495	65	3,259
Aisan Industries	180,807	60	2,591
10 Subsidiaries Average	230,587	77	73,379
Other Automakers			
Mazda	278,742		27,395
Honda	228,483		27,969
Isuzu	198,845		15,199
Suzuki	235,974		11,321

Sources: Kaisha shikihō *and* yūka shōken hōkokusho.

Note: *The employee figures for Nissan and Toyota represent annual averages. Other employee totals indicate fiscal-year-end levels.*

mon in Japan during the early 1980s and which facilitated increases in manufacturing automation. General Motors even founded its new Saturn subsidiary in 1985 specifically to take advantage of the modular concept for product design and manufacturing, after deciding in 1984 to consolidate the body manufacturing and assembly operations of its four car divisions into two groups: one for large cars, and one for small cars.[14]

Worker Output and Compensation

Even though low degrees of vertical integration and product complexity exaggerated the efficiency of Japanese autoworkers, in comparison to their counterparts in the United States and Europe, Nissan and Toyota managed real and dramatic increases in productivity during the 1960s and 1970s. At the time of the Korean War, the Japanese employees averaged 2 vehicles per year, the same level of productivity reached during the 1930s. Output was mainly standard-size trucks, twice the size and weight of small cars, and both firms made a majority of the components in house. As the production of small vehicles increased, and as Nissan and Toyota made more units of each type, nominal productivity rose to about 10 vehicles per worker by 1958-1959—the level of the American automobile industry during the early 1980s (see Table 44 and Appendix F).

But, while the actual number of vehicles American autoworkers produced remained about the same or even declined between the 1960s and the 1980s, productivity continued to improve in Japan. As early as 1965, even adjusting for differences in vertical integration, each Toyota worker was producing 70 percent more vehicles per year than employees at General Motors, Ford, Chrysler, or Nissan, where each worker made the equivalent of between 4 and 5 complete vehicles (Table 48). The performance of Toyota was especially remarkable given that its production volume was only 5 percent that of General Motors. Nissan employees worked fewer hours and were not as efficient as Toyota employees, although Nissan, using largely American techniques, by 1965 had nearly matched the American automakers in vehicle productivity at merely 3 percent of General Motors' level of production.

As production volumes (adjusted for vertical integration) rose 5-fold at Toyota and 6-fold at Nissan between 1965 and the early 1980s, productivity tripled—to the point where, by 1979-1980, Nissan workers were producing about 2.5 times more vehicles per year than their American counterparts, and Toyota workers more than 4 times

Table 48: Vehicle Productivity and Production Scales Adjusted for Vertical Integration, 1965-1983

(A = vehicles per worker; B = change in the scale of production; C = relative scales of production, with GM as 100)

	GM			Ford			Chrysler			Nissan			Toyota		
FY	A	B	C	A	B	C	A	B	C	A	B	C	A	B	C
1965	5.0			4.4			4.5			4.3			8.0		
		1.0	100		1.0	44		1.0	21		1.0	3		1.0	5
1970	3.7			4.3			3.9			8.8			13.4		
		0.7	100		1.2	72		1.2	34		3.7	16		2.8	21
1975	4.4			4.0			4.1			9.0			15.1		
		0.8	100		1.0	55		1.2	30		4.1	16		3.7	25
1979	4.5			4.2			4.3			11.1			18.4		
		1.1	100		1.3	54		0.8	15		5.6	16		4.8	24
1980[a]	4.1			3.7			4.5			12.2			17.8		
		0.8	100		1.0	51		0.6	14		6.1	23		4.8	31
1983[a]	4.8			4.7			5.1			11.0			15.0		
		0.9	100		1.1	53		0.6	13		5.8	20		4.5	26

Sources: Annual reports, yūka shōken hōkokusho, *and Table 46.*

Note: [a]*GM and Ford figures for 1980 and 1983 assume the same levels of vertical integration as in 1979. Productivity for GM and Ford as stated above, therefore, would be exaggerated if, as occurred at Chrysler, vertical integration actually declined between 1979 and 1983 (see Table 46).*

as many vehicles. Production scales at the American automakers between 1965 and 1983 rose only marginally or declined, along with output per worker, whereas a significant drop in productivity at the leading Japanese automakers came only after production declined following the imposition of "voluntary" quotas on Japanese car exports to the United States in 1981. Even in 1983, however, Nissan and Toyota workers were still 2 and 3 times as productive in terms of vehicles produced per year as employees at General Motors, Ford, and Chrysler.

Although there were many reasons for the productivity increases in Japan, two factors, in addition to less vertical integration, contributed to the higher levels of actual worker output. One was greater "capacity utilization" in Japan after 1965; growing demand for Japanese vehicles helped managers operate factories and equipment at rates close to or even above potential output levels calculated for a standard number of working hours. While capacity utilization in the American automobile industry dropped from 96 percent in 1965 to 60 percent in 1982, before rising to 76 percent in 1983, Nissan operated at rates between 82 and 97 percent. Toyota was consistently over 100 percent—using overtime, unscheduled extra shifts, higher-than-standard line speeds, and increases in actual capacity and output before readjusting capacity estimates to achieve these times.[15] In addition, Japanese consistently worked more hours than Americans—approximately 10 percent more per year between 1965 and 1983, including overtime; this allowed managers to hire fewer employees overall, resulting in higher annual output per capita.[16] Part of the difference in hours worked was a result of labor contracts, although absenteeism was also much higher in the United States and this required managers to keep on extra workers.[17]

Capacity utilization, to a large extent, is a measure of management efficiency in manufacturing; adjusting for differences in utilization, along with potential differences in hours worked (in addition to vertical integration), provides a measure not of actual output per worker per year but of hourly productivity unaffected by rates of operation. Assuming that the American automobile industry as well as Toyota operated at Nissan's level of capacity utilization, with roughly the same number of annual employee hours, Toyota workers were still 1.5 times as productive as American autoworkers in 1965 and 2.4 times as productive by 1970; Nissan workers increased their productivity from 10 percent below the American level in 1965 to 90 percent above in 1970. Nissan continued to maintain nearly a 2-fold advantage through 1983, while Toyota workers in 1983 were 2.2 times more productive than American autoworkers, as opposed to 2.7 in 1979 (Table 49).[18]

Compared to 1965, moreover, Nissan increased the physical output of its workers more than 150 percent by the early 1980s. The level of increase at Toyota, which was already highly productive in

Table 49: Vehicle Productivity Adjusted for Vertical Integration, Capacity Utilization, and Labor-Hour Differences, 1965-1983

FY	GM, Ford, Chrysler[a]	Nissan	Toyota
Vehicles per Employee			
1965	4.7	4.3	6.9
1970	4.6	8.8	10.9
1975	5.3	9.0	13.7
1979	5.5	11.1	15.0
1983	5.7[b]	11.0	12.7
Scale of Increase			
1965	100	100	100
1970	98	205	158
1975	113	209	199
1979	117	258	217
1983	121	256	184
Relative Scale (U.S. = 1.0)			
1965	1.0	0.9	1.5
1970	"	1.9	2.4
1975	"	1.7	2.6
1979	"	2.0	2.7
1983	"	1.9	2.2

Source: Derived from Table 48 and Appendix G.

Notes: [a]This column indicates average figures for GM, Ford, and Chrysler, based on worldwide data.

[b]As in Table 48, the 1983 figures for GM and Ford, but not for Chrysler, assumed the vertical integration levels of 1979.

1965, was 117 percent before the import quotas, while productivity in the American automobile industry, according to this measure, rose only 21 percent between 1965 and 1983. Represented graphically, there was a conspicuous stagnation in productivity (adjusted for integration, utilization, and labor-hour differentials) and production volumes (adjusted for vertical integration) at the American automakers after 1965, while huge increases in output at Nissan and Toyota helped them to match and then surpass American productivity levels during the early or mid-1960s, at merely a fraction of American manufacturing volumes (Figure 4 and Table 48).[19]

Compared to physical units, however, there was a much smaller discrepancy in the "value" that American and Japanese autoworkers "added" during the course of manufacturing. Value added measures the difference between the net revenue (sales) of a firm and the cost of procured materials, services, and components. Divided by the average number of employees in a given period, value-added productivity indicates how much, in monetary terms, each worker has contributed to materials and components through processing and assembly. Since these calculations reflect labor costs, a lower percentage of value added accounted for by payrolls and benefits indicates higher productivity in physical terms. On the other hand, restraints on Japanese imports caused car prices, profits, and value added at the American automakers to rise during 1981-1984 more than they would have in an open market.[20]

In 1960, Ford workers (worldwide) were twice as productive in net value added as employees in the Nissan or Toyota groups, although only 17 percent more productive than Toyota workers.[21] By 1980, value-added productivity at Ford had declined by 10 percent while more than doubling in the Nissan and Toyota groups. As a result, these Japanese workers in 1980 were between 23 and 66 percent more productive than Ford employees. Nissan and Toyota workers considered separately from subsidiaries showed even higher output, since the subsidiaries were smaller firms and usually engaged in more labor-intensive processes, including both components manufacturing and final assembly. Productivity at subsidiaries, nonetheless, surpassed gains at both Nissan and Toyota, which was already highly productive in terms of value added per worker during the 1960s (Tables 50 and 51). Only after the institution of retrenchment measures and new design and investment programs in the United States, in addition to the quotas on Japanese imports, did profit margins recover sufficiently for Ford workers to exceed their

Figure 4: Adjusted Vehicle Productivity and Change in Production Scales, 1965-1983 (———— indicates vehicles per worker; ------ indicates change in scale of production)

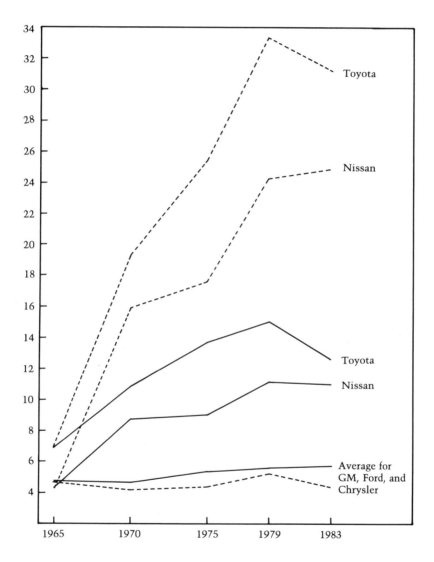

Source: Vehicle productivity derived from Table 49; change in production scales derived from Table 48 (column B).

value-added productivity level of 1960 and cut Nissan's lead in this area during 1983 to 7 percent. Toyota workers in 1983, however, were still twice as productive as Ford workers in terms of value added, while employees throughout the highly integrated Toyota group were nearly 50 percent more productive.

Table 50: Net Value Added per Employee, 1960-1983

FY	Ford	Nissan / N. Group		Toyota / T. Group	
1983 Dollar Values					
1960	31,272[a]	16,712	14,630	26,039	16,194
1965	35,950[a]	14,305	13,148	24,978	17,714
1970	33,308	24,392	22,973	35,937	27,339
1975	35,822	22,316	21,021	35,066	26,395
1980	28,018	37,914	34,420	46,475	38,920
1981	28,741	43,420	38,584	59,665	46,462
1982	30,395	38,469	34,555	58,694	45,124
1983	37,235	39,835	37,088	73,897	54,929
Scale of Increase (Constant Values)					
1960	100	100	100	100	100
1965	115	86	90	96	109
1970	107	146	157	138	169
1975	115	134	144	135	163
1980	90	227	235	178	240
1981	92	260	264	229	287
1982	97	230	236	225	279
1983	119	238	254	284	339

Table 50: (continued)

FY	Ford	Nissan / N. Group		Toyota / T. Group	
Relative Scale (Ford = 100)					
1960	100	53	47	83	52
1965	100	40	37	69	49
1970	100	73	69	108	82
1975	100	62	59	98	74
1980	100	135	123	166	139
1981	100	151	134	208	162
1982	100	127	114	193	148
1983	100	107	100	198	148

Sources: Nihon Seisansei Honbu, Fuka kachi bunseki; yūka shōken hō-kokusho *(Toyota); and annual reports (Ford).*

Notes: Exchange rates are based on purchasing-power parity data for small cars ($1.00 = 260 yen in 1975) found in Irving Kravis et al., World Product and Income, *p. 53. Rates for other years and constant values were found by using the Japanese and U.S. consumer price indices for private transportation (automobiles and related expenses). See Appendix H.*

aThe Ford value-added figures for 1960 and 1965 are estimates based on the assumption, derived from later annual reports, that total labor costs were 15% higher than nominal payrolls. Ford did not report total wages and benefits for these two years.

A more striking statistic derived from value-added data is the difference in labor's share—that part of value added attributable to wages and benefits, rather than operating profits. In 1960, 67 percent of value-added productivity at Ford came from labor, compared to only 33 percent at Nissan and 23 percent at Toyota (Table 52). In other words, in 1983 dollar equivalents, Ford workers in 1960 produced only $10,000 in value beyond their own wages and benefits, compared to over $11,000 at Nissan and $20,000 at Toyota (Table 53). By 1983, labor's share had risen to 85 percent at Nissan, compared to 50 percent at Toyota, and profit margins had dropped to

Table 51: Net Value-Added Productivity (VAP) at Nissan and Toyota Subsidiaries, 1960-1983 (number of firms and employees; 1000 yen in constant 1983 values)

| | Nissan Subsidiaries (N) | | | | Toyota Subsidiaries | | | | |
FY	Firms	Employees	VAP	Scale	Firms	Employees	VAP	Scale	N = 100
1960	2	3,700	1,811	100	6	15,800	2,130	100	118
1965	3	8,800	2,062	114	6	24,200	2,214	104	107
1970	3	15,100	3,994	221	7	42,300	4,057	190	102
1975	4	20,300	4,607	254	7	48,600	4,583	215	99
1980	6	29,300	5,342	295	8	58,900	6,197	291	116
1981	6	31,100	5,258	290	8	62,600	6,158	289	117
1982	6	31,600	4,872	269	8	64,700	5,918	278	121
1983	6	31,500	5,425	300	8	66,600	6,495	305	120

Source: Fuka kachi bunseki.

Notes: Constant values found by using the Japanese consumer price index for private transportation. *See Appendix H.*

The years in which subsidiaries appear in this table follow their first public filing of corporate reports and inclusion in the Fuka kachi bunseki series. For the Nissan group, these were Nissan Auto Body and Nissan Diesel in 1960; add Aichi Machine in 1965, Nihon Radiator in 1975, Atsugi Auto Parts and Kantō Seiki in 1980. For the Toyota group, these were Aichi Steel, Toyota Auto Body, Kantō Auto Works, Toyoda Machine Works, Nippon Denso, and Toyoda Automatic Loom in 1960; add Aisin Seiki in 1970 and Toyoda Gōsei in 1980.

Table 52: Labor's Share of Value Added, 1960-1983 (%)

FY	Ford	Nissan	Toyota
1960	67	33	23
1965	70	42	31
1970	81	50	37
1975	94	65	43
1980	122	69	56
1981	111	69	49
1982	104	75	50
1983	87	85	46

Source: Same as Table 50.

Table 53: Value Added per Employee Minus Labor's Share, 1960-1983 (1983 dollar values)

FY	Ford	Nissan	Toyota
1960	10,320	11,197	20,050
1965	10,785	8,297	17,235
1970	6,329	12,196	22,640
1975	2,149	7,811	19,988
1980	—	11,753	20,449
1981	—	13,460	30,429
1982	—	9,617	29,347
1983	4,841	5,975	39,904

Source: Derived from Tables 50 and 52.

Table 54: Operating Profits, 1965-1983 (%)

FY	Nissan	Toyota	GM	Ford	Chrysler
1965	8.8	13.2	9.4	11.2	8.9
1970	7.4	10.3	2.6	6.8	0.2
1975	4.6	9.7	3.5	1.8	−0.1
1980	4.1	5.6	−2.1	−6.1	−13.1
1981	4.2	7.4	0.6	−3.3	−2.6
1982	3.2	6.2	1.6	−1.3	0.9
1983	1.8	7.4	7.4	4.1	7.6

Sources: Yūka shōken hōkokusho *and annual reports.*

Notes: Operating profits are defined as pre-tax earnings (excluding any extraordinary income or expenses associated with non-operating categories, such as interest payments or receipts) divided by sales.

The percentages for Toyota are based on the sales of Toyota Motor Sales through 1982 and include operating profits from both firms.

less than half the levels of the early 1960s (Table 54). But Nissan employees still produced nearly $6000 each in value beyond wages and benefits, while Toyota workers contributed almost $40,000 each. In contrast, labor's share exceeded 100 percent of value-added productivity at Ford during 1980-1982, reflecting the company's operating losses.

Clearly, wages and benefits rose substantially at Ford—more than 50 percent between 1960 and the early 1980s—despite drops in value-added and vehicle productivity prior to 1983. Even though labor costs at Nissan and Toyota doubled between 1960 and 1983, value-added productivity increased by even larger margins. During 1983, moreover, Nissan and Toyota workers still cost their employers only about $26,000 per year—considerably less than the $32,489 per year that Ford workers worldwide cost their employer in 1983[22] (Table 55).

Fixed Assets
A comparison of fixed assets divided by an estimate of hours worked indicates that Nissan and Toyota matched and then passed General

Motors, Ford, and Chrysler in vehicle productivity at lower levels of investment. In fact, Toyota workers in 1965 produced 1.5 times as many vehicles each per year, adjusted for integration, utilization, and labor-hour differences between Japan and the United States, with merely 80 percent as many fixed assets per labor hour as at the

Table 55: Average Annual Wages and Benefits per Employee, 1960-1983

FY	Ford	Nissan	Toyota
1983 Dollar Values			
1960	21,769[a]	12,592	13,775
1965	26,008[a]	8,691	11,143
1970	26,208	14,743	16,002
1975	31,889	16,276	17,046
1980	35,185	21,697	21,742
1981	33,115	23,414	22,978
1982	31,993	24,242	24,404
1983	32,489	26,073	25,632
Scale of Increase (Constant Values)			
1960	100	100	100
1965	119	69	81
1970	120	117	116
1975	146	129	124
1980	162	172	158
1981	152	186	167
1982	147	193	177
1983	149	207	186

Table 55 (continued)

FY	Ford	Nissan	Toyota
Relative Scale (Ford = 100)			
1960	100	58	63
1965	"	33	43
1970	"	56	61
1975	"	51	53
1980	"	62	62
1981	"	71	69
1982	"	76	76
1983	"	80	79

Sources: Same as Table 50.

Notes: Exchange rates are based on general-consumption purchasing-power parity data ($1.00 = 271 yen in 1975) found in Kravis et al., pp. 178-179. Rates for other years found by using the Japanese and U.S. consumer price indices (see Appendix H).

[a]*The Ford figures for 1960 and 1965 are estimates, based on the same assumption used in Table 50.*

American automakers (Tables 49 and 56). Toyota's products and product mix were simpler than at automakers in the United States, although this was still a remarkable achievement and about to be duplicated at other Japanese producers. Nissan in 1970, for example, showed nearly twice as many vehicles per worker as the American firms, with 10 percent less investment per estimated labor hour.

As output rose 5 or 6 times at the Japanese automakers between 1965 and 1983, Nissan and Toyota expanded investment per worker at equivalent levels (also see Appendix I); this helped boost and then maintain productivity levels, as well as improve manufacturing quality. In contrast, even though American automakers had already lost their productivity advantage by the mid-1960s, investment at General Motors, Ford, and Chrysler increased at far lower levels. One result was that, in 1983, compared to their American counterparts, each worker at Nissan and Toyota had at least twice as many fixed assets—property, plant, and equipment—despite the publication of statistics by MITI that indicated the contrary.[23] Yet the amount of fixed assets required to produce 1 vehicle, based on purchasing-power parity data for capital equipment, was roughly comparable in Japan and the United States by the late 1970s, even adjusting for differences in integration and capacity utilization (Table 57). This suggests, rather clearly, that it was not capital that was at least twice as productive in the Japanese automobile industry, but labor.

The magnitude of these changes at the leading Japanese and American automakers can be seen as well in comparisons of figures from a base year, such as 1965, with 1980 or 1979, before quotas on Japanese imports began (Table 58). Production levels, adjusted for vertical integration, increased 379 percent at Toyota and 510 percent at Nissan. Meanwhile, as sales declined at General Motors, Ford, and Chrysler, vehicles per worker, adjusting for integration, fell as much as 18 percent at General Motors and 16 percent at Ford. Adjusting for capacity utilization and labor-hour differences, there was a 21-percent increase in vehicle productivity in the American automobile industry between 1965 and 1979, but this was far less than the 184-percent rise at Nissan and the 84-percent increase at Toyota (which was far more productive than Nissan in 1965). There was also a 30-percent decrease in capacity utilization in the U.S. automobile industry, and approximately a 10-percent increase at Nissan and Toyota—even though rates of growth dropped at the Japanese automakers after the mid-1960s. While labor costs rose faster in Japan than in the United States, increases in physical and value-added productivity kept pace at Nissan and Toyota, and rises in fixed investment per employee were approximately 4 times as high as in the United States. There was far less relative investment at the U.S. automakers, even though automobile manufacturing, by the early 1980s, had become more capital intensive; not surprisingly, labor costs rose while actual vehicle and value-added productivity declined, along with profits.

The Productivity-Cost Advantage
Differences in scale economies, suppliers, levels of investment, utilization rates, and labor policies also contributed to the productivity differential between the leading Japanese producers. Between 1960 and 1983, the Toyota group had an advantage in value-added productivity over the Nissan group of about 25 percent, while Toyota

210

employees were more than 50 percent as productive in value added and vehicle output, compared to Nissan workers. This translated directly into a cost advantage over Nissan of approximately 275,000 yen or $1200 per unit; the average car that Nissan made in 1983 cost the company 1,228,000 yen ($5500), compared to 952,000 yen ($4300) at Toyota.[24]

Toyota achieved high productivity and low costs with utilization rates that averaged 15 to 20 percent higher than Nissan (see Appendix G and Table 65), a production share about 5 percent higher, and 50 percent more plant and equipment per capita. At equivalent levels of capacity utilization, Toyota's advantage over Nissan in vehicle productivity was still about 30 percent between 1965 and 1983. In addition, Toyota's 8 main subsidiaries averaged 12 percent more in net value added per capita than Nissan's 6 main subsidiaries during

Table 56: Fixed Assets (at Cost) per Estimated Labor Hour, 1965-1983

FY	GM, Ford, Chrysler	Nissan	Toyota
1983 Dollar Values			
1965	16	11	12
1970	20	17	25
1975	19	26	32
1980	25	35	43
1983	28	55	69
Scale of Increase (Constant Dollar Values)			
1965	1.0	1.0	1.0
1970	1.3	1.5	2.1
1975	1.2	2.4	2.7
1980	1.6	3.2	3.6
1983	1.8	5.0	5.8

Table 56 (continued)

FY	GM, Ford, Chrysler	Nissan	Toyota
Relative Scale (U.S. = 1.0)			
1965	1.0	0.7	0.8
1970	"	0.9	1.3
1975	"	1.4	1.7
1980	"	1.4	1.7
1983	"	2.0	2.5

Source: Derived from Appendixes G and I.

Notes: Exchange rates are based on purchasing-power parity data for capital formation ($1.00 = 299 yen in 1975) found in Kravis et al., pp. 178-179. Rates for other years and constant values found by using the Japanese and U.S. price deflators for domestic non-residential fixed investment (see Appendix H).

The same assumptions hold for this table as for the appendixes. In addition, I adjusted Toyota's estimated employee hours upward, assuming that there was more overtime than at Nissan, and that this additional amount roughly equaled the level of capacity utilization at Toyota above 100% in any given year.

1960-1983 (see Table 51). Given the greater discrepancy between the productivity of Toyota and Nissan workers, compared to their subsidiaries, it appears that Toyota more effectively transferred value added from subsidiaries or other suppliers to itself. The benefits of lower costs for materials, components, or services such as final assembly thus accrued to Toyota as it sold cars and trucks at retail prices.

In contrast, by the end of the 1970s, managers at General Motors, Ford, and Chrysler found their companies suffering from low productivity in terms of vehicle units or sales, too much value added coming from payrolls and benefits, and profit margins that were minuscule or nonexistent. The increasing popularity of larger vehicles, combined with lower "break-even" points at the American automakers and quotas on car imports, helped restore earnings dur-

Table 57: Fixed Assets per Vehicle Produced, 1965-1983

Adjusted for Vertical Integration

FY	GM	Ford	Chrysler	Nissan	Toyota[a]
1983 Dollar Values					
1965	7,173	8,618	6,544	6,126	3,799
1970	12,092	9,266	8,454	4,418	4,287
1975	9,392	10,149	7,537	6,405[b]	4,805
1979	7,424	8,543	8,598	6,165	6,322
1983	11,819	11,148	12,094	10,796	10,075
Relative Scale (GM = 100)					
1965	100	120	91	85	53
1970	"	77	69	37	35
1975	"	108	80	68	51
1979	"	115	116	83	85
1983	"	94	102	91	85

Adjusted for Integration and Capacity Utilization

FY	GM, Ford, Chrysler	Nissan	Toyota[a]
1983 Dollar Values			
1965	8,030	6,126	4,397
1970	9,816	4,148	5,280
1975	8,055	6,405[b]	5,270
1979	7,165	6,165	7,705
1983	10,450	10,796	11,853

Table 57: (continued)

FY	GM	Ford	Chrysler	Nissan	Toyota[a]
Relative Scale (U.S. = 100)					
1965		100		76	55
1970		"		42	54
1975		"		80	65
1979		"		86	108
1983		"		103	113

Sources: Annual reports (English versions for Nissan and Toyota); Table 48; Appendix G.

Notes: [a]Figures for Toyota prior to 1983 are adjusted upward by 9% to account for the fixed assets of Toyota Motor Sales; this was the level of Toyota Motor Sales' fixed assets in the 2 years prior to the merger.

[b]Includes an estimate of 50% for accumulated depreciation not listed in Nissan's 1975 report. This estimate is based on data from other years.

See Table 56 for an explanation of purchasing-power parity exchange rates.

ing 1983-1984.[25] Yet the inability of American firms to compete in an open market with the Japanese in small-car production was not a problem with a simple solution: It involved product mixes, company unions, as well as the structure and management of the American manufacturing systems. For example, vertical integration may have made General Motors and Ford more efficient when they competed between themselves or with smaller American or European producers. But this strategy offered no advantage over the Japanese in the 1970s and 1980s, once they perfected production systems characterized by worker productivity that was twice as high as in the United States, lower total labor costs, and higher levels of subcontracting within cohesive groups but to firms with low wage scales—to which the Japanese automakers could transfer many of the manufacturing costs and operating expenses that American (and European) firms had to pay themselves.

Productivity rose at Nissan and Toyota for a combination of reasons. First of all, between the mid-1930s and the early 1960s, they

Table 58: Comparison of Productivity/Management Measures, 1965 and 1980 (% change)

Measure	GM	Ford	Chrysler	Nissan	Toyota
Production (Nominal)	– 2	– 4	–41	+651	+577
Production (Adjusted for VI)	–16	– 4	–44	+510	+379
Vehicles per Worker (Adjusted for VI)	–18	–16	0	+184	+123
Vehicles per Worker (Adjusted for VI, CU, LH)[a]	+21 (average)			+156	+ 84
Value-Added Productivity	–15[b]	–12	–53[b]	+165	+ 86
Costs per Worker	+22[b]	+35	+33[b]	+150	+ 95
Fixed Assets per Employee	+18	+17	+87	+197	+254
Fixed Assets per Estimated Labor Hour	+60 (average)			+220	+260
Fixed Assets per Vehicle (Adjusted for VI)	+42	+43	+86	+ 3	+ 58
Fixed Assets per Vehicle (Adjusted for VI, CU)[a]	–11 (average)			+ 1	+ 75
Capacity Utilization	–30 (average)[c]			+ 9	+ 11

Sources: Tables 48-50, 55-57; Appendixes G-1; and annual reports.

Notes: VI = Vertical Integration, CU = Capacity Utilization, LH = Labor Hours
[a]Indicates comparison between 1965 and 1979.
[b]Excludes the value of employee benefits.
[c]Industry average, rather than the average for GM, Ford, and Chrysler.

214

successfully transferred and modified American and European manufacturing technology—knowledge of production techniques as well as equipment—even though they were still small-scale producers by international standards. Then, after 1965, Nissan and Toyota vastly increased the scale of their operations while shifting from large trucks to small cars. Greater economies of scale offered opportunities to learn more about automobile manufacturing, to lower total costs further, and to improve productivity from levels that, by 1980s American standards, were already high during the mid-1960s. Large profit margins and low employee compensation, as a percentage of value added or in comparison to the leading American automakers, contributed to the ability of Nissan and Toyota to invest at higher levels than their foreign competitors. Decreasing vertical integration within the parent firms in Japan made it possible to expand nominal production 600 percent between 1965 and 1980 while raising per capita fixed investment only about a third as much. Nissan and Toyota were able to concentrate even more on final assembly or subassembly production, and take advantage of rising productivity and far lower wage scales at subsidiaries and other subcontractors.

While benefiting enormously from decades of government protection, to the credit of Japanese managers and public officials, firms such as Nissan and Toyota did not become less efficient producers as a result: They built new factories and improved their manufacturing techniques, and those of their suppliers. By the end of the 1960s, both had eliminated the manufacturing-cost advantage of American and European automobile producers. Increases in productivity corresponded to but did not keep pace with the rise in production volumes, although this was predictable, given the industry's experience with diminishing returns from additional investment. Most significant, however, was the ability of the Japanese to continue raising productivity and reducing manufacturing costs, while improving product designs, product diversity, and quality.

A study of the British automobile industry that became a handbook for company executives in the United States and Europe, published by George Maxcy and Aubrey Silberston in 1959, predicted that manufacturing costs would drop around 40 percent as production increased from 1000 to 5000 units annually, another 15 percent from 50,000 to 100,000 units, 10 percent from 100,000 to 200,000, and only around 5 percent thereafter. This meant that most savings would end after 100,000 units of production per year by a single, integrated company, and that no gains were likely after 1,000,000 units since, they maintained, at these volumes a firm was merely duplicating equipment.[26]

According to this thesis, which assumed (as was largely the case in the American automobile industry during the 1960s and 1970s) that there would be no major changes in product mix or production technology, Nissan and Toyota should have exhausted the major benefits of mass production by the early 1960s. Both passed 50,000 units in 1957, 100,000 in 1959-1960, and 200,000 in 1961-1962, although they took until 1968-1969 to top 1,000,000. Nissan reduced its manufacturing costs per unit by 31 percent as volume rose from 23,000 in 1955 to 130,000 in 1960, and another 6 percent by 1965, when annual production reached 350,000 units (Table 59). These figures correspond, more or less, to the Maxcy and Silberston estimates.

Table 59: Manufacturing Costs per Vehicle at Nissan, 1955-1983

FY	Vehicle Production	Scale of Production	Scale of Unit Costs	Savings (%)
1955	23,000	1	100	—
1960	130,000	6	69	+31
1965	350,000	15	63	+ 6
1970	1,400,000	62	55	+ 8
1975	2,100,000	92	57	− 2
1980	2,650,000	115	62	− 5
1983	2,518,000	109	74	− 12

Source: Yūka shōken hōkokusho.

Note: This is a simple index of total manufacturing costs divided by vehicle production and deflated by the Japanese wholesale price index for industrial commodities (see Appendix H). It does not adjust for non-automotive production costs, and does not include administrative or other non-manufacturing costs.

While managers in the United States and Europe were led to believe that further gains would be 5 percent or less, Nissan cut its costs per unit another 8 percent as production rose to 1,400,000 vehicles by 1970. Only at this point did economies of scale or other factors produce no more savings; Nissan's unit costs rose 2 percent during the next five years, despite another doubling of output. One reason why costs rose was that Nissan introduced 10 new car and truck models between 1971 and 1980, adding to the complexity of its product mix.[27] Part of the early savings was also due to the shift from standard-size trucks to small cars. Yet Nissan still increased sales and productivity to an extent that appeared to be unmatched by any other automaker, except for Toyota.[28] The main reason for this performance is that managers at Nissan, as well as at Toyota and other Japanese automakers, realized even during the 1960s that modifications of traditional manufacturing technology would render obsolete the Maxcy and Silberston thesis. In the words of Nissan's former president, Iwakoshi Tadahiro, it was "innovation" that would "make it difficult to argue conclusively about economies of scale in the automobile industry."[29]

This observation, made in 1968, was equally true in 1983. Nissan and Toyota workers had twice as many fixed assets as their counterparts in General Motors, Ford, and Chrysler, but capital requirements per vehicle were similar, and the Japanese continued to produce twice as many vehicles per worker. Nissan and Toyota made more small cars and had greater control over the complexity of their product lines. It still appears, however, that much of the 2-fold productivity differential stemmed from the techniques Nissan and Toyota developed, prior to 1970, to manage their technological, capital, and labor resources to raise worker output and lower costs far beyond the levels expected or achieved outside of Japan, at both high and low levels of production.

POSTWAR FACTORY MODERNIZATION AND EXPANSION

Differences in productivity between Nissan and Toyota appeared gradually after 1950. Both firms introduced new equipment during the 1950s and built several new plants during the 1960s and 1970s as demand for cars continued to grow. When purchasing machinery, Nissan tended to emphasize high-speed, single-function machine tools, automated equipment, and computers—which should have provided an advantage in productivity over Toyota. They did not, due mainly to the greater dispersion of Nissan's manufacturing facilities, smaller and less efficient suppliers that did not integrate their operations with Nissan as closely as Toyota's suppliers did with Toyota, and less cooperation from the Nissan union in allowing tight cycle times or rapid line speeds, and the liberal use of overtime.

Nissan's manufacturing system as it existed in the early 1980s centered on seven factories in domestic Japan. Five devoted their operations primarily to the final assembly of cars and trucks; two focused on engines, transmissions, steering and axle subassemblies. Nissan located six of the plants in Tokyo or neighboring prefectures. Tochigi and Yoshiwara were approximately 50 miles in opposite directions from the main factory in Yokohama. Oppama, Zama, and Murayama were within 10 to 20 miles of the Yokohama factory, while Kyūshū was more than 500 miles to the southwest (Table 60).

Even though Nissan concentrated its production facilities in the metropolitan area of Tokyo and Yokohama, these were considerably more dispersed than Toyota's factories and suppliers, which were clustered in or close to Toyota City. The layout of Nissan's manufacturing system contributed to lower productivity, compared to Toyota, since it required more workers to transport parts and materials, and more supervisors to manage the various facilities. Nissan also had more difficulty coordinating deliveries of parts and supplies with final assembly due to urban traffic and the distances separating plants and subcontractors.

Facilities Rationalization
Nissan began the postwar period with the most advanced manufacturing equipment in the Japanese automobile industry. While the Yoshiwara plant was a major target during World War II because it made aircraft engines, the Yokohama plant escaped unharmed and Tsurumi, a mile away, had only minor damage. Nissan's dispersal of equipment during 1945 and the burial of machinery from the Yokohama plant, as protection against air raids, actually did more damage to equipment than American bombs.[30] Even with the loss of some machinery, however, Nissan in the late 1940s had twice as many machines per direct worker as the average for machinery industries in Japan as a whole. Equipment in good operating condition during 1946 included precision forging machinery, automatic die-cutters, casting and molding machines, large stamping presses, single-function machine tools for making engines, transmissions, gears, and other key components, and conveyor lines for vehicle and engine assembly.[31]

Table 60: Nissan Factories, 1984

Factory Name	Prefecture	Opened	Employees	Functions (Manufacturing and Assembly)
Yokohama	Kanagawa	1935	6,708	engines, axles, casting, forging, machine tools
Yoshiwara	Shizuoka	1943	5,273	transmissions, steering subassemblies, transaxles
Oppama	Kanagawa	1962	5,948	car assembly
Zama	Kanagawa	1964	5,995	car assembly, machine tools
Murayama[a]	Tokyo	1966	5,647	car assembly, forklifts, axles, machine tools
Tochigi	Tochigi	1971	7,952	car assembly, casting, forging, axles
Kyūshū	Fukuoka	1977	4,533	truck and car assembly, casting, forging, axles
Ogikubo-Mitaka[a]	Tokyo	1966	1,468	rocket engines (Ogikubo), textile machinery (Mitaka)
			43,524	

Sources: "Nissan Jidōsha no gaiyō" (1984) and yūka shōken hōkokusho.

Note: [a]Acquired in the 1966 merger with Prince Motors.

Yet Nissan took seventeen years after the resumption of production operations in the autumn of 1945 to complete a reorganization of company factories that allowed workers to specialize in specific components and vehicle lines. This was necessary because, at the beginning of the Korean War, Nissan had eight small factories compared to one large plant for Toyota, which was far easier to operate. The U.S. Army delayed Nissan's "rationalization" program by requisitioning a significant portion of its facilities and not returning them until 1955-1958.

Nissan's original Yokohama plant consisted of three sites; the first and second were adjacent, while the third was a mile away in Tsurumi ward. The first site handled major production operations for Nissan trucks—forging, body stamping, and final assembly. The second was primarily a casting factory, and the third manufactured steel. In September 1945, GHQ requisitioned 7 percent of the land and 14 percent of the buildings at the first site, 80 percent of the land and buildings at the second, half of those at the third, and all of another facility in the nearby Hamamatsu-chō section of Tokyo.[32] The U.S. Army took these facilities not to penalize Nissan but because they were close to the Yokohama and Tokyo wharfs.[33] But the requisitions presented a substantial burden to the automaker, already short of space and on the verge of bankruptcy.

Toyota had its own financial difficulties during the late 1940s and was behind Nissan in most areas of manufacturing, except for casting, which Toyoda Automatic Loom had perfected prior to World War II. Toyota also relied far more than Nissan did on general-purpose machinery and tools that were less efficient for mass production. Since the Americans took no interest in Toyota's land-locked facilities, however, it was able to upgrade and expand production operations years before Nissan. Furthermore, to make up for less specialized equipment, Toyota managers after the war concentrated on improving manufacturing techniques to lower costs and raise productivity. They succeeded.[34]

Nissan reopened its Osaka plant in October 1945 to make malleable cast-iron parts such as transmission cases, brake drums, valves, cylinder blocks, and cylinder heads. Once Yokohama opened the next month, Nissan used leftover parts to assemble 50 standard-size trucks in November and 150 in December, although, to resume full-scale production, it had to acquire more factory space to manufacture components and materials. Management began by purchasing two small factories in Yokohama during the spring of 1946. Company engineers converted one into a casting and machine processing shop, and the other into a facility to house machinery from the Hamamatsu-chō factory that Nissan used to rebuild vehicles and engines for the U.S. Army. Nissan also rented two steel manufacturing plants from the Naigai Steelworks; these became the automaker's Tokyo Steelworks. In addition, Nissan lent manufacturing equipment to Nihon Shipbuilding (later renamed Nihon Auto Body) and asked it to produce steel cabs until a new body shop was ready in the Yokohama plant during 1950. Shin-Mitsubishi Heavy Industries assisted Nissan as well by making Datsun bodies until 1955.[35]

Of the 12,500 vehicles Nissan's eight factories produced in 1950, 55 percent were standard-size trucks, 34 percent small trucks, 7 percent small cars, and 4 percent buses. This large variety of models, given the company's total output, made it all the more essential for Nissan to reorganize its manufacturing system. The Yokohama plant had 3800 workers, nearly half of all employees in the firm, and assembled Nissan trucks while making parts for this line and for the Datsun. Yoshiwara (1700 workers) assembled Datsun models, manufactured parts for these and the Nissan line, and rebuilt vehicles for the American military. But Nissan's other facilities were small and inefficient: Atsugi (400), a few miles outside of Tokyo and Yokohama, made gears and screws; Tsurumi (370), in the city of Yokohama, produced sheet steel and did repair work; Funehori and Sunawachi (400), in Tokyo, manufactured steel; Osaka (100) did casting; and Kashiwao (90) repaired vehicles for GHQ in Yokohama.[36]

Nissan management would have liked to concentrate all production in the main Yokohama plant, but this was impossible while GHQ held major portions of it. The Nissan union further complicated matters by opposing the relocation of employees because of the severe shortages of housing and food in many areas of Tokyo and Yokohama. Yet the company still managed to construct a new body shop for its truck lines in Yokohama, move parts production for Nissan trucks from Yoshiwara to Yokohama, close the smaller facilities in Totsuka and Kashiwao, and consolidate repair work in Tsurumi before closing this factory in 1951.[37]

Nissan also introduced new equipment during the late 1940s, including Japan's first infra-red drying machine, which was useful to repair foreign cars because it reduced the time required for paint to dry from 3 or 4 hours to only 7 minutes. After discontinuing repair work for GHQ, Nissan placed the equipment in Yoshiwara's new Datsun body shop—an improvement in paint-drying technology that was essential to increase car output. Nissan acquired other machinery at bargain prices from discarded stocks of equipment that the government took from the defunct Japanese army and navy for reparations. Once its financial situation improved, Nissan then began a program in November 1950 to buy or repair 1475 machines over 3 years, at a cost of 362,000,000 yen ($1,000,000). The easing of government restrictions on foreign exchange and imports also made it possible for Nissan to purchase American machine tools for the first time since the 1930s. The Japan Development Bank gave the automaker a loan of 60,000,000 yen ($167,000) exclusively for this purpose, while the United States provided $56,000 through the counterpart aid fund to import manufacturing equipment for military vehicles that Nissan sent to the U.S. Army in Korea: the Nissan Patrol, a copy of the jeep that Nissan later turned into a civilian sports vehicle, and the Nissan Carrier, a truck designed to transport troops and weapons.[38]

Although it kept some land on the third Yokohama site until the end of 1958, the American authorities returned most of the requisitioned land and buildings in June 1955, freeing Nissan to complete additional reorganization and expansion plans between 1955 and 1960.[39] During 1955-1956, the company moved gear manufacturing from Atsugi to Yokohama and Datsun axle production to Yoshiwara from Yokohama, then closed the Osaka plant. Then, in 1957, Yoshiwara replaced Yokohama as the factory responsible for producing transmissions, steering columns, Datsun engines, crankshafts, and cylinder blocks. The following year, Nissan enlarged the Datsun painting and body shops in Yoshiwara while constructing another shop for transmission cases. A new casting factory in the Yokohama plant also opened early in 1960 and enabled Nissan to close the Totsuka facility, which had made truck engines to supplement the output of the main Yokohama plant.[40]

By the end of 1961, Nissan had finally succeeded in centralizing its manufacturing operations around Yoshiwara and the main plant in Yokohama. Half of the Yokohama facility did stamping, welding, painting, and assembly for Nissan trucks; the other half did machining, casting, and parts manufacturing for engines and other major subassemblies. Nissan reorganized Tsurumi, which had made the Austin from 1953 to 1959, to function as part of the Yokohama plant while it assembled the Cedric. Yoshiwara continued to specialize in the Datsun line. Nissan had no more available space, however, so additional expansions of capacity required more factories, beginning with Oppama in 1962 and Zama in 1965. Nissan then acquired Murayama from Prince in 1966, and added Tochigi in 1971 and Kyūshū in 1977.

The New Generation of Manufacturing Plants

Oppama, the first assembly plant Nissan constructed after 1945, marked the company's transition from being a manufacturer of trucks to a mass-producer of small cars. It cost 14 billion yen ($39,000,000), considerably more than Nissan's paid-up capitalization of 11.3 billion yen ($31,000,000) in the fall of 1960, when management decided on the final layout.[41] But Oppama was essential because the introduction of the Datsun 310 in 1959 had brought more orders to Nissan than it could handle. In fact, the operating rate for the Datsun line rose from 94.2 percent of factory capacity in 1959 to 113.6 percent in 1961, a company record that stood through the early 1980s.[42] In addition, Toyota's opening of the Motomachi plant in 1959 made it imperative for Nissan to construct a factory capable of large-scale production to remain competitive in manufacturing costs.

Nissan management decided to build modern shops for body stamping, welding, and painting, and two assembly lines devoted exclusively to small cars, while equipping Oppama with some of the most advanced production machinery in the world, including shell-molding equipment, a 2000-ton forging press, automatic grinding machines, and 34 fully automatic body-stamping presses, 8 of which were portable and easy to switch among different jobs. The American architectural and construction consultants, Giffels and Barry (Giffels Associates), of Southfield, Michigan, who had designed manufacturing facilities for Ford, did the final layout for the plant. A Chicago company, Clearing, designed and built the body-stamping line with equipment so advanced that Nissan had difficulty persuading American officials to approve the sale.[43] The Washington Import-Export Bank's two loans to Nissan, guaranteed by the Industrial Bank, of $3,000,000 in 1959 and $11,000,000 in 1961 to purchase American equipment, paid for over a third of the total cost of the factory and roughly equaled the machinery and tools it required.[44]

But, while Oppama displayed Nissan's ability to match the manufacturing systems of foreign competitors, years elapsed between the time executives recognized the need for a new facility and it actually opened. Once completed, moreover, Oppama was already too small—just when the demand for new cars in Japan was beginning to expand as rapidly as the entire economy. Toyota, on the other hand, had anticipated the growing car market by building a factory to specialize in small cars three years ahead of Nissan. After orders for the Crown exceeded expectations, President Ishida and other executives decided to purchase the Koromo (Motomachi) site of Tōkai Aircraft in July 1958. A year later they had a new plant in operation.

Nissan had difficulty finding a suitable location—at the right price—in the crowded cities of Yokohama and Tokyo. This was the major reason for the delay in building a new factory.[45] Kawamata, while still an executive director in 1956, had recognized the need for a new car plant but preferred to wait for a large site that would provide ample room to expand. He was unable to find this in Yokohama. Then, since automobile sales stagnated in 1958 after growing rapidly for several years, as president, Kawamata shelved plans for a car factory until an opportunity came to buy Fuji Motor's Oppama complex in Yokosuka, another port city nearby Yokohama.[46]

Nissan executives were fortunate to hear from Kawazoe Sōichi, who had been with the company during the 1930s, that the 1,400,000-square-meter site would be available. After a stint with Manchuria Motors and eight years as a prisoner of war in China, Kawazoe had gone to work for Yamamoto Sōji at Fuji Motors in 1953. He was still interested in returning to Nissan, however, and knew that the company was looking for a location. Since the U.S. Army, which gave contracts to Yamamoto's company, was about to phase out its ordnance depot at Oppama, he contacted his old firm and took President Kawamata, Managing Director Iwakoshi, and Director Ishihara on a tour of the site in fall 1958. While this gave Nissan a head start over other prospective buyers, company executives deliberated for months over the investment—even though the price was a "bargain," according to Kawazoe—because they still wanted to explore the possibility of expanding the Yokohama facilities or finding less expensive real estate.[47]

Even after tentatively deciding in October 1958 to buy the tract, Kawamata and other members of the board of directors took until May 1959 to approve the purchase. Another four months went by before they agreed on a bid to submit to the Ministry of Finance, which was managing the sale. This gave Toyota a chance to open Motomachi and allowed 72 other firms to join in the bidding. The

Ministry still granted the sale to Nissan in November, although another four months elapsed before the company decided on a design. Construction began in February 1961 and took a year to complete (Table 61).

Oppama's small size was mainly due to Kawamata's reluctance to risk too much money. Matsuzaki Shirō, who did most of the planning, had managed the production and engineering departments

Table 61: Motomachi and Oppama Chronology, 1956-1962

Year (Month)		
1956		Both Nissan and Toyota recognize the need to build new factories to specialize in small cars.
	(10)	Toyota files an application with the Ministry of Finance to purchase the site owned by Tōkai Aircraft in Koromo.
1958	(7)	The Ministry of Finance grants formal approval for the purchase to Toyota.
	(9)	Toyota begins constructing the Motomachi (Koromo) plant.
	(10)	Nissan makes a preliminary decision to buy the Oppama site.
1959	(5)	Nissan's board of directors confirms the decision to buy the Oppama site.
	(8)	Toyota opens the Motomachi plant.
	(9)	Nissan files an application with the Ministry of Finance to purchase the Oppama site owned by Fuji Motors.
1961	(2)	Nissan begins constructing the Oppama plant.
1962	(3)	Nissan opens the Oppama plant.

Sources: Nissan Jidōsha sanjū nen shi, *pp. 428-429, and* Toyota Jidōsha sanjū nen shi, *pp. 466-470.*

in the Yokohama factory during 1955-1959, before Kawamata made him chief of the staff planning office in 1959 and elevated him to company director in 1961. His team suggested a monthly capacity of 20,000 units to accommodate Datsun sales and to give Nissan a substantial cost advantage over Toyota, but Kawamata wanted 5000 units, the same as Motomachi's original scale. When the Nissan engineers balked at changing their designs, the president brought in Giffels and Barry to "check over" the plant's layout.[48] Matsuzaki's direct superior, Sasaki Sadamichi, who headed Oppama's preparations and construction office and then managed the plant after it opened, agreed that Nissan should build a larger facility but they failed to convince Kawamata. Giffels and Barry suggested a compromise of 7000 units per month, based on the argument that American automakers designed plants with projected operating rates of only 70 percent. Kawamata still wanted a smaller scale, however, and as president he prevailed.

Sasaki went off to the United States during the summer of 1960 to buy machinery based on a monthly capacity of 5000 units; company engineers compensated by operating a second shift as soon as the factory opened formally in March 1962. This doubled Oppama's output but was still insufficient, prompting Nissan to begin constructing the Zama plant in March 1964, which management could have postponed for several years had it built Oppama to the scale company engineers originally wanted.[49]

To be fair to Kawamata, even Nissan's top engineers underestimated the growing demand for cars. Matsuzaki, who went on to head the preparations office for Zama and then manage the plant during 1964-1966, designed it to make small trucks. Yet Zama also operated at capacity as soon as it opened, with two shifts of 2400 workers, and the company had to expand it almost immediately to produce station wagons in 1965.[50] Nissan then acquired the Murayama plant in 1966, which Prince had opened four years earlier with a monthly capacity of 13,000 cars and 20,000 engines. But, since it took several years to integrate Prince's two main car lines, the Skyline and Gloria, with Nissan's competing model, the Cedric, Murayama did not add directly to Datsun capacity. This made it necessary for Nissan to expand Murayama and then begin constructing another factory in Tochigi prefecture during 1968. While Nissan did not complete the new plant until 1971, it managed to open parts of Tochigi in stages: the aluminum casting shop in fall 1968, metal casting and machine processing in 1969, and forging in 1970.[51]

Automation and Robotics

During the 1950s, Nissan engineers hoped to raise productivity and compensate for the dispersal and smallness of their factories by leading the industry in the introduction of conveyors, transfer machinery, and other automated or high-speed equipment. Toyota purchased similar machines but in fewer numbers and used them along with older equipment, while experimenting with manufacturing techniques. While Nissan worked extensively on production management and quality control as well, its programs focused on American production methods that were needed to use the new equipment.

For example, to make crankshafts, rear axle shafts, universal joints, and similar components, Nissan switched, during 1955-1962, from drop-hammer forging to more efficient press-forging technology which required faster standard times and different techniques for machine operation, maintenance, and handling materials. Austin cooperated with Nissan to introduce, in 1956, new casting techniques, which later helped the Japanese company to equip Oppama with fully automated casting machinery to make shell cores and manual manipulators to handle materials. After 1962, Nissan was then able to upgrade the casting shops in Yokohama and Yoshiwara by itself with automated equipment comparable to Oppama's.[52] In addition, production managers had to revise their schedules completely after the belt conveyors Nissan installed in Yokohama during 1958 linked stamping machines and tripled operating speeds, while stamping shops in Oppama and Zama doubled and then tripled Yokohama's earlier output levels with equipment that changed dies in less time and used conveyors to remove scraps automatically. Nissan later developed even faster body-stamping presses with Hitachi Shipbuilding and installed them during the early 1970s.

Nissan started to automate engine manufacturing and assembly in 1956, with the introduction of four transfer machines in Yokohama, and transmission cases in 1958, with two transfer machines in Yoshiwara. Nissan then increased its level of automation by mixing transport equipment and electronic or hydraulic regulating switches with machinery to assemble cylinder heads, blocks, and pistons. Hitachi Seiki and Toshiba built much of the new equipment and designed it to have especially low setup and cycle times. These features allowed workers to make various parts for different engines on the same lines, although mixing production complicated scheduling, prompting Nissan to computerize all phases of production control during the second half of the 1960s.[53]

While Nissan also led the Japanese automobile industry in the application of industrial robots and computers, this was consistent with its emphasis on automation dating back to the 1930s. By the late 1970s, Zama had become a showpiece for domestic and foreign tourists by assembling over 500,000 cars a year with only 6000 workers and several hundred robots automatically performing up to 97 percent of all operations on lines such as body welding. In October 1984, Nissan even replaced 30 human workers with 25 robots on Zama's Sunny assembly line—the first case of using robotics so extensively in the automobile industry.[54]

Nissan began experimenting with fixed-sequence robots in the mid-1960s to automate spot and arc welding and then developed a variable sequence manipulator during 1967 to handle materials. Its first programmable robots, however, were Unimates—numerical control mechanical arms invented in the United States. Nissan bought several from Kawasaki Heavy Industries in the autumn of 1969, only a year after Kawasaki began making robots under license from Unimation. Nissan tried a few in Oppama but had difficulty getting the Unimates to do even simple spot-welding jobs properly, forcing company engineers to spend years adjusting and modifying the machines. Four years later Nissan still had just 34 of the programmable robots. By this time it had begun to experiment with them in Zama, Murayama, and Tochigi, as well as Oppama, although large-scale deployment started only after 1976. By the end of 1983, Nissan had around 1400 programmable robots, including numerical control models developed in house, capable of following a routine outlined on punched tape run through microcomputers (Table 62). Spot-welding jobs occupied 88 percent of the robots in company plants, assembly and materials handling 5 percent, painting 5 percent, and other functions, mainly sealing, another 2 percent.[55] Nissan also used robots to do jobs such as place seats in cars, handle front windshields, and put spare tires in rear trunks. Other robots served as "tire fitters"—fixed machines with mechanical arms that located wheel-hub bolts and placed tires on automatically—which Hitachi made specifically for the automaker.[56]

Even by 1979, Nissan had enough robots in place to worry union leaders about their impact on jobs, especially since the days of steadily increasing sales seemed to be over and there was at last a danger of too much production capacity. Shioji Ichirō, the union chief, continued to raise the issue as management installed more robots than any other automaker in the world and finally persuaded President

Table 62: Number of Playback Robots in Operation at Nissan Plants, 1975-1983

1975	50
1976	85
1977	210
1978	240
1979	405
1980	540
1981	730
1982	1,000
1983	1,400

Source: Nissan Motor, "Data File 1984," p. 30.

Ishihara to sign a memorandum in March 1983, effective for one year and renewable by mutual consent. Management agreed to submit to the union, in advance, any plans to introduce more robots or other new manufacturing technologies that incorporated micro-electronics, and not to go ahead with these plans if the installation of such equipment appeared likely to result in the dismissal or layoff of union members. Nissan also promised to train employees to operate and maintain any new equipment.[57]

This agreement was the first of its kind in Japan, although the other Japanese automakers, who were hastily introducing robots to catch up with Nissan while slowing down their rates of new hiring, refused to issue similar memoranda, for obvious reasons. In spot welding, even a robot made in 1981 performed a typical operation in about 1.5 seconds. While an experienced worker was just as fast, the typical robot in 1985 cost about 10,000,000 yen (or $40,000 at the general exchange rate of 250 yen to $1.00), approximately 1.7 times as much as the average worker. A robot used on 2 shifts thus paid for itself in less than a year.[58] Robots also did not tire and their work was more precise, which aided quality control, although there were still problems with maintenance, such as failures in control equipment and jigs that held work in place. In a 1981 survey, 3 out of 4 units broke down before completing 1500 hours of operation, and nearly 1 in 3 experienced difficulties before 100 hours.[59] Yet the economic advantages of robots were likely to increase throughout the 1980s as Japan's blue-collar workers became more expensive and shorter in supply, and as robots became more reliable and cheaper to buy or lease.

Toyota: A Centralized, Integrated System
Not only did Toyota start its postwar program of factory modernization and expansion ahead of Nissan, but it had several advantages: a single, large manufacturing plant; half a dozen subsidiaries located nearby; and a more cooperative union. These factors helped management to experiment with production techniques that proved to be just as important in raising productivity as Nissan's acquisition of expensive, specialized machine tools, transfer machinery, computers and, eventually, robots.

The year 1950 was a watershed for Toyota in several ways. The longest strike in the company's history ended peacefully. Kamiya Shōtarō established Toyota Motor Sales and this helped coordinate manufacturing volumes and sales more precisely, eliminating overproduction. Kamiya also began laying a base for an effective national sales network. In addition, although tie-up negotiations with Ford broke down after the outbreak of the Korean War in June, visits to American plants gave Toyota executives the confidence to build small cars independently.

After Ford invited Toyota executives to study its American operations, Managing Director Toyoda Eiji led a group that remained in the United States from July to October 1950. A second team, headed by Managing Director Saitō Naoichi, continued from October to January 1951, analyzing Ford facilities, machine tool manufacturers, and parts subcontractors. Toyoda Eiji and Saitō Naoichi compared notes back in Japan and then drew up a 5-year plan to double production capacity to 3000 units per month without increasing personnel. Toyota exceeded this goal after spending 6.1 billion yen ($17,000,000) by March 1956; about a quarter of this sum went to machinery imports, mainly from the United States. While loans from the Japan Development Bank and other institutions funded the program in its early stages, Toyota financed nearly half through equity capital, mostly in the form of amortization, retained earnings, and capitalization increases.[60]

Toyota used the first year of the plan to repair old machinery and replace or modify inefficient equipment for manufacturing standard-size trucks. During the next two years, management focused on increasing car-production capacity by purchasing body-stamping equipment, automatic spot-welding machines, high-speed Keller machinery for making dies, and new conveyors for painting and final assembly lines. In the last two years of the plan, Toyota installed more automated equipment in machine processing and final assembly, including a small transfer machine for drilling holes in engine blocks.[61]

All the Japanese automakers launched modernization programs during the first half of the 1950s, but none matched Toyota in results. This was due mainly to Toyota's successful experiments in production management techniques to accompany the new investment, although foreign tie-ups also preoccupied Nissan, Isuzu, Hino, and Shin-Mitsubishi. Toyota's monthly capacity stood at 5000 units in October 1956, compared to 1750 when the 5-year plan began. Most of the increase was for cars. Although the average number of employees during 1951-1955 stayed at around 5000, new machinery and operating methods lowered the number of casting workers by 30 percent and reduced costs in this shop by 25 percent; in stamping by 20 percent; and in forging by 15 percent. Productivity improved from 2 vehicles per employee in 1950 to 10 in 1956, including the 600 workers at Toyota Motor Sales.[62]

As production expanded during the 1950s, Toyota shifted its priorities from improving capacity and basic manufacturing technology to developing an integrated, mass-production system that was as continuous as possible from forging and casting through final assembly. During the two years that followed the 1954 tie-up with Canadian Nickel Products, which taught Toyota ductile iron-casting techniques, the automaker introduced automated shell-molding equipment, abandoned hammer forging, and installed a modern forging press. Between 1956 and 1960, Toyota added several 2000- and 2500-ton presses, rotary and high-speed tunnel furnaces, and then installed high-frequency induction furnaces during 1960-1961 while switching to cold forging to make bearing caps, piston pins, and ball-joint studs.[63]

Toyota also modified its older universal machine tools and used them along with newer equipment purchased during the 1950s. Adding pneumatic or hydraulic jigs, and attachments such as limit or relay switches and electromagnets to serve as automatic regulators, made it possible, by 1953, for 1 worker to operate from 10 to 17 machines. This allowed the company to raise productivity inexpensively while introducing transfer machinery more gradually than Nissan did. Toyota finally purchased a large number of transfer machines when it opened Motomachi in 1959; as at Nissan, Toyota engineers made each machine independent and installed automatic devices to store work in process so that, if one machine developed a problem, workers did not have to shut them all down. Toyota's main plant also received 3 transfer machines in 1960 to process joint-yoke retainers, rear-axle housings, and various engine parts, although Toyota did not put cylinder-block and crankshaft machining on similar equipment until 1965.

While Toyota subcontracted car bodies prior to 1953, from that year on it introduced new stamping presses and die-making machinery to produce more bodies in house. The company bought 15 hydraulic stamping presses from Japanese and American firms in 1953 alone, and installed spot-welding machines simultaneously. After a year of studying American die manufacturing techniques, Toyota built a new die shop in 1957, using Keller equipment that greatly reduced the time needed for model changes. Toyota installed other stamping machines with the 1957 model change for the Crown and placed high-speed Danley presses in Motomachi during 1959-1960. As simple modifications of the American equipment enabled workers to change the dies for these presses 3 and 4 times as fast as autoworkers in the United States, die setup time in the main plant dropped from 2 or 3 hours during the mid-1950s to only 15 minutes by 1962—by far the fastest time of any automaker in the world.[64] This made it economical to produce different models on one assembly line and saved Toyota from having to invest in additional facilities.[65]

Through improvements in productivity and expansions of existing facilities Toyota met rising orders from 1960 through 1965 with only 2 factories. Both operated at 115 percent of the capacity listed for 1 shift, and Motomachi took on an increasingly large share of Toyota's output as car sales rose. Body, painting, and casting shops containing high-speed machinery, a modern transport system for materials and work in process, television cameras to monitor production lines, and automatic inspection devices, provided a capacity of 5000 units per month, the same as the main Koromo plant, although Toyota engineers designed Motomachi so that they could easily expand it.[66] No less than 6 months after Motomachi opened in August 1959, Toyota started a second phase of construction to enlarge the body shop and to build new body-stamping and machine shops. The company finished these in 8 months then added a second assembly line and a machine tool shop exclusively for the Publica in 1961, other assembly and die-making shops in 1962, a second painting line and a third machine shop in 1963. Toyota also expanded Motomachi's stamping and plating shops during 1964-1965 while installing automatic Delta welding machines in the body shop.[67]

Toyota completed 3 new plants in or adjacent to Toyota City between 1965 and 1968, and 5 more during 1970-1979 (Table 63). By 1984, exactly half of its 10 factories assembled cars and trucks, while the other half concentrated on engines, transmissions, and suspension systems. Kamigo, opened in November 1965, was Toyota's first factory to specialize in engines. Transfer machines allowed continuous processing from casting though assembly, although Kamigo still used some universal machine tools to add flexibility to its machining operations.[68] Takaoka, finished in December 1966, assembled cars at an initial rate of 16,000 units per month with only 1200 employees on each of 2 shifts. This was the earliest Toyota factory to combine automatic welding and painting machines and to contain a control system that utilized an IBM 1440 computer to monitor all processes from parts storage through final assembly.[69] Toyota tested the new automated equipment and computers at Kamigo and Takaoka before installing similar machines in subsequent factories such as Tsutsumi, completed in 1970, the third of Toyota's 3 main facilities for car assembly. While later plants incorporated even more automated systems, computers, and robots, Toyota waited until the 1980s to utilize this type of equipment as extensively as Nissan did.

Toyota managers, led by Ōno Taiichi, the executive in charge of production management during the 1960s and 1970s, were initially skeptical about robots. They heard of the difficulties Nissan had with its first Unimate models; furthermore, Ōno did not believe that the industrial robots of the 1960s and early 1970s fitted into Toyota's manufacturing system. Toyota required machinery and workers to do a variety of jobs with minimal preparation time, and efficiency fell sharply when machines broke down because factories contained few buffer stocks of components to keep assembly lines running while equipment was being repaired. Ōno also felt that production operations at Toyota were sufficiently rationalized and automated by 1970 through transfer machines and other devices,

Table 63: Toyota Factories, 1984

Factory Name	Opened	Employees	Functions (Manufacturing and Assembly)
Honsha (Main)	1938	2,326	truck and bus assembly, prefabricated housing
Motomachi	1959	5,095	car assembly
Kamigō	1965	3,346	engines, transmissions
Takaoka	1966	5,727	car assembly
Miyoshi	1968	2,081	suspension subassemblies
Tsutsumi	1970	5,570	car assembly
Myōchi	1973	1,679	engines, suspension cast parts
Shimoyama	1975	1,679	engines, emission control equipment
Kinuura	1978	1,969	transmissions, drive trains
Tahara	1979	3,429	car and truck assembly
		32,901	

Sources: "Toyota 1984: jidōsha sangyō no gaikyō" and yūka shōken hōkokusho.

Note: All factories are in Aichi prefecture.

and that large numbers of expensive robots with questionable capabilities were unnecessary. Only as these machines improved did he agree to introduce more of them, and then mostly to replace retiring workers or to eliminate dangerous or tedious jobs. After he retired in 1978, however, Toyota increased the number of robots it had in operation from a few hundred to 1300 by the end of 1984, slightly less than at Nissan.[70] But Toyota still required the machines to adapt to Ōno's system and purchased or developed robots of various sizes that were relatively inexpensive and easily programmed to do different jobs.[71]

Why the Initial Investment?
While Nissan and Toyota completed an impressive modernization of their prewar facilities during the 1950s and then opened a whole new generation of assembly plants in the 1960s, in retrospect, their growth was no more or less remarkable than the expansion of the entire Japanese economy after 1955. In fact, they were already 2 of Japan's larger firms by the late 1950s. Both ranked among the top 15 Japanese companies in sales during 1958 and made the top 10 in 1962, even though on an international scale Nissan and Toyota were still medium-size producers, ranking behind General Motors, Ford, Chrysler, International Harvester, Volkswagen, Fiat, Daimler-Benz, the British Motor Corporation, American Motors, Renault, and Citroen.[72]

Prior to the 1970s, Nissan and Toyota focused on domestic sales but grew faster than other Japanese automakers because they had more resources to prepare for the shift in demand from large trucks to small trucks, and then to small cars. Kawamata, Kamiya, Ishida, and other executives still did not believe during the early 1960s that Nissan and Toyota would overtake their foreign competitors so quickly, and they consistently underestimated the need for plant capacity when building Motomachi, Oppama, and later factories such as Zama. It was clear that the Japanese market had room to expand, although no one knew how much this would be or when it would stop. Yet managers invested in new plant and equipment because, first, they expected growth in domestic sales to continue for several years at least, and they hoped to lower costs by increasing production and then by earning foreign exchange through exports.

Comparisons of income and the number of automobiles per capita with other countries provided statistical evidence that automobile sales in Japan were far below their potential, even though Japan was smaller and more crowded than many Western nations, and citizens had relatively good access to mass-transportation facilities. Nissan, for example, published the following table in a 1959 company newsletter, to suggest how sales would rise as personal income increased to the levels of the industrialized Western countries (Table 64). In 1958, Japan had a higher per capita income than Mexico or South Africa, but Mexico had 3 times as many automobiles per person and South Africa 8 times as many. The average income in the United States was 9 times that of Japan; Americans had 50 times as many cars and trucks per person. A later table, cited in the Toyota company

Table 64: National Income and Automobile Ownership, 1958

	Per Capita Income		People Per Automobile	
Country	US$	Scale (Japan = 1)	Number	Scale (Japan = 1)
Japan	226	1	131	1
U.S.A.	1927	9	2.6	50
Switzerland	1187	5	12	11
Sweden	1184	5	7.5	17
Britain	1147	5	8	16
Belgium	1116	5	11	12
Denmark	809	4	7.7	17
France	763	3	9	15
W. Germany	695	3	17	8
Netherlands	618	3	20	7
Italy	381	2	30	4
Mexico	220	1	50	3
South Africa	208	1	16	8

Source: Nissan News *97:6 (May 1960).*

history, pointed out that per capita income tripled in Japan between 1959 and 1964, while the number of people for each automobile dropped from 131 to 45, but that this was still far below the 2.6 individuals per vehicle in the United States.[73]

Even though Nissan management introduced second shifts only in 1959 and did not calculate factory capacity on this basis until several years later, its production lines for the Datsun operated at 95 percent of capacity during 1955-1959 and at 107 percent for the next five years. With extra shifts, plenty of overtime, and rapid increases in factory capacity, Toyota's capacity utilization rate went from 115 percent during 1960-1964 to 150 percent between 1965 and 1969 and stayed well over 100 percent, with two shifts, during the 1970s and early 1980s (Table 65). Even though Nissan and Toyota appear to have understated their actual capacity, these statistics are significant because they influenced investment decisions. According

Table 65: Capacity Utilization at Nissan and Toyota, 1955-1983 (%)

FY Period	Nissan	Toyota
1955-1959	95.1[a]	90.2
1960-1964	107.1[a]	114.8
1965-1969	92.2	149.2
1970-1974	85.7	100.3
1975-1979	92.3	107.3
1980-1983	89.4	106.9

Source: Yūka shōken hōkokusho.

Notes: [a]*These rates exclude the Nissan line of standard-size trucks. Capacity utilization for these vehicles was 63.0% during 1955-1959 and 111.1% during 1960-1964.*

The Toyota rates prior to 1969 are so high because they were calculated on the basis of 1 shift, even though overtime and partial shifts were used extensively. Prior to 1965, Nissan also calculated capacity utilization on the basis of 1 shift. For a discussion of how the Japanese calculated capacity utilization see the first section and the notes in this chapter.

Table 66: Capacity Utilization in Manufacturing Industries, 1959-1963 (%)

Industry	1959	1960	1961	1962	1963	1959-1963
Automobiles	98	114	132	115	156	123
Iron and Steel	99	100	100	91	99	98
Rolling Stock	87	89	115	73	90	91
Radio Equipment	90	92	93	83	95	91
Cotton Textiles	94	97	92	71	79	87
Cement	86	87	88	85	74	83
Plate Glass	92	83	83	63	83	81
Rubber	132	160	188	104	120	141
Petroleum Refining	93	95	73	83	89	86

Source: Iwakoshi, p. 192.

to Nissan's president from 1973 to 1977, Iwakoshi Tadahiro, high operating rates were a major reason why he and other automobile executives bought more plant and equipment than managers in any other manufacturing sector in Japan between 1955 and 1962. His 1968 study noted that the automobile industry as a whole produced at nearly 123 percent of capacity during 1959-1963 and at over 156 percent in 1963, considerably higher than iron and steel, the second leading industry in this category (Table 66). These rates practically guaranteed high returns on invested capital; and, not surprisingly, automobiles ranked far above the average for manufacturing industries between 1954 and 1962 in operating profits and in the rate of growth for assets and sales[74] (Table 67).

But, while investment in the Japanese automobile industry between 1955 and 1963 alone increased more than 13-fold, over twice the level for manufacturing industries in general and exceeding all other major manufacturing sectors, utilization rates indicate that Nissan and Toyota built new facilities not so much in anticipation of future sales as to accommodate demand that already existed (Table 68). The investment policies of Kawamata and other executives were

Table 67: Comparison of Major Manufacturing Industries, 1954 and 1962 (100,000,000 yen, nominal values) Scale: 1954 = 1.0

Industry	Assets			Sales			Profits		
	1954	1962	Scale	1954	1962	Scale	1954	1962	Scale
Automobiles	689	5,009	7.3	327	2,636	8.1	20	277	13.9
Shipbuilding	1,594	8,423	5.3	531	2,402	4.5	16	133	8.3
Electrical Machinery	2,474	16,655	6.7	1,116	6,831	6.1	57	471	8.3
General Machinery	856	4,061	4.7	347	1,631	4.7	7	151	21.6
Iron and Steel	4,451	19,482	4.4	1,752	5,632	3.2	18	100	5.6
Petroleum Refining	844	4,278	5.1	729	2,457	3.4	55	35	0.6
Chemicals	3,256	12,332	3.8	1,680	4,595	2.7	93	216	2.3
Textiles	4,538	9,891	2.2	2,340	4,854	2.1	93	180	1.9
All Manufacturing	22,854	99,628	4.4	11,469	40,972	3.6	501	2,099	4.2

Source: Iwakoshi, p. 187.

Notes: The total number of manufacturing companies considered was 420 in 1954 and 401 in 1962. The number of automobile companies was 12 in both years, including body assemblers and the larger components manufacturers. Petroleum refining was not included under manufacturing in 1954.

Table 68: Major Industries' Equipment Investment Index, 1955-1963
Scale: 1955 = 1.0

Category	1955	1956	1957	1958	1959	1960	1961	1962	1963
Automobiles	1.0	2.4	4.0	3.2	5.4	12.1	10.6	12.7	13.6
All Machinery	1.0	2.1	3.3	2.8	4.3	7.9	10.9	9.6	8.2
Iron and Steel	1.0	3.0	5.2	5.1	7.7	11.1	13.9	11.1	8.9
Petroleum Refining	1.0	2.8	2.2	1.5	2.0	3.8	5.7	4.9	5.6
Chemicals	1.0	2.2	2.6	2.2	2.8	4.4	6.0	5.2	5.8
Paper and Pulp	1.0	2.2	2.7	1.7	3.1	4.3	4.2	3.1	2.7
Synthetic Fibers	1.0	1.4	1.9	2.0	2.7	2.8	4.0	4.6	7.6
All Industries	1.0	1.8	2.2	2.0	2.4	3.4	4.3	4.0	3.9
All Manufacturing	1.0	2.2	2.7	2.2	3.2	5.1	6.8	5.9	5.7
Heavy Manufacturing	1.0	2.3	3.2	2.8	4.1	6.4	8.5	7.3	7.0

Source: Kodaira, p. 292.

actually conservative, because demand forecasts were below sales. Motomachi, Oppama, and other new plants all were relatively small, at first, and not intended to match the scale economies of American factories; Nissan and Toyota saw the European automakers as their chief international competition.[75] Only toward the end of the 1960s did Toyota executives begin to contemplate the possibility of some-day catching General Motors in production volume.[76] Nissan man-agers, meanwhile, carefully studied foreign automakers such as the British Motor Corporation and Volkswagen, and concentrated the rest of their efforts on reducing Toyota's advantage in sales and productivity.

SUBSIDIARIES AND OTHER SUPPLIERS

When automobile demand began to expand rapidly during the mid-1950s, Nissan, Toyota, and the other Japanese automakers faced a choice: make more components themselves, found additional sub-sidiaries, or recruit more suppliers from existing firms, such as from the former aircraft industry. The last option required the least capital and was the fastest way to build up a parts network. By the 1980s, such a large portion of manufacturing expenses had come to depend on subcontracting that the efficiency of subsidiaries and other sup-pliers ultimately determined retail prices, the quality of final prod-ucts, and the competitiveness of Nissan, Toyota, and the other Japanese automakers, at home and abroad.

The Decision Against Vertical Integration

For more than seven decades after the appearance of the Ford Model T in 1908, managers in the American automobile industry believed that vertical integration made them more efficient by reducing de-pendence on other firms for materials and components and by low-ering their vulnerability to opportunistic overcharging.[77] Engineers at Nissan and Toyota studied the American automobile industry during the 1930s and adopted this philosophy as well; actually, they had little choice because only a handful of Japanese companies made machine parts and high-quality steel. During the late 1950s, how-ever, Nissan and Toyota departed from one of the most fundamental strategies of automobile manufacturing: They increased their de-pendence on firms over which they had little or no financial control.

The Japanese saw certain disadvantages to the manufacturing sys-tem that supported the American automobile industry. First of all, vertical integration required huge amounts of capital to buy out firms or to expand in-house capacity. While Japanese automakers were highly profitable during the 1950s and early 1960s, company executives hesitated to invest large sums because they could not be sure to what extent the domestic market would grow, despite the high potential demand. To subcontract more was, essentially, a policy of caution. Less manufacturing in house reduced the need for employees, machinery, warehouses, and operating capital, especially if subcontractors agreed to hold stocks of parts and deliver them frequently, and in small loads, only as the automakers requested.

Managers at Nissan and Toyota also realized that in-house manufacturing offered no benefits if it was possible to purchase components of equal or better quality from other firms for less money. Even though nearly all subcontractors in the Japanese automobile industry during the 1950s and 1960s had only a few hundred or at most a few thousand employees, Nissan and Toyota gambled that, through specialization and lower wage scales, even small firms would be able to produce high quality components at comparable or lower costs than themselves. American automakers cooperated with or helped form specialized firms as well but preferred to absorb profitable operations as corporate divisions or consolidated subsidiaries. At the same time, American managers tried to reduce the procurement costs that remained through competitive bidding—asking a number of companies to submit bids on contracts and giving orders to suppliers offering the lowest prices. This resulted in savings on specific items but did not guarantee stable supplies, high quality, or cooperation beyond existing contracts to solve design or engineering problems that often showed up later.[78]

If suppliers were unreliable or expensive, it made sense to integrate vertically, whatever the fixed costs. Yet increased levels of outside manufacturing led to lower costs and higher productivity in Japan because Nissan and Toyota made this strategy work. They risked time more than money to help their suppliers, and learned how to control firms, sometimes without investing in them directly, by dispatching executives, providing technical assistance and loans of equipment or money, and arranging purchases of all or nearly all a company's output for extended periods of time.[79]

Development of a Components Industry
The absence of an independent machine-parts sector to make automobile components was perhaps the most difficult obstacle for

Japan's automakers to overcome after 1950 because this limited their production levels while keeping manufacturing costs high and the quality of domestic cars low. Compared to domestic competitors, however, Toyota was in the best position to expand production capacity, since it already had a large group of subsidiaries founded in the 1940s. As these firms grew in size and improved their manufacturing operations, they increased Toyota's ability to lead the industry in price cuts and profits. In addition, nearly all these subsidiaries became popular during the late 1950s for investors in the Japanese stock markets, providing capital to the Toyota group that was not available to Nissan since Nissan Diesel and Nissan Auto Body were the only Nissan subsidiaries to sell shares to the public prior to the mid-1960s.[80] Nissan received assistance from the Industrial Bank to locate and invest in suppliers, although most of these companies were much smaller than Toyota's subsidiaries.[81]

The origins of the Japanese auto parts industry date back to the establishment of Japan GM and Japan Ford in the mid-1920s. Prior to this, the few domestic automakers in the country purchased most of the components they did not make from the United States. The American subsidiaries imported parts as well, in the form of knock-down sets, but a small local industry developed to supply components for maintenance and repairs to Japanese dealers. Around 1930, Japan GM and Japan Ford also started to subcontract the manufacturing of simple items to Japanese companies in response to pressures from the Japanese government to decrease their imports. The volume of their purchases expanded after MCI raised the tariff on parts imports in 1931. Since the American subsidiaries needed components that fit their vehicles exactly, the Japanese auto parts industry began using American standards and technology, with many parts copied directly from the originals.

In 1930, approximately 30 Japanese companies did metal stamping, casting, forging, machine processing, plating, and sheet-metal fabrication. All were small or medium-size firms, although suppliers for 2- and 3-wheel vehicle manufacturers, which also expanded production during the 1930s, gave a boost to automobile parts capacity. In addition, during the early and mid-1930s, large enterprises such as Hitachi and Mitsubishi Electric began to make facsimiles of electrical parts for automobiles made in the United States and Europe, and new companies such as Bridgestone Tire, Riken Piston Ring, and Nihon Radiator began to produce other essential items.[82]

The 1936 automobile manufacturing law required parts makers

to apply for licenses along with Japan's 3 authorized vehicle producers, but MCI waited until 1938 to draft legislation specifically to assist these smaller firms. The 1938 law then provided subsidies for 136 suppliers while requiring them to improve the quality and level of standardization or interchangeability of automotive components. Although MCI instituted other controls in 1940 that encouraged companies to specialize, all the suppliers in the industry came under the jurisdiction of a control association for parts manufacturers in 1941. This merged with the automobile industry control association three years later.[83]

The small number of independent manufacturers, combined with the 1936-1938 legislation and wartime controls, encouraged the parts industry to develop around specific automakers. While the capacity of these firms was small by postwar standards, it was adequate to produce trucks for the military during World War II. After 1945, there was little incentive for Nissan, Toyota, Isuzu, or Hino to expand their parts networks, since production in the domestic automobile industry remained below the 1941 peak until 1953. Prior to the mid-1950s, suppliers also followed the lead of original-equipment manufacturers and produced repair or service parts for U.S. Army vehicles and components for the Korean War special orders. This work provided income and helped standardize specifications for the industry, especially since GHQ and the Japanese government promoted industry standards based on components for Chevrolet and Ford trucks.[84]

The requirements of the parts industry changed once production levels for automobiles started to expand after 1953. Each automaker that intended to maintain its share of this growth had to secure a stable and adequate supply of materials and components. Nissan, Toyota, and the other domestic manufacturers increased in-house capacity for essential subassemblies and bodies, but they also doubled their efforts to organize independent suppliers. Okumura Shōji, who had served as the assistant general manager of Nissan's production planning department during the mid-1950s, noted three reasons why Nissan and Toyota recruited subcontractors rather than increase their levels of vertical integration: to avoid the capital expenditures necessary to produce a wider variety of components in large quantities; to reduce risk by maintaining low factory capacity in case sales for the industry slumped; and to take advantage of the wage scales in smaller firms.[85]

MITI also became involved in promoting the parts industry in 1952 by arranging loans from the Japan Development Bank for equipment modernization and expansion. While most of these funds went to the larger firms, for all parts manufacturers, the number of labor hours required for operations such as casting, forging, stamping, and machine processing fell by more than 40 percent between 1956 and 1959. The Japanese steel industry also cut its prices for basic materials to levels lower than in the United States and West Germany by 1959.[86]

Further improvements in productivity for parts manufacturers were limited to some extent by the size of these firms. Even in the early 1960s, more than 70 percent of the 314 manufacturers of automobile components in Japan had less than 500 employees, although 84 companies that had 500 or more workers accounted for 75 percent of parts production by value.[87] Productivity at these larger firms in particular rose throughout the 1950s and 1960s as they received direct assistance from Nissan, Toyota, and other Japanese automakers, in addition to foreign companies such as Robert Bosch and the Bendix group (Table 69). Higher productivity then made it possible for the Japanese automakers to demand price reductions from all their suppliers of around 10 percent a year during the late 1950s and early 1960s.[88]

Rapidly increasing productivity took place as well at the subsidiaries of Nissan and Toyota, where value-added productivity tripled between 1960 and 1983 (see Table 51). Some of the improvement came from greater economies of scale and more experience in manufacturing. But another factor was the assistance Nissan and Toyota provided to install more automated equipment and to institute better methods of product engineering, cost accounting, production management, and quality control. Toyota was particularly successful in improving the operations of its subsidiaries, although the larger size of these companies also helped to explain their productivity advantage over Nissan's subsidiaries. Nissan Diesel and Nissan Auto Body showed more value added per worker during the first half of the 1960s than Toyota's main subsidiaries, but only because they had one-fourth the number of employees in the Toyota companies and their primary business was final assembly. In the period from 1975 to 1983, Toyota's 8 largest subsidiaries averaged almost 20 percent more in value added per employee than Nissan's 6 main subsidiaries.

Table 69: Tie-ups with Foreign Companies in the Japanese Auto-Parts Industry, 1951-1964

Japanese Firm	Date	Foreign Firm	Component
Diesel Kiki	1951	Bendix Aviation (US)	heavy-duty brakes
	1955	Robert Bosch (W. Germany)	fuel-injection pumps
Aizō Industries	1952	Laham Werken (W. Germany)	engines
Nippon Denso	1953	Robert Bosch (W. Germany)	electronic parts
	1955	"	fuel-injection pumps
	1956	"	spark plugs
Nihon Air Brake	1955	Bendix-Westinghouse (US)	pneumatic brakes and clutches, steering subassemblies
Mikuni Shōkō	1955	Wilhelm Barrier (W. Germany)	engine-starter instruments
Tōyō Rubber	1959	General Tire (US)	pneumatic springs
Yazaki Instruments	1959	Kinzle Apparate (W. Germany)	tachometers
Nippon Hatsujo	1959	Henrich Pielsen (W. Germany)	rubber springs
Usui International	1959	Bundy Tubing (US)	Bundy wheel tubes
Fuji Valves	1960	Thompson Ramo Woolridge (US)	engine valves
Sumitomo Electric	1960	Firestone Tire (US)	pneumatic springs
Atsugi Auto Parts	1961	Fichtel and Sachs (W. Germany)	automatic vacuum clutches
	1962	Thornton Products (US)	universal joints

246

Shingawa Industries	1961	Fichtel and Sachs (W. Germany)	automatic vacuum clutches
Nihon Dia-Clevite (NDC)	1961	Clevite (US)	bearings
Koito Works	1962	Internation General Electric (US)	shield-beam headlamps
Tochigi-Fuji Industries	1962	Thornton Axle (US)	theft locks
Nissan	1962	Thornton Products (US)	theft locks
Mitsubishi Electric	1962	S. Smith and Sons (Britain) Allgemeine Electricitats (W. Ger.)	electromagnetic clutches throttles
Sumitomo Electric	1963	Dunlop Rubber (Britain)	disk brakes
Fuji Thompson	1963	Standard-Thompson (US)	thermostats for auto air conditioners, regulators for temperature, pressure, and air flow
Shinkō Electric	1963	Bendix Corp. (US)	electromagnetic clutches and brakes
Tokyo Filters	1963	Glacia Metal (Britain)	oil cleaners
Mitsubishi Electric	1963	Electric Auto-Lite (US)	A.C. dynamos and cell motors
Akebono Brakes	1964	Bendix Aviation (US)	brakes, disk brakes
Kayaba Industries	1964	Bendix Aviation (US)	brake linings
Jidōsha Kiki	1964	Bendix Corp. (US)	universal joints

Source: Iwakoshi, p. 93.

The Toyota Group Strategy

The Toyota group in 1984 included 10 subsidiaries that employed over 73,000 workers, compared to 46,000 in 17 Nissan subsidiaries (Table 70). In addition, Hino and Daihatsu assembled several hundred thousand Toyota vehicles, while Toyoda Spinning and Weaving, which was closely affiliated with Toyoda Automatic Loom, devoted nearly half of its sales to automobile parts.

Kiichirō established all Toyota's main subsidiaries except the Kantō Auto Works and Toyoda Automatic Loom, which predated the automaker. As a general strategy he believed with the Americans that an automaker should have direct access to essential parts and materials to guarantee supplies and quality. Toyota's board of directors formally adopted the policy of self-sufficiency and issued a directive to managers on the subject early in 1940.[89] The method Kiichirō chose to implement this was the same one his father had used to found Toyoda Automatic Loom and which he employed to launch Toyota: Kiichirō began by setting up departments or factories to specialize in particular products or functions such as steel, electrical components, machine tools, or body stamping. Later, he incorporated these factories as nonconsolidated subsidiaries, since this format offered greater possibilities for expansion and fund-raising than maintaining them as in-house departments.

Kiichirō began with steel after various experiments during the early 1930s indicated that he would not be able to produce reliable engines or gears without higher-quality steel materials. His machine tool operators had to change cutting tools after every lot of 12 or 13 gears if they used Japanese materials, while with American or German steel the tools lasted through lots of 30. He set up a steel department in Toyoda Automatic Loom during 1935 to correct these problems after obtaining advice from Honda Kōtarō, a professor at Tōhoku University and Japan's leading expert on ferro-alloys, and L.H. Berry, an American specialist. Berry concluded that the grains in the iron ore available in Japan were too large, prompting Kiichirō to go to China in a futile search for higher-grade ore. But Kiichirō, and other Japanese metallurgists working for him, still learned enough to upgrade the quality of the steel Toyoda Automatic Loom manufactured, to expand the department, and to make it into an independent subsidiary in 1940, the present Aichi Steel.[90]

Kiichirō's second concern was machine tools. When he first prepared Toyoda Automatic Loom to make automobiles, he had refused to buy standardized equipment and asked American and Japanese suppliers to make customized machine tools that could be adjusted to accommodate design changes; these were somewhere in between single-function and universal machine tools. After he had at least one tool of each type that he needed, Kiichirō decided he could save money by manufacturing additional machine tools in house. The machine tool shop he founded in 1937 became especially valuable after Japan stopped importing American machinery in the late 1930s. Kiichirō then built a new factory in Kariya and detached it as the Toyoda Machine Works in 1941.[91]

Nippon Denso, the largest Toyota subsidiary during the early 1980s, with over 29,000 employees, dated back to 1936, when Kiichirō established another shop in Toyoda Automatic Loom to make electrical parts. He later built a factory in Kariya to produce starters, electric motors, distributors, spark plugs, and coils, and then in 1943 added a plant for radiators. These two facilities became the nucleus of Nippon Denso when Kiichirō incorporated it separately in 1949. Through a tie-up during the 1950s with Robert Bosch of West Germany, Nippon Denso expanded into car heaters, engine-regulating equipment, and fuel-injection systems for diesel engines, and then added air conditioners, exhaust-gas and automotive-safety equipment, and various other electronic components during the 1960s.[92]

Other firms in the Toyota group that originated as company departments included Toyota Auto Body, separated in 1945 from Toyota's truck body plant in Kariya, and Aisin Seiki, previously named Tōkai Aircraft, which manufactured airplane engines before switching to automobile transmissions, brakes, and related components after World War II. Toyoda Gōsei began in 1943 when Kiichirō decided to make his own tires and other rubber products; he detached this factory in 1949 and merged it with another local firm. Toyota also separated its cotton-spinning division in 1950, the present Toyoda Spinning and Weaving, although this was actually a reconstruction of the original company Sakichi founded in 1918.

Toyota added other firms to its group after World War II such as the Kantō Auto Works, incorporated in 1946, formerly an independent company in Yokohama that repaired automobiles and made bus bodies and electric vehicles. Toyota became the largest shareholder during 1948 after deciding it wanted a subcontractor in the Tokyo area to manufacture car and van bodies. Toyota invested in local suppliers as well, although the only subsidiaries not founded by Kiichirō with a thousand or more employees in 1984 were the Koito Works (est. 1936), a supplier of automotive light fixtures to

Table 70: Toyota Subsidiaries, 1984

Company (established)	Employees	Prefecture	Shares(%)[a]	Sales Itemization (%)
Toyoda Automatic Loom (1926)	6,400	Aichi	23.0	automobile assembly (25), forklifts (28), engines (20), car air-conditioner parts (19), looms (8)
Aichi Steel (1940)	3,463	"	21.2	rolled steel (77), forged steel (23)
Toyoda Machine Works (1941)	3,552	"	24.9	machine tools (37), auto parts (58)
Toyota Auto Body (1945)	6,576	"	40.4	cars (36), vans (45), trucks (8), auto parts (11)
Aisin Seiki (1949)	7,971	"	21.3	auto parts (93), home appliances (7)

250

Nippon Denso (1949)	29,210	"	21.5	electronic components (27), heating and air-conditioning equipment (39), radiators (7), fuel-injection control equipment (10), injection pumps (4), meters (7)
Toyoda Gōsei (1949)	4,630	"	47.1	rubber (61), plastic components (37)
Kantō Auto Works (1946)	5,727	Kanagawa	49.1	assembly of Corolla (27), Corona (7), Mark II (11), Crown (10), Sprinter (21), Carina (14), others (10)
Koito Works (1936)	3,259	Shizuoka[b]	20.7	lighting fixtures (93), aircraft parts (2)
Aisan Industries (1938)	2,591	Aichi	24.3	carburetors (59), valves (12), throttle housings (8)

Source: Kaisha shikihō (*summer 1984*).

Notes: [a]*Indicates shares held by Toyota.*
[b]*Koito Works' head office is in Tokyo; its factory is in Shizuoka.*

Toyota as well as to Nissan, and Aisan Industries (est. 1938), a manufacturer of carburetors and engine valves.[93]

Toyota not only led the Japanese automakers in founding subsidiaries; it was also the first to organize unaffiliated subcontractors. Toyota began an early suppliers' association in 1939 by arranging for 20 local companies to meet under the name of the Toyota Subcontractors Discussion Group (Toyota Jidōsha Shitauke Kondan Kai), sometimes called the Toyota Cooperative Association (Toyota Kyōryoku Kai). To facilitate materials rationing during the war, Toyota reorganized the group in 1943 as the Kyōhō Kai.[94] After World War II, it expanded the association on a regional format; the 3 main branches had 160 members by 1958. Although some of these firms were not exclusive Toyota suppliers, membership in the association changed little between the 1950s and the early 1980s. Approximately 220 firms participated in 1984, of which 80 percent had plants in Aichi or surrounding prefectures.[95]

Toyota acquired additional assembly capacity and product design capabilities through tie-ups with Hino and Daihatsu beginning in 1966-1967. Hino, which specialized in large trucks, especially diesels, was a suitable partner, since Toyota did not make this type of vehicle, and the Mitsui and Tōkai Banks were shareholders and creditors of both automakers. Cooperation focused initially on small-vehicle development, manufacturing, and sales. Hino began producing a Publica van model in March 1967 after sending a team of engineers and 1200 workers from its main plant in Tokyo to observe Toyota's methods of manufacturing and production management, and helped design a pickup truck that Toyota introduced in April 1967. The tie-up with Daihatsu involved similar cooperation in design and manufacturing and made it unnecessary for Toyota to expand into minicars. Daihatsu also took over assembly of the Publica sedan and joined with Toyota to develop new subcompacts, starting with the 1969 Publica, which used many of the same components as Daihatsu's Consorte Berlina.[96]

The Nissan Group Strategy
In contrast to Toyota, Nissan established control over several suppliers mainly through stock investments and executive dispatches (Table 71). Managers did this not only to save on equipment investment and personnel expenses; they also believed that it would be too difficult and expensive to establish entirely new firms from scratch. In fact, Nissan succeeded in separating only one in-house

factory, a gear plant with 168 employees completed during 1954 in Atsugi, Kanagawa prefecture. This firm, named Atsugi Auto Parts, subsequently diversified into propeller shafts, pressure plates, pistons, clutches, and universal joint assemblies following tie-ups with Fichtel and Sachs (West Germany) in 1961 and Thornton Products (United States) in 1962.[97]

Geography and the GHQ requisitions hindered Nissan's attempt to match Toyota's network of subsidiaries after World War II. Since managers were reluctant to build new facilities to manufacture parts because of the premium on real estate in the vicinity of Tokyo and Yokohama, Nissan had to disperse parts production and assembly among the various plants it either owned or leased, even though it would have been easier to lower costs with specialized factories or subsidiaries.[98] On the other hand, there were probably more companies near Nissan facilities to provide components or help with assembly than anywhere else in Japan.

Nissan Diesel, for instance, which had about 7000 employees during the early 1980s and manufactured large and small trucks, buses, and diesel engines for the Nissan group, originated in 1950 as Minsei Diesel, the former motor vehicle division of an independent truck and ship engine manufacturer, Minsei Industries. Diesel trucks and buses were in greater demand than gasoline models after World War II, but Nissan had no experience with diesel engines. Company executives and officials from the Industrial Bank worried that this would restrict the automaker's truck business, so Nissan began buying diesels from Shin-Mitsubishi Heavy Industries. The Industrial Bank saw an opportunity to help both Nissan and Minsei Industries, and arranged for Nissan to buy engines in 1949. The bank then oversaw the separate incorporation of the motor vehicle division as Minsei Diesel. This continued to provide diesel engines and also began to assemble the Nissan Patrol and Carrier in 1950 after former Nissan Managing Director Gotō Takayoshi, designer of the original "Datson," joined the firm as president. Nissan invested directly in Minsei Diesel during 1953 and established a joint-venture sales company when President Asahara took on the post of Minsei Diesel chairman in 1956. Kawamata succeeded him as president in 1959, and Nissan Executive Director Harashina Kyōichi took over in 1960, at which time the subsidiary changed its name to Nissan Diesel.[99]

Nissan Auto Body, which also had about 7000 employees during the early 1980s, began in 1949 as Shin-Nikkoku Industries, based

Table 71: Nissan Subsidiaries, 1984

Company (established)	Employees	Prefecture	Shares(%)[a]	Sales Itemization (%)
Nissan Diesel (1950)	6,685	Saitama	46.4	large trucks (42), mid-size (10), small (21); engines (12), service parts (15)
Nissan Auto Body (1949)	7,200	Kanagawa	47.9	small cars (62), trucks (32), buses (4)
Atsugi Auto Parts (1956)	4,314	"	40.4	engine parts (35), drive-train parts (30), steering and suspension parts (35)
Nihon Radiator (1938)	4,839	Tokyo	40.8	radiators (24), heaters (25), air conditioners (28)
Kantō Seiki (1956)	3,041	Saitama	43.6	measuring instruments (28), plastic parts (31), wire harnesses (12), electronic parts (13)
Japan Electronic Control Systems (1973)	1,100[b]	Gunma	54.2[b]	electronic engine components
Aichi Machine Industries (1949)	4,403	Aichi	38.7	engines (56), chassis (39)
Japan Automatic Transmission (1970)	1,300[b]	Saitama	65.0[b]	automatic transmissions

Company		Location	Nissan share (%)[a]	Products
Ichikō Industries (1939)	3,074	Tokyo	22.4	headlamps (62), mirrors (27)
Fuji Ironworks (1955)	1,103	Shizuoka	34.0	transmissions (80), axles (11)
Kasai Industries (1948)	1,128	Tokyo	24.5	doors (53), plastic parts (25)
Fuji Kikō (1944)	1,503	"	31.1	miscellaneous auto parts (100)
Jidōsha Denki (1947)	1,545	Kanagawa	20.2	motor parts (63), control equipment (37)
Daikin Works (1950)	1,597	Osaka	33.6	clutches (84)
Ikeda Bussan (1948)	1,572	Kanagawa	48.8	seats (82), interior components (16)
Tochigi-Fuji Industries (1949)	770	Tochigi	21.0	auto parts (28), door locks (28)
Tokyo Sokuhan (1949)	585	Kanagawa	49.0	auto parts (58), measuring instruments (25)

Sources: Kaisha shikihō *(summer 1984) and Nissan's Public Relations Department.*

Notes: [a]*Indicates shares held by Nissan.*
[b]*1983 figures.*

on another firm that had manufactured bus bodies, automobile parts, and engines for use in agriculture. Both Nissan and Toyota subcontracted bus bodies to Shin-Nikkoku; Nissan added gasoline tanks in 1950 and standard-size trucks the following year after it was unable to handle a large order from the Japanese police reserves. Then, in 1951, Nissan management opted to buy out the Industrial Bank's investment in Shin-Nikkoku, which amounted to 87 percent of its outstanding shares. Nissan director and head of the Yokohama plant, Murakami Takatarō, joined Shin-Nikkoku as president and took along the chief of Yokohama's production planning department, Miura Yoshinobu, who subsequently became a director of the new subsidiary. Nissan afterwards asked Shin-Nikkoku to manufacture Datsun sedan bodies and do body assembly, painting, and brake assembly for Datsun trucks and Patrol and Carrier models. Kawamata became chairman in 1956; six years later Shin-Nikkoku changed its name to Nissan Auto Body. In 1964, it began manufacturing the Datsun sports car line, the now-famous "Z" series.[100]

Nihon Radiator, incorporated in 1938, was Japan's top manufacturer of radiators and second largest producer of mufflers during the early 1980s. While it began supplying these components to Nissan during World War II, the automaker did not invest in Nihon Radiator until 1954. Nissan then transferred equipment it owned to manufacture radiators to the new subsidiary and sent the assistant manager of the Yokohama plant, Fukumoto Shūsaku, who became president of Nihon Radiator in 1965, to the company as an executive director. In 1954, Nissan also signed a contract with Nihon Radiator to purchase all of its output; this subsequently became a common practice in the Nissan group. Nihon Radiator later added car heaters and air conditioners to its product lines. With assurances that Nissan would need as many of these components as possible, the subsidiary doubled its capacity every few years for two decades by building factories nearby each of Nissan's new assembly plants, including a truck factory in Tennessee opened during 1983.[101]

Nissan added most of the other firms in its group during the later 1950s and the 1960s. Kantō Seiki, which also established a plant in Tennessee during 1984, was originally a supplier of precision instruments and plastic components that Nissan invested in during 1956 to save it from bankruptcy. Nissan also became the major shareholder in several small companies that manufactured headlights and other light fixtures, transmissions, interior components, clutches, and items such as seats that were difficult to produce in house. In addition, Nissan tried separating the Tokyo Steel Works as an independent subsidiary but Daido Steel, a manufacturer associated with the Industrial Bank, purchased the company in 1957. This worked to Nissan's advantage, however, since Daido Steel had a much larger capacity than the Tokyo Steelworks and agreed to supply specialty steel to Nissan on a long-term basis. The company later became a subsidiary of Nippon Steel; both Nissan and the Industrial Bank maintained their investments and in 1984 ranked as Daido Steel's second and third largest shareholders.[102]

Two other companies added during the early 1970s provided automatic transmissions and electronic components. Japan Automatic Transmissions (Nihon Jidōhensōki) began in 1970 as a joint venture involving Nissan, Toyo Kogyo, and Ford. The two Japanese companies divided a 50-percent interest. Ford owned the other half and provided patent rights to an automatic transmission its engineers had designed with General Motors and Borg-Warner, although, since Toyota had acquired the patent through a 1968 joint venture between Aisin Seiki and Borg-Warner, Aisin-Warner, Nissan was still two years behind in acquiring an automatic transmission. The other firm that Nissan added, Japan Electronic Control Systems (Nippon Denshi Kiki), was a joint venture formed during 1973 with Robert Bosch and Diesel Kiki, a fuel-injection pump maker associated with Isuzu. Nissan had started importing electronic fuel-injection equipment from West Germany in 1971 as part of its strategy to reduce engine pollutants. The new subsidiary manufactured the components in Japan, and subsequently diversified into electronically controlled exhaust-gas systems and similar equipment.[103]

The Industrial Bank, during 1968, also arranged for Nissan to invest in Fuji Heavy Industries. The bank was a major creditor and shareholder of both firms but it was mainly interested in helping Fuji Heavy Industries because sales of Subaru minicars were dropping due to increasing competition from firms like Honda and Suzuki. In addition, MITI was encouraging companies to merge or cooperate, and Toyota was putting pressure on Nissan to expand its group after aligning itself with Hino and Daihatsu. Nissan and Fuji Heavy Industries then established a joint management council in 1969 to coordinate their manufacturing operations, and the latter started assembling Datsun Sunny models at the rate of 100,000 a year beginning in 1970. The two companies also worked together during the 1970s and early 1980s on rocket engine contracts that Nissan received from the Japanese government but, unlike Toyota,

Hino, and Daihatsu, Nissan did not cooperate with Fuji Heavy Industries in marketing or product development.[104]

Following the example Toyota set during the 1930s, Nissan first attempted to organize its primary subcontractors in 1949 by forming the Nissan Kyōryoku Kai (Nissan Cooperative Association). This broke up during the 1953 strike, but the company tried again and, by 1958, had brought together nearly a hundred firms in what came to be known as the Nissan Takara Kai (Nissan Treasure Association). Nissan reorganized this in 1963 by grouping firms into separate branches, according to their specialties, to facilitate the implementation of programs to provide technical assistance to the members. Most of the 109 firms participating during the early 1980s dealt mainly or exclusively with Nissan.

While some Nissan managers viewed the Takara Kai as a mechanism to impose across-the-board price reductions for parts and materials on suppliers, they also used it to help firms improve their operations.[105] For example, Takara Kai meetings during 1959-1960 included instructions on job standardization, factory rationalization, cost accounting, and quality control. During much of the 1960s, they focused on value analysis, a technique originally developed by General Electric's purchasing department in 1947 to study product designs, materials, and manufacturing methods to reduce systematically the costs of procured components. The Takara Kai also held annual conferences and published results of the value-analysis programs.

Nissan engineers were especially interested in having suppliers adopt continuous-processing techniques and reduce manufacturing costs for items not suited to mass production. Quality control experts also urged firms to replace sampling inspection, which consumed time and labor without adding value, with continual checking by shop workers during the manufacturing process. Due to these and other assistance programs, and to increasing manufacturing volumes, procurement costs to Nissan for the 1963 Datsun 410 dropped by 30 percent compared to the previous model, and 70 percent for the 1966 Datsun Sunny, which Nissan used as a test case for a comprehensive value-analysis program that coordinated all aspects of design with in-house and outside manufacturing.[106]

In addition, Nissan found the Takara Kai useful to coordinate procurement with member firms and parts delivery with final assembly. The company first experimented with joint procurement in 1960 by purchasing sheet steel with Nissan Auto Body, and extended this cooperation in subsequent years, particularly during the 1970s, to other items and to other firms. In 1963, Nissan also began to synchronize final assembly with deliveries by Takara Kai members that had the most reliable records for service and quality. While it took until the mid-1970s to coordinate deliveries with a majority of firms in the association, other programs Nissan offered to suppliers continued to bring improvements in productivity and manufacturing quality.

To increase parts supply while reducing procurement costs, Nissan established a staff office in 1967 to provide direct assistance to Takara Kai members on technical questions, management policy, product planning, factory layout, and the use of computers. It then set up computer link-ups with 60 firms during 1967-1969 to computerize parts procurement, production and delivery scheduling, and to facilitate the sharing of technical information. An industrial engineering group Nissan formed in 1971, composed of specialists from its procurement and production management departments, provided extra guidance to suppliers on productivity and production management. Demand for this assistance grew so large that in 1972 Nissan reorganized the 122 employees working in the industrial engineering group into a separate staff department for outside products control.[107]

For independent firms that supplied components such as electrical parts, tires, steel, and piston rings, Nissan set up another organization in 1966, the Shōhō Kai, primarily as a "goodwill" forum.[108] This originally consisted of 31 companies that were not exclusive suppliers of Nissan, such as Hitachi, Mitsubishi Electric, Matsushita Electric Industrial, Asahi Glass, Bridgestone Tire, Daido Steel, Hitachi Metals, and Riken Piston Ring. Fifty-four members belonged to the association in 1983, including several that were also in Toyota's parts organization.

A close relationship with Hitachi was a major reason why Nissan did not acquire a subsidiary to compete directly with Nippon Denso, Japan's largest manufacturer of electrical and electronic automotive components. Hitachi began supplying electrical components and carburetors to Nissan during the 1930s after manufacturing heavy transport equipment such as locomotives and cranes. Once automobile demand reached high levels during the 1960s, Hitachi established a formal automobile-parts division in 1964 and a marketing subsidiary, Hitachi Automobile Appliances Sales, in 1968.

While Hitachi sold components to Isuzu, Hino, Fuji Heavy Industries, Honda, and Daihatsu, as well as to Nissan, it played an especially important role in improving the electrical and electronic technology in the Datsun line during the 1960s. Nissan began using Hitachi electric generators in 1960, air conditioners, radios, and liquified gas equipment for taxis in 1962, automatic chokes in 1963, transistorized spark plugs in 1965, starters and distributors in 1966, and cassette radios in 1968. Nissan also invested in Jidōsha Denki (Automobile Electric Industries, est. 1947), a Hitachi subsidiary that manufactured engine regulator equipment and other electrical components (see Table 71).

Hitachi assisted Nissan in developing pollution control devices adequate to meet government standards in Japan and the United States. After learning in 1963 that Nissan was planning to export large numbers of cars to North America, Hitachi even entered into a tie-up with an American firm to acquire technology and information regarding regulations that the United States government intended to impose on engine pollutants. Nissan and Hitachi then launched a joint research project to reduce carbon monoxide and hydrocarbon levels for Datsun export models, using an air-injection system for cars and a combination of measures to lower fuel consumption for trucks. The new American regulations went into effect in 1965 for domestically manufactured cars and in 1968 for imports. While the Datsun passed in 1966, two years ahead of schedule, Hitachi added air pumps to engine valves on Datsun export models to reduce emissions further, and continued to experiment with pollution and automotive safety equipment during the 1970s and 1980s.[109]

Nissan began an in-house research program for car electronics during the early 1960s, and Hitachi helped Nissan to lead the Japanese automobile industry in the application of this technology. One result of the research and development effort related to integrated circuits they began in 1969 through a joint committee was the application of semiconductors to A.C. motor regulators. Another committee set up in 1971 focused on electronic technology for emissions control and safety devices such as a skid control system Nissan introduced in 1971. Hitachi also contributed software for electronic engine control equipment Nissan began offering in 1979.

During the early 1980s, Hitachi and one of its subsidiaries, Hitachi Chemical, another member of Nissan's Shōhō Kai, cooperated on research related to silicon ceramic materials for engine parts such as pistons and cylinders Nissan hoped to apply in the future. This continued the long tradition of cooperation and mutual procurement between Nissan and the Hitachi group that extended from transfer machines to industrial robots, electric automobiles and forklifts, special batteries, and computers for production control. Even Hitachi Shipbuilding, a prewar Hitachi subsidiary that became independent after 1945, provided Nissan with custom-made body-stamping presses and ships to transport cars and trucks to North America during the 1960s and 1970s.[110]

While Nissan and Toyota both developed extensive supplier networks, each followed a different strategy: Toyota relied mainly on subsidiaries detached from the company during the 1940s based on specialized factories; Nissan required assistance from the Industrial Bank to recruit suppliers on an ad hoc basis during the 1950s and 1960s. Nissan also benefited from a close relationship with Hitachi but, even during the early 1980s, it continued to rely on smaller firms than Toyota did to manufacture components or to provide assembly services. In addition, Toyota's suppliers integrated their production operations and delivery schedules more closely with Toyota than Nissan's suppliers did with Nissan. In both groups, however, the general shortage of automobile-parts manufacturers, while demand expanded rapidly during the late 1950s and 1960s, and the deliberate efforts of managers either to establish subsidiaries or to bring suppliers into formal organizations, encouraged more cooperation between suppliers and original-equipment manufacturers than was common in the United States, and promoted long-term relationships rather than short-term contracts based on competitive bidding. High levels of cooperation and relatively close geographic proximity then became essential to the production management systems which Nissan and Toyota perfected between the late 1940s and the 1970s—with Toyota taking the lead in devising a combination of techniques that changed the way automakers around the world managed their manufacturing operations.

CHAPTER FIVE

PRODUCTION MANAGEMENT: LARGE VARIETY IN SMALL (OR LARGE) VOLUMES

THE TOYOTA REVOLUTION

During the early 1980s, a dozen assembly plants turned out Toyota automobiles at the combined rate of more than 800 per hour. Toyota purchased rolled steel and other materials, made a brief inspection at receiving, and sent them through forging, casting, stamping, or plastic molding processes. Steel destined for forging and casting received heat treatment and machine processing before becoming engines, transmissions, and steering subassemblies, while other materials went directly to stamping shops to become frames and bodies, which then moved through separate assembly and painting shops. Outside suppliers, at appropriate stages, introduced electrical or electronic parts, radiators, rubber products, bearings, batteries, seats, and hundreds of other items (Figure 5).

Toyota managers were responsible for coordinating deliveries of components and subassembly manufacturing with the schedules of final assembly lines, where workers quickly joined engines, transmissions, steering components, and frames with body shells. Inspectors checked the completed vehicles, made adjustments in the engines, carburetors, brakes, or emissions systems as necessary, and sent them on to dealers. To manufacture a small car, from basic components (excluding raw-materials processing) through final assembly, Toyota and its subcontracors took approximately 120 labor hours, compared to between 175 and 200 in the United States for a comparable vehicle.[1]

While productivity varied at different automakers around the world, the manufacturing process of an automobile changed surprisingly

262

Figure 5: Toyota Process Flow Chart, 1984

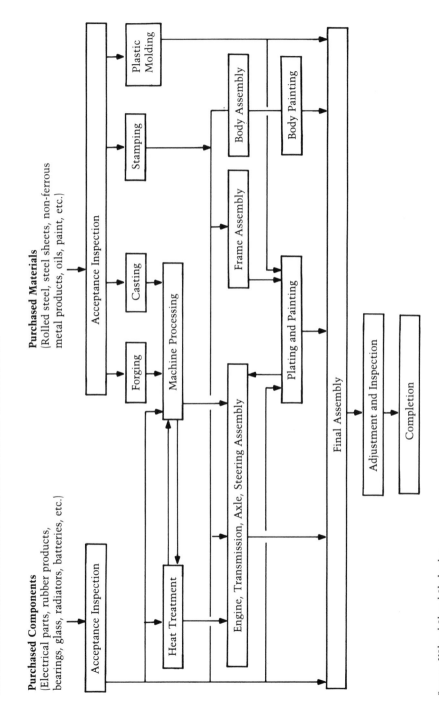

Purchased Components
(Electrical parts, rubber products, bearings, glass, radiators, batteries, etc.)

Purchased Materials
(Rolled steel, steel sheets, non-ferrous metal products, oils, paint, etc.)

Acceptance Inspection

Acceptance Inspection

Plastic Molding

Stamping

Forging

Casting

Machine Processing

Heat Treatment

Frame Assembly

Body Assembly

Body Painting

Engine, Transmission, Axle, Steering Assembly

Plating and Painting

Final Assembly

Adjustment and Inspection

Completion

Source: Yūka shōken hōkokusho.

little between Ford's introduction of the Model T in 1908 and the early 1980s. The Japanese, reacting originally to shortages of space and low production volumes, developed the practice of consolidating various shops under one roof rather than building separate facilities for casting, body stamping, final assembly, or other distinct operations. But all companies—American, European, and Japanese—had process flows and manufacturing shops that looked more or less alike to the casual observer, except for the larger piles of components common in American plants.

A chief concern of manufacturing engineers at automakers since the beginning of the industry was to coordinate or synchronize the deliveries of materials and parts with the production of subassemblies and the requirements of final assembly lines. The process was complicated, not because automobile technology itself was difficult, but because a single vehicle contained thousands of large and small components that required thousands of workers to produce. Coordinating in-house manufacturing with supplies from outside the company was especially difficult when hundreds of subcontractors contributed parts, materials, or assembly services—a problem especially severe for Japanese automakers once they began expanding production and subcontracting levels after the mid-1950s.

Henry Ford and other American managers discovered that it was possible to smooth out the process flow by keeping "buffer" stocks of parts or subassemblies. If equipment broke down or if workers discovered defective components, they were able to take extra parts from stock and the line continued. It was left to production management specialists to determine the most economical balance between retaining buffer stocks, "just in case" something went wrong, and reducing total inventory levels to prevent piles of unused components from consuming any more operating capital than necessary. Manufacturing with buffer stocks of only a few hours or a day required precise control over all phases of production and supply. This reduced inventory carrying costs but involved the risk that, if the system broke down, workers and machines would be kept idle. To prevent this, most automobile manufacturers, even in the early 1980s, preferred to keep enough parts on hand to cover several days, depending on the size, cost, and availability of the component.

Companies based their scheduling on lead times, or how long it took to manufacture or procure each part or subassembly. Computers were a logical aid to these calculations because of the large number of parts in an automobile and the difficulty of coordinating so many manufacturing processes and components. Nearly all automobile producers, including Nissan and Toyota, introduced electronic calculators during the 1950s and computers in the 1960s to estimate materials requirements and to generate schedules for production lines, suppliers' deliveries, and shipments to dealers. Computerization refined the technique of "pushing" materials and components through the various stages leading to final assembly; yet most companies found that work in process and buffer stocks accumulated whenever subsequent stations were unable to handle parts or materials that previous stations forwarded. The line flow also carried assembly mistakes or defectives onto the next process, especially when rapid conveyor speeds and computerized controls made it difficult to stop one line because of its connection to previous and subsequent processes. Defectives continued down the line until workers or inspectors noticed them, if they noticed them at all.

In 1948, Toyota began deviating from the most fundamental manufacturing technique in the American automobile industry: It decided not to "push" materials and components but to have final assembly lines "pull" them through the system. The company made this change gradually, shop by shop, over a period of fifteen years or more. The arrows in Toyota's flow chart did not reflect this because, in a physical sense, everything moved forward. But Toyota turned around the conceptualization and management of the flow by allowing final assembly to control the ordering or, in effect, the reordering, of all parts and materials as workers completed each vehicle. Nothing was pushed forward, because workers moved backwards to previous stations to take only what they needed, "just in time" for their operation. Toyota also decided to attach small paper (sometimes metal) signs, which it called *kanban* in Japanese (both syllables rhyme with the "Khan" in "Genghis Khan"), to pallets or containers of components. The kanban accompanied all parts in transit and also signaled machine operators or suppliers to provide more components. Workers checked for mistakes as they took the parts they needed, eliminating large numbers of inspectors, and corrected defectives in process, eliminating large rework or reject piles.

For the system to work properly it was necessary to produce and receive components in lots as small as possible; Toyota's objective was to have one station provide components to the next quickly, while the subsequent station used them up just as quickly, with no stockpiling. Since small lots were uneconomical without low lead times, and low lead times required machinery that did not take long to set up for different jobs, Toyota had to modify its equipment and job routines. Once it did this, however, small lots made it possible to produce a growing variety of models in small volumes, at less cost than before, due to savings in inventory carrying costs, personnel, and fixed investment. Moreover, Toyota gradually found ways to combine the advantages of small-lot production with economies of scale in manufacturing and procurement. The result was an ability to produce a variety but still limited number of automobiles in large volumes at low cost.

Reversing the process-information flow to create a "pull" system, setting up equipment rapidly, and producing in small lots without buffer inventories, were "revolutionary" techniques. They altered the conventional American assumption that mass production of components in lots as large as possible was the best way to manufacture an automobile because it kept machines and workers operating and avoided frequent resetting of equipment and dies. Yet, to a large degree, the changes Toyota made were "evolutionary" adaptations to the circumstances surrounding the company and to domestic market needs. All Japanese automakers became more efficient because they had to modify American mass-production techniques to produce in smaller numbers. Volume requirements were extremely low in Japan during the 1950s, yet the domestic market called for an increasing number of different car and truck models.

The entire Japanese automobile industry in 1950 produced only 30,000 vehicles—about one and a half days' production in the United States. American methods and equipment, to the extent they were transferable to Japan at all, worked best for standard-size trucks. Since Nissan and Toyota made these in thousands of units, with relatively few variations and model changes, it was possible to produce a large number of components at one time and to store them for future weeks or months. As production scales rose during the 1950s, and as Nissan and Toyota added small- and mid-size trucks and cars, a new problem arose: how to produce more models in small volumes with American equipment designed to manufacture in lots of hundreds of thousands, if not millions. All managers of Japanese automobile factories during the 1950s and 1960s dealt with this problem by reducing setup and lead times to accommodate smaller lots, while shortages of capital and warehousing space prompted companies to reduce inventories by coordinating deliveries, subassembly production, and final assembly as closely as possible.

Toyota not only pioneered many of the manufacturing techniques that characterized the Japanese automobile industry during the 1980s. It also achieved the smallest lots, the lowest inventories, the shortest setup and lead times, and the highest profits. Neither kanban nor the "pull" concept were essential to produce in small lots or to reduce buffer stocks; their function was to facilitate inventory control and to expose slack or waste in the manufacturing process. But since "just-in-time" production—no buffers, and workers taking only what they needed when they needed it—also required intimate cooperation among different shops, factories, and suppliers, the geographic concentration of manufacturing facilities and suppliers helped Toyota implement these manufacturing techniques more quickly and effectively than the other Japanese automakers.

Toyota, in fact, changed the American concept of productivity. Prior to 1948, Toyota workers tried to make as much as possible; if they exceeded the day's schedule, so much the better. Once management instituted the rule of working only for the next process, however, workers had to view overproduction as wasteful because it created unneeded inventory and this consumed operating capital. By the end of the 1970s, it was clear to companies around the world, in a variety of industries, that Toyota had found ways to extract maximum "value added" from its workers. Many firms in Japan and abroad attempted to study Toyota's production techniques, as best as they could from the outside, to improve worker output and lower unit costs. The engineer who devised Toyota's postwar production system, and four younger members of the company's production control department, made the task of other firms easier by publishing outlines of their basic techniques during 1977-1978.[2] Still lacking, however, was an historical explanation: Why, when, and how did the "revolution" occur?

THE TOYOTA PRODUCTION SYSTEM

The individual most responsible for developing Toyota's system of production management after 1945, including the famous kanban, was Ōno Taiichi, an engineer without a college education but with a remarkable ability to analyze manufacturing operations and eliminate unnecessary practices or worker motions. He was born in 1912 in Dairen, Manchuria, the son of a Japanese ceramics technician who worked in the laboratories of the South Manchuria Railway. His father moved the family to Aichi prefecture (central Japan) toward the end of World War I and enrolled his son in a local middle school. Ōno subsequently attended the Nagoya Higher Industrial School, which was not a university in Japan's prewar educational system but resembled a combination technical high school and junior college. He studied mechanical engineering, graduated in 1932, and went to work at Toyoda Spinning and Weaving as a production engineer in cotton thread manufacturing.

Ōno applied to work in a Toyoda company because Kiichirō was an acquaintance of his father; there happened to be an opening in Toyoda Spinning and Weaving.[3] He joined Toyota only because the automaker absorbed Toyoda Spinning and Weaving in 1943 to concentrate more resources on automobile manufacturing. Ōno worked in production management for two years, managed assembly and machine shops from 1945 to 1953, and then accepted a promotion to company director in 1954. He went on to head the Motomachi factory, the main plant in Toyota City, and Kamigo during the 1960s. When he retired from Toyota as an executive vice-president in 1978, Ōno moved back to his original firm, Toyoda Spinning and Weaving, as chairman, although he continued to visit subsidiaries to find ways of making their operations as efficient as he had made Toyota's (Table 72).

While Ōno had no specific interest in manufacturing automobiles, as a student in Nagoya he visited the assembly plant General Motors built nearby in Osaka and remembered being impressed by Ford's concept of "high productivity, high wages." He also found that the basic principles Toyoda Spinning and Weaving used to manufacture thread applied equally well to automobiles: control production costs, reduce defectives, and utilize automation or mechanical devices to raise productivity without eliminating the ability of human workers to adapt to different jobs.[4] "The Toyoda automatic loom," recalled Ōno in his 1978 manual on the Toyota production system, "was a concrete textbook right in front of my eyes." The machine was well known throughout the world for stopping automatically when thread ran out, a feature that prevented operator mistakes and the production of defectives, and which led the Platt Brothers of England to buy the patent rights in 1929.[5] Not coincidentally, eliminating "waste" became Ōno's single most important objective when he took charge of production management at Toyota after World War II.

Small-Lot Production
In retrospect, it was important that Ōno started out in 1943 with no formal experience in automobile manufacturing because he carried with him no prejudices in favor of American methods. He used

Table 72: The Career of Ōno Taiichi

1912	Born in Dairen, Manchuria
1932	Graduated from the Nagoya Higher Industrial School, mechanical engineering course, and entered Toyoda Spinning and Weaving
1943	Entered Toyota when it absorbed Toyoda Spinning and Weaving
1945	Promoted to manager of an assembly shop in the manufacturing department, general assembly section, of the Koromo factory
1947	Promoted to manager of the No. 1 machine shop (engines) in the manufacturing department; postponed this appointment to serve on the executive committee of the Toyota union from February 1947 to March 1948
1948	Returned to the No. 1 machine shop as shop manager
1953	Promoted to general manager of the manufacturing department for engines, transmissions, and vehicle assembly
1954	Promoted to company director
1960	Promoted to general manager of the Motomachi factory
1962	Promoted to manager of the No. 2 assembly department
1963	Promoted to general manager of the main factory
1964	Promoted to managing director
1965	Moved to general manager of the Kamigo factory
1970	Promoted to executive director
1975	Promoted to executive vice-president
1978	Retired from Toyota except as a consultant to the company; moved to Toyoda Spinning and Weaving as chairman

Sources: Toyota Motor Corporation, Public Affairs Department (Tokyo), and yūka shōken hōkokusho.

common sense, and various analytical techniques, to improve the company's manufacturing operations. After working in Toyota for only five years, Ōno became convinced that Ford's original system—producing a limited product line in massive quantities, and making each lot of components as large as possible to gain maximum economies of scale—contained two fundamental flaws. One was that only Ford's final assembly line achieved anything resembling a continuous process flow, the ideal of all factory managers. Henry Ford developed a system to mass-produce one model, with no variations, which he sold in volumes reaching millions per year. His strategy was to attract customers with low prices and to earn a small profit on each vehicle. Ford offered no options or annual model changes because his manufacturing system relied on enormous dies and presses and specialized machine tools, which required a great deal of time, manpower, and money to change.

With this type of equipment, Ford naturally found it most economical to manufacture in lots as large as possible. Ford would stamp, for instance, 500,000 right-door panels in a single run and store them until the final assembly lines called for more right doors, rather than switch dies frequently to make different components as needed. But lots of this size created massive inventories and took up enormous amounts of warehousing space and operating capital, especially when sales fell below production or if equipment broke down and other problems developed to disrupt the process flow. Manufacturing components in such huge volumes also generated many defectives, since workers made mistakes or grew lax in quality control through sheer monotony and the knowledge that there would always be spare parts and reject piles.[6]

The second flaw Ōno observed in the Ford system was its inability to accommodate consumer preferences for product diversity. Demand for different models, equipment, and colors became increasingly important in the American car market during the 1920s and 1930s, and allowed General Motors to replace Ford as the world's largest automaker in 1927 by offering, beginning in 1923, several car lines at stratified prices, with optional features and annual model changes.[7] Yet Ōno did not believe that General Motors abandoned mass-production techniques; in his view, the company merely adjusted to the market by establishing several body shops and allowing a variety of body shells on its final assembly lines. General Motors, like Ford, still tried to make as many standardized, interchangeable components as possible for its different car lines, and to produce components in lots as big as possible and then stock them rather than change equipment frequently. Managers were able to do this because annual model changes were largely cosmetic, involving a mere reshaping of sheet metal for the outer body shells.

Ōno took General Motors' strategy one step further. He extended the idea of small-lot production, which he found in the American company's body-stamping shops and on its final assembly lines, throughout Toyota's entire production system.[8] The "flexibility" of small lots eventually made it easier for Toyota to add more model lines and optional equipment during the 1950s and 1960s, to vary features such as emissions-control equipment or left-hand drive for different export markets, and to adjust production levels in times of slack demand or "oil shocks." Initially, however, Ōno simply wanted to reduce costs by eliminating unnecessary inventories and production.

Eliminating Waste and Idle Time
Toyota's high costs and large operating deficits directly after World War II worried company and bank officials because they saw no improvement unless Toyota found a way to enter the car market. Demand for military trucks no longer existed, and American vehicles were flooding Japan. Management decided on four measures: convert unnecessary stocks of materials and parts into cash and prevent additional inventories from building up; limit the budget to incoming revenues and avoid bank loans as much as possible; place branch factories on separate budgets from the main plant in Koromo; and institute strict cost-accounting procedures throughout the firm. Toyota then detached all non-automotive departments, conducted several staff reorganizations during 1946-1950, and adopted a 5-year plan in 1948 with specific proposals to raise productivity, reduce inventories, and cut operating expenses.[9]

Ōno, then the head of the machine shop that made engines, became a central figure in the 5-year plan after convincing senior executives that he could raise productivity while reducing personnel and manufacturing costs. Top management made his department a "model shop"; Ōno and his staff subsequently set out to analyze each job routine and each machine, and to eliminate "waste" in operations. He took a fresh look at cycle or tact times, the number of minutes and seconds required to make a certain part or to complete a set operation, and reexamined equipment operating rates, defective production rates, unprocessed inventory levels, and inspection techniques. Then he drew up revised operation tables with higher standards and recalculated the amount of labor and inventory necessary to manufacture a given number of vehicles. He coordinated these new estimates with separate studies that Toyota's cost accounting section conducted.[10]

While Ōno felt that Ford's concept of mass production was inappropriate for Toyota, the "time and motion" studies he used to examine workers and machines came from the United States. His first encounter with these techniques occurred during 1937-1938 when a supervisor at Toyoda Spinning and Weaving asked him to study the latest American management methods and to report on those he thought would be useful for manufacturing thread. Ōno read several textbooks and articles that contained a variety of ideas and theories, but nothing practical. He then decided that the best way to improve the Toyoda factory was to put the textbooks aside, go to the shop floor, and study the plant and workers in operation.

Ōno did not have much chance to experiment with production management concepts at Toyoda Spinning and Weaving because the company was already operating smoothly and relied exclusively on Sakichi's automatic loom. Furthermore, textiles was an industry in relative decline during the 1930s and war years, since the Japanese government gave priority to heavy industries related to armaments. But Ōno's reputation as an expert in production management preceded him into Toyota; and, as soon as he joined the automaker, he took charge of revising standard operation sheets to make it easier for unskilled workers, many of them women, to perform more efficiently. While he concentrated on cycle times and process routing, he also became concerned about the accumulation of in-process inventories between production stations. He received a promotion to manager of the machine shop in 1947, but was elected to serve as a union official for a year and did not return to the machine shop until April 1948.[11]

One of the ideas Ōno had was to redistribute worker motions and cycle times to eliminate idle time for a series of workers, and then either remove one or more of them or have the last person on a line take over some of the tasks of his neighbor, and so on down the line. While American engineers invented this technique along with time and motion studies, Ōno applied it with much more rigor. He was determined to eliminate all unnecessary movements and to allow no idle time, for machines or workers. He also decided to revise cycle times according to production requirements. When demand was slow he dropped line speeds, cut out workers, and tightened job routines and cycle times. He made employees work even faster when there were many orders, although he set line speeds high to begin with and always permitted a surplus of equipment, which facilitated productivity increases because workers had a lot of machines to support them. This made it possible to raise output quickly by adding more workers or overtime, without having to introduce additional equipment.[12]

Another of Ōno's "rationalizations," and a key reason for the rise in productivity at Toyota during the 1950s, was his decision to make a distinction between the operating time of a machine and the working time of its operator, and then to have each worker operate more than one machine. Toyota had followed the American system prior to his arrival in the machine shop: Workers at distinct stations specialized in operations such as lathe processing, milling, boring, or welding. Americans even established different unions and job classifications for dozens of specialties, making it difficult for managers to adapt their work force to changing production requirements. It was obvious that, with so many single-function machines and operators, production volumes had to be huge to pay the costs of equipment and personnel. Yet it also seemed to Ōno that, in times of slow demand or low production, specialization resulted in idle time that could be eliminated if machinery and workers did more than one job each. Nor did all machines require constant attention when running, though employees considered themselves to be working while they waited for machines to finish. Ōno concluded that this was another source of waste.

Toyota's firing of 2000 workers in 1950 gave an immediate boost to productivity by reducing personnel. The Korean War orders then placed more demand on Toyota's single factory than it was able to handle and forced Ōno to test his ideas on productivity and costs at rising levels of output. But his problems were just beginning, because most of the war orders did not call for "mass production" of any one item. Unlike the period prior to 1945, during 1950-1951 Toyota suddenly found itself making several different car and truck lines, as well as a variety of metal ordnance components, all in small volumes and with shortages of labor and operating capital. To raise productivity during 1948-1949, Ōno had asked each employee to operate 2 machines rather than 1; he made this possible by placing machine tools in parallel lines or in "L" formations. To accommodate the new orders in 1950, he asked each worker to operate 3 and 4 machines arranged in a horseshoe or rectangular configuration according to the series of processes in the production flow, rather than by the type of machinery.[13]

Ōno and other Toyota managers followed the same principle Sakichi built into his automatic loom—use automation or mechanical devices to make work simpler and to prevent mistakes—and implemented four changes. The first was to remove handles from machine tools and jigs that required workers to hold on continuously and to replace them with pneumatic or hydraulic chucks to keep work in place while freeing the hands of the operators. The second was to add limit switches to turn machines off automatically when they completed an operation. The third was to centralize or automate lubrication so that workers did not have to lubricate each machine constantly. The fourth was to create a section to grind machine tools for operators and to have the machine-tool room deliver tools to workers just as they were finishing an operation, eliminating the need for workers to leave their stations. These and other measures made it possible for one man to operate as many as 17 machines by 1953, although the average for the machine shop during the 1950s was between 5 and 10.[14]

The type of equipment Kiichirō purchased in the 1930s helped Ōno because it was relatively easy to modify. American firms, and Nissan, preferred single-function machine tools and large stamping or forging presses because they offered a cost advantage when manufacturing standardized components at high volumes, and required less skill to produce goods of a predictable standard and quality. But Kiichirō opted for universal machine tools capable of performing several operations on various types or sizes of material because he expected to change designs frequently and manufacture in low volumes.

For example, a worker might use a general-purpose lathe to bore holes in an engine block and then to do other drilling, milling, or threading operations without moving the block to different stations for each process. This was not assembly-line manufacturing but was somewhere in between "batch" and "job shop" production. American automakers, and Nissan, attempted to move beyond this technology by having specialized machines perform each of these operations individually, but specialized machinery, though faster and cheaper at high volumes of production, was expensive at low volumes because the cost of the equipment was high to begin with. It became even more expensive to operate if workers frequently had to change cutting tools or dies for different components because the changeover usually took hours and could shut down an entire factory.

While Toyota bought specialized machinery during the 1950s, Ōno found that it was possible to make older machinery, with different functions and capacities, perform repetitive operations almost automatically by adding feeding devices, limit switches, timers, and other attachments, on the principle of the Toyoda automatic loom. These devices also helped control work-in-process inventories by shutting off machines after they finished a set number of parts. A limit switch allowed Toyota to use a press capable of punching holes in, say, 90 pieces of metal per minute, with a bending machine that processed only 60 units per minute. In an American factory, or at Nissan during the 1950s and 1960s, workers would have operated the first machine for two-thirds of a month and then let it remain idle for the final third, while the second machine used up the stocks of punched components. Toyota, in contrast, eliminated stockpiling by operating the punching press for 2 minutes, resting it for 1, operating it for 2, and so on.[15] Furthermore, during the period when the machine was not operating, Toyota made workers do jobs such as preventive maintenance or helping other employees.

Nissan engineers during the 1950s considered Ōno's changes in the machine shop simply as an attempt to use old or general-purpose machinery more efficiently. They preferred to stay with faster, specialized equipment, and to introduce transfer machinery, which also allowed a few operators to control dozens of machines simultaneously.[16] But Ōno believed that Toyota's production volumes were not high enough until the 1960s to warrant the investment in transfer machinery, especially since simple techniques to reduce idle time for workers and machines brought major rises in productivity and savings in manufacturing costs. In addition, while Toyota bought transfer machinery for Motomachi and newer factories, he found that it was possible to eliminate waste by applying the same type of analysis used in the machine shop to equipment and cycle times in casting, forging, body stamping, subassembly production, and final assembly.[17]

The Just-in-Time Pull System

Along with compressing cycle times to raise line speeds and making workers do more than one job at a time, the other technique Ōno applied successfully was to reverse the process-information flow.

Not only did he ask workers to go back to previous stations to take only the materials or parts they needed, but he established the rule that no one was to make more parts than the next station could handle immediately. It occurred to him that, by reversing the information and conveyance flow and limiting production to small lots, he could identify waste in manufacturing, transport, buffer stocks, equipment operation, worker motions, defectives production, inspection, and finished product inventories.[18] Yet the pull system had two consequences, in addition to exposing slack in the system. First, it made mass production in large lots inconvenient, because stations were able to handle only so much work at one time without building up work-in-process inventories. Second, it made long lead or setup times for equipment stand out as an obstacle to manufacturing in small lots, which Ōno believed were the key to tightening the process flow. Therefore, he wanted everything—conveyance and in-house production—to operate on a "just-in-time" basis, and he used the English term to emphasize this.[19]

"Just-in-time" referred to an idealized, continuous process flow where each station made one component and passed it on to the next station, only as needed. In theory, this cut work-in-process inventory to the bare minimum—one unit. In practice, Ōno made Toyota workers produce not single components but small lots, with the product mix at final assembly determining the size of each lot. The inherent limitations of this technique were that, to be economical, it required reliable machinery with rapid setup times and workers willing and able to do a variety of jobs. Furthermore, if production on a certain line fell behind schedule, rather than allow buffer stocks, he scheduled all lines downward until workers corrected the problem. This placed Toyota's production and supply system in such precise coordination that the tardiness of one supplier or the breakdown of one machine disrupted an entire plant. For this reason, Ōno made machine operators go through preventive maintenance procedures and perform different machining operations as necessary rather than in large lots that would stay around as inventory until later processes required them.[20]

Ōno credited Kiichirō with first promoting the idea of "just-in-time" production and parts delivery. When Kiichirō founded Toyota in 1937 he set up a preparations office to coordinate production planning so that the machine shop received materials only for one day's needs at a time. The assembly shop then completed only the number of vehicles that corresponded to the machine shop's output.

Once military orders increased, Kiichirō decided there was no reason to restrict production when output levels were low and the company was trying to produce as many trucks as possible. After completing a new assembly plant in Kariya during 1940, he changed the production control system by assigning numbers to lots of parts for vehicles scheduled to be finished by a certain date, which made it possible to keep track of a lot's progress throughout the process flow.

Although Toyota continued to use the lot numbers until Ōno introduced kanban during the 1950s and early 1960s, Kiichirō was never satisfied with this system because work-in-process inventories and buffer stocks always piled up at the beginning and the end of production lines or series of stations. After 1940, workers produced in lots as large as possible; but, even though bottlenecks and stockpiling occurred whenever downstream stations were not ready to receive components, Kiichirō still believed the company had to produce as much as possible, so he kept stocks of 1 to 2 months' supply for most components, the same level as Nissan and American firms.[21] After joining Toyota in 1943, Ōno observed these bottlenecks and inventories time after time and realized that they were caused by the lack of coordination among parts and subassembly production, deliveries from suppliers, and final assembly. He took five years to come up with a solution: Reverse the process-information and conveyance flow. Then previous stations would no longer have to wait for subsequent stations. Not only did this eliminate stockpiles down the line; if workers had to wait for parts, they knew immediately where the delay was—the previous station.

The reversal technique was not easy to implement in a manufacturing system that involved thousands of workers and components. Nor was it new. Some factories in the United States had already tried systems in which workers reordered parts when stocks reached a certain low level; to some extent, subsequent processes "pulled" components from previous stations, although conveyance was typically in a forward direction. In addition, American producers of military aircraft during World War II tried a pull system after they had to raise output levels drastically in a short period of time and found it difficult to manage the conveyance of components. Their idea was simply to copy the principle of the supermarket, whose customers do not keep large stocks of food at home but go to the local store to select items only when they need them. The supermarket, in turn, carefully controls its inventory and replaces items only as it sells them. In a factory, it was possible to view the "next" process or station as the customer and the "previous" process as the supermarket; with subcontractors, the factory was the customer and suppliers were the supermarket.[22]

Ōno read about the "supermarket method" and the American aircraft industry in a Japanese newspaper after the end of World War II and thought it possible to apply that technique throughout Toyota's entire production system, including deliveries from suppliers. Not until 1948 did he have a chance to try it, and then just in the machine shop.[23] In-process stocks, as opposed to inventories of finished vehicles, were not a major problem in Toyota until the mid-1950s since it was possible to manage parts supplies of a month or more because production levels were low. While Ōno worried about what would happen when volumes increased, during 1948-1949 he was most concerned with shortages of materials and the unpredictability of deliveries from suppliers.

Toyota's factory often sat idle for the first half of a month waiting for critical components. Then, once the components arrived, workers would have to meet an entire month's production schedule in two weeks. A few years of this convinced Ōno and other managers of the need to coordinate deliveries with assembly and to establish a more constant manufacturing pace, spreading out production evenly throughout the month. As an expert in calculating cycle times, Ōno knew how long his shop took to make an engine, but he needed the cooperation of other managers and subcontractors to implement a "just-in-time" schedule and to introduce this and other concepts that made it work throughout the company.[24]

While Ōno did not reorganize Toyota's system of production management by himself, the extension of his techniques corresponded to his movements, between 1948 and the mid-1960s, from one shop or factory to another and up the ladder into top management. In 1950, Toyota divided its single factory into two manufacturing departments: one for the machine processing of engines and transmissions, as well as for assembling vehicles; and another for casting and forging components. A production control office in the final assembly shop supervised the feeding of parts and materials into the lines and the scheduling of the various production processes.[25] Ōno, while still head of the machine shop, had reversed the conveyance flow and coordinated machine processing with engine subassembly and final assembly in one of the manufacturing departments by the end of 1950.[26] Other Toyota managers then coordinated the body manufacturing and assembly shops by 1955, following the principle of a pull system.

Toyota also worked at adapting suppliers to the idea of the supermarket or "just-in-time" production during 1954-1955. Prior to 1954, Toyota's procurement department had ordered components in volumes of one to two months' supply. Vendors delivered to Toyota's inspection department, which checked the goods, stored a portion, and sent the rest to the factory. The procurement system implemented during 1954-1955 required suppliers to deliver daily. While the procurement department still ordered components and materials in one-month lots, it now drew up precise schedules of daily requirements, with the cooperation of factory departments, and insisted that suppliers deliver only when requested and directly to the factory. This eliminated intermediate inspection and warehousing, released Toyota workers from having to transport stock from the warehouse to the factory, and insured that components stored at the factory remained at the level of one day's needs or less.[27]

Toyota thus had four of its most important production techniques already in place by 1955, not including the kanban, which it started to use in 1953 but only on a limited basis. First, workers in machine processing, body manufacturing, and assembly went back to previous stations and took only those parts or materials they needed and could process immediately. Second, workers produced only what the next station required. Third, Toyota reduced the number of automatic conveyors in its factories and required workers to carry parts from one station to the next in small conveyance lots. This last change added more flexibility to the intra-factory transport system; shutting one conveyor down affected too many workers unnecessarily, and conveyors in general held work in process that Ōno preferred to have on machines or in the hands of employees. But, rather than abandon conveyors completely, Toyota limited them to early processing operations in casting and forging until deciding to use them with Motomachi's transfer machines in 1959. Fourth, for convenience, Toyota limited conveyance lots within the factory to components for 5 vehicles at a time. Forklifts, trailers, and carts then replaced small trucks that Toyota had used inside the building to transfer piles of components.[28]

The machine shop began reducing in-process and buffer inventories after Ōno reversed the process-information and conveyance flow in 1948. As other shops followed suit, Toyota eliminated all stockpiling of components next to production lines by 1958. This increased the amount of available space on shop floors and made the factory safer by removing hazardous stockpiling. If parts ran out or exceeded the 5-unit limit, or if other problems developed, management asked workers to stop the lines. Ōno first gave this authority to employees in the engine assembly shop during 1950 and then to workers on the final assembly line in 1955. Toyota refined the "line-stop" technique in 1957 by installing lights—yellow to request assistance from a supervisor, red to stop the line, and green to indicate all was well—that workers had access to through buttons near their stations. Toyota placed these lights (which it called the *andon* system) in Motomachi and all subsequent factories.[29]

While Toyota still used small conveyance lots during the early 1980s, the original 5-vehicle limit never applied to production. Lot size in shops such as stamping and forging depended on the requirements of final assembly and the capability of equipment to change dies quickly. For major orders containing components that factories used continuously, Toyota took advantage of mass-production principles and manufactured in relatively large lots. Stamping and forging presses often made components in runs as big as 10,000 units at a time, after sales expanded into the millions during the late 1960s; workers then advanced these components to subsequent processes in small batches. During the 1950s and 1960s, Toyota also encouraged subsidiaries and other primary subcontractors to manufacture in small lots. Even small firms were able to comply without extensive new investment, because this type of production required only minor adjustments in equipment to be economical, although Toyota left it to primary suppliers to teach the new system to secondary and tertiary subcontractors.[30]

As a logical extension of the pull system or the principle of "the next process takes," and as a result of the 1950 agreement with its bankers, Toyota allowed Toyota Motor Sales (and its sales division after the 1982 merger) to take the lead in production planning.[31] Toyota Motor Sales not only received orders from dealers but, during the mid-1950s, it began providing critical data for long-term production planning by conducting surveys of several tens of thousands of people twice a year to estimate demand for Toyota cars and trucks. It supplemented these with five or six smaller surveys. Toyota drew up annual production plans after analyzing the forecasts with Toyota Motor Sales, and then set its monthly production schedules two months in advance of the actual manufacturing. Toyota reviewed these plans one month and then ten days in advance, and used computers to draw up plans for equipment, personnel, and supplies. Managers then waited until firm orders came in from dealers before drawing up daily schedules four days ahead of production. By the late 1960s, Toyota had acquired the ability to revise production schedules at the last moment by sending out delivery instructions to subcontractors only after making up the final schedule.[32] (Figure 6). This allowed managers to adjust production levels or model mixes on the morning of or evening before production, whereas firms such as General Motors, which relied on tight computer scheduling, fixed assembly plans about five days in advance and normally did not have the option of introducing changes at the last minute.[33]

During the late 1950s, Toyota also began modifying its daily production schedule and assembly sequencing to reflect monthly sales orders as closely as possible to insure that workers produced only what was necessary and that the company did not store finished vehicles or components for long periods. If an assembly shop had to make 10,000 Coronas in one month—say, 5000 sedans, 2500 hardtops, and 2500 station wagons—Toyota used a computer to arrange daily production in the same ratio as the monthly schedule. Dividing by 20 working days, and assuming one 8-hour shift, daily output would consist of 250 sedans, 125 hardtops, and 125 station wagons. Although the cycle time for each vehicle determined the exact sequence so that managers were able to distribute jobs evenly, Toyota tried to make the final assembly mix fit the 2:1:1 ratio: sedan, hardtop, sedan, station wagon, sedan, hardtop, sedan, station wagon, and so on. In contrast, most other American and Japanese automakers, before mixed assembly became popular at plants making low-volume models by the early 1980s, would have required workers to spend the first half of the month making 5000 sedans, the third week making hardtops, and the fourth making station wagons, stockpiling vehicles until they had enough of each model type to begin shipping to dealers.[34]

Mixing final assembly offered several advantages. It insured against a build-up of inventory, which could occur if dealers canceled large orders for one type of vehicle. Since the scheduling was flexible enough to change the mix daily, Toyota adjusted production levels downward or upward more quickly than other companies as orders or cancelations came in from dealers.[35] Mixed-model runs also saved floor space and cut work-in-process inventory, because a factory met orders with fewer assembly lines. Fewer lines made it easier to co-

Figure 6: Toyota Production Planning and Procurement System, 1977

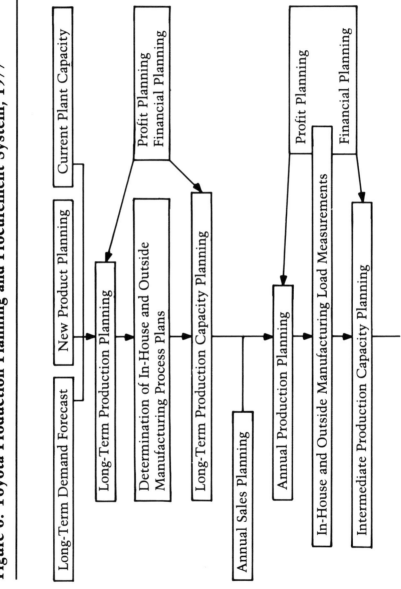

Monthly Orders

Monthly Production Planning

Short-Term Production Planning and Preparations

Daily Orders

Production Scheduling (Delivery Dates to Dealers)

Assembly Routing

Vehicle Assembly

Delivery Instructions for Large Subassemblies

Parts Processing and Assembly

Materials Delivery Instructions

Outside Parts Delivery Instructions

(Note: Dotted lines indicate instructions carried by kanban)

Source: Sugimori et al., p. 560.

283

ordinate different stations, reduced the need for line supervisors, and made it possible to distribute jobs and schedule cycle times more evenly throughout the day since there were no prolonged changes in job requirements. The smaller production lots that sequencing generated also lessened the monotony of assembly work, and this improved quality control.[36]

The only drawback to mixing models in assembly and having previous processes manufacture in small lots was that machines and workers had to be able to switch from one job to another quickly. Compared to manufacturers in the United States and Europe, all Japanese automakers developed this capability, in varying degrees, during the 1950s and 1960s, after serving a closed market that required an increasing number of car and truck models. Each discovered that the key to accommodating diversity was to manufacture in small lots, and that only fast machinery setup and production lead times made this type of production economical.

Lot Size and Rapid Equipment Setup
Modifying equipment and making special arrangements with suppliers for frequent deliveries thus allowed Toyota, and other Japanese automakers, to revise American assumptions regarding economical lot sizes and buffer inventories. From World War I through the early 1980s, American business schools, as well as economics and engineering departments, taught prospective managers to use a formula known as the "economic order quantity" (EOQ). This was supposed to determine the optimal lot size for reordering or producing components by calculating at what point the costs of holding inventory offset gains made by economies of scale in ordering or manufacturing. If equipment required hours to reset for different jobs, neither workers nor machines were able to produce anything during this changeover period, and subsequent processes also had to wait. Carrying inventory, even though it consumed operating capital, was usually more economical than trying to reorder or produce components frequently. But Ōno realized that, if a company procured or made parts often, without incurring extra costs or creating idle time, then it was more efficient (profitable) to order or manufacture in small lots. This is what Toyota and, to a lesser extent, every Japanese automaker accomplished. They increased the real cost of holding inventory (*I*) in the standard EOQ equation.[37]

Prior to 1955, Toyota needed from 2 to 3 hours to change stamping dies (the time still taken by many American and European automobile manufacturers in the 1970s and early 1980s). Toyota cut this to 15 minutes by 1962 and to as little as 3 minutes by 1971.[38] Toyota was not alone in doing this, however; Japan Steel and Shin-Mitsubishi Heavy Industries also devised rapid setup techniques during the 1950s for steel processing and shipbuilding.[39] In addition, Nissan lowered its average setup times from several hours in 1955 to between 30 minutes and an hour by 1960, and then to about 10 minutes by the early 1980s, for the same reason as Toyota and other Japanese firms: to reduce production and procurement lot sizes once manufacturing levels rose so high that keeping supplies for a month or so became too expensive.[40] In comparison, typical stamping plants for hoods and fenders in the United States, Sweden, and West Germany during 1977 required from 4 to 6 hours to change dies, according to Toyota's production control department. As a result, these foreign plants found it economical to manufacture in lots equivalent to 10 or 30 days' supply, and to reset equipment only once a day or every other day. In contrast, Toyota took an average of 12 minutes to change dies, which it did 3 times per day, and produced in lots of only 1 day's supply for most components.[41]

It is one of the great ironies in the history of production management and technology transfer that the idea of rapid setup, in addition to the time and motion studies that the Japanese used to cut cycle and idle times, were American. Ōno first saw Danley stamping presses with rapid die-change features on a trip to the United States during the mid-1950s. As he bought several for the Motomachi plant he asked himself why Americans and Europeans still took several hours to change stamping dies with Danley equipment, and concluded that this was because they chose to produce in large lots. Since changes were infrequent due to large lots, foreign automakers were able to reset equipment during breaks between shifts. Workers then became accustomed to taking hours to do a job that, with preparations in advance and adjustments of the machinery and dies, should have taken only a few minutes. To Ōno it was simply a matter of chance that the Japanese market was small and companies wanted to produce a variety of models but were unable to afford large supplies of parts or specialized assembly lines before the 1960s. Yet it still required deliberate planning to modify equipment and job routines, mix assembly runs, and manufacture parts in smaller lots for different vehicles.[42]

While Ōno was the main person promoting rapid setup techniques in the company, in 1955 Toyota also hired an outside consultant,

Shingō Shigeo, to study die setup systematically, reduce changeover times further, and then teach these and related production techniques to Toyota suppliers. Shingō, a 1930 graduate of the Yamagata Higher Industrial School (later Yamagata University), had joined the Japan Management Association (Nihon Nōritsu Kyōkai) in 1945 as a consultant and lecturer on production management before going to work for Toyota. Shin-Mitsubishi Heavy Industries also hired him in 1956, giving Shingō an opportunity to help the shipbuilder cut its lead time for producing a supertanker from 4 to 2 months. He continued as a consultant at Toyota for several years, however, and invented a term that became widely used in the Japanese automobile industry: the "single setup," referring to setup times requiring only a single digit, that is, less than 10 minutes.[43]

Studying how workers changed dies and machine tool equipment at several companies, including Toyota, Shin-Mitsubishi Heavy Industries, and Toyo Kogyo, enabled Shingō to break down the time required for these operations into four areas: preparing materials, dies, jigs and tools (30 percent of total setup time); removing and replacing old dies (5 percent); centering and measuring new dies and fixtures (15 percent); testing and adjusting equipment (50 percent).[44] Then he composed eight general suggestions to expedite setups on any type of equipment:

(1) To reduce setup time by 30 to 50 percent, distinguish which preparations do not require stopping the machine, and then make all possible preparations while a machine is running.

(2) Modify equipment, including dies and tools, so that workers can complete as many preparations as possible without stopping the machine.

(3) Standardize the parts of dies and machinery that function in the setup process to eliminate the need for readjustments and to make the changeover job more routine.

(4) Design clamps or fasteners to eliminate bolts or screws so that workers can easily tighten or loosen them.

(5) Use standardized intermediate jigs that fit on a piece of work while a machine is operating and that workers can easily set up once they finish a job.

(6) Train workers responsible for changing dies or tools to operate in coordination or in teams to save time.

(7) Eliminate adjustments of new dies, which consume at least 50 percent of setup time, by designing equipment to fit properly the first time or with one touch, like a cassette,

or by adding limit switches and jigs in specific locations so that workers can check the accuracy of the setup at a glance, while they insert new dies or tools.

(8) Mechanize the setup process by using hydraulic or pneumatic attachments for dies and by using stamping machines that have electric motors controlling the height of their shafts.

Toyota reduced its average setup time from several hours to 2 hours simply by standardizing all dies and using rollers or carts to move dies and other fixtures. Mechanizing part of the setup process, such as adjustments of the height of machinery, cut the time from 2 hours to 18 minutes. After devices to reduce adjustments once a die was in place lowered the time from 18 to 14 minutes, Toyota achieved further reductions by redesigning equipment and dies on the principle of the cassette.[45] In addition, both Nissan and Toyota discovered that it was easier to change dies on medium-size or small stamping presses, so they purchased numerous smaller machines in place of a few larger presses.

Toyota engineers also studied lead times and broke these down into three elements: production time for the supply lot to each process; waiting time between processes; and conveyance time between processes. One way they reduced production times was to improve coordination between the quantity and timing of production in different processes. Reducing the size of production and conveyance lots lowered the time workers spent waiting for machines or for parts to arrive. During the early 1960s, younger engineers working under Ōno also developed a formula to calculate lead times by multiplying processing time by demand for a particular component, subtracting the product from total operating time, and dividing the remaining figure into total setup time. Toyota engineers then determined lot sizes by multiplying demand for a component by total lead time. These and other formulae made it easier to perfect the kanban system and to introduce it throughout company factories and to suppliers.[46]

Kanban: Manual Controls Over the Process Flow
The kanban system operated rather simply. Each component had a predetermined, although elastic, number of production-ordering and withdrawal (conveyance) kanban. In-house withdrawal kanban accompanied parts or materials moving from one process to another; production-ordering kanban signaled in-house workers to make or

get more components, or told subcontractors what and how much to make, and when and where to deliver (Figure 7). Stations produced only as many components as there were kanban, and only as frequently as workers exchanged kanban, which they attached to containers (usually small carts or pallets). As with the entire process-information flow, the beginning point of the exchange was the last station on the final assembly line, and the exchanges continued in reverse order (Figure 8).

For example, a materials handler covering a station that had to attach front hoods to body assemblies went back to the previous station and picked up a pallet containing 5 of the components. When the user emptied the container, it was a signal for the materials handler to return it to the station that stamped the hoods (or to the gate where a supplier delivered them). A worker at the previous

Figure 7: Types of Kanban

In-House Conveyance or Withdrawal Kanban

Store Shelf No. 5E215	**Item Back No.**	**Preceding Process**
Item No. 3567 S07	A2-15	Forging B2
Item Name		**Subsequent Process**
Drive Pinion		Machining M6
Car Type SX 50BC		

Box Capacity	**Box Type**	**Issue No.**
20	B	418

In-House Production-Ordering Kanban

Store Shelf No. F26-18	**Item Back No.**	**Process**
Item No. 56790-321	A5-34	Machining
Item Name		
Crankshaft		
Car Type SX 50BC		

Figure 7: (continued)

Subcontractor Production-Ordering Kanban

Delivery Times		Store Shelf to Deliver	
9:30 AM	10:00 PM	E-1-2	
2:30 PM	3:00 AM	Item No.	Car Type
Name of Subcontractor		28100-66070	BJ-1
Nippon Denso		Item Name	Box Type
Store Shelf of Subcontractor		Starter	S
5-middle		Item Back No.	Box Capacity
Receiving Company		469	2
Toyota/Assembly Line 2		Gate to Receive	
		55	

Source: Yasuhiro Monden, "Adaptable Kanban System Helps Toyota Maintain Just-in-Time Production," pp. 30, 36.

station removed the withdrawal kanban, hung it on a rack, and replaced it with a production-ordering kanban. When the station made or received enough hoods to fill the pallet again, a worker replaced the withdrawal kanban and a materials handler from the next station came back and retrieved it. The worker at the station then attached a production-ordering kanban to another pallet, refilled it, and so on.[47]

While Ōno began using kanban in the machine shop after he took over as head of the No. 1 manufacturing department in 1953, these were no more than small paper strips on which workers wrote numbers to mark components and provide processing information to prevent mistakes in handling. Toyota gradually extended the functions of the kanban after designing them in different sizes, colors, and shapes to facilitate the identification of components. By the end of the 1970s, kanban had become so famous that Japanese and non-Japanese journalists, scholars, and businessmen were referring to Toyota's entire collection of manufacturing techniques as the "kan-

Figure 8: Kanban Flow Chart

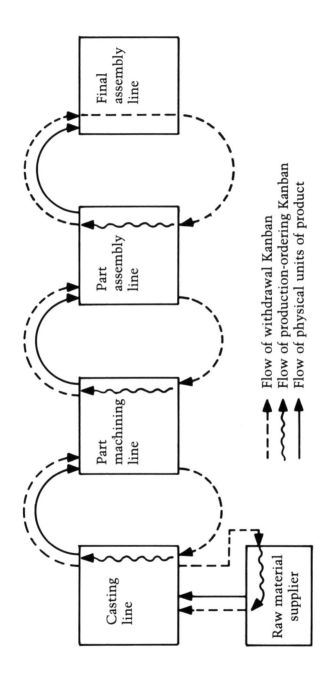

Source: Yasuhiro Monden, "Adaptable Kanban System Helps Toyota Maintain Just-in-Time Production," p. 34. Reprinted with permission from Industrial Engineering magazine, May 1981. Copyright @ Institute of Industrial Engineers, 25 Technology Park/Atlanta, Norcross, GA 30092.

ban system." But these paper and later metal signs were only one part of an integrated system characterized by a flow of processing information backward from final assembly, "flexible" machinery and workers, tightly rationalized job routines, low lead and setup times, and small lots for manufacturing, in-house conveyance, and deliveries from subcontractors. The physical exchange of the kanban was, however, central to the Toyota system. Not only did they identify each component and each vehicle assembled, but, according to Ōno, the kanban controlled inventories of work in process and finished goods by preventing over production; reduced the production of defectives by eliminating buffer inventories and making defects or assembly mistakes immediately affect the next processes; and served as a mechanism to make any problems in the production system highly conspicuous, including defectives, overproduction, and inefficient conveyance or equipment setup.[48]

Ono's first chance to apply the kanban system broadly within Toyota came when President Ishida made him the manager of the Motomachi plant in 1959; he then directed every department in the factory to adopt kanban for conveyance and process control. In the main plant Ōno had already converted the machining, body-stamping, and body-assembly shops but, since many parts and materials came from shops that did not use kanban, the system had only a limited impact on inventories. When Ōno became manager of the main plant in 1962, he extended the kanban to forging and casting, and then brought suppliers into the system between 1962 and 1965.[49]

While Ōno and other shop managers first determined the number of kanban to use by trial and error, by the early 1960s they had devised a formula to make the estimates more accurate. This considered demand per unit of the component (D), waiting time for the kanban (Tw), processing time for the component (Tp), the capacity of each standardized container (a), and a policy variable (n) that corresponded to a shop's ability to maintain a production schedule despite outside interference (Table 73). The main objective of the formula was to help managers keep lead times, container capacity, and the policy variable as small as possible because these values translated directly into work-in-process inventory.

The equation was supposed to describe an idealized conveyor line controlled by final assembly and operating in a continuous process flow, with kanban serving to link all stations. Managers calculated demand by averaging out or leveling production orders to avoid large variations; they also limited the value of the container capacity and

Table 73: Toyota's Kanban Formula

$$y = \frac{D\,(Tw + Tp)\,(1 + n)}{a}$$

y = the number of kanban
D = demand (units per period)
Tw = waiting time for kanban
Tp = process time
a = container capacity (not more than 10% of daily requirement)
n = policy variable (not more than 10% of daily requirement)

Source: Sugimori et al., pp. 561-562.

the policy variable to no more than 10 percent of the daily require-ment for a particular component. Since the number of kanban (y) usually remained fixed even if demand (D) changed, the value of ($Tw + Tp$), which equaled the lead time, dropped when D decreased in value. In practice, this resulted in frequent overtime at less efficient shops or suppliers. Toyota also allowed lead times to expand when demand decreased but then reduced the number of workers. In ad-dition, shop supervisors had the authority to increase the policy variable (or, in extreme cases, the number of kanban) to accom-modate longer lead times, but managers tended to measure a shop's efficiency by the size of the policy variable.[50]

The kanban system was able to handle variations of 10 to 30 percent in monthly demand merely by changing the frequency of kanban exchanges, rather than by increasing the number of kanban or lot sizes. Sudden or larger changes in demand created problems because these required an expansion of the number of kanban and personnel, and revisions of all cycle times. The system worked best when Toyota (and Toyota Motor Sales prior to the merger) correctly estimated, several months to a year in advance, what demand would be within a range of 30 percent, because production engineers then had ample time to prepare equipment, workers, and kanban, and fill orders without too much or too little capacity.[51]

Shingō also used an ordering-point (OP) formula to estimate the impact of the kanban, and the other Toyota techniques, on inventory levels. He took the number of vehicles that a company wanted to make in one day (*a*), the time required to produce the necessary parts (*P*), the minimum level of necessary stocks (*b*), and the size of the manufacturing lots for the parts (*Q*), so that $OP = a (P + b)$ (Table 74). Gradually reducing production lead times for components, the sizes of manufacturing lots, setup and preparation times, and the levels of parts stocks eliminated work-in-process inventories almost entirely as Toyota cut the ordering point for the needs of the next production period to one day's supply.[52] As a result, Toyota managers did not have to worry about inventory build-up, daily production planning, or comparing production estimates with actual output, since it was sufficient merely to determine lot sizes and the number of kanban, and then watch the exchange signal for more components. In "push" systems, if planning departments overestimated needs, or if any one process fell behind, inventories increased.[53]

The kanban system did not work well if a large number of defects appeared in process or in delivered components. To minimize mistakes in components manufacturing or assembly for new models, Toyota relied on strict off-line pre-production preparations and spent approximately 12 hours over a 2-week period training workers. In the event that a few defects still appeared, there was usually enough inventory in the system to keep the process flow moving, as long as workers followed specific procedures to lessen their impact.

For example, if a worker discovered a defective component in final assembly that neither he nor a supervisor could repair on the spot, he marked the vehicle and then had the component fixed or replaced after the vehicle came off the line. There was also immediate feedback on errors to the responsible stations, communicated verbally through a loudspeaker or by a supervisor, or signaled by a yellow or red light. If a defective component was made in house, if possible, an identical component was borrowed from another lot or pallet (which then served as a small buffer inventory), although the responsible station still had to make a replacement. In the case of a supplier, if one part in a delivered pallet was defective, Toyota rejected the entire pallet, providing someone noticed the problem before a station actually began using the pallet. If the defective component was discovered in process, Toyota used the rest of the parts but took a similar component from another pallet and asked the supplier to send a replacement part with its next delivery, which was usually within a few hours. In this way, Toyota made every effort to keep the flow moving and to reduce the need to stop its production lines.[54]

Table 74: Ordering-Point System

Step	Production Method	1 Day's Needs	Production Time for Parts (days)		Minimum Stocks	Ordering Point	Lot Size (supplied parts)	Maximum Stocks	Number of Pallets
		a	P	a·P	b	a·P + b	Q	Q + b	n
1	Regular	100	15	1500	500	2000	5000	5500	110
2	Reduce production time by process revisions, such as better synchronization	100	12	1200	500	1700	5000	5500	110
3	Reduce the size of parts lots and production time by revising equipment setup	100	6	600	500	1100	1000	1500	30

4	Reduce production time by cutting waiting time for parts deliveries	100	3	300	500	800	1000	1500	30
5	Reduce minimum stocks by leveling the process flow	100	3	300	200	500	1000	1200	24
6	Further reduce the size of parts lots by cutting setup times again	100	2	200	200	400	400	600	12
7	Eliminate stocks	100	1	100	0	100	200	200	4

Assumptions: —The number of vehicles needed for 1 day's production is 100.
 —Each pallet contains 50 parts, and a kanban is attached to each pallet.
 —The production time for parts changes if the lot size is reduced, although this does not necessarily reduce the time needed for conveyance and waiting for processes to finish.

Source: Shingō Shigeo, Toyota seisan hōshiki no IE-teki kōsatsu, p. 250.

Rejection of Computer Controls

It was not simply the efficient exchange of kanban that kept inventories low at Toyota. An interrelated system of production techniques—the pull concept; synchronized parts production, deliveries, and final assembly; low setup and lead times; small lots for manufacturing, procurement, and conveyance—found the most economical level of inventories by themselves. Companies with longer setup and lead times, on the other hand, found it cheaper to produce and order in larger lots, even though this required larger inventories and a complex system of procurement and warehousing. With bigger lots and inventories, Nissan and many other automakers in Japan, the United States, and Europe needed to have customized "materials requirement planning" (MRP) systems to generate master schedules and bills of materials and to coordinate all phases of production and supply.[55]

American engineers and computer specialists began developing MRP programs in the early and mid-1960s to find ways to order and schedule production with the lowest possible inventories and final costs. Nissan and Toyo Kogyo in Japan were among the first automakers to institute these systems, which relied on "real-time on-line" processing initially designed for banking and airline reservations. In "real-time" operations, at least in theory, high-speed central computers and terminals placed on the shop floor made it possible to get responses to inputs of information almost instantaneously, so that the computer was able to direct the flow at each production line and control the feeding of materials and parts into the system. Many managers in the Japanese and American automobile industries during the 1960s and 1970s believed that "real-time" production control, as opposed to the use of computers merely to calculate schedules for production and parts supply, or to keep track of inventories, was far superior to any type of manual scheduling.

Yet MRP programs had problems even in 1980s. To be effective, they required extremely precise information on lead times and intermediate costs, while it was rare for companies to maintain such accurate information and to update it constantly for themselves, let alone for dozens or hundreds of suppliers. The computer also injected rigidity into production control because cost and timing estimates required that companies behave in the future exactly as data indicated they were behaving in the present. Since MRP systems had difficulty accommodating intermediate processing or supply delays, managers found it economical to carry buffer inventories, but these stocks then made it impossible to cut operating costs to the same degree as a firm with smaller lots and lower inventories. While production control programs were being developed during the 1980s to adapt to changes in the assembly process more easily, the software and hardware were expensive because they had to link all factories and major suppliers. And these systems still failed to prevent inventory from building up due to data and operational problems, and were likely to push defectives forward because they did not contain any physical checks on the process flow.[56]

In Ōno's opinion, one of the most important benefits of Toyota's techniques was that they reduced the need to rely on computers for production control and parts procurement. Kanban in particular made it possible to change the production mix or volume, within certain limits, without having to reprogram a central computer and revise an entire schedule for processing and parts supply. The kanban required accurate estimates of lead times, but managers were able to adjust these values easily while the manual exchange of kanban determined the process flow and the level of inventories. Moreover, a kanban-type of pull system was far cheaper to install and simpler to modify than an MRP system. To be effective, Toyota's system required short setup and lead times as well as suppliers that delivered frequently and in small loads. But, while buying all new equipment would have been prohibitively expensive, Toyota engineers found that minor modifications in machinery and preparations routines allowed almost any machine tool to change cutting tools or dies more quickly.[57]

Toyota engineers had years of experience with computers and computerized production control before deciding around 1970 to use computers only to coordinate overall production scheduling and to determine information for the kanban, which workers continued to prepare and exchange manually (sometimes riding bicycles because of the size of Toyota's manufacturing plants). In 1953, Toyota acquired an IBM electronic calculator that processed punched cards and used it for routine administrative tasks, such as to keep personnel records. Over the next several years, it began utilizing the calculator for inventory control, materials-cost computations, parts ordering, equipment scheduling, and monitoring deliveries of components. Toyota was also one of the first Japanese firms to lease an IBM 650 computer in 1960, which it applied even more extensively to production planning, materials and equipment planning, inventory control, and office administration. Toyota then replaced the

650 with an IBM 7074/1401 in 1963 and a "third-generation" 1440 (equipped with integrated circuits) in 1966.[58]

Since the IBM 1440 processed data from terminals quickly enough to affect the process flow on several production lines simultaneously, Toyota tried to use "real-time processing" in the Takaoka assembly plant to coordinate body manufacturing, painting, and final assembly. Later, Toyota experimented with similar systems in Motomachi during 1969 and Tsutsumi in 1970. Despite believing that computerized controls would make it easier to manage the growing volume and complexity of orders for domestic and export customers, Toyota engineers found that the computer tended to "push" work-in-process, including defectives, onto subsequent stations, increasing inventories and complicating quality control.[59]

Even as mainframes and software systems for "real-time" or instantaneous processing improved during the 1970s, Ōno in particular preferred to have daily process flow information proceed not by computer orders but by the exchange of kanban for the simple reason that "the real world doesn't always go according to plan."[60] He and other managers also realized that it was unnecessary to buy costly software and computer systems when the kanban provided accurate information, almost instantaneously, on changes in production capacity, operating rates, and manpower—as long as these data corresponded to movements on the final assembly lines, and workers followed directions. It even seemed to Toyota managers that letting final assembly regulate previous processes kept inventories at lower levels than were possible with the best MRP systems, because they removed processing to a distant point—the central computer.[61]

Rapid Inventory Turnover
While Toyota did not achieve complete control over inventories and procurement costs until suppliers began using kanban between 1961 and 1965 to regulate their deliveries, Ōno began coordinating deliveries from subcontractors with production lines in the Koromo factory during 1949 to eliminate intermediate warehousing. Then he gradually familiarized these firms with how kanban worked by tagging all delivered parts and then by making suppliers deliver only when they received the kanban. During the middle and late 1960s, Toyota also taught its management techniques to main subsidiaries and synchronized their production lines with its own, although most other subcontractors continued to produce in large lots, without adopting their own internal kanban systems or the other production

techniques Toyota used. After 1973, however, the rising costs of energy and materials, and the high domestic inflation that followed the first oil shock, prompted Toyota managers to insist that all suppliers adopt the kanban system and related techniques to reduce lot sizes, inventories, and, therefore, manufacturing costs.

Companies in or near Aichi prefecture were the first suppliers to integrate their internal production lines with Toyota's, since they were almost entirely dependent on the automaker for orders. During the late 1970s and early 1980s, Toyota asked subcontractors in other parts of Japan to adopt its system. Firms in the Tokyo area were usually the last to convert their production lines and management systems; most were not exclusive Toyota suppliers. But another reason for their reluctance to follow Toyota was that the kanban system required several deliveries a day, sometimes in the middle of the night, directly to Toyota factories. This was not so difficult for companies in or near Toyota City, especially since some firms located near to each other cooperated by forming "car pools" to reduce the number of trips that any one of them had to make.[62] The system placed a greater burden on subcontractors with factories in other parts of Japan, although most found that Toyota's techniques resulted in higher productivity and more stable, if not higher, operating profits.[63]

The Toyota concept of inventory control spread gradually throughout the Japanese automobile industry, although major subsidiaries as well as Daihatsu and Hino were the only companies in the industry to adopt pull-type, kanban systems during the 1960s. Nissan, relying on a push-type system, began reducing inventories as production volumes rose after 1955 rather than storing large amounts of components that kept huge sums of capital tied up in unproductive stockpiling.[64] But not until after the 1973 oil shock did Nissan and other firms in the Japanese automobile industry attempt to match Toyota in lowering inventories, since it had become clear that savings in carrying costs offered protection against sudden declines in demand. By the early 1980s, most Japanese automakers (as well as many other Japanese manufacturing firms) operated with little on-hand inventory, compared to their foreign competitors.

One source of evidence for this trend was the National Research Council, which published a study in 1982 citing parts inventory levels at assembly plants in Japan and the United States. This found that most Japanese automakers operated with only 1 or 2 hours of supplies for components such as heaters, radiators, and brake drums, in contrast to 3 to 5 days' supply in the United States, where automobile plants usually received components from several different states and even from different countries, such as Canada and Mexico—thus making a "just-in-time" system extremely difficult to implement. American firms also averaged supplies for 6 days of other components that Japanese automakers stocked for only 11 hours. As a result, total work-in-process inventories per completed vehicle in 1980 averaged $74 in Japan and $584 in the United States.[65] In addition, low in-process inventories not only saved on operating costs, but they allowed the Japanese to build assembly plants from 20 to 40 percent smaller than American factories with the same capacity.[66]

Despite the impressions created by studies reporting only industry averages, however, not all Japanese automakers operated with equally effective "just-in-time" production and parts-delivery systems. Inventory turnover rates (average inventories divided by sales) varied widely throughout the industry between 1960 and the early 1980s, though these statistics also reflected how quickly firms sold finished vehicles. Different structural characteristics or levels of vertical integration also made it difficult to compare companies precisely; in fact, Toyota engineers greatly exaggerated their efficiency by publishing figures claiming a turnover of 60 and 70 times annually—excluding the substantial finished-goods inventories of Toyota Motor Sales![67] Prior to July 1982, Toyota sold all its production immediately to Toyota Motor Sales, which then distributed vehicles to dealers. Combining their balance sheets brought down Toyota's actual turnover by two-thirds, although the resulting figures were still higher than Nissan's, and both Nissan and Toyota turned over their inventories faster than General Motors, Ford, Honda, Fuji Heavy Industries (Subaru), or Isuzu.

Inventory turnover at Toyota and Toyota Motor Sales increased from 8 times annually in 1955 to 12 by 1962 and then to over 18 in 1963 as Ōno extended the kanban system throughout the main plant and Motomachi. Once suppliers joined the system, turnover rose to 28 in 1966, about the same as in 1982. Between 1960 and 1982, Toyota averaged a turnover of 24 times annually, compared to 14 for Nissan and 8 for General Motors and Ford, although all these companies, including Toyota (which streamlined its accounting system after the merger with Toyota Motor Sales), showed substantial improvements in 1983 (Table 75). Nissan raised its turnover from under 5 in 1955 to nearly 17 in 1963, despite operating with equipment and techniques that required more buffer stocks than Toyota did to be economical, but then dropped to an average of 14 between 1964 and 1978. Only in 1979, following cost increases after the second oil shock, did Nissan management devote more attention to cutting inventories.[68]

Daihatsu and Hino copied Ōno's techniques in the late 1960s, although Daihatsu established a new sales company and this exaggerated its turnover rates. On the other hand, even during the early 1980s, Fuji Heavy Industries, Honda, and Isuzu had yet to

Table 75: Inventory Turnover Comparison, 1955-1983

FY	Nissan	Toyota	FY	Nissan	Toyota
1955	4.5	7.7	1970	12.5	23.5
1956	7.2	14.9	1971	14.4	22.8
1957	6.1	10.6	1972	17.3	25.8
1958	5.9	9.8	1973	15.8	24.2
1959	8.9	10.9	1974	11.0	20.5
1960	12.0	10.4	1975	13.5	21.1
1961	13.9	11.0	1976	13.3	24.2
1962	14.5	12.4	1977	13.3	26.9
1963	16.6	18.4	1978	13.5	28.4
1964	14.9	20.7	1979	16.7	27.4
1965	12.7	20.9	1980	17.4	22.5
1966	13.2	27.7	1981	15.1	21.3
1967	14.0	28.6	1982	16.2	28.5
1968	14.5	27.8	1983	19.4	36.3
1969	14.8	26.7			

Table 75: (continued)

Period	Nissan	Toyota	GM	Ford	Chrysler
1955-1959	7	11	7	9	9
1960-1964	14	15	7	8	9
1965-1969	14	26	7	7	8
1970-1974	14	23	6	7	6
1975-1979	14	26	8	9	6
1980	17	23	8	7	5
1981	15	21	9	8	6
1982	16	29	9	9	7
1983	19	36	12	11	11

Sources: Annual reports and yūka shōken hōkokusho.

impose effective controls on inventories and production and thus had turnover rates that were not much higher than General Motors or Ford. Furthermore, while Mazda operated an effective low-inventory system patterned after Toyota, it did not institute this until the late 1970s.[69] Major subsidiaries of Toyota, and of Nissan, also increased their inventory turnover during the 1960s and 1970s, although Kantō Auto Works, Toyota Auto Body, Nissan Auto Body, and Aichi Machine, which registered the highest rates in the industry, merely assembled vehicles and sold them to Toyota or Nissan, without holding large amounts of buffer stocks, work in process, or finished vehicles (Table 76).

Despite Toyota's lead in raising inventory turnover, management did not set specific rates as goals and Ōno preferred to measure a company's efficiency by its profit margins.[70] But, while he believed that lower inventories reduced costs and resulted in higher earnings, this was not always the case. Toyoda Automatic Loom doubled its inventory turnover rate from 14 in 1976 to 29 in 1979, although its operating profit margins fell from 7.3 to 7.1 percent. Nihon Radiator recorded profit rates of 7.4 percent in 1975, with a turnover of 12

Table 76: Inventory Turnover in the Nissan and Toyota Groups, 1965-1983

	1965-1969	1970-1974	1975-1979	1980-1983
Toyota Group				
Toyota Auto Body	27	52	41	43
Toyoda Automatic Loom	9	11	20	26
Kantō Auto Works	19	76	72	70
Nippon Denso	13	12	14	19
Aichi Steel	6	8	7	10
Aisin Seiki	14	17	29	30
Toyoda Machine	6	4	6	7
Toyoda Gōsei	—	—	39	42
Daihatsu	17	20	32	36
Hino	10	16	20	21
Nissan Group				
Nissan Auto Body	28	36	51	68
Nissan Diesel	8	8	8	9
Nihon Radiator	—	11	15	21
Kantō Seiki	—	—	22	23
Aichi Machine	16	24	32	32
Atsugi Auto Parts	—	—	15	20
Fuji Heavy Industries	8	7	9	10
Other Automakers				
Honda	11	12	12	13
Mazda	13	10	14	20
Isuzu	12	10	10	10

Source: Fuka kachi bunseki.

Table 77: Operating Profits and Inventory Turnover

(inventories/sales, profits/sales)

FY	Toyoda Automatic Loom		Nihon Radiator		Mazda (Toyo Kogyo)	
	Inventory	Profits(%)	Inventory	Profits(%)	Inventory	Profits(%)
1975	9.1	6.0	12.4	7.4	8.8	−2.9
1976	14.3	7.3	12.2	6.6	11.4	0.8
1977	21.2	6.7	13.8	4.8	12.1	0.7
1978	28.1	7.3	17.8	4.1	14.8	1.1
1979	29.0	7.1	21.2	3.9	20.9	3.2
1980	26.9	6.3	19.6	3.7	21.7	3.3
1981	23.4	5.7	19.1	4.1	20.1	2.8

Source: Fuka kachi bunseki.

times, and 3.7 percent in 1980, with a turnover of nearly 20 times. Mazda recovered from major losses during the early 1970s but, even with turnover rates of around 20 during 1979-1981, profits were just 3 percent of sales, albeit this represented a marked improvement over 1975 (Table 77).

Other examples include General Motors, Ford, and Chrysler. All had higher operating profits than Nissan in 1965 with inventory turnover rates only half as high. General Motors even matched Toyota in profitability during 1983, with a turnover rate that was merely one-third as high (Tables 54 and 76). This was because, as Ōno conceded, a company's profitability ultimately depends on the salability of its products. In the case of General Motors and other American automakers during 1983-1984, the limited supply of Japanese cars and a 25-percent duty on imports of light trucks helped to shift demand to American producers while raising prices and even profit margins. As a general rule, however, realization that manufacturing efficiency was of little benefit if a company neglected market needs prompted Toyota to devote the same attention to product design and marketing as it did to production and inventory control techniques.[71] Most firms in the Japanese automobile industry, including Nissan, were unable to do this as effectively. Yet, even without guarantees of higher profits, manufacturing companies throughout the world had come to recognize by the early 1980s that the advantage of low inventory systems lay in their ability to adjust to drops in demand without tying up capital in unproductive stockpiling. This characteristic was especially important for companies in the small-car market, where competition was intense and profit margins were usually lower than for larger models with more options.

The Impact on Labor

If there was a flaw in the Toyota system, then it was the toll exacted from workers in company plants and suppliers. Ono and his assistants, beginning in 1948, subjected every process, machine, and worker to rigorous analyses to eliminate "waste"—which they defined as anything that did not contribute to "value added."[72] One book that a Toyota worker published in 1982 even maintained that the "just-in-time" pace in the Toyota group led to more major accidents (resulting in a loss of 4 or more days of work) than in other Japanese automakers, and an unusually high number of suicides among the blue-collar work force.[73] Another book, published in 1973 and sold widely in Japan for a decade, stated these same charges and had a Japanese title that translated as "The automobile factory of despair: diary of a seasonal worker."[74]

The author of "The Automobile Factory of Despair," Kamata Satoshi (1938-), was a graduate of the literature faculty of Waseda University, one of Japan's most prestigious private universities, as well as a professional journalist who kept a diary while working at Toyota between September 1972 and February 1973. It is no secret that Kamata went to Toyota to write an article critical of the company, so there is some bias built into his story. He began by noting that Toyota was careful to give rigorous physical examinations to new employees, and that managers refused to hire women as factory laborers. But, contrary to popular impressions of the Japanese as contented, proud employees, he insisted that Toyota workers were more likely to feel a sense of "despair" and loneliness because of their job routines and the company's tendency to treat them as "human transfer machines."

Kamata's days began with a meeting before the official starting time. Line workers then had to spend the next eight to ten hours in the space of approximately one square yard, with only a short break for lunch, all their movements precisely prescribed, and no time to speak to neighbors or even to begin understanding what part each worker played in the production process. Supervisors were slow to add help and preferred to raise line speeds, assign extra tasks or machines to workers, and keep everyone late for overtime. These policies not only contributed to accidents when workers grew weary; they left employees without any sense of control over their jobs or lives. "Rationalizing" worker movements to increase value added was fine, wrote Kamata, except that men were not machines. Three of the six temporary workers that entered with him quit before their contracts expired, while several others took the unfortunate route of suicide as a way out.

Toyota officials admitted some of these charges and dismissed others. Engineers in the production control department claimed, in 1977, that Toyota's accident rate was half that in the American automobile industry and low by international standards, although they did not publish any figures.[75] Ōno denied, in an interview with this author, that his policies were directly responsible for the suicides of workers, and pointed out that if they had been, "I would have been locked up by the police long ago." Yet the inventor of Toyota's production techniques acknowledged that shop managers were slow to add workers to the lines when production orders rose; instead, they usually shortened cycle times and increased the exchange rate of kanban. Workers hated this and the technique of operating several machines at once, recalled Ōno, who admitted that he never felt the need to try operating several machines simultaneously to see how easy or hard it was.[76] Ōno also encountered considerable resistance from workers during the 1950s when he began switching to the new system, because they had been trained to specialize on one machine and saw the request to operate several different machines as retrogressive. Moreover, employees were accustomed to considering a machine's operating time as part of their working time—which Ōno did not. Other problems arose when workers did not possess the skills to adjust various types of equipment.[77]

The reforms in the machine shop were one of the main issues in the 1950 strike. "Had I faced the Japan National Railways union or an American union," Ōno mused, "I might have been murdered." As it turned out, he was able to control the Toyota union, partly because management threatened to fire dissident workers, which it did in 1950, and partly because he was personally close to the union leaders.

Ōno had postponed a promotion to head the machine shop in 1947 to serve on the union's executive committee. He left the union when he entered management the following year. Since he knew the union leaders, he was able to convince them not to reject his program outright. By the end of 1955, the year following the collapse of the short-lived industrial union in the Japanese automobile industry, Ōno claimed that he had overcome most of the opposition to the new production techniques. But, despite his obvious genius as a production manager, Ōno still considered his success in controlling the union to have been the most important advantage Toyota gained over its domestic and foreign competitors. These included Nissan, because even its second union challenged management policies, Ōno asserted, and this hindered Nissan's attempt to match Toyota in productivity or profitability—reducing the impact of Nissan's earlier introduction of transfer machinery and quality control techniques.[78]

THE NISSAN PRODUCTION SYSTEM

Engineers at Nissan faced the same problems as their counterparts in Toyota after 1945: how to manufacture a rising number of cars and trucks at the lowest possible cost, at low volumes. As a solution, Nissan instituted a limited version of "just-in-time" parts delivery and production between the mid-1950s and early 1960s, learned to produce in smaller lots than American firms, and reduced setup times and inventory levels. Yet, even in the early 1980s, Nissan differed from Toyota in several areas. It did not employ a "pull" system and reverse the process-information or conveyance flow, and it produced in relatively large lots, as long as warehousing space was available. In addition, Nissan managers, as well as union officials (at least until 1983), chose to rely more on automation and computers to raise productivity than production-management techniques such as a complete kanban system or the job-cycle rationalization measures and rapid line speeds that Toyota employed.[79]

The Preference Toward Automation
Nissan's company history characterized the firm's manufacturing operations prior to 1960 as "lot" production: a small variety of models, compared to the period after 1960, manufactured in small volumes.

The product mix varied more than during World War II and became increasingly complex as orders rose for military vehicles during the Korean War, then for Datsun cars and trucks thereafter. Nissan did not begin "mass-producing" cars in volumes reaching the tens of thousands until the 1959 Datsun 310, and it did not have to manufacture more than one car line until it introduced the 1960 Cedric. But rising sales and subcontracting levels during the 1950s still created problems on the shop floor because managers preferred to keep 1 or 2 months' supply of components and store them next to production lines, although sales were low enough for the inventory problem to take second place in priority to improving the company's level of "mechanization" or automation (Table 78).

During the Austin tie-up, which taught Nissan how the British designed and manufactured small cars, including the use of transfer machines to produce engines and transmissions, Nissan purchased new high-speed, specialized machine tools from the United States and studied the latest factory management techniques. After 1959, production requirements changed: Nissan had to manufacture in much larger volumes. Production engineers focused on improving the flow on assembly lines by introducing more conveyors in older plants, and by purchasing new equipment for the Oppama factory. With the opening of Zama in 1964, Nissan then began to rely heavily on computers to coordinate subassembly production, final assembly, and parts supply as sales volumes rose and the product mix became more complex with options and different sets of emissions-control equipment for export models.

The second half of the 1960s thus brought on different problems for manufacturing engineers than earlier years: how to accommodate increasing product complexity in growing volumes, and how to lower costs to compete in export markets. Whereas Toyota's strategy was to refine the kanban system and extend this to suppliers, Nissan's approach was to perfect its use of computers to synchronize production and deliveries of parts and materials. During the 1970s, as manufacturing volumes and product complexity rose further, Nissan improved its computer systems, linked factories to main suppliers through "on-line" terminals, and added highly automated equipment, including programmable robots. Management expected these measures to bring the same results as Ōno's techniques, although Toyota's more centralized factory system and supply network, as well as tighter job cycles, faster equipment setup, more overtime, and more equipment per capita, increased inventory turnover and helped each Toyota worker produce more vehicles, value added, and profits than employees at Nissan.

Yet Nissan managers decided, in the early 1950s, not to copy Toyota's manufacturing techniques. While each company closed its factories to the other's employees around 1953, Matsuzaki and other Nissan engineers found out from looking at blueprints of Toyota's new machinery and attachments, provided by machine-tool manufacturers that made equipment for both automakers, how Ōno was compressing standard cycle times and arranging machinery to make employees work faster while operating several machines simultaneously. Nissan engineers had learned to use high-speed, single-function machine tools before World War II, and they wanted to introduce more of this equipment during the 1950s. Transfer machinery was thus Nissan's answer to Ōno's line rationalizations in the machine shop, according to Matsuzaki, although he admitted that Nissan managers also hesitated to compress cycle times too much, or rely too heavily on overtime, because the union leaders preferred to achieve productivity increases through automation.[80] Kanao Kaiichi (1919-), a mechanical engineer educated at Waseda University who entered Nissan in 1946 and was the executive vice-president in charge of production management and manufacturing quality control during the early 1980s, confirmed that Nissan's historical experience with equipment and production management made some of Ōno's techniques unsuitable; but he insisted as well that differences in geographic location between the two firms was another critical factor.[81]

Geography affected how Nissan and Toyota reacted to the problems of production management because worker consciousness of labor and management distinctions was lower in Japan's rural areas than in the Tokyo area, at least in the opinion of Nissan executives. They confronted union leaders who wanted a greater role in running the company than Toyota executives did, and they hesitated to order extensive overtime without prior notice. Like automakers in the United States and Europe, Nissan scheduled production and overtime assignments a month in advance; if a shop fell behind, managers resorted to only limited amounts of overtime before carrying work over to the next day. Toyota, in contrast, insisted that workers stay until they filled the day's orders, and resorted to overtime whenever sales were brisk or previous stations fell behind final assembly. Furthermore, Nissan permitted buffer stocks and allowed excess or "idle" time when calculating standard cycle times to make sure the

Table 78: The Development of Production Management at Nissan, 1945-1975

	1945-1960	1960-1965	1965-1970	1970-1975
Market	Automobiles still in introductory phase; more trucks than cars in demand.	Increased sales and competition among domestic firms; improved performance required of cars.	Popularization of cars among the general public.	Maturity period of sales. New focus on safety and anti-pollution devices. Internationalization of operations and products.
Production	Small variety, small volumes (lot production)	Small variety, large volumes.	Large variety, large volumes.	Larger variety, larger volumes
Technology	Focus on improving mechanization (transfer machinery, specialized machine tools).	Focus on extending the use of conveyors on assembly lines.	Focus on synchronization of production with parts supply, and on increasing automation.	Extension of synchronization to all operations and development of total control systems along with robots.

310

On-Line Computer Systems	Limited use of punched-card IBM calculators, mainly for accounting	Introduction of computers into offices using EDP card base and HITAC 301 and IBM 650 hardware.	Further use of computers in offices and for production control using magnetic tape and HITAC 3010, IBM 1401, HIDIC 100, and SDS 910 hardware.	Introduction of 3rd generation (IC) computers; development of total control systems using HITAC 8400 and IBM 1401 hardware	Further development of a total control system and the extension of computers to all operations, using HITAC 8500 and 8700, IBM 370, and HIDIC 500 and 700 hardware.

Source: Nissan Jidōsha shashi, *p. 374.*

311

process flow continued without delays. This looser type of scheduling was the rule rather than the exception in the Japanese automobile industry, insisted Kanao: Toyota was unusual, not Nissan.

On the other hand, Nissan modified American practices that were inconvenient. For instance, managers took advantage of lower production volumes than in the United States, and the absence of union restrictions on job classifications, by making workers operate different types of machinery, even though workers still operated only one machine at a time. Graham-Paige also taught Nissan to have its maintenance personnel specialize in electrical, mechanical, and hydraulic equipment, though the Japanese company eliminated these categories after installing robots in the late 1960s. Robots combined components from all three areas, whereas it took too much time to decide into which category a problem fell and then call in a maintenance crew, only to find often that the difficulty was another crew's responsibility. Toyota encountered the same problem but solved it by subcontracting specialized maintenance work—another factor that exaggerated the vehicle-unit productivity of its employees.[82]

Nissan, like Toyota, reduced setup times for stamping presses during the 1950s and 1960s by attaching rollers to heavy dies, automating die conveyance from storage areas, and redesigning equipment to allow dies to slip in and out of machines more easily.[83] But, since Nissan did not try to produce in lots as small as Ōno wanted, company engineers had no incentive to lower setup times to the same extent as Toyota did until they began following the Toyota system more closely during the 1970s. Nissan management, while believing that it had to adapt to the different market requirements in Japan, continued to look to the United States for advances in manufacturing technology: "We were Americanized," explained Matsuzaki.[84] Nissan thus led the Japanese automobile industry in importing American technology and equipment: specialized machine tools and time and motion studies during the 1930s, transfer machinery and new production-management techniques during the 1950s, computerized production and inventory control systems as well as industrial robots during the 1960s and 1970s.

The Importation of American Production Techniques
American engineers, led by William Gorham in 1934, showed Nissan how to conduct time and motion studies to determine the best ways to use Datsun production equipment. Nissan even experimented

with movie cameras in 1939 to analyze workers and machinery in final assembly, forging, casting, and stamping.[85] According to Igarashi Tadashi (1906-), who entered Nissan in 1935 and rose to vice-chairman before retiring in 1977 to head Atsugi Auto Parts, these prewar studies were "extremely primitive"; the time calculations relied on stopwatches and were only approximations. Yet Nissan needed new standards because it had to switch from producing the small-size Datsun line to standard-size trucks. Workers did not make the transition smoothly and management had difficulties computing wages, although the company solved most of these problems by 1939 and truck production proceeded smoothly until the later years of the war.[86] After 1945, Nissan resumed its introduction of American techniques, focusing on those developed during the second half of the 1930s and World War II, to improve process control and to generate new data for equipment and personnel planning as well as for recalculating monthly premiums for workers. The U.S. Army assisted, after asking Japanese automakers to provide trucks and other military vehicles for the Korean War, by urging Nissan to adopt "work factor analysis" and other techniques such as statistical quality control to improve manufacturing quality and efficiency.[87]

Work factor analysis was a refinement of earlier time and motion studies that Frederick Taylor and Frank Gilbreth had pioneered prior to 1930. W.G. Holmes and A.B. Segur, production management specialists working for Philco Radio and RCA during the late 1930s and early 1940s, developed more precise techniques for analyzing worker motions and cycle times by using high-speed strobe cameras and electrical measuring instruments. Their objective, similar to Taylor and Gilbreth, was to find an "economic" work pace that was not too tiring for employees. While Nissan and Toyota engineers were familiar with Taylor and Gilbreth, they did not receive detailed explanations of work factor analysis and the new cameras or measuring instruments until after World War II.

Ueda Takehito, a Japanese engineer formerly employed at Tokyo Keiki, a small precision instruments manufacturer, studied the Holmes and Segur techniques during the Occupation and then became a consultant to several Japanese firms, including Hitachi and Nissan. Thirty companies in the Tokyo area—led by Fujitsu, Hitachi, Fuji Electric, NEC, Columbia, and Toshiba—formed a work-factor-analysis study group in 1951 to examine these techniques and applications in more detail; other firms established branch organizations in Nagoya and Osaka. During the Korean War, they became the first

Japanese firms to apply work factor analysis to daily job routines, although Nissan was merely a few months behind and instituted a series of programs between 1950 and 1955 to improve process control and to standardize all manufacturing operations. While managers again needed the new techniques and equipment to recalculate standard times for premiums, they also wanted to study ways of reducing production costs and to determine whether it was more economical to make particular components in house or to subcontract.[88]

Matsuzaki and other Nissan engineers also learned the economic order quantity formula and used it to decide when to reorder components and how many to buy, or how many to produce in one lot. Their rule of thumb for in-house production was to make as many of a part as there was warehousing space, but the EOQ curve continued to call for around a month's supply of most components, even during the early 1960s—a level that became increasingly impractical as production volumes rose and Nissan ran out of storage facilities. While faster setup times and closer coordination with suppliers reduced on-hand stocks to an average of 2 or 3 weeks by the mid-1960s, for the next decade, Nissan did nothing to lower inventories further. The domestic recession in 1965, and the difficulty of assimilating Prince's lines while adjusting to new computerized systems, preoccupied managers until slower growth in sales during the 1970s provided new incentives to lower costs.[89]

Inventory and Process Controls
Although Nissan made less progress than Toyota in reducing inventories, its first attempts to lower in-house stocks began in 1954. On-hand parts supplies in the Yokohama factory had become a major problem because Nissan used one line to assemble standard-size trucks, Datsun orders that Yoshiwara was unable to handle, as well as the Patrol and the Carrier. Since accumulations of parts on the floor made resupplying the line difficult, and workers had trouble keeping track of which components went into which models, managers became convinced during 1954-1955 that Nissan had to improve coordination with suppliers and methods of introducing components into final assembly.

First, Nissan established the Yokohama Transport Company as a joint venture with Shin-Nikkoku Industries (Nissan Auto Body), Minsei Diesel (Nissan Diesel), and several other subcontractors. Sixty full-time employees and 75 to 100 part-time workers staffed the new firm, which owned a fleet of 40 trucks to transport materials and parts from suppliers to Nissan factories. After GHQ returned requisitioned facilities in 1955, Nissan held an in-house conference to discuss ways to improve intra-factory conveyance and to make on-hand supplies easier to handle, and sent observers to see how foreign automakers dealt with similar problems of storage and conveyance. The conference, which met 17 times between June and October 1955, ended with the establishment of a conveyance rationalization committee in November 1955 and the appropriation of 40,000,000 yen ($100,000) to buy forklifts and trailers. Management allocated another 200,000,000 yen ($500,000) in 1956-1957 to modernize warehousing and transport facilities in the Yokohama and Yoshiwara plants. At the same time, Nissan engineers used work factor analysis and similar techniques to examine work schedules and process flows to improve the conveyance of parts and materials, allocate trailers and forklifts, and reduce the number of workers engaged in these functions.

In 1955, Nissan also adopted an American technique called "marshaling" to ease the confusion in the Yokohama factory. This involved building a control room on the second floor of the plant, above the middle of the assembly line, to house a main control board and several "sub-control" boards to direct the main line and the flow of subassemblies and parts deliveries. While some managers hesitated to remove the control center from the shop floor, the second-story control room made it possible to coordinate the flow better and relieved some of the pressure that mixing models had created with rising production volumes, before computers performed this same function automatically during the 1960s.[90] Improvements in process control and parts supply, along with rapidly rising sales, enabled Nissan to raise its inventory turnover from 4.5 times in 1955 to 7.2 in 1956 and then to 12.0 in 1960 (Table 75).

Nissan Auto Body, Nissan Diesel, Nihon Radiator, and Atsugi Auto Parts were the only companies during the 1950s and early 1960s to synchronize their deliveries with Nissan's final assembly lines. To expand this practice, Nissan management decided in 1963 to ask 40 members of the Takara Kai to deliver more frequently and directly to Nissan's factories, according to the assembly line schedules. To determine the number of components required per day Nissan used the formula $Yi = (Aij) (Xj)$, with Yi as the number of parts (i) needed in one day, Aij as the number of parts used in vehicle j, and Xj as the number of units produced of the same vehicle.[91] The

Takara Kai firms also formed a production committee to draw up detailed cost estimates, which Nissan applied to product planning, job scheduling, storage and conveyance planning, and decisions on manufacturing in house versus subcontracting. Nihon Radiator, Atsugi Auto Parts, Nihon Air Brake, and Riken Piston Ring were the most active companies on the committee, which helped reduce Nissan's procurement costs and raise inventory turnover to 16.6 times in 1963.[92]

Mixing Computers and Kanban

Nissan's efforts to regulate the process flow and parts supply through American techniques culminated in the introduction of systems for computerized production control and materials requirement planning in the 1960s, utilizing advanced American computers and software. Nissan, like Toyota, was also one of the first Japanese companies to acquire IBM equipment. After leasing a punched-card IBM calculator in 1952 for office administration, over the next five years Nissan gradually extended its use of the machine to computing and storing statistics on service parts, procurement, deliveries, personnel, and general accounting. Management even established a committee in 1956 to study applications for production control. Several years elapsed before this was practical technologically, although in 1959 Nissan switched from punched cards to magnetized cards (EDP or "electronic data processing" cards), which facilitated the use of computers for more complex calculations and larger amounts of data related to production control, materials and equipment planning, sales forecasting, and production planning.

Nissan's computerization program became as advanced as that of any automaker in the world during the 1960s. In 1961, it acquired a transistorized IBM 650 computer and a HITAC 301 and added an NCR 390 in 1962 and two HITAC 3010 models (built by Hitachi but based on an RCA model), in 1963 to monitor production and parts supply in the Oppama and Yoshiwara plants. Management subsequently decided to introduce a fully computerized production control system in the Zama factory and asked three firms to bid on the contract: Hitachi, IBM Japan, and Scientific Data Systems (SDS), a company located in California, which designed sophisticated scientific computers and software for NASA before Xerox absorbed it in 1969.

When Hitachi decided it was unable to write the software, IBM Japan became the leading candidate, since it had provided equipment and advice to Nissan in the past and was already developing production control programs. But SDS won the contract by offering to make Zama an experimental factory containing the world's most advanced control system for automobile assembly. Zama opened in December 1964 with an SDS 910 computer controlling production schedules, equipment planning, parts supply, and the assembly flow, in addition to monitoring quality control data throughout the factory. Nissan guarded Zama closely and refused to admit visitors when it first opened, despite several requests from General Motors and other foreign automakers. The plant manager at the time, Matsuzaki, considered Zama's computerized system to be Nissan's ultimate "answer" to the kanban.[93]

While the agreement with SDS did not stop Nissan from leasing, in 1965, the first IBM computer to use integrated circuits, the model 360, Nissan engineers decided to use this for computer-aided design and to buy Hitachi hardware for production and supply control. The SDS and IBM software was not fully compatible with Hitachi mainframes, so Nissan allowed Hitachi to study and copy the programs.[94] Although Matsuzaki claimed in 1983 that he "felt bad" about this, Japan lacked adequate copyright protection for software and Hitachi's action was not illegal, at least not in Japan during the 1960s. Hitachi then took several years to design comparable software but, when it was ready in 1969, Nissan installed Hitachi systems in Zama, Oppama, and Murayama, utilizing HIDIC mainframes with integrated circuits and teletype terminals to direct parts supply, subassemblies production, painting, and final assembly[95] (see Table 78). Hitachi also sold its production control system, based originally on SDS and IBM programs, to other Japanese customers, such as Isuzu.[96]

Nissan adopted more sophisticated computerized controls in 1971, starting with an "order entry system" (OES) that employed a Hitachi mainframe to coordinate vehicle orders with materials and components procurement, in-house parts production, transport, and final delivery of completed automobiles to dealers. This reduced the lead time needed to produce a vehicle from 1 or 2 months to as little as 1 week, with an average of about 2 weeks. Also in 1971, Nissan introduced a "total plant production system" (TPPS) to monitor in-process stocks and to calculate the lowest possible levels for the process flow to continue.[97] Nissan's inventory levels immediately reflected the influence of the new systems: Turnover rose from 12.5 times in 1970 to 17.3 in 1972. Yet frequent, unpredictable changes in orders after the first oil shock caused stocks to build up and turnover to drop to only 11 times in 1974. Turnover stayed at around 13 for several years, until Nissan management renewed its efforts to reduce inventories in 1979 (see Table 75).

Parts stocks were again the major problem. They had become increasingly difficult to regulate due to the dispersal of Nissan's factories and suppliers, and the lack of strict controls on deliveries and buffer inventories. Even when managers tried to schedule deliveries at the last moment to keep stocks at the lowest possible levels, intermediate stations accumulated inventories as trucks got caught in traffic jams or, for other reasons, were unable to arrive on time. While this occurred rarely at Toyota because of its rural location and because the manual exchange of kanban "pulled" materials and parts through the system, computers tended to "push" them through at Nissan even when stations had more stocks than they needed or when subsequent lines had shortages of critical components.[98]

Nissan's solution, after several years of experimenting in selected shops, was to introduce a limited kanban system during the late 1970s. Managers called this the "action plate method" (APM) because they did not want to copy the name kanban, although these plates or signs were clearly a version of Toyota's subcontractor production kanban. Within its factories, Nissan continued to relay processing or conveyance information instantaneously by computer, whereas Toyota used kanban to trigger processes to begin. To suppliers able to reach its factories within 10 to 20 minutes, however, Nissan relayed delivery orders by on-line computer terminals, and switched only those firms located farther away to APM, which they exchanged manually. Nissan also retained buffer inventories of a few days or even a week for critical components, because managers gave priority to insuring that production lines did not stop. Nor did managers encourage workers to stop assembly lines if they noticed defects, since this upset the computer scheduling. Instead, they asked workers to alert inspectors to problems by attaching white markers, and then to take replacement parts from stockpiles. If a line had to stop because of a major equipment or supplier failure, computers usually rescheduled production for the next shift instead of keeping workers on overtime, even though this practice contributed to higher inventory levels.

Main suppliers with plants or warehouses near Nissan's factories had delivered more than once a day since the early 1960s. Even during the 1980s, however, Nissan allowed firms located farther away to deliver less frequently and in larger loads, despite the APM system. This made life easier for distant subcontractors but added more unneeded stocks to Nissan's inventory. Most of Nissan's suppliers also continued to manufacture in relatively large lots, compared to the Toyota group, without synchronizing production with Nissan's final assembly lines to the same degree as Toyota's suppliers. Nissan made suggestions to members of its Takara Kai but did not enforce changes in their methods of production management, whereas Toyota instituted "just-in-time" scheduling throughout its production and supply network during the 1960s. Toyota's production system relied on extremely close relations with suppliers, concentration in a rural area, rapid equipment setup, and the full cooperation of workers. To devise and implement these techniques also required a "fanatic," Matsuzaki mused, "an Ōno Taiichi." Nissan simply did not have one.

CHAPTER SIX

QUALITY CONTROL: MANUFACTURING AND DESIGN

There are at least two ways to interpret quality control (QC). A simple approach focuses on manufacturing and inspection to insure that products meet predetermined standards for precision, performance, or appearance. Another, broader interpretation sees QC as the identification of consumer preferences, the incorporation of these into product designs, and the institution of controls ranging from manufacturing to procurement and customer service. The second interpretation also assumes the existence of measures to insure that pre-production testing eliminates as many design or material defects as possible, and that engineers design a given level of quality, determined by what consumers desire and are willing to pay for, into a product. A company then tries to maintain this level throughout the manufacturing process without relying on large inspection departments to check for and adjust product quality after production.

THE AMERICAN AND JAPANESE APPROACHES

Japanese automakers, during the early 1960s, began to interpret QC in the second, broader sense. Although some firms had better results than others, and several American or European companies exhibited QC programs that were as effective as any in Japan during the early 1980s, in general, Japanese automakers developed extensive QC procedures in response to a series of quality problems during the 1950s and 1960s, while competitors abroad tended to maintain narrower programs that focused on inspection and process control in manufacturing. By the early 1980s, QC programs in Japan also differed from programs in the United States or Europe by their emphasis on simple rather than complex statistical methods, and on other techniques that were relatively easy for production workers to learn and

320

apply. These techniques allowed Japanese automakers to shift much of the responsibility for maintaining quality in processing from inspection or QC staff departments to workers on the shop floor.

The U.S. Army introduced statistical QC (SQC) techniques to Japanese academics, engineers, and managers during the late 1940s, along with production management and personnel administration concepts developed during World War II. While GHQ wanted to aid the recovery of Japan's economy, it also needed companies to produce electrical equipment, trucks, and other items up to American standards for U.S. troops stationed in Japan and Korea. QC methods that the American army promoted consisted mainly of statistical random-sampling techniques to facilitate inspection without having to check every component in every lot of goods a factory made. Military inspectors, and civilian managers, had gained extensive experience in the use of these methods by 1945 after mass producing aircraft and other ordnance for the American armed forces.

NEC, Toshiba, Fuji Electric, and Hitachi were the first Japanese companies to apply American production management and QC techniques. GHQ gave special assistance to electrical equipment firms because it wanted to set up a new communications network throughout Japan but found serious defects in the quality of Japanese telephone equipment. Strict American standards for military vehicles also forced Nissan, Toyota, and Isuzu to attend QC lectures and to adopt higher quality standards and new inspection techniques. But quality problems in the postwar Japanese automobile industry were far too severe to be solved merely through better methods of inspection, or even through improvements in manufacturing process controls. Quality suffered from inferior materials and faulty designs at original equipment manufacturers and at the myriad small and medium-size subcontractors that supplied them. To satisfy American inspectors during the 1950s, and consumers in Japan and abroad during the 1960s, Japanese automakers had to find and correct quality problems at their source. This required an extension of QC programs from inspection to process control, and then to design and market analysis.

The Introduction of Statistical QC

American companies prior to World War I controlled manufacturing quality by having machine operators or foremen conduct visual or manual inspections of all work, either in process or after production. Since this method consumed too much time and labor for production in large volumes, American factories experimented with statistical random sampling to test the average quality of lots by selecting a few components and comparing them with processing standards that management found acceptable. A lot passed if the average variation fell within certain limits, even though a lot might still contain a few defectives. If a lot was unacceptable, inspectors checked every piece and placed defectives in rework or reject piles, depending on the severity of the problem.

Walter A. Shewhart (1891-1967), a Bell Laboratories researcher with a PhD in physics, designed a control chart in 1924 in an attempt to distinguish the normal variation in manufacturing introduced by chance causes from the excessive variations introduced by assignable causes such as worker error or faulty machinery. This percent-defective table or histogram began the SQC movement as Western Electric and other American companies applied the Shewhart chart to sampling inspections. Shewhart's 1931 book, *Economic Control of the Quality of Manufactured Product*, was the first major treatment of the subject, although other American and British specialists made significant contributions to the field of statistical sampling during the 1920s and 1930s.[1]

To teach QC methods to the Japanese after World War II, GHQ recruited William E. Deming (1900-), a PhD in physics from Yale who had worked for the U.S. Department of Agriculture and the Census Bureau during 1927-1946 as an expert on statistical sampling. A private foundation established in Japan during 1946, the Japanese Union of Scientists and Engineers (Nihon Kagaku Gijutsu Renmei, abbreviated in English as JUSE), became a major center for the Japanese QC movement by cooperating with GHQ, hosting American specialists, offering lecture series and awards, providing Japanese consultants to private firms, and publishing the leading QC journals in Japan. JUSE's membership consisted of scientists and engineers from universities, government agencies, and business; many of the members had previously belonged to another organization, the Greater Japan Engineering Association (Dai Nippon Gijutsu Kai), which GHQ dissolved after World War II. The Japan Standards Association (Nihon Kikaku Kyōkai, abbreviated in English as JSA), established in 1945, and the Japan Management Association (Nihon Nōritsu Kyōkai, abbreviated in English as JMA), established in 1942, also introduced QC techniques through public lectures, although indirect links to Keidanren, the largest business organization in Japan, helped JUSE become an especially effective center for the Japanese QC movement.[2]

While GHQ started the Japanese QC movement by providing direct guidance to NEC (Nippon Denki) in 1948, the first public lectures on QC began in 1949 under the auspices of the Japan Management Association, the Japan Standards Association, and JUSE. JUSE also founded a QC research group in June 1949 to study SQC techniques systematically, and then began publishing a monthly journal in 1950, *Hinshitsu kanri* (Quality Control, 1983 circulation of 15,000). In addition, during 1950 JUSE hired Deming to speak in Tokyo, Osaka, Fukuoka, and Nagoya; 500 engineers and middle managers (department and section heads) responsible for manufacturing or inspection attended seminars to hear explanations of control charts and inspection sampling. Deming also had his basic text on QC methods translated into Japanese, and donated the royalties to JUSE to establish a QC award that JUSE named the Deming prize and gave out each year, beginning in 1951, to the company with the most outstanding QC program. The foundation made other awards for personal contributions to the QC movement and added a second company prize in 1957 for small and medium-size firms.[3]

Another reason why executives in Japanese companies became interested in QC was the efforts of the founder and first chairman of JUSE, Ishikawa Ichirō (1885-1970), who ranked among the most influential business leaders in the country. Ichirō, after graduating from the University of Tokyo's department of applied chemistry in 1909, taught at the university for several years and then entered Dai Nippon Fertilizer, a company that Aikawa Yoshisuke acquired during the mid-1930s and later renamed Nissan Chemical. Ichirō served as president of Nissan Chemical during 1941-1943, as head of the control association for the chemical industry from 1942 until the end of World War II, and then as the chairman of Keidanren from 1948 to 1956. In addition to starting JUSE's QC lecture series in 1949 and heading the committee that gave out the Deming prize, he managed Showa Denko after this chemical firm became involved in a notorious industrial pollution case in 1948, helped found the Japan National Broadcasting Corporation (NHK) in 1948, and sat on the boards of the Japan Standards Association from 1949 to 1965, and the Japan Atomic Energy Research Institute.[4]

Yet it was Ichirō's son, Kaoru (1915-), who made an even larger contribution to the QC movement in Japan after 1950 as a scholar, teacher, and private consultant affiliated with JUSE. Ishikawa Kaoru (hereafter referred to as Ishikawa) also studied chemistry at the University of Tokyo, received a doctorate in engineering in 1958, and taught at the university from 1947 to 1976, before becoming president of Tokyo's Musashi Institute of Technology in 1978. In addition to writing a series of texts during the 1950s and 1960s on QC methods, sampling, testing, and product variability which did much to introduce these subjects to the Japanese in their own language, he received an individual Deming prize in 1952 and served as the chief QC consultant to Nissan between the late 1950s and the early 1980s.[5]

After graduating from college in 1939, Ishikawa entered the navy and received an assignment to work at a Nissan Chemical subsidiary, where his father was chairman, to study coal liquification and explosives. He returned to the University of Tokyo after the war but was unable to continue his research and decided to study applied statistics for use in manufacturing. Ishikawa then joined JUSE's QC research group in Tokyo in 1949, even though he was unfamiliar with QC techniques, because GHQ had given JUSE access to the latest American manuals and textbooks on statistical methods. Ishikawa then began offering classes at the University of Tokyo during the early 1950s on applied statistics. His concern with quality problems in Japanese factories convinced him to undertake a broader study of QC techniques and then to become a consultant.[6]

The First Total QC Movement
Ishikawa Kaoru and other Japanese academics and managers went through several stages in developing a distinctive approach toward QC during the 1950s and 1960s. During the Occupation, they concentrated on the basic techniques that American experts emphasized—statistical sampling, control charts, and related methods to inspect lots and make adjustments in manufacturing processes or equipment to reduce defect levels. Then, as Japanese automakers and other firms learned how to use these tools by the mid-1950s, they began studying the ideas of American experts such as Deming and J.M. Juran, who stressed the need to expand QC programs to cover all manufacturing operations as a supplement to process control and production management, and to move the responsibility for controlling quality to workers on the shop floor and away from inspectors and QC staff engineers. During the second half of the 1950s and the early 1960s, other American experts, such as A.V. Feigenbaum, head of the QC department at General Electric, also

started to promote the concept of "total quality control" (TQC)—
which called for companies to devise operating frameworks to act
on statistical data to remedy QC problems and to extend QC programs to market research, product development, design, and procurement.[7]

While many American companies had trouble going beyond the
first stage, Japanese automakers started moving toward the concept
of "TQC" during the late 1950s and early 1960s. But a distinct
Japanese QC movement did not really begin until companies modified the statistical techniques and methods of controlling quality
that American firms practiced. Japanese consultants and academics
had no problem understanding American statistical techniques, although middle managers and workers who lacked specialized training in engineering or mathematics found them to be too difficult.
Deming had recognized the same problem in the United States and
encouraged Ishikawa and other Japanese experts, during a 1954 lecture tour, to teach the more complicated methods only to experts
with technical backgrounds and to show a few basic concepts to
everyone else. Few American managers attempted this type of program, however, because they had become accustomed to relying on
quality engineers and inspectors. But Japanese companies, faced with
processing, design, and material defects, and limited in their financial abilities to cover mistakes or to maintain large inspection departments, decided to try implementing some of the ideas that Japanese
professors and QC consultants had learned from Deming, Feigenbaum, and Juran.[8]

Ishikawa also arranged to have NHK's public radio station begin
broadcasting courses on simple QC techniques in 1956. These were
so successful that NHK offered a QC lecture series on its educational
television channel in 1957 and sold 110,000 copies of a text that
accompanied the series. JUSE followed this in 1960 with a two-
volume QC manual for factory foremen (*Shokuba kumi-chō no tame
no hinshitsu kanri tekisuto*), and devoted its March 1960 issue of
Quality Control to high-school teachers to help them educate students headed for blue-collar careers in the basic QC tenets. JUSE
then started another monthly journal in 1962 specifically for factory
workers and foremen, *Genba to QC* (The shop and QC), which it
renamed *FQC* in 1973 for *Factory Quality Control* (1983 circulation
of 135,000).[9]

Along with increasing the QC responsibilities of shop workers
came a tendency among Japanese firms not to rely on random sampling inspection as a valid test of quality. Inspection did not elim-

inate defects; it merely caught them after the fact. Defects were expensive to produce since they had to be fixed or discarded. Although statistical analyses were helpful if companies used the data to modify processing techniques or equipment to prevent defects, this application of SQC was easier to explain in theory than to implement in the factory, since most workers lacked training in statistical methods.

Japanese managers in the automobile industry who switched to sampling inspection during the Occupation found that workers still produced defects, and that better manufacturing quality did not solve problems stemming from faulty designs or materials. Recognition during the 1960s that original equipment manufacturers had to improve the components manufactured in house and procured from suppliers was another major step in the development of QC in Japan because it brought departments not responsible for manufacturing—market research, product planning, product design, prototype design, pre-production testing, and procurement—directly into formal QC programs.[10]

This broad approach to QC was built on the ideas of American QC experts, although Japanese firms experimented with these concepts, and Japanese consultants made several important modifications. For instance, when Feigenbaum used the term *total quality control* in a fall 1956 issue of the *Harvard Business Review* and in a 1961 book, *Total Quality Control: Engineering and Management* (translated into Japanese the same year), he argued that QC programs should focus on defect prevention rather than inspection, and that managers should make quality the responsibility of the worker. He also encouraged American firms to set up TQC systems that involved all departments and aimed at satisfying consumer definitions of quality. Yet he found that his interpretation of QC did not catch on in the United States because few American managers were ready to commit themselves to comprehensive QC programs. Most were reluctant to act on statistical data to make substantive improvements in quality and hesitated to take corrective measures such as to reject entire production lots that were below standard if doing so would shut down a factory, place tighter controls on design and testing before production, or rebuild and replace machinery on a regular basis to upgrade processing technology.[11]

Managers in Japanese companies also had little or no experience with QC concepts and methods prior to the postwar Occupation, and many were reluctant to devote much time or effort to QC lectures and formal programs until the 1960s. The majority of Japanese who attended JUSE's QC seminars during the 1950s were production engineers and inspection department specialists.[12] Like Deming, however, Feigenbaum had more impact in Japan than in the United States. Ishikawa recalled that he and other Japanese consultants not only read Feigenbaum's book and articles but they adopted the term *TQC* during the early 1960s while encouraging Japanese companies to expand their QC programs into non-manufacturing areas.

Yet even Japanese managers had difficulty implementing Feigenbaum's ideas because, according to Ishikawa, he still relied too much on specialized statistical techniques and left the problem of enforcing QC programs to engineers, without suggesting ways to involve all employees simply and effectively. Japanese companies and consultants had struggled throughout the 1950s to improve quality only to find that a few QC experts and lectures did not change product quality or the overall operations of a firm. This experience convinced them that obscure statistical methods or abstract discussions of QC concepts were useless insofar as most factory workers or managers were concerned. The Japanese thus felt a need to experiment with different QC techniques; rather than abandon the concept of total QC, however, Ishikawa coined another term in 1968, *company-wide QC*, to emphasize that all employees should participate in QC programs and that companies should rely less on QC staff functions and add to QC programs methods for managing and coordinating cost control, production management, inventory control, market analysis, and design.[13]

While government protection from foreign competition reduced the need to improve quality and vehicle performance during the 1950s and 1960s, the prospect of large exports stimulated Japanese automakers to develop better QC and production management systems. The small scales of production in the domestic automobile industry, and more flexible job specifications, also made it easier to experiment with QC programs prior to 1970, although it was significant as well that Japanese automakers did not switch to mass-production techniques which probably would have eliminated the advantages of smaller manufacturing or procurement lots than were common in the United States. Instead, they added capacity by subcontracting more components and final assembly, and building more factories of easily manageable scales, containing only a few thousand employees each. At the same time, Japanese automakers tightened up process and inventory controls while increasing the responsibilities of workers and raising levels of automation in manufacturing and inspection.

Japanese QC: Characteristics and Explanations
One of the primary features of Japanese QC was its lack of reliance on formal inspectors or quality staff. In fact, while QC and inspection departments were relatively large in the United States, even during the early 1980s, since they had extensive responsibilities for testing quality and implementing corrective measures, Japanese automakers started reducing the number of inspection and QC personnel by the early 1960s. In the mid-1950s, Nissan and Toyota also gave employees the authority to stop assembly lines when they noticed defectives or errors, and began stressing that each process had to work directly for the next process, with workers checking continuously for defects. Fewer buffer stocks than in the United States, and closer coordination between different processes and with suppliers, eliminated large margins for error and contributed to the development of manufacturing systems that caught defects in process or prevented them entirely, with a minimum of inspection and QC staff. High levels of subcontracting, a major source of poor quality in the 1950s and 1960s, eventually became an asset as suppliers evolved into specialized producers of one or two components manufactured at levels of quality that more integrated automakers, such as General Motors and Ford, had trouble matching.[14] Once suppliers became reliable sources of components by the 1970s, Nissan, Toyota, and other Japanese automakers made suppliers do most of their own inspections, further reducing the need for original equipment manufacturers to maintain large inspection or QC departments.

During the 1960s, QC staffs in the leading Japanese automakers shifted their main functions from assisting inspection departments to coordinating training programs, monitoring progress in different factories and departments, guiding suppliers, and conducting the more technical quality tests. By the early 1980s, Japanese automobile manufacturers had developed a reputation for superior quality in manufacturing and design while the average American assembly plant, according to a recent consultant's study, had 2.3 times more workers assigned to QC (including inspection) departments, as well as to other functional areas, than Japanese factories with identical capacities.[15] Furthermore, even while conducting many of their own inspections, Japanese employees did enough maintenance, janitorial, and other work to reduce overall personnel levels in assembly, supervision, production scheduling, and materials control to less than half of those in comparable American facilities (Table 79).

Along with this movement of inspection functions from company

Table 79: Assembly Plant Comparison: Japan-United States, ca. 1980 (employees)

Function	Japan	United States	Ratio Japan = 1.0
Quality Control	156	359	2.3
(inspection)	(120)	(302)	(2.5)
(emissions)	(26)	(37)	(1.4)
(engineering)	(10)	(20)	(2.0)
Production Control	95	310	3.3
(scheduling)	(11)	(66)	(6.0)
(materials)	(56)	(216)	(3.9)
Product Engineering	22	6	0.3
Manufacturing Engineering	132	411	3.1
(maintenance)	(62)	(207)	(3.3)
(janitors)	(10)	(114)	(11.4)
Production	1324	2640	2.0
(painting)	(250)	(421)	(1.7)
(assembly)	(641)	(1603)	(2.5)
Management Staff	33	132	4.0
Grand Total	1762	3885[a]	2.2
Hours Per Small Car	14	31	2.2

Source: Harbour and Associates, Inc., "Comparison of Japanese Car Assembly Plant Located in Japan and U.S. Car Assembly Plant Located in the U.S.," pp. 70-72.

Notes: [a]Total includes 27 union officials.

Figures in parenthesis are examples of subcategories and do not always equal the totals for the individual major functions.

staff to factory workers during the 1960s, Japanese automakers began paying increasing attention to how consumers viewed quality. Deming and Feigenbaum had suggested, in the 1950s, that companies determine quality specifications according to what customers wanted at a given price. But many large American companies tended to design products according to what they wanted to sell, rather than according to what surveys indicated consumers wanted. Managers usually measured quality by the statistical conformity of manufactured products to engineering specifications, or equated improvements in quality with reductions of "inherent variability" in manufacturing operations to less than specified limits.[16] Americans introduced this concept of "quality" into Japan when GHQ set up industrial standards for finished goods, materials, and engineering during the Occupation, and the Japanese government adopted these standards in 1949 through formal legislation.[17] Japanese companies followed GHQ's guidelines to get military contracts but, after the Korean War, they switched to more fluid specifications that reflected the limited ability of Japanese consumers to pay for quality. Managers also wanted to modify in-house engineering standards every few years to reflect changes in market requirements and national income.

Their experiences after World War II with American procurement caused many Japanese managers to dislike fixed industrial standards or parts specifications based on rigorous statistical limits. Automakers in particular did not have the funds to produce vehicles of a higher quality than domestic consumers needed or that did not aim at a clearly defined market. Even during the 1950s, increasing competition between Nissan and Toyota encouraged design engineers to incorporate costs in quality decisions and to cooperate more closely with market research departments than they had in the past. As Japanese automakers became better able to distinguish design quality from inspection and then from process control, they created systems, under the prodding of consultants such as Ishikawa, that treated QC as a continual process of revising product specifications to suit changing consumer preferences.

Both Nissan and Toyota combined market research, product design, and testing in their QC programs during the 1950s and early 1960s as they developed new car models for domestic and export sales. Toyota especially benefited from Toyota Motor Sales' surveys of dealers and taxi drivers before it put out the 1954 Crown and the 1957 Corona. Export models also required extensive revisions after market research and road tests in the United States revealed that specifications design engineers thought were adequate would not appeal to American consumers. Nissan and Toyota then redesigned their cars for export, even before this was profitable, by fitting them with larger engines, 4-speed transmissions, and left-hand drive.[18]

Ishikawa offered several reasons why Japanese firms managed to introduce broader QC programs than in the United States while "failing" to adopt the QC practices or staff department functions that appeared to work in American companies. Most important, he believed, was Japan's weak tradition of specialization in industry. Japanese companies never felt comfortable with the Taylor system of creating a rigid set of rules for job routines to distinguish responsibilities among workers and between labor and management. The absence in Japan, after the mid-1950s, of powerful industrial unions, which enforced job classifications in the United States, also allowed managers to rotate employees freely and to assign them multiple tasks. Furthermore, the "vertical" character of personal relationships in Japanese society, reproduced in companies, made it seem natural for managers to make QC primarily a "line" rather than a "staff" function, and to extend the responsibility to maintain quality to the factory level while reducing the roles of staff specialists.

Other cultural or social characteristics appear to have aided Ishikawa's efforts to develop effective QC programs in Japan. High educational levels, and good mathematics instruction in secondary schools, made it easy to teach basic concepts and simple statistical techniques to all workers. The small number of graduate schools in Japan allowed firms to train engineers and managers as they saw fit. Many employees also stayed with one company for their entire careers; managers responded by training them extensively and treating worker education as a profitable investment, while "life-time" employees usually applied themselves to acquiring skills for the firm more seriously than transient workers did. Ishikawa also felt that life-time employment, and the emphasis on seniority rather than performance to determine wages, were other positive factors in Japanese companies because QC programs seemed to work best when employees had motivations other than money alone.

Yet Ishikawa believed the Japanese would not have produced such effective QC programs without having devoted more time and effort to them than most foreign companies. While American and European firms adopted formal QC or "zero-defect" programs during the early 1960s, these focused on process control and the elimination of defects in manufacturing, and consisted mainly of brief training sessions lasting from 5 to 10 days, with little or no follow up. Several Japanese organizations began offering extensive QC courses as early as 1949. JUSE's basic training program, for instance, consumed 5 days per month for 6 months and included both classroom lectures and factory visits. JUSE consultants then recommended procedures so that companies could set up in-house QC training programs for new employees and for other workers to continue studying.[19]

Japanese consultants and managers also became convinced, during the 1960s, that no QC measures would achieve significant results without the enthusiastic support of top management. Ishikawa came to this conclusion after realizing that Matsushita and Toyota, the companies he felt had the best QC programs in Japan between the mid-1960s and the early 1980s, had executives who maintained their enthusiasm for two decades and effectively transmitted their commitment to subordinates.[20] And, even though competition to increase sales was probably the underlying motivation behind the promotion of QC programs, managers also worked toward the Deming prize—which Nissan won in 1960, Nihon Radiator (in the small and medium-size firm category) and Nippon Denso in 1961, Toyota in 1965, and Toyota Auto Body in 1970. This encouraged senior executives and entire companies to take an active interest in QC programs because JUSE and the Japanese media publicized the awards nationally.

To be eligible for the Deming prize, a firm had to apply to JUSE, explain its QC policies and programs, and present evidence of progress in each department. JUSE then sent an examination committee to interview executives and employees, and to visit factories. Members of the QC research group staffed the committees, although consultants working with particular companies did not participate in the examinations of those firms. For example, Ishikawa, since he worked with Nissan, was on the committee that visited Toyota in 1965, while Mizuno Shigeru, a professor at the Tokyo Institute of Technology (Tōkyō Kōgaku Daigaku) and the leading QC consultant for Toyota, was a member of the group that examined Nissan in 1961.[21]

The prize committees relied on check lists and gave out awards according to point totals. While they focused on process control in manufacturing during the early 1950s, JUSE gradually added to its criteria and required companies to implement comprehensive QC programs to win the award.[22] During the early 1980s, the Deming check list contained ten categories: company policy toward QC and the application of statistical methods; organization and operation of the QC program, including QC circles (called quality circles in the United States); training and diffusion of QC methods within the company and among suppliers; collection, dissemination, and application of information affecting QC; analysis of QC problems; standardization practices; production management and cost control; quality assurance measures, from product development to safety, process improvement, inspection, procurement, and servicing; programs to measure the effectiveness of QC procedures and to deal with results; and long-term company planning, in particular that relating to the future promotion of QC.[23]

QC Circles

The Deming prize criteria reflected the relatively minor role that QC circles played in quality-improvement programs, despite the considerable attention they drew during the 1970s and early 1980s in the United States and Europe as one of the key elements in the Japanese approach to QC. Japanese managers and QC experts, and organizations such as JUSE, added to the mystique surrounding QC circles by encouraging the impression that these groups sprang up "spontaneously" as Japanese workers came together in the early 1960s to discuss quality problems and solutions.[24] While some workers expressed interest in QC on their own initiative, the idea to form QC circles, and even the name for these groups, came from Ishikawa and co-editors of JUSE's monthly journal for foremen.

The editorial committee for the journal, *Genba to QC (FQC)*, of which Ishikawa was chairman, coined the term *QC circle* in May 1962 to promote the shift of QC and inspection responsibilities to the shop floor and the improvement of company methods for personnel administration and worker training. They believed it would be possible to involve workers further because the Japanese public had already received several years of general education in QC concepts and basic techniques through the NHK radio and television programs. JUSE started the journal to continue this education by presenting simplified explanations of QC methods and sample problems or reports on results in specific companies. But the editors worried that foremen were unaccustomed to studying after they left school, and felt that foremen, and regular employees, would be more likely to study if they met in groups of ten or so, perhaps once a week or twice a month, to discuss the journal or specific problems in the shop. In addition, the committee hoped that groups would encourage workers to apply the QC methods discussed in the journal and JUSE manuals, especially those involving statistics, in cases where individuals might be reluctant to experiment with new techniques on their own. It was common in Japanese schools for students to organize study groups to prepare for exams; even Ishikawa and other professors and engineers had participated in a group during the late 1940s and the 1950s to research American SQC techniques. Why not have study groups in the factory?[25]

In 1962, Matsushita was the first Japanese company to establish QC circles. Toyota followed the next year and had around 50 by the end of 1963, when JUSE set up a "QC Circle Headquarters" to register groups throughout the country and to manage an annual convention. Local branches of the headquarters, organized in 1964, assisted companies that wanted to form QC circles by giving lectures and seminars, and providing materials and films. While total registrations throughout Japan increased from 215 in 1963 to 3702 in 1965 and then to over 180,000 by 1984, average membership per circle rose from 3.8 workers in 1963 to 15.5 in 1965, before declining to 8.5 in 1984 (Table 80).

Despite the reputation of QC circles in Japan and elsewhere, and his role in inventing them, Ishikawa admitted that they did little to improve quality without the support of a comprehensive "quality assurance" program throughout a firm and its supply network.[26] Nissan and Toyota officials also conceded that QC circles functioned primarily to increase employee participation in company operations and to boost morale by allowing employees to work in groups to solve problems.[27] Nissan claimed, nonetheless, that QC circle activities saved the company 40 billion yen ($160,000,000) between 1978 and 1984 (see Table 80). This worked out to about $5000 per circle, an amount typical of other firms in Japan, according to a JUSE survey.[28]

Additional Stimulus: The 1969 Recalls
Increasing the responsibilities of workers on the shop floor still did not solve quality problems at suppliers; it took major government recalls in Japan during 1969 to persuade Japanese automakers to devote adequate attention to identifying and correcting quality or safety problems in procured components before production, without attempting to solve them merely with superficial changes in manufacturing or inspection procedures.[29] The United States Congress

also contributed to the development of QC in Japan by passing safety legislation in 1966 that led to the discovery of 411 defects or hazards and the recall of 13,500,000 vehicles by mid-1968. Japan's automakers fared surprisingly well in the American recall since nearly all of the cited vehicles were Volkswagen, General Motors, Ford, and Chrysler products. But the Japanese Ministry of Transport set up a similar system during 1968-1969 and then announced in June 1969 that it had identified defects in 2,500,000 cars, trucks, and motorcycles made in Japan. While the Ministry cited 12 companies, Toyota, Honda, and Nissan accounted for almost 75 percent of the defective vehicles. Toyota had the dubious distinction of leading the industry with 28.4 percent of the recalled vehicles, compared to 23.6 percent for Honda and 21.5 percent for Nissan (Table 81).

Companies traced most of the problems to suppliers. More than 500,000 Toyota Coronas, in addition to 350,000 Daihatsu and Mazda cars, suffered from brake-pipe corrosion, while the Toyota Crown and Corolla models had defective front-brake hose fixtures and floor shift levers. Nissan models, including the Datsun Bluebird and two mid-size car lines acquired from Prince in 1966, had faulty carburetor and fuel-pump fixtures, defective pedal rods, and brake-fluid leaks. Overall, brakes accounted for approximately 30 percent of the 58 defects, steering wheels 16 percent, power-drive trains and suspension systems 12 percent each, and body components 8 percent. Causes of the defects fell into four categories: design (39 percent), assembly (23), processing (22), and materials (16).

Recalls in the United States and Japan did not necessarily reflect a decline in quality, since many resulted from increased safety and quality standards, and government requirements that automakers notify customers of defects and offer to repair them. Nor was cost-cutting always a factor. Toyota's main difficulty, for instance, was with a lead plating that a supplier placed on brake pipes; this cost as much as zinc or tin platings that other Japanese firms used but proved to be less resistant to corrosion. Honda's recalls all came from brake hoses provided by one of two suppliers of the component in Japan, and this firm happened to use a faulty ozone process.

Yet some of the defects indicated that Japanese automakers had pushed suppliers to reduce costs too rapidly. As an increasing number of firms entered the domestic car market during the 1960s, original equipment manufacturers required subcontractors to lower prices approximately twice a year, often regardless of their expenses. Several problems stemmed from the substitution of inferior materials

Table 80: QC Circle Statistics, 1963-1984

	Japan		Toyota		Nissan					
Year[a]	Number	Members[b]	Number	Members	Number	Members	Participation[c]	Resolved Themes	Total Savings[d]	Savings Per Circle[d]
1963	215	3.8	—	—	0	—	—	—	—	—
1964	1,015	14.8	50	N.A.	0	—	—	—	—	—
1965	3,702	15.5	78	"	0	—	—	—	—	—
1966	5,593	13.6	150	"	0	—	—	—	—	—
1967	9,334	12.3	169	"	38	N.A.	N.A.	N.A.	N.A.	N.A.
1968	13,609	12.2	811	"	290	"	"	"	"	"
1969	20,894	12.1	1,410	"	815	"	"	"	"	"
1970	28,041	12.0	1,842	"	2,728	6.7	65	0.3	400	.147
1971	37,475	11.3	2,459	"	3,256	6.8	76	0.4	500	.154
1972	46,222	10.9	3,038	"	3,462	7.1	80	0.4	530	.153
1973	54,034	10.6	3,257	"	3,701	7.1	86	0.7	500	.135
1974	59,934	10.3	3,365	"	4,088	7.2	87	0.6	520	.127

Year										
1975	68,559	10.1	4,195	"	4,125	7.3	89	0.8	700	.170
1976	75,276	10.0	3,458	"	4,215	7.5	92	1.5	1,030	.244
1977	79,204	9.9	3,984	"	4,007	8.2	96	2.4	1,370	.342
1978	86,482	9.7	3,925	"	4,068	8.6	97	4.1	3,270	.804
1979	95,690	9.5	4,159	"	4,161	8.7	97	7.4	5,260	1.264
1980	104,155	9.4	4,308	"	4,162	8.5	99	20.2	4,720	1.134
1981	116,686	9.2	4,644	"	4,180	8.7	99	40.6	8,100	1.938
1982	133,033	9.0	4,968	6.3	4,153	8.9	99	14.1	4,730	1.139
1983	154,654	8.8	5,283	6.5	4,132	9.1	99	4.7	6,460	1.563
1984	180,684	8.5	5,850	5.9	4,064	9.2	99	5.4	7,530	1.853

Sources: QC Circle Headquarters (JUSE); Public Relations Departments of Nissan and Toyota; Nissan Motor, Quality Control Department, "QC sākuru katsudō no ayumi" and "Data File 1984"; Toyota Jidōsha, Kōhō handobukku.

Notes: ªFigures are as of April of the listed year, except for 1963-1965 in the Japan column, which indicate totals for December, July, and June, respectively.

ᵇAverage members per circle.

ᶜPercent of factory workers.

ᵈ1,000,000 yen, in nominal values.

Table 81: Japanese Recalls of June 1969

Manufacturer	Defects	Vehicles	%	Nameplates	Type of Defects
Toyota	10	698,513	28.4	Corona (530,000) Crown Corolla	brake-pipe corrosion front-brake hose fixtures floor shift lever
Nissan	11	528,403	21.5	Bluebird (220,000) Gloria Skyline	carburetor and fuel-pump fixtures pedal rod brake-fluid leak
Honda	9	578,617	23.6	N360 (130,000) LN360 (50,000)	front-brake hose "
Daihatsu	5	194,987	7.9	Fellow (120,000) Hi-Jet	brake-pipe corrosion "
Toyo Kogyo	1	150,812	6.1	Carol	brake-pipe corrosion
Fuji H.I.	3	96,887	3.9	Subaru Samba Subaru 1000	steering design carburetor fuel leak
Suzuki	5	69,264	2.8	Fronty 360	heater hose

		Units	%	Models	Defects
Isuzu	3	49,737	2.0	Florian / TX Truck	floor shift lever / weak rear-axle shaft
Mitsubishi	5	35,302	1.4	Colt 1000F / Colt 1500	front-wheel suspension components / steering subassembly
Aichi Machine	1	31,000	1.3	Koni	front-brake hose
Hino	3	18,868	0.8	KM300 Truck	battery wiring
Nissan Diesel	2	4,154	0.2	Large Truck / Large Bus	propellar-shaft bearing / battery-charging equipment wiring
Total	58	2,456,544	100.0		brakes (30%), engines (22), steering (16), power drive (12), suspension (12), body (8); design (39), assembly (23), processing (22), materials (16)

Source: Tōyō keizai, 28 June 1969, No. 3479, pp. 61-62.

Note: Vehicles refer to the number of recalled units; % indicates what portion of the total number of recalled vehicles each manufacturer was responsible for.

or changes from arc welding to less expensive spot welding, or to reductions in the number of spot welds. Other defects reflected insufficient testing for long-term endurance, especially in extremely hot or cold climates and in areas that used rock salt in the winter.

Industry analysts writing in the Japanese media, and government officials in MITI and the Ministry of Transport, accused Toyota, Nissan, Honda, and the entire motor vehicle industry of giving priority to increasing sales through lower prices. This provoked a debate over the need to balance safety with cost reductions, although company engineers stressed the impossibility of producing a vehicle completely free of defects at any price, and noted that consumers' desires for cars requiring a minimum amount of maintenance made it difficult to offer assurances on quality and safety. Yet the June 1969 recalls cost the industry between $14,000,000 and $17,000,000 just for repairs, production delays, and customer notifications. Rather than oppose the government through extensive litigation, or damage their reputations any further, companies quickly set up repair programs and corrected most of the defects before exporting cars to the United States. Some defective vehicles reached Korea and Australia, although during the 1970s Japanese automakers instituted measures to avoid a repeat of June 1969, which proved to be so effective that the next largest recall in any one year through mid-1983 affected only 160,000 vehicles (in 1977).[30] In addition, the recall rate for Japanese cars sold in the United States during 1976-1980 was merely one-third that of American automobiles.[31]

While nearly all of Japan's automakers and components producers had established QC measures by the late 1970s that practically eliminated major defects in manufacturing or design, not all firms in the industry were equally adept at identifying consumer preferences and incorporating these into design, or at maintaining a high level of enthusiasm among workers and managers. QC programs also tended to vary according to the attitudes of top executives, different systems of production management, and occasional discrepancies in the quality of procured components. While these differences also accounted for variations in the steps managers took to organize their QC programs, when companies won Deming prizes or fared well in recalls, word spread quickly and firms imitated one another; this helped spread the best practices throughout the industry. The precise sequence and timing varied among the leading Japanese automakers and their subsidiaries, although QC programs in the Japanese automobile industry went through at least ten stages of development between 1950 and the early 1970s:

(1) Study of American statistical methods for sampling inspection that GHQ promoted for vendors of goods for the U.S. military.

(2) Gradual shift of QC activities from inspection, which attempted to catch defectives after production, to process control, which tried to eliminate defectives in manufacturing.

(3) Establishment of QC staff departments and the teaching of QC concepts and techniques to middle managers, engineers, and production workers.

(4) Additional training of employees through in-house programs supplemented by a national effort to educate the Japanese public, beginning with high-school teachers and students, in basic QC concepts and techniques.

(5) Reduced usage of lot inspections by random sampling and rejection of the idea of an "acceptable quality level" that permitted the existence of a few defectives within a lot; and a return to the pre-1950 practice of inspecting all components. To accomplish 100-percent inspection, companies installed automatic devices as well as simplified QC techniques, taught these methods to all production workers, and added inspection duties to the job routines of production workers while reducing the size of staff inspection and QC departments.

(6) Formal shift of responsibility for manufacturing quality from staff departments for inspection or QC to the factory level, focusing initially on foremen and then increasingly on QC circles, which also assisted management in training workers and maintaining discipline and morale, in addition to solving problems in manufacturing or design quality, maintenance, and safety.

(7) National competition among companies to improve their QC programs and to achieve at least intra-industry recognition for QC excellence, which the Deming prize symbolized.

(8) Shift in the focus of QC activities from process control to eliminating defects in design or materials, and to guaran-

teeing customer satisfaction by closely integrating market research, pre-production testing, product planning and development, procurement, and customer servicing.

(9) Shift of design quality from standards geared toward Japanese consumers to international markets, especially the United States.

(10) Intensive instruction in QC methods to all suppliers and insistence that they provide components free from defects, which eliminated the need for original equipment manufacturers to conduct lengthy vendor inspections.

THE NISSAN GROUP

To attract customers during the 1950s, while Toyota relied on the industry's largest distribution network and the rapid introduction of new models at low prices, Nissan became known for automated manufacturing and engineering quality. Part of Nissan's reputation resulted from a history of associating with foreign companies; part also came from establishing the first QC program in the Japanese automobile industry and from becoming the first automaker to win the Deming prize. Nissan's reception of the award in 1960 was significant for the entire industry, because product quality among domestic automakers had been poor in previous years, allowing manufacturers of steel, electrical equipment, chemicals, and textile machinery to dominate the prize throughout the 1950s.[32] For Nissan to lead its domestic competitors in QC was not unusual, however, since company engineers had consistently looked to the United States for the latest production technology. QC was an American invention; as a matter of course, Nissan took an interest in the subject and began to study QC techniques during the Occupation.[33] In contrast, Toyota preferred to concentrate on production management and did not devote an equal amount of attention to QC methods until the 1960s.

Sampling Inspection and Process Control
In 1949-1950, Nissan executives set the goal of raising manufacturing quality to American standards to sell trucks to the U.S. Army and to prepare for exports.[34] Manufacturing quality was already on the decline at Nissan after World War II because it had to spread out production in several small locations. As part of an attempt to correct this, company managers sent two workers from the Yokohama factory's inspection department, Asano Shūzō and Yamazaki

Hirohisa, to the JUSE and JSA lectures in 1949, before experimenting with American sampling inspection techniques in the Atsugi plant beginning in June 1950. Atsugi was a good test facility because it was small and made only gears and screws; it also produced more defectives than other factories and thus contributed to quality problems throughout Nissan's assembly plants. The new inspection methods, combined with higher precision standards, replaced more casual checks of components by Nissan's inspection department and succeeded in reducing the number of defectives coming out of Atsugi within a few months.[35]

The Yokohama factory also had difficulty meeting quality standards set by the U.S. Army. In particular, after manufacturing a set of rear engine-support brackets that GHQ returned, Nissan managers decided to follow the advice of American quality experts working for the Army who suggested that Nissan not rely only on limit gauges for inspection but, instead, adopt statistical lot sampling throughout the company. This incident also convinced the members of Yokohama's inspection department to found a QC group in 1951 to study sampling inspection techniques more intensively, even though the head of the department, Ōkura Tsutomu, later found the statistical methods too difficult for anyone "except scholars."[36] Other Nissan managers realized that American QC techniques had not reduced manufacturing defects; Atsugi's inspection department had merely improved its ability to catch defectives after production.[37] But, since sampling inspection lowered the number of substandard items that came out of the plant, management had Yokohama's machine processing department adopt the same procedures, with a similar result of fewer complaints about defectives within a few months.

The improvements at Atsugi and Yokohama persuaded Nissan to set up a QC office in Yokohama's inspection department during 1954 to work in conjunction with branch offices in the inspection departments at Atsugi and Yoshiwara and to coordinate quality testing and control procedures in all company factories.[38] Asano and Yamazaki took up new posts in the QC office, which was now responsible for assigning tasks to factories and manufacturing departments, providing guidance in worker training, establishing QC regulations and standards, compiling QC manuals, conducting quality tests and research, and recording inspection data. The office also organized a series of lectures during 1954-1955 to introduce QC concepts and techniques to all Nissan's department and section heads, foremen, engineers, and procurement department staff. While QC staff members gave most of the lectures, to discuss "QC thinking," quality testing and planning, and the use of control charts and sampling inspection techniques, they brought in outside lecturers such as J.M. Juran (July 1954), William Deming (December 1955), several JUSE experts, and Nishibori Eisaburō (1903-), a consultant with the Japan Management Association (JMA) and a 1936 PhD from Kyoto University, who had worked for Toshiba during the late 1930s and studied QC techniques at RCA during 1939, before advising Nissan on its QC program during 1955-1956.

Although their main QC activity during the first half of the 1950s was to compile approximately 1000 control charts to determine processing limits for components manufactured in house, Nissan's factories and manufacturing departments also formed committees to monitor progress in reducing defectives, discuss problems related to QC, and advise the QC staff on how to solve them. The QC office and factory inspection staff took samples and conducted quality tests, and cooperated with production engineers to determine quality specifications, processing limits, and standard values. Foremen, or other workers that supervisors in each manufacturing department designated to take charge of QC measures, recorded the inspection data, compiled the control charts, and posted them in the shops. Other foremen and workers responsible for analyzing the data made adjustments in machinery or processes and then took a second set of measurements, drew up new control charts, and made additional adjustments if necessary. A QC council that met weekly in each section brought together the personnel (usually engineers) in charge of control charts, the section chief, other engineers involved in QC procedures, and representatives from each factory's inspection department. A QC liaison committee, consisting of members from the section's QC council and the QC staff office, oversaw worker training.[39]

According to Yamashita Yoshitaka, the head of Nissan's QC office during the mid-1950s (which also directed the publication of a special issue on QC in the company's technical journal during February 1956), most workers and their superiors did not understand how to use techniques such as control charts. Still he felt that the charts, and the entire QC effort, had made workers more conscious of quality and defects in manufacturing.[40] Prior to 1950, Nissan had separated inspection from manufacturing; factories focused on production, and inspection departments determined if components met standards. Even though inspectors checked all parts and subassemblies, lax standards and procedures allowed too many defectives to pass through the system until the U.S. Army convinced Nissan during the Korean War to adopt statistical sampling for in-house manufacturing and procurement.[41] The new QC program brought manufacturing departments directly into the inspection process because they had to cooperate with inspectors and QC staff members to draw up control charts and to make adjustments in production. The application of statistical sampling, with higher standards and better process controls, enabled Nissan to cut its overall defectives rate in half during 1954-1955.[42]

Nissan's procurement staff also started to offer guidance to subcontractors on QC during 1953-1954, but only the larger firms with adequate standardization procedures, and the ability to invest more in new equipment or to take other measures to improve their operations, responded well. Most of Nissan's 50 main suppliers in 1956 had between 20 and 50 employees; and, although firms of this size accounted for just 30 percent of procured components, they produced a greater share of defects. Nissan's insistence that all suppliers lower prices on a regular basis even caused quality to decline at many of the smaller suppliers, forcing Nissan to set up a special program for small firms in the summer of 1955 to teach them how to use control charts, statistical inspection, and modern accounting methods. Yet managers still had difficulty enforcing quality standards after discontinuing the program, prompting the head of Nissan's purchasing department, Director Hori Kōjirō, to threaten suppliers that did not match American firms in quality while reducing prices with a loss of orders from Nissan.[43]

Even sales personnel began participating in the QC program. Nissan established a market research section during March 1955 in the domestic sales department which contained several statistics experts. Although their job focused on market surveys, the company also used them for quality testing and to assist the QC office and design engineers in providing information on consumer preferences for quality specifications and pricing. Nissan had previously conducted few consumer surveys and had used market research to aid sales rather than to formulate design standards.[44]

Yet the managers responsible for Nissan's QC program, while expressing broad goals and even some ideas that would later become central to successful QC efforts, continued to focus on statistical measures that few workers and suppliers were able to utilize effectively. One such manager was Igarashi Tadashi, who headed the QC program in Nissan from 1953, when President Asahara promoted him to company director and head of the Yokohama plant, until 1977. For instance, Igarashi noted in a preface to the 1956 issue on QC in Nissan's technical journal that "the consumer must determine design quality" and that manufacturing must meet this demand with a level of quality that is economical in terms of retail prices and production costs. This comment reflected the idea that QC was more than just an extension of inspection, although Igarashi subsequently qualified his statement by admitting that, in practice, he preferred to limit the objectives of Nissan's QC program to developing a "statistical way of thinking"—the same approach that most American firms followed during the 1950s and 1960s.[45]

Yamashita, in 1956, also showed a desire to extend QC measures beyond inspection when he made a careful distinction between "general QC" and "statistical QC," and asserted that general QC should be thought of as "quality management," organized as an activity throughout the firm. In addition, he cautioned workers not to equate quality control with statistical measurements. But Yamashita still maintained that establishing a broad QC program for the entire company was merely an "ideal" toward which Nissan should work; and he argued, along with his boss, Igarashi, that workers should concentrate on developing a more "statistical way of thinking" while learning to use control charts, frequency distributions, sampling inspection, and variance analysis.[46]

Broadening the QC Effort

A lack of coordination among company departments and functions, a dependency on QC staff and inspection personnel, and limited programs at suppliers, continued to hinder Nissan's QC efforts throughout the 1950s and to restrict its effectiveness outside of inspection and manufacturing. Not until President Kawamata organized a planning committee in February 1958, consisting of managing directors and higher executives, with special subcommittees for export policy, cost reduction, and procurement, did Nissan make a serious attempt to diffuse a "QC way of thinking" among all employees, to establish a system to carry out QC functions in several departments, and to organize procedures to check on the company's progress. The planning committee began Nissan's second QC effort in 1959 by adopting a new program specifically to prepare for the Deming prize examination, which consisted of inspections of company factories and offices, and questions that JUSE experts directed randomly at employees. Nissan also asked Ishikawa Kaoru to be its chief quality consultant.[47]

According to Matsuzaki, Nissan decided to rely more on outside experts in 1959-1960 than in previous years to distinguish QC training from the superior-subordinate relationships within the firm and to make it appear less obligatory. The QC office began by arranging an extensive lecture series between April and July 1959 to instruct factory section chiefs and foremen, and then other section heads, assistant managers, engineers, and selected office staff, in the latest QC concepts and techniques. Since all managers and workers had to be prepared for the prize committee, the Deming examination motivated everyone to study. QC instruction and self-study then became a mandatory part of work routines for all Nissan employees. The QC office divided the company into 30 groups for the classes and lectures it conducted throughout 1959, and supplemented these with literature on the program and basic QC methods. The planning committee also established a QC committee in June 1959, headed by Managing Director Igarashi, to oversee QC policy and to coordinate solutions to QC problems. The QC committee then formed subcommittees for standardization, quality assurance, and manufacturing control to study specific quality problems and to recommend solutions.

President Kawamata played an important role by setting priorities for the new QC effort in a policy statement on 4 September 1959. First, he noted that product quality had to conform to the market and consider price as well as quality. He also criticized the company's previous lack of initiative in product development. Second, he declared that Nissan would shift its standards for product quality from the domestic market to the international market. Third, to tie in product design more closely with product planning and market research, he authorized the establishment of joint conferences to coordinate these functions and announced an expansion of the research department so that it could play a larger role in product development. Fourth, he called for increased standardization in design, manufacturing, and procurement, an area that he felt Nissan had seriously neglected during the 1950s. Fifth, Kawamata directed each department to set up a system for "quality assurance" to control and guarantee quality in design and to handle customer complaints. While he still wanted inspection to serve as the main control on quality, he called for a better exchange of information among departments to ease the burden on inspection and to improve the level

of technology throughout the company. Sixth, he ordered a contin-
uation of employee instruction in QC methods and concepts to raise
"quality consciousness" and to promote "the correct way of QC
thinking." Finally, Kawamata asked all departments to cooperate in
implementing these objectives and to follow "the principle of giving
priority to the next process."

Implementation of Kawamata's program took several forms. Nissan held QC conferences for middle managers between September
and December 1959, set up new manufacturing standards by January
1960, and organized a conference in March 1960 to examine customer complaints about new models. Outside consultants conducted inspections of Nissan plants in September and December
1959, and in February 1960, to monitor the introduction of these
measures. The QC committee also received over a hundred complaints regarding quality from within the company; these prompted
Nissan to upgrade quality standards, reduce the time required for
new product development, decentralize responsibility for product
quality, and expand planning functions. Kawamata also set the goal
of matching the European automakers in product quality and prices
within five years.[48]

An article in Nissan's company newsletter discussed a conference
held in September 1959 and reported on how middle managers in
various departments intended to interpret and carry out the new QC
program.[49] The head of Nissan's personnel department, Komaki Ma-
sayuki, was chairman of the meeting. Section and department chiefs
attending from the QC office, engineering, inspection, market research, assembly, body manufacturing, chassis design, cost accounting, machining, forging, and outside-parts inspection all agreed that,
prior to 1959, Nissan had viewed QC mainly as the statistical control
of manufacturing processes. Terazawa Yoshio, manager of the QC
office in 1959, expressed the philosophy behind the new effort in
pointing out that, however important statistics were, "for the quality
of products to improve, all work in the company must improve. If
there is too much reliance on statistical methods, workers tend to
believe that QC does not apply to them individually."

Other participants in the conference admitted that, after years of
training, most workers still did not know how to use control charts,
and that there was no direct coordination between the charts or the
identification of defectives and measures to stop operations until
Nissan corrected the problems. As a result, too many defectives

moved on to subsequent processes. Everyone seemed to agree that Nissan had made progress in reducing defectives, either through inspection or process controls. But Yamashita Yoshitaka, former head of the QC office and chief of the section for outside-parts inspection in 1959, maintained that Nissan had difficulty controlling quality outside of manufacturing because QC measures up to 1959 had not extended throughout the company. He and others felt this would now change, because Kawamata had made QC a top priority; the commitment of the president placed an obligation on other senior executives and department managers, and on lower managers and personnel, to carry out the new program.

Nissan managers also decided to devote more attention to coordinating product planning and QC measures to eliminate defects or undesirable features in design, before they got to manufacturing. Kobayashi Kazuo, head of the planning department, claimed that the 1959 QC lectures showed him how important it was for planning to focus on the identification of consumer preferences, before the company considered questions of technology, product utility, or costs. The manager of the inspection department, Murakami Yukio, added that he intended to deemphasize the importance of inspections in maintaining quality and to shift QC functions to design and manufacturing departments by treating inspection as only one part of a "quality assurance system." He also wanted to limit his department's activities to conducting simple quality checks of finished vehicles that would reflect how customers examined new cars.

Other department and section heads attending the September 1959 conference described similar plans to implement the new program. The personnel department was organizing sessions to instruct employees in QC methods, job standardization, and daily work scheduling. Market research promised to channel more information from dealers on consumer preferences to the design department. Purchasing offered to instruct subcontractors in QC and standardization, and to pay greater attention to the smaller firms that had the most serious quality problems. Cost accounting described a new, easily understandable method for graphing costs and announced it would provide graphs directly to factory managers to help them identify the location of cost overruns. The department had previously published cost data in a more complicated form and then left it to production personnel to interpret and act on the information. Matsuzaki, head of the engineering department in 1959, offered his encouragement to everyone by insisting that "QC is not especially difficult; it's a matter of common sense. With the correct instruction, all employees should be able to carry out the program."

Shortly after instituting this new QC program, Nissan won the 1960 Deming prize for reducing the production of defectives through statistical inspection, higher engineering standards, and improvements in manufacturing process controls. Between 1960 and 1964, however, the company tripled its production volume, introduced several new car and truck models, and reorganized its factory system by opening Oppama and Zama while turning Yokohama into an engine plant. The QC measures and process controls that had sufficed in earlier years were no longer adequate.

The first response of Nissan executives was to tighten process controls by creating a centralized production management department in 1964 that combined the planning office with several departments responsible for production. At the same time, they relegated QC to the status of a section in the production management department, although this arrangement lasted only two years. Increasing exports to the United States, and new American safety and pollution regulations, persuaded Nissan managers to reestablish QC as a separate staff office in 1966, headed by Executive Vice-President Igarashi. Nissan also expanded the office's functions to include problems related to vehicle safety, exhaust emissions, maintenance, and parts control, in addition to overseeing a worldwide quality assurance program to receive customer complaints from Japan and abroad, and to make certain that the company provided adequate service. Inspection departments in each factory continued to check materials, parts production, assembly operations, and finished vehicles, while two sections in the QC office (which became a staff department in 1973) dealt with various quality problems. One section was responsible for consumer complaints, vehicle safety, emissions, and other problems that affected in-house departments; the other handled parts procurement and inspection, provided guidance to subcontractors, and supervised the quality assurance program for the entire Nissan group.[50]

Another change at Nissan was the gradual integration of quality checks into the production process rather than continued reliance on inspection departments to determine if components met standards. This concept was not new. Ōno Taiichi had limited Toyota's use of statistical sampling since the Korean War while insisting that workers inspect all components, on the conviction that this was the best way to guarantee quality. Nissan, in contrast, adopted random-sampling inspection, and only in 1962 did it begin returning to 100-percent inspection. In making this change, Nissan was merely following the advice of Ishikawa and other Japanese professors who, during the QC lectures at Nissan during 1959, had encouraged managers to make production workers do their own inspections. Nissan managers had few ideas of their own on the subject of QC, but they were flexible enough to try shifting inspection duties to employees or automatic devices on the shop floor.[51]

Nissan began experimenting with the self-inspection technique in the spring of 1962, using 25 major subassemblies for brakes, steering, suspensions, axles, and wheels. Staff inspectors checked other components, until Nissan expanded the list to 55 in 1970 and then to 192 in 1973. Since conducting all these inspections manually would have consumed too much time and labor, Nissan added devices to assembly and processing equipment to perform simple quality checks automatically, such as by measuring specifications and preventing defective components from fitting into subsequent machines or jigs. In 1961, Nissan also started to attach inspection numbers to parts to keep a record of manufacturing lots. It coordinated these with vehicle serial numbers in 1969 and computerized the data in 1971 to facilitate the rapid identification of quality problems in specific lots.[52]

Nissan still did not emphasize self-inspection to the same extent as Toyota, which had begun moving inspection duties to production workers around 1950. Even in 1982, Nissan continued to rely more on staff inspection and employed one inspector for every 600 or so vehicles assembled in house, compared to one inspector for more than 1000 vehicles at Toyota (Table 82). This difference also contributed to the higher productivity of Toyota workers.

QC Circles
QC circles contributed to the shift toward in-process inspection by reinforcing the training employees received in QC methods. In both Nissan and Toyota, however, the circles appeared and proliferated as a result of careful planning by outside consultants and in-house managers. Toyota formed the first QC circles in the automobile industry around 1963; it still had only 169 in 1966, when management started a campaign to eliminate customer complaints and defects due to processing deficiencies or errors in manufacturing. Toyota grouped workers into QC circles and had them take up quality prob-

Table 82: Inspection Staff Comparison—Nissan and Toyota, 1982

	Nissan	Toyota
In-House Assembly	1,684,000	1,910,000
Inspection Staff	2,644	1,800
Vehicles/Inspector	637	1,061

Sources: *The Public Relations Departments of Nissan and Toyota; interviews with Ōno and Kanao.*

Note: *The in-house assembly figures are based on the estimate that Nissan assembled 70% of its output in-house, and Toyota 60%.*

lems as monthly projects, with the results posted on bulletin boards.[53] Bolstered by the enthusiastic support of top executives, the number of circles in Toyota rose to 811 by early 1968, encouraging other firms to adopt this practice as well (see Table 80). Nissan, for instance, even though it had practically abandoned the QC program after 1960 and fallen several years behind Toyota in establishing QC circles, passed Toyota in circle registrations during 1970 and then led the industry in forming QC circles throughout the 1970s. Toyota started a new "total quality control" program for in-house factories and subsidiaries in 1969 but took until 1980 to overtake Nissan in QC circle registrations.[54]

Ishikawa initiated the QC circle movement in Nissan after he visited the Zama plant in 1966 to observe its computerized production control system and felt that the factory could improve quality by involving shop workers more directly in studying and applying QC concepts. After Nissan again asked him to serve as a quality consultant, Ishikawa helped organize 38 QC circles in Zama by the end of the year. He modeled these after Matsushita's circles and had them use the journal *Genba to QC* and discuss specific quality problems in the Zama plant.[55] Murayama formed Nissan's next QC circles in 1967; workers in this factory were relatively easy to organize since they had participated in an American-style "zero-defect" program that Prince instituted in the early 1960s to eliminate processing errors.[56]

Once Nissan started to organize QC circles at other factories, their numbers rose from 815 in 1969 to 2728 in 1970, compared to

1842 at Toyota. By 1974, the number of QC circles in Nissan had stabilized at around 4000, while a rise in the average membership per circle from 7.2 in 1974 to 9.2 in 1984 allowed the factory workers participating to increase from 65 percent in 1970 to 99 percent in 1980 (see Table 80). Toyota preferred to have more circles with fewer members; in 1984, it registered 5850, with an average of 5.9 workers per circle, although Nissan's circles met around 3 hours per month, as opposed to 2 1-hour sessions per month at Toyota.[57]

In addition to specific efforts by consultants and managers to promote QC circles, another reason why they became so popular at Nissan and Toyota was that, around 1969, both companies began to pay workers to attend meetings. In the early 1980s, Nissan even allowed employees to claim up to 2 hours per month in overtime for this activity, although the average Nissan worker spent only 1 hour per month beyond regular hours in QC circles.[58] Similarly, Toyota offered workers 200 yen per hour to attend QC circle meetings prior to 1971; thereafter it paid regular wages and overtime plus a bonus of 300 yen per hour.[59]

The systems Nissan and Toyota used to manage QC circles during the 1970s and early 1980s were similar and relied on QC circle offices from the corporate level to intra-section groups in factories, and on independent committees from the corporate level down to company sections (Figure 9). At Nissan, top management set general objectives and monitored QC circle activities indirectly through semi-annual meetings, while the QC department took charge of specific planning and coordinated company policies and goals regarding QC. The corporate QC office compiled statistical data on QC circles, published a QC circle manual, planned and supervised employee training programs, managed the company budget for QC circle activities, supervised and assisted plant and departmental QC circle offices, evaluated achievements and gave out awards, managed an annual QC circle convention, provided guidance to affiliated firms, and coordinated Nissan's circle activities with those of external organizations such as JUSE or other companies. The plant, department, and lower-level QC circle offices registered QC circles and supervised their activities in coordination with the independent committees. Activities consisted mainly of selecting and analyzing themes, and presenting results. QC circles also held study meetings and recreational activities, and submitted suggestions to management on how to improve quality or other aspects of company operations.[60]

Analyzing a set number of themes or projects each year, covering

Figure 9: Nissan's QC Circle Operational Organization Chart, 1981

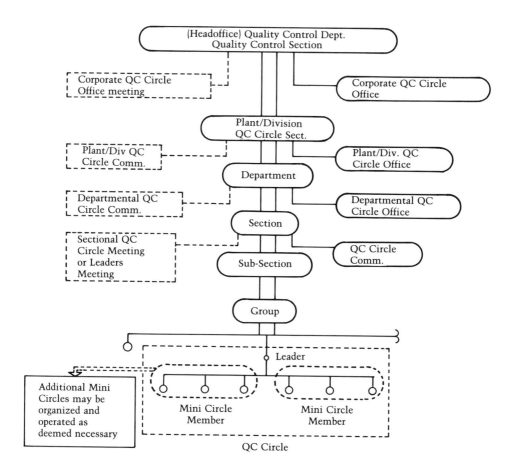

Source: Shigeru Tsujita, "The Promoter's Role in QC Circle Activities," p. 6.

a variety of topics, consumed most of the time Japanese workers spent in circle meetings. In 1981, 29 percent of the projects Nissan's circles discussed dealt with costs and efficiency, 22 percent with quality and process control, and another 26 percent with equipment maintenance. The remainder concerned safety (18 percent) and morale (5 percent) (Table 83). While a comparable percentage of themes in Toyota covered costs and efficiency or safety, its circles devoted 13 percent more of their projects to quality, 11 percent less to maintenance, and none, at least officially, to morale. The Toyota circles also served to improve worker attitudes by increasing opportunities to participate in company operations, although management did not consider low morale to be a serious problem. In contrast, Kanao Kaiichi, the Nissan executive vice-president in charge of manufacturing QC and production management in 1983, felt that, during the 1970s and early 1980s, Nissan had come to use QC circles more to deal with morale difficulties than quality control.[61]

To analyze quality problems, Nissan's QC department (the QC office before 1973) provided basic training in methods such as procedural check sheets, cause-effect or "fishbone" diagrams (that Ishikawa invented to map out the fundamental reasons for quality problems in processing or materials), quality graphs, and Pareto diagrams to determine the "vital few" areas where most quality prob-

Table 83: QC Circle Themes at Nissan and Toyota, 1981 (%)

	Nissan	Toyota
Quality and control procedures	22	35
Costs and efficiency	29	30
Safety	18	20
Equipment maintenance	26	15
Morale	5	—
Total	100	100

Sources: Nissan Jidōsha, "QC sākuru katsudō no ayumi," p. 4; and Toyota Jidōsha, Kōhō shiryō (1982), p. 34.

Table 84: QC Circle Techniques at Nissan, December 1981 (%)

Method	Currently Using	Know How to Use	Cannot Use
Pareto diagrams	15	60	25
Cause-effect diagrams	80	19	1
Check sheets	88	12	0
Histograms	36	61	3
Dispersion charts	20	72	8
Control charts	18	70	12
Graphs	86	12	2

Source: "QC sākuru katsudō no ayumi," p. 12.

lems occurred. While most employees learned to apply at least a few of these techniques, management efforts to make QC circles cover as much material as possible resulted in a decline in the number of workers who fully understood statistical methods. An internal survey in December 1981 indicated that, while 85 percent of Nissan's factory workers regularly used check sheets, graphs, and cause-effect diagrams to solve problems in QC circles, just 22 percent (including multiple answers) used histograms, dispersion charts, control charts, and Pareto diagrams, and a rising percentage of workers did not understand Pareto diagrams (25 percent), control charts (12), or dispersion charts (8) (Table 84). In addition, factory surveys noted serious discrepancies in the performance of QC circles at different facilities.[62]

The response of Nissan management to the decreasing effectiveness of QC circles contributed to the company's morale problems during the early 1980s. Pressure from managers on circle leaders to accomplish more in their meetings increased the number of themes they completed successfully from 0.3 in 1970, when circles spent much of their time studying, to nearly 41 in 1981—causing both employees and their superiors to complain that Nissan had come to stress "quantity" over "quality," and that workers were actually accomplishing less than when QC circles took on fewer projects.[63] Management subsequently allowed the number of themes resolved in one year to drop to 4.7 in 1983. Not only was this closer to the 3.4 themes that Toyota's circles averaged during the early 1980s but Nissan estimated that, while the number of themes its circles dealt with in 1984 was merely one-ninth the level of 1981, financial savings per circle declined by only a few percent[64] (see Table 80).

In 1980, when Nissan also asked employees and QC circles to contribute more suggestions on how to improve the company, management encountered similar complaints of stressing "quantity" over "quality." Nissan had introduced a suggestion system in 1955, copying Toyota, which had borrowed the idea from Ford in 1951, but then let the system lapse by the late 1950s due to low levels of participation.[65] Even Toyota received an average of only 1 suggestion per worker annually during the 1950s and 1960s, until contributions rose dramatically after management combined the suggestion system with QC circle activities during the 1970s (Table 85). Toyota workers submitted nearly 33 suggestions apiece in 1982. Like QC circle attendance, the practice stopped being voluntary after the 1960s; managers set quotas, kept records of who submitted suggestions, and used these data when determining bonuses. Staff superiors also gave out awards for suggestions and criticized workers who failed to contribute their share.[66]

Nissan tried to revive its system during the later 1960s by involving QC circles, but suggestions grew from 148 in 1969 to 1655 five years later, compared to the nearly 400,000 that Toyota employees submitted in 1974. Nissan finally revived the individual-suggestion system in 1978 and started a new effort to obtain more proposals from QC circles, resulting in over 22 suggestions per worker in 1980, in addition to more than 163,000 from QC circles. These surpassed Toyota's figures, although Toyota management responded with a new promotion effort of its own during the early 1980s that doubled the number of employee suggestions between 1980 and 1982 to 1,900,000. While Toyota workers appeared to accept higher quotas for suggestions, Nissan workers and the union reacted adversely and pressured management to focus on the "quality" of employee suggestions, which subsequently dropped at Nissan from nearly 1,300,000 in 1980 to about 660,000 in 1981, before rising above 800,000 in 1983.[67]

Table 85: Employee Suggestion Systems at Toyota and Nissan, 1951-1983

FY	Toyota			Nissan		
	Suggestions	% Adopted	Suggestions per Worker	Suggestions (New System)	% Adopted	Suggestions per Worker	QC Circle Suggestions
1951	789	23	0.1				
1955	1,087	53	0.2				
1960	5,001	33	0.6				
1965	15,968	39	0.7				
1969	40,313	68	1.1				148
1970	49,414	72	1.3				552
1971	88,607	74	2.2				767
1972	168,458	75	4.1				1,387

Year						
1973	284,717	77	6.7				1,366
1974	398,091	78	9.0				1,655
1975	381,438	83	8.5				3,032
1976	463,422	84	10.4				4,911
1977	454,522	84	10.2				9,761
1978	527,861	88	11.7	134,157	37	2.4	25,323
1979	575,861	91	12.7	533,448	52	9.5	73,711
1980	859,039	94	18.6	1,267,222	66	22.4	163,013
1981	1,412,565	94	29.5	663,362	70	11.6	62,173
1982	1,905,642	95	32.7	667,865	77	11.5	21,566
1983	1,655,858	96	28.2	827,859	80	14.0	20,025

Sources: Toyota Jidōsha, Kōhō shiryō (1982), p. 33, and Kōhō shiryō handobukku (1984), p. 35; the Public Relations Department of Nissan Motor; "Data File 1984," p. 31.

Suppliers: The Case of Nihon Radiator

Nissan, like other Japanese automakers during the 1950s and 1960s, had mixed success in attempts to extend its QC programs to subcontractors. QC and procurement specialists instructed suppliers on manufacturing process controls and basic QC techniques, but they limited their efforts mainly to primary subcontractors. The constant need for more components at lower prices made it difficult to terminate contracts or to enforce quality standards, although, after the June 1969 recalls, Nissan reviewed the QC practices at most of its suppliers and issued new guidelines for parts specifications, inspection procedures, materials, and manufacturing process controls. During 1970, Nissan specialists checked to see if companies had complied and provided extensive instructions in QC methods or set up quality assurance programs at firms with inadequate controls. Nissan then gave its larger suppliers access to a computerized parts-data system, established a QC circle committee in the Takara Kai in 1970 to organize QC circles in suppliers under a 3-year program, and began monitoring the Datsun Sunny to test the effectiveness of the new QC procedures. In addition, during 1973, suppliers started to introduce the same type of automated inspection equipment used in Nissan plants, some of which incorporated minicomputers.[68]

Despite these measures, Nissan took until the mid-1970s to solve quality problems in procured parts that resulted from designs and materials, rather than faulty processing. Most of these defects appeared or worsened as Nissan forced suppliers to reduce prices, or as customers used exported vehicles in countries with different climatic conditions. Even Nihon Radiator, a leader in QC techniques within the Takara Kai after winning the 1961 Deming prize for small and medium-size firms, suffered from severe quality problems during the late 1960s and the 1970s in its basic product lines.

As a major subsidiary of Nissan since 1954, Nihon Radiator had participated in Nissan's QC instruction program during the mid-1950s. After Nissan announced in 1959 that it intended to win the Deming prize, Nihon Radiator declared its intentions to compete for the award and set up a system to prepare for the examination. Ōyama Takashi, president of Nihon Radiator between 1949 and 1965, and his successor, Fukumoto Shūsaku, who left Nissan during the 1950s to join the subsidiary as an executive director, initiated the QC program and personally supervised its implementation. Nihon Radiator then applied for the 1960 prize, in the regular category for large firms, but lost to Nissan. Ōyama and Fukumoto immediately brought in Ishikawa to design a study program that continued through 1961 and succeeded in capturing the next Deming prize. Nihon Radiator also used the publicity it received from the award to advertise the company's name in preparation for opening shares to the public.[69]

Nihon Radiator had relatively few difficulties with manufacturing defects during the remainder of the 1960s, but it did switch to inferior designs and materials to lower production costs. During 1967-1968, the substitution of thin sheet steel in place of thicker steel to construct radiator cores resulted in a virtual flood of complaints from customers around the world, who found that holes developed too easily in the radiator cores, causing water to leak out and engines to overheat. While the company returned to a thicker sheet steel during the early 1970s, its radiators also tended to corrode quickly in hot climates. Correcting this required a higher quality paint. Nihon Radiator's mufflers also corroded due to road salt used in North America and Europe; to solve this, the company had to switch to aluminized sheet steel during 1971-1972.

Engineers at Nihon Radiator had been studying aluminum materials as a general remedy for corrosion problems but had difficulty perfecting the appropriate welding techniques. When they tried using aluminum heat exchangers in 1970, loose welds resulted in leaks and additional corrosion. Nihon Radiator finally purchased furnaces during 1973-1974 to bake aluminum welds in a vacuum, solving the welding problem and permitting a wider use of aluminum materials. But the large number of complaints that came in during the late 1960s and early 1970s convinced managers at Nissan and at Nihon Radiator that all suppliers had to establish quality assurance systems to cover manufacturing, designs, materials, and servicing. Nihon Radiator set up a new QC office and adopted stricter procedures during 1972-1973 to check the materials and designs of each product line to eliminate as many defects as possible before production.[70] Other subsidiaries and suppliers subsequently established similar programs, although Nihon Radiator continued to be a leader in QC within the Nissan group throughout the 1970s and early 1980s.

THE TOYOTA GROUP

While Toyota waited until 1961 to establish a formal QC program, the concept of design quality and quality assurance as functions separate from inspection and process control already had a long history in the company. In fact, Toyota continued to maintain a staff office for "supervision and improvement" to study customer complaints and work on solving problems in design, manufacturing, or procurement, from 1937 through the early 1980s.[71] As at Nissan, the first opportunity for Toyota employees to study QC formally came in 1949, when several members of the company's inspection department, joined by staff members from the supervision and improvement office in 1950, attended the lectures that JUSE and other Japanese organizations sponsored. Toyota then held an in-house QC lecture series during 1951; the inspection department followed this up the next year by forming a QC group and instructing factory workers on control charts and machine process testing. Toyota then established an independent QC committee in 1953 and specialized subcommittees for different areas of manufacturing, but the inspection department remained responsible for QC procedures, such as control charts and product or machine testing.[72]

Limited Use of Sampling Inspection
Between 1954 and 1960, Toyota managers largely ignored QC as a separate function and devoted themselves to improving the company's ability to manage production operations. A major reason for this was that Ōno did not believe random sampling was an effective way to test quality. Toyota had enough manufacturing defects to convince him that "all components should be inspected"; lot sampling simply allowed too many defects to pass through the inspection system. Since Ōno did not want to waste labor by having a large inspection department to check all components in addition to finished vehicles, during the late 1940s and the 1950s he began asking production workers to conduct their own inspections.

Ōno's policy led to a minor clash with GHQ during the Korean War, when officials from the U.S. Army visited Toyota and insisted that the company use higher standards and sampling inspection. Ōno agreed to allow the inspection department to adopt these procedures, but only as formal checks to supplement the inspections of workers in his shop. American officials criticized him for being "ignorant of QC," although Toyota engineers found that in-process self-inspection was the best way to insure against manufacturing defects leaving the factory without employing a large inspection staff. As Toyota adopted this technique for all manufacturing departments by the 1960s, the number of inspection personnel gradually dwindled since they had, according to Ōno, "so little to do."[73]

It was actually Nissan's victory in the Deming competition, and the publicity the company received, that inspired Toyota executives to seek the award themselves and launch a 5-year QC program in 1961. They asked Mizuno Shigeru, a professor at the Tokyo Institute of Technology and a colleague of Ishikawa Kaoru in JUSE, to direct the exam preparations, though Toyota managers modeled their plan on the system that won the 1961 Deming prize for their electrical and electronic components subsidiary, Nippon Denso. While this departed from common practice in Japanese manufacturing industries, where parent firms usually provided guidance on technology and manufacturing techniques to their suppliers, Toyota managers were willing to learn from Nippon Denso.[74]

The Nippon Denso Model

Following the recommendations of American and Japanese QC experts, during the 1950s Nippon Denso established a program that combined processing controls with design and cost controls, in addition to self-inspection and other techniques such as the use of committees to supplement QC staff personnel. The inspection department began to learn statistical QC techniques in 1950 and to compile control charts in 1951, along with other firms in the electrical equipment and automobile industries. Inspectors adopted random sampling and similar testing methods in 1952, when the Japanese government authorized Nippon Denso to manufacture electrical components for telephones. Hayashi Torao, president from 1949-1967, and other top executives were especially anxious to follow American procedures because they wanted to fill orders for the American military. Strict industrial standards for electrical equipment producers that GHQ and the Japanese government adopted during the Occupation forced the company to raise its manufacturing and product standards.[75] In addition, the tie-up with Robert Bosch, Inc., between 1953 and 1956, to manufacture electronic components and other automobile parts encouraged Toyota's subsidiary to improve standardization procedures in manufacturing processes and product design.

Nippon Denso initiated a 5-year program in 1954 that included the compilation of an in-house QC manual and training for company employees and subcontractors to improve inspection methods, standardization, and process controls. In 1956, management established a QC staff office, an independent QC committee to oversee the program, and an office for supervision and improvement, similar to Toyota's, to deal with customer complaints. To test the effectiveness of the program, company specialists began monitoring the magnet manufacturing department in 1957. Since this showed a substantial decrease in defectives production, later in the year management set up separate committees for each product line. At the same time, to centralize supervision functions, Nippon Denso combined the QC office, the supervision and improvement office, and its management research department into a single planning and administration office.

During 1957-1958, Nippon Denso deemphasized inspections of finished goods and tried to improve process controls while extending QC measures to design and prototype manufacturing. In addition, factories purchased new precision measuring equipment and automatic inspection devices in 1958 to help workers conduct their own inspections; supervisors designated one or more workers in each manufacturing section to take charge of QC procedures and to watch for defects. Factories, as well as the design, purchasing, and sales departments, then established control sections in 1959, directly under the department managers, to supervise quality checks during processing. To insure that plants received components and materials free from manufacturing defects, the company founded an organization for subcontractors, grouped them by their specialties, and sent staff experts to examine member firms and provide technical guidance on manufacturing, product design, and QC procedures.

Nippon Denso made several important changes in its QC program before undergoing the Deming examination. In 1960, in-house QC experts completed a new manual for foremen and workers; foremen then took over the responsibility of instructing the company's 5100 employees in QC concepts and procedures from the control sections in each manufacturing department. Outside lecturers came in to discuss QC concepts and techniques with middle managers, while another team of in-house QC specialists visited subcontractors to supervise their training programs. Control sections relinquished their QC responsibilities to a new QC staff office that Nippon Denso established to implement another 5-year plan beginning in 1961. This program combined cost control with other QC functions by organizing cost-control committees and separate supervision committees for each major product line, in addition to forming committees for product planning and new-product development, and separating research from the general manufacturing department. The electric-plug and oil-cleaner departments served as test cases to monitor the effectiveness of the new organization and procedures.

The Deming committee, when it gave the 1961 award to Nippon Denso, cited the company's efforts to coordinate long-term planning, job standardization, flexible process controls (despite a large number of product lines), parts procurement, and new-product development. MITI also recognized the firm's achievements in factory management and standardization by awarding Nippon Denso its annual prize for electrical equipment manufacturers in 1960 and again in 1964. This was the model that Toyota managers had before them when they revived Toyota's QC effort and drew up their own 5-year plan in 1961.

The Toyota Program

Toyota's QC office directed the first phase of its new program. This lasted from June 1961 through December 1962 and focused on manufacturing quality while including several specific goals: to introduce broad QC concepts throughout the company, cut the defective rate in half (which Toyota did by the end of 1962), raise quality standards while lowering costs, and continue shifting inspection functions from the inspection department to production workers. Mizuno Shigeru, Ishikawa Kaoru, Nishibori Eisaburō, and other Japanese experts from the University of Tokyo and the Tokyo Institute of Technology assisted the QC staff in another lecture series, which consumed 1860 hours before ending in June 1965, to instruct foremen, factory workers, and managers on TQC thinking and the standard QC tools: Pareto diagrams, Ishikawa cause-and-effect diagrams, histograms, control charts, and correlation diagrams.[76]

At the beginning of the second phase (January 1963 to August 1964), Toyota management set the goal of winning the Deming prize by the end of the 5-year program. In a major organizational change, a new planning office replaced the QC office and took on extensive authority over staff and line departments so that it could design a control system for the entire company by function rather than by department. After setting up the outlines of this system, Toyota management merged the planning office with its research department in February 1964 to form a new planning and research office.

To direct the third phase of the program (September 1964 to September 1965), Toyota established a "QC promotion headquarters" that assumed all QC supervision responsibilities and completed the system to link line and staff managers. Executive Vice-President Toyoda Eiji, who headed the QC promotion headquarters, and Managing Directors Toyoda Shōichirō and Umehara Hanji, who served as vice-chairmen, set policy for quality assurance, cost control, personnel administration, and office administration (Figure 10). A standing committee of 5 (later 10) members from various company departments and sections, including the directors of the general control and promotion departments that the committee established directly beneath it, supervised QC planning, research, policy implementation, and QC instruction. In addition, 8 promotion committees for product planning and design, manufacturing preparations, outside-parts procurement, the main plant, Motomachi, Toyota Motor Sales, and company offices in Toyota City, Nagoya, and Tokyo, covered various other line and staff functions and had direct responsibility for QC training and QC circles.[77]

Toyota managers came up with the idea of having a promotion center, according to Ishikawa, to strengthen horizontal relations among departments and to encourage different sections to cooperate. Dual controls over QC activities by committees responsible for functions extending throughout the firm, and for specific factories or offices, offered top management a broader base to oversee the implementation of the QC program and to establish a quality assurance system to deal quickly with customer complaints or other problems involving product quality. This organization also improved communication among different departments and facilitated the rapid circulation of suggestions on how to improve company operations from departments to senior executives.[78]

When Toyota received the Deming prize in November 1965, two months after the conclusion of the 5-year program, the award committee cited the company for linking Toyota Motor Sales, in-house departments, subcontractors, customer service, new-product development, and cost-control measures in a comprehensive "quality assurance" system.[79] Furthermore, in contrast to Nissan, which let QC activities decline after winning the Deming, Toyoda Shōichirō launched a new program in 1966 that divided the functions of the temporary QC promotion headquarters among a new general planning office, the procurement control department, and a new quality assurance department. The quality assurance department then absorbed the office of supervision and improvement, and established a control office and separate sections for general administration, measurements, testing, vehicles, metal materials, and non-metal materials.[80]

The new program attempted to promote similar quality assurance measures for the entire Toyota group, although initial efforts cen-

Figure 10: Toyota's QC Promotion Center and Committees, 1964-1965

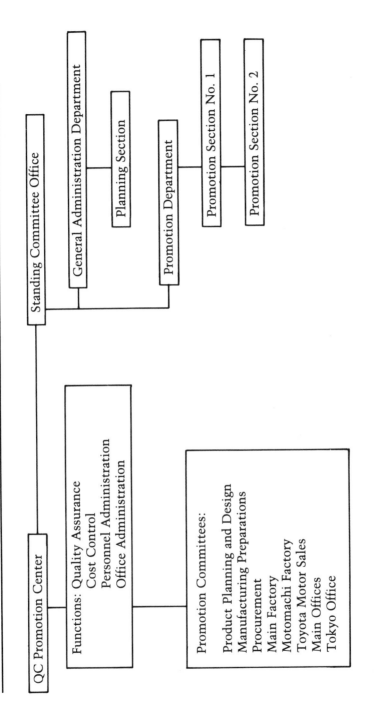

Source: Toyota Jidōsha sanjū nen shi, *p. 510.*

tered on 34 of Toyota's largest suppliers, divided into three categories. The first category consisted of main subsidiaries: Toyoda Automatic Loom, Toyoda Machine Works, Nippon Denso, Aisin Seiki, Toyota Auto Body, Kantō Auto Works, and Toyota Motor Sales. They formed a QC liason conference with Toyota that included an executive committee formed by the top executives of each member firm responsible for QC programs, and a secretariat composed of middle managers to carry out the committee's policies. The executive committee met once every two or three months, while the secretariat worked closely with Toyota's quality assurance department and met monthly. Toyota's procurement control department took charge of the 27 firms in the other two categories of subcontractors. In addition, an "All-Toyota QC Conference," started in November 1966, brought together representatives from 70 subsidiaries and subcontractors, as well as from Toyota, Toyota Motor Sales, and Toyota dealers. Through these measures, and the awarding of the Deming prize to several Toyota suppliers between 1966 and 1970—Kantō Auto Works, Kojima Press Industries (for small and medium-size firms), and Toyota Auto Body—the Toyota group gained a reputation for having the most effective QC program in the Japanese automobile industry.[81]

Even these controls did not prevent suppliers from producing defective brake tubes and other defective components, which resulted in Toyota's leading Japan's automakers in recalled vehicles during 1969. As at Nissan and other firms, this experience prompted Toyota managers to reexamine the designs and materials of components to prevent as many future defects as possible. Toyota managers also decided to supplement formal testing with competition within the group to improve product designs by establishing two "All-Toyota" QC awards for suppliers in 1969: one for quality excellence, and another for improvement. The examination categories focused on QC policy, quality assurance measures, productivity increases, long-term company policy, cost-control procedures, and technological development.[82] Whereas Nissan management did not offer a similar prize for its parts group until 1982, these annual awards and examinations encouraged Toyota's suppliers to maintain active QC programs throughout the 1970s and into the 1980s.[83]

QC Management: A Critical Comparison
While the recall system instituted during the late 1960s uncovered major flaws in components that all of Japan's automakers used, the

apparent inadequacy of existing QC programs struck managers at Nissan and Nihon Radiator particularly hard, since they had ranked their firms among the quality leaders in the industry. In Nihon Radiator's case, quality declined as a result of too much emphasis on cost reductions and inadequate pre-production testing in a variety of climatic conditions. Although Nissan had to take responsibility for quality problems at its suppliers, it seems that early success in QC, and the reception of Deming prizes when the examination committee still interpreted QC as process control, had an adverse affect on both Nissan and Nihon Radiator. Once they won the awards, managers and employees lost their enthusiasm for QC measures— precisely when firms such as Matsushita and Toyota were beginning to interpret QC more as a total company and group responsibility extending from market research to design, and only then to manufacturing or procurement.

Although Nissan managers discussed various ways to expand their QC programs during the middle and late 1950s, according to Igarashi, they relied almost entirely on Japanese consultants for ideas and did not always absorb or adopt the advice given. Perhaps as a result of this lack of initiative, between 1960 and the early 1980s Nissan's QC program declined from being the "best" in the industry to merely "average"—in Ishikawa's estimation, more effective than Isuzu or Mitsubishi, but not as good as Toyota, Honda, or Hino. In manufacturing process control, or in the infrequency of vehicle repairs, Ishikawa ranked Nissan alongside Japan's QC leaders of the early 1980s, but he maintained that Nissan fell behind Toyota and Honda in establishing a parts network known for high quality in manufacturing, and in general "design quality": identifying and satisfying consumer preferences for specific design features.[84]

Ishikawa blamed Nissan management for the company's lack of enthusiasm for QC after 1960 and its manifestation in quality problems in procurement, greater demand for Toyota vehicles, and a decline in QC circle activities as well as the tendency of foremen to dominate them. He believed Nissan's problems stemmed from both President Kawamata's loss of interest in QC after 1960 and from the presence of too many engineers in top management educated at the major national universities, especially the University of Tokyo, who tended to overlook QC and other fundamental manufacturing principles in favor of product design, research, or "fancy" manufacturing technologies that employed high levels of automation. In contrast, Ishikawa found that Toyota executives, including

Toyoda Eiji and his cousin Shōichirō, as well as lower-level technical personnel, paid more attention to the basics of QC and production management, and cooperated much more closely with QC consultants, especially after Nissan won the Deming prize. He also praised the efforts of Toyota and Toyota Motor Sales to match vehicle designs and performance with consumer preferences.[85]

In addition to Toyota's consistent advantage in total production, exports, and best selling models, ratings of new cars published in *Consumer Reports* tended to confirm Ishikawa's assertion that Toyota pulled ahead of Nissan in "design quality" during the 1970s. A 1968 issue, for instance, judged the Toyota Corona and the Datsun PL510 to be roughly equal; Toyota's advantage in engine performance offset superior handling and steering in the Datsun. The 1971 Datsun PL510 continued to rate better in handling than Toyota's competing model although, between 1973 and 1983, Toyota cars, except in 1976, received higher ratings than Nissan models, mainly due to superior handling at high speeds and in emergencies, smoother engine performance, and more comfortable rear seating (Table 86).

Table 86: *Consumer Reports'* Small Car Ratings, 1968-1983

Year	Models	Rank	Notes
1968	TOYOTA CORONA	1	Toyota advantage in
	DATSUN PL510	1	engine performance;
	Opel Kadett 1500	2	Nissan advantage in
			handling and steering.
1971	DATSUN PL510	1	Datsun advantage in high-
	TOYOTA CORONA	2	speed handling.
	Chevrolet Vega	2	
	Ford Pinto	3	
	VW Super Beetle	3	
	AMC Gremlin	4	
1973	AMC Gremlin	1	Toyota advantage in
	TOYOTA CARINA	2	power train noise level,
	Chevrolet Vega	3	rear accommodations,
	DATSUN 610	4	handling with a full
	Mazda RX3	5	load or in emergencies,
	Ford Pinto	6	and driver vision.

Table 86: (continued)

Year	Models	Rank	Notes
1976	VW Rabbit	1	Datsun advantage in ride
	DATSUN B210	2	comfort and gas
	TOYOTA COROLLA	3	mileage.
	Ford Pinto	4	
1978	Chevrolet Chevette	1	Toyota advantage in
	TOYOTA CORONA	2	engine performance and
	DATSUN 510	3	rear seating.
	Dodge Omni	4	
1980	VW Rabbit	1	Toyota advantage in
	TOYOTA COROLLA	2	emergency handling,
	Chevrolet Chevette	3	interior comfort, and
	DATSUN 310	4	engine performance.
1983	TOYOTA COROLLA	1	Toyota advantage in
	NISSAN PULSAR	2	engine performance,
	Mitsubishi Tredia	2	shifting, emergency
	Plymouth Horizon	3	handling and handling
			precision, and ride
			comfort.

Source: Consumer Reports *issues of September 1968, p. 498; January 1971, pp. 15-16; January 1973, p. 417; June 1976, pp. 361-362; July 1978, p. 382; January 1980, pp. 28-34; and August 1983, p. 398.*

Note: These ratings do not indicate the "best" cars in a given year but merely rank comparable models examined in issues that compared Nissan and Toyota models.

Nissan Executive Vice-President Kanao Kaiichi, who was also chairman of Japan's Quality Control Association in 1983, explained that he and other Nissan managers did not really lose interest in QC after winning the Deming prize. Rather, he claimed that there was internal resistance to continuing the program; top executives and other employees simply became tired after nearly two years of preparations for the examination. Once the company had the prize in hand, no one wanted to start another, more comprehensive effort to expand the program to involve marketing more closely or to make certain that Nissan focused its definition of quality on consumer desires rather than process control in manufacturing. But Kanao admitted that the responsibility for interpreting QC narrowly, and for letting Toyota develop an edge in determining how consumers viewed quality, rested primarily with senior executives during the 1960s and 1970s. They did not make QC a top company priority after 1960, although President Ishihara attempted to rectify this in 1982 by engaging Ishikawa to head a new QC effort in the Nissan group.[86]

Matsuzaki also admitted that Nissan tended to view QC mainly as product and manufacturing quality, and that no one took the initiative to organize a QC program that linked all levels of management and subcontractors, as Toyota did during the mid-1960s. While he criticized Kawamata and other top executives for not believing that a new QC program was necessary after Nissan won the Deming prize, he was especially hard on Igarashi, who headed Nissan's QC effort from the mid-1950s through the late 1970s but showed no personal expertise or genuine enthusiasm for the program.[87] In his own defense, Igarashi maintained that President Asahara put him in charge of QC during 1953 not because he was an expert but because he was manager of the Yokohama plant and a new company director. Unfortunately, he became "too busy" to learn the finer details of QC and had to delegate this responsibility. Moreover, since the Deming examinations during the late 1950s and early 1960s focused on manufacturing process controls, that is how Igarashi continued to interpret QC and instruct his subordinates to interpret it.[88]

Matsuzaki was one of the few managers in Nissan to realize the importance of establishing a broad QC program. Yet he had several excuses of his own for not doing more for the movement personally. Kawamata made him a company director only in 1961 and never promoted him to a higher position, and then he left Nissan in 1971 to head a subsidiary. During the first half of the 1960s, Matsuzaki also had to open the Oppama and Zama factories, and was not closely involved with manufacturing when Nissan made key decisions regarding the QC program. As a general explanation for Nissan's attitude toward QC, however, Matsuzaki believed that company engineers and managers had followed American companies too closely, while Igarashi and others felt that QC was too "plain" or "simple" a concept to be enthusiastic about, even though everyone studied for the Deming examination. Only later did they realize how important it was for senior executives to interpret and set policy for such a basic function as QC and that, for a program to operate effectively throughout the company and its supply network, and over a long period of time, someone in top management had to push it. Toyota had both Ōno Taiichi in production management and Toyoda Shōichirō at the head of its QC effort to make sure that managers and workers took QC measures seriously. In contrast, neither Kawamata nor Igarashi were capable leaders for Nissan's program, yet they determined company policy and attitudes toward QC throughout most of the 1960s and 1970s.[89]

This is not to say that there were major problems with the quality of Nissan products. To the contrary, many automakers the world over would have been more than pleased to produce automobiles as durable and marketable as Nissan had come to manufacture by the 1970s. In the intensely competitive world of the Japanese automobile industry, however, Nissan was only second best; and it fell to this position after being the first domestic automaker to introduce almost the entire assortment of American manufacturing techniques—from special-purpose machine tools and time and motion studies prior to World War II; to highly automated equipment, statistical quality control, and even computers and robots, during the 1950s and 1960s. In retrospect, it appears that Nissan's reliance on direct technology transfer from the United States and Britain caused managers to become more dependent on foreign techniques and less innovative in process development—including production management and quality control—than their counterparts at Toyota.

CONCLUSION

A venture in the automobile industry during the 1930s seemed to be almost an impossible dream to many businessmen and government officials in Japan, because of American domination of the Japanese and world markets. Yet the founders of Nissan and Toyota persisted; and their late entrance into a mature industry made it possible to learn from older automakers in the United States and Europe, and to concentrate more on technology transfer and process innovation rather than new product technologies. At the same time, government protection from foreign competition, along with creativity in the management of technology and people, were equally necessary for success. As the domestic industry grew, the Japanese turned historical disadvantages stemming from the initially backward state of their technology, and the low level of demand for cars prior to 1960, into competitive advantages in the international marketplace. While overcoming inefficiency made managers acutely aware of costs and productivity, Nissan, and especially Toyota, devised policies for subcontracting, production management, quality control, and other areas of operations that, by the early 1980s, had persuaded managers around the world to rethink some of their most basic assumptions. Whatever the future of automobile manufacturing in Japan, this contribution to managerial theory and practice, for both product and production technology, was likely to be permanent.

Japanese engineers first mastered American truck technology during the 1930s and then small-car technology from Britain, France, and Germany during the 1950s. By the end of the 1960s, Nissan and Toyota had surpassed American productivity levels as well as learned how to produce small cars that compared favorably in quality, performance, and price with European vehicles. By the end of the 1970s,

374

Americans and Europeans had become painfully aware of just how much the Japanese had improved their ability to compete in the automobile industry; but stories of miracles and rapid growth usually omitted the fact that the development process required decades and involved, moreover, a unique mixture of technology transfer and process innovation.

Japanese engineers employed two methods to learn how to design and manufacture automobiles: direct technology transfer, which required formal tie-ups with foreign automakers and parts manufacturers, or direct assistance from foreign engineers; and indirect technology transfer, which involved the selective copying of designs and manufacturing techniques from various foreign producers, and the importation or copying of machinery. Most Japanese automakers used both methods at one time or another, although Nissan, Isuzu, Hino, and Mitsubishi relied mainly on tie-ups, while Toyota, Honda, Fuji Heavy Industries (Subaru), Suzuki, Prince (which merged with Nissan in 1966), Daihatsu, and Mazda (except for the Wankel rotary engine) relied mainly on indirect technology transfer.

Both direct and indirect technology transfer made it possible for Japanese firms to enter the automobile industry and to market their products internationally, especially since more than a dozen Japanese auto-parts makers also benefited from tie-ups with firms in the United States, West Germany, and Britain during the 1950s and early 1960s. Yet each method had disadvantages as well as advantages. Tie-ups were the fastest way to introduce vehicles comparable to foreign models. But the case of Toyota suggests that a firm relying on indirect technology transfer, when supported by in-house research and development efforts focused on the analysis of foreign products, gained several benefits denied to firms relying mainly on tie-ups.

First, indirect technology transfer enabled Toyota engineers to copy proven technologies selectively from different manufacturers and to incorporate advanced features before Nissan or other Japanese automakers introduced these through foreign assistance. Tie-ups, on the other hand, locked Nissan into designs that, while adequate, were not always the most advanced in the industry or suited to local market conditions. Second, indirect technology transfer provided experience in designing vehicles and solving engineering problems that Toyota found useful for developing new products or improving existing models. Third, relying on in-house engineers prevented Toyota from acquiring a bias toward manufacturing techniques or equipment better suited to larger markets in the United States or Europe.

Several factors contributed to the effectiveness of indirect technology transfer and helped Toyota set world standards for productivity and profitability during the 1970s and early 1980s: the concentration of its production facilities and suppliers in one rural area, a large group of manufacturing subsidiaries founded during the 1940s, a highly cooperative company union, and a specialized sales company (until 1982). Yet, as important as these factors were to Toyota's performance, a tradition of independent experimentation, combined with the careful analysis of foreign automakers, was a major reason why Toyota innovated in production management more than Nissan and other Japanese, American, or European firms, even though Nissan also modified American manufacturing technology to raise productivity to twice the levels common in the United States during the 1970s and early 1980s.

Any claims that the Japanese lack creativity or the ability to innovate should be put to rest. The history of the automobile industry in Japan is full of innovations—not so much in product technology, where they were largely unnecessary due to the advanced state of the industry elsewhere, as in manufacturing strategy, production management, and quality control. But even in vehicle design it took imagination to make a truck into a car after World War II, a time when foreign automakers treated trucks and cars as totally separate products. This was a simple but practical response to the situation Japanese automakers faced in the 1950s: They had accumulated experience in making trucks for the military but not in making cars, and they had little money to design or manufacture components for separate car and truck lines.

During the 1950s, government protection against imports allowed Nissan and Toyota to sell small trucks fitted with car body shells, despite awkward looks and high prices, to Japanese taxi drivers. It then turned out, ironically, that these hybrid vehicles were better suited to Japan's rough, unpaved roads than high-quality European cars such as the Austin. To sell vehicles in the United States during the 1960s and 1970s required new types of body structures, more stylish exteriors and interiors, more powerful engines, smoother handling, synchromesh 4-speed transmissions, and other features widely available in the United States and Europe. Japanese firms upgraded product standards and quality through forming tie-ups, studying European vehicles, and analyzing consumer surveys taken in Japan and the United States. Yet their experience with trucks, and the need to accommodate poor road conditions, helped the Japanese build automobiles with sturdy chassis and suspension systems. At the same time, Nissan, Toyota, and other automakers followed Volkswagen's lead in concentrating on one or two basic models retained from year to year and improved incrementally, rather than adopting the American practice of annual model changes. While low sales and limited experience in product development made frequent model changes impractical during the 1950s and 1960s, even after 1970 the Japanese continued this departure from one of the most successful marketing and product strategies in the history of American business.

But clearly the most "revolutionary" changes the Japanese made in what Americans and Europeans had considered a stable technology came in manufacturing. On the one hand, it seems that the experience of technology transfer itself created a "bias" within Japanese automakers toward process development rather than product innovation; but it also appears that this tendency remained even after the Japanese reached comparability in small-car design with European automobile producers.

The decision of Nissan and Toyota during the mid-1950s to subcontract more components, rather than expand in-house capacity to meet new demand, stands out as the most significant departure from American practice because, when implemented successfully, it resulted in consistently high nominal productivity in house and low manufacturing and operating costs. Subcontracting so extensively brought with it the risk of poor quality, and this was a major difficulty until the early 1970s. Japanese managers solved this problem by organizing suppliers into groups and controlling even unaffiliated firms by dispatching executives, extending long-term contracts, buying the entire output of factories, providing loans of money or equipment, and offering technical guidance in design, accounting, cost control, production management, automation, and quality control. The true payoff came as the shifting of components manufacturing and even large portions of final assembly to outside firms with lower wage scales reduced personnel expenses, fixed investment requirements, and inventory carrying costs.

The need to produce a variety of models in a small domestic market evoked another creative response in process technology: rapid machine setup and mixed assembly and manufacturing. These techniques facilitated production in small lots, which made it possible to raise capacity-utilization rates by producing a variety of models with a limited amount of equipment and personnel. Small lots then made it easier for managers to reduce inventories, especially when suppliers were nearby and delivered frequently and in small loads. Companies also reduced personnel costs by broadening job routines. Rising production scales in the 1960s and 1970s, as well as the accumulation of experience in small car manufacturing, cut production expenses further and enabled the Japanese to manufacture a limited number of car and truck lines, with few options, for less than it cost foreign competitors to produce comparable vehicles.

In quality control, Japanese automakers deserved credit more for recognizing good advice than for inventing new procedures. Managers followed the suggestions of American and Japanese consultants to move the focus of QC from inspection to process control, and then to product design. Japanese QC programs also shifted inspection functions and QC responsibilities from staff departments to the shop floor and from departmental to functional committees, and extended quality controls to non-manufacturing departments to link market research and design with in-house production and procurement. But managers and workers in Japan still deserve at least half the credit for the thoroughness and novelty of their QC programs because they alone were responsible, on the operating level, for the perfection, implementation, and maintenance of these techniques.

Accounting for the source of creativity that the Japanese displayed in production and operations management is far more difficult than describing the results. Innovation certainly required impressive engineering skills acquired through universities, company training programs, or individual study. Toyota's history suggests that indirect technology transfer encouraged a more radical response to the problem of applying American production technology to the smaller Japanese market than did tie-ups or direct technology transfer. Yet the combination, during the 1960s and 1970s, of American-style automation Nissan introduced into Japan in the 1930s and 1950s, with the production management techniques Toyota pioneered between the late 1940s and the mid-1960s, eventually made both Japanese automakers more efficient.

Ōno Taiichi, who joined Toyota after having neither experience in automobile manufacturing nor any contact with American engineers, faced the challenge of producing a large number of models at low volumes of output to meet the demands of the Japanese market after World War II. To raise productivity and lower manufacturing costs, he decided to experiment with rapid equipment setup, mixed production scheduling, a "pull" system, tight cycle times, little or no buffer inventories, and manual controls on the process flow and the reordering of components. The fact that both Nissan and Toyota made similar improvements in American manufacturing technology by moving toward rapid setup, lower inventories, broader job classifications, and tighter coordination between final assembly and components production or delivery, indicated that these techniques were effective solutions to a more fundamental dilemma: how to accommodate the factory's preference for product standardization and mass production to the Japanese market's requirement for a variety of products in small amounts.

Some of the difference in the performance between Nissan and Toyota was due to factors beyond the control of Nissan managers, such as geographical location. Yet the impact of Ōno Taiichi confirmed the notion that individuals could indeed make an enormous contribution even in a large Japanese firm that prided itself on maintaining a "family" atmosphere. Ōno did not have a college education but he possessed extraordinary talent as a manufacturing engineer, uncanny insights into production and inventory problems, and a thorough, intuitive understanding of what firms such as Ford and General Motors had done before him.

Of equal importance was persistence. It took 15 years or more to perfect the process techniques that made Ōno and Toyota famous. Many engineers might have given up long before completing the program to introduce kanban and "just-in-time" manufacturing, or they might not have even tried to convince top executives, as Ōno did in the late 1940s, to adopt these measures in the first place. All the managers above Ōno responsible for production, beginning with the company founder, Toyoda Kiichirō, deserve credit for allowing a highly intelligent but relatively inexperienced young man to take on such a task. Nor was the case of Ōno so exceptional: Toyota executives were equally foresighted in providing another manager, Kamiya Shōtarō, with extensive responsibilities in marketing. Yet, the cases of Nissan and Toyota also suggest that stereotypes of decision making in Japanese firms as being "from the bottom up," that is, with initiatives rising upward from the lower ranks of the company, rather than "top down," need review. Most key decisions and initiatives at both firms came from top executives or from talented middle managers who were close to reaching the board of directors.

The observations in this study about the effectiveness of Toyota's policies and managers are not meant to detract from the achievements of Nissan, which became one of the world's largest and most competitive automakers. But Toyota's performance throughout its history has been so outstanding that some Nissan engineers even attributed their competitor's edge to "luck" in finding men like Ōno and Kamiya. No doubt "luck" played a role but there was also more openness in Toyota, more leeway for personnel at all levels to operate without fear of reprimands from superiors or recriminations from union officials, which was not present at Nissan in the early 1980s. From all accounts, this atmosphere never existed in the company, despite Nissan's longstanding, and laudable, commitment to match or surpass the product engineering and manufacturing technology of any firm in the United States or Europe.

The Nissan case illustrates a general point which applies equally well to automobile manufacturers in the West: There was nothing particularly "wrong" with American vehicles and mass-production technology during the 1970s and early 1980s; it was only that the Japanese had mastered small-car designs and low-cost production techniques precisely when demand for small cars was expanding in the United States. And there was nothing "wrong" with Nissan's strategy of directly importing technology from the United States during the 1930s and from Britain during the 1950s. Given the technological lead of companies in these nations, Nissan's strategy was understandable and even intelligent. It was simply that Toyota, without the constraints in product development and manufacturing technology that a direct tie-up created, but with a unique combination of managers, workers, suppliers, and geographical conditions, perfected a system to produce and sell a few more cars per worker per year.

It is tempting but unjust to insist that Toyota and the Japanese automobile industry in general were merely "lucky"; there is some indication of this, as in the "oil shocks" of the 1970s, but too much evidence of hard work, planning, as well as trial and error. It is also too simple to explain the performance of these firms by saying that a late entrance into the automobile industry provided a fundamental advantage, since the Japanese were then able to copy superior technologies selectively. Although Nissan, Toyota, and other Japanese automakers transferred technology, selectively, and learned a great deal from watching the operations of more experienced manufacturers, the opportunity to borrow and learn was available to established automakers in other countries as well. All that was required for a firm to begin improving its products and operations was for top management to perceive that improvement was necessary. This was lacking in the American automobile industry during much of the 1960s and 1970s, probably due to the domination of General Motors since the late 1920s, the stability of company market shares, and the unfortunate confidence of managers that the public would continue to buy standard-size American products as long as the outer bodies changed on a regular basis. It took a new factor in the marketplace—Japanese competition—to alter American assumptions about marketing, design, manufacturing, and labor.

While Japanese companies demonstrated enviable skills in the management of automobile technology and the necessary business operations to support this, to a large extent their achievements rested on the creation of an environment that greatly reduced the chances of failure: protection against imports, and company unions. Yet, to the lasting credit of Japanese managers and government officials, protectionism and low labor costs did not perpetuate inefficiency: Nissan, Toyota, and other Japanese automakers consistently reduced prices and improved product quality after 1950 due to a combination of intensifying domestic competition, rapidly expanding demand, the controlled introduction of foreign technology, indirect technology transfer, exposure to international markets through exports, and process innovation inspired by necessity and circumstance.

In labor relations, Japanese managers and white-collar workers headed for managerial posts truly feared the power of industrial unions created during the late 1940s and early 1950s. They made a deliberate effort to break up the labor federation that had achieved major wage hikes for all Japanese autoworkers during the Korean War and threatened to limit management's control over production scheduling and union meetings. But the 1954 collapse of the industrial union in the Japanese automobile industry was not a cultural accident; it was planned and well orchestrated. The result was a huge drop in wage levels throughout the industry, the maintenance of especially low wages at subcontractors, the increased use of inexpensive, temporary workers and suppliers, and the implementation of long-term programs to raise productivity and quality while lowering costs. And, despite higher levels of productivity during the early 1980s, Japanese autoworkers, especially in small subcontractors, still had much lower incomes than their counterparts in the United States.

Differences in unions also affected the competition between Nissan and Toyota. Union opposition was a major reason why Nissan did not try to compress cycle times, raise line speeds, or use overtime to the same extent as Toyota, even though these techniques contributed to Toyota's higher productivity and operating profits. This comparison suggests that, had the industrial union in the Japanese automobile industry survived, or had strong company unions emerged at firms other than Nissan, it would have been much more difficult for Japanese managers to implement the kinds of techniques that Ōno, a former union official, convinced the Toyota union to accept. Demands from Japanese autoworkers for a greater share of the tremendous wealth they produced or for less strenuous job routines probably would have resulted in companies with a smaller advantage over American or European automakers in productivity and costs, just as a policy of free trade in Japan during the 1930s or 1950s might have prevented the Japanese automobile industry from beginning at all.

American automakers in the early 1980s were already making the transition to smaller, more fuel-efficient vehicles and adopting Japanese-style production techniques and labor agreements focusing more on job security than wage hikes. The Japanese, in turn, were internationalizing their manufacturing operations by establishing plants abroad or forming joint ventures with foreign firms. The American automobile industry benefited from limitations on Japanese imports from 1981 through March 1985, which resulted in reduced output in Japan and higher prices for American consumers. The future competitiveness of American automakers, to a large extent, depended on how well they had taken advantage of this protectionism to introduce new design programs and cost-reduction measures, such as cutting back on personnel, shutting obsolete facilities, installing more modern equipment, and implementing tighter inventory controls and limitations on wages and benefits. On the other hand, the future of Japan's automobile industry rested on the ability of the Japanese to overcome or adapt to political restrictions on their exports, such as by moving even more production overseas, and to maintain an edge in small-car design, production costs, and quality—while the rest of the world studied their methods and products intensively.[1]

It is clear, however, that a major obstacle to internationalizing manufacturing operations was the extraordinarily high reliance of the Japanese—for 70 percent of the manufacturing costs for each car they produced—on outside suppliers that paid lower wages. While the absence of an industrial union made it possible for a "pyramid" of subcontractors with declining wage scales to exist in Japan, the decision to "disintegrate" vertically was integral to the productivity and cost advantage of the Japanese, whether the comparisons focused on physical or value-added output, fixed assets per vehicle, or inventory turnover. Toyota in particular was likely to have difficulty duplicating its production system outside of Toyota City. In fact, not even Nissan had been able to copy the Toyota system, due to more dispersed facilities and suppliers, urban traffic, union resistance, and a greater reliance on automation and computerized production control. It was no coincidence that firms relying less on the kanban and "just-in-time" techniques—including Nissan, which opened a plant in Tennessee during 1983, and Honda, which established a car factory in Ohio during 1982—were more willing to experiment with manufacturing abroad.

By 1984, political pressures and threats of "local-content" legislation to insure that cars sold in the United States contained a majority of components made domestically had persuaded even Toyota to commit itself to producing cars in the United States, starting with a joint venture with General Motors that promised to limit the Japanese automaker's financial risk. Yet the movement of Nihon Radiator, Kantō Seiki, Nippon Denso, and several other Japanese auto-parts manufacturers into the United States to supply the American plants of their parent firms suggested that another Japanese strategy was to transfer abroad as much of the domestic manufacturing system as possible. Managers in Japan, however, were still reluctant to have their American plants unionized by the United Automobile Workers and, as in the case of Nissan and Honda, they preferred to locate factories in areas where it was possible to avoid unionization.

Both the American and Japanese automobile industries were destined to continue competing for world leadership in production volume throughout the 1980s, although expansion of automobile output was problematic for the Japanese. Not only did Japan's automakers have more capacity than foreign governments would prefer them to use, but the Japanese also faced increasing competition from American and other producers. Yet the length of time Japan had required to build up its automotive assembly and components industries suggested that nations such as Korea or Brazil, unless they proved even more adept at transferring technology than Japan, would require years to design their own high-quality vehicles and manufacture them with economies of scale large enough to counter Japan's advantage in productivity, quality control, and unit costs, especially as the Japanese moved to even higher levels of automation to offset their own rising wage levels. While another open question was whether the Japanese would be able to innovate in design or export larger vehicles (which were becoming more popular in Japan during the early 1980s), something they had not been required to do much of in the past, there was little doubt that Nissan, Toyota, and other Japanese automakers such as Honda and Mazda had the engineering skills, motivation, and financial resources to continue improving their product lines and manufacturing operations well into the future. The most pressing questions centered not on Japan but on the determination of managers and workers in the United States and Europe to respond to a challenge that, to Japanese and non-Japanese alike, had once seemed beyond the limits of imagination.

Appendix A: Four-Wheel Vehicle Supply, 1916-1939

(vehicles, %, knock-down sets)

Year	Domestic Production Units	%	Vehicle Imports Units	%	Knock-Down Set Imports Units	%	Total Units
1916	—	—	218	100.0	—	—	218
1917	—	—	860	"	—	—	860
1918	—	—	1,653	"	—	—	1,653
1919	—	—	1,579	"	—	—	1,579
1920	—	—	1,745	"	—	—	1,745
1921	—	—	1,074	"	—	—	1,074
1922	—	—	752	"	—	—	752
1923	—	—	1,938	"	—	—	1,938
1924	—	—	4,063	"	—	—	4,063
1925	—	—	1,765	33.9	3,437	66.1	5,202
1926	245	2.2	2,381	21.1	8,677	76.8	11,303
1927	302	1.8	3,895	23.1	12,668	75.1	16,865
1928	347	1.1	7,883	24.2	24,341	74.7	32,571
1929	437	1.3	5,018	14.4	29,338	84.3	34,793
1930	458	2.0	2,591	11.4	19,678	86.6	22,727
1931	436	1.9	1,887	8.4	20,199	89.7	22,522
1932	880	5.5	997	6.2	14,087	88.2	15,964
1933	1,681	9.7	491	2.8	15,082	87.4	17,254
1934	2,787	7.5	896	2.4	33,458	90.1	37,141
1935	5,089	13.8	934	2.5	30,787	83.6	36,810

Appendix A: Continued

	Domestic Production		Vehicle Imports		Knock-down Set Imports		Total Units
1936	12,186	27.5	1,117	2.5	31,058	70.0	44,361
1937	18,055	35.4	1,100	2.2	31,839	62.4	50,994
1938	24,388	56.7	500	1.2	18,093	42.1	42,981
1939	34,515	100.0	—	—	—	—	34,515

Knock-Down Set Import Shares (%)

	Japan Ford	Japan GM	Kyōritsu (Chrysler)
1925	100	—	—
1926	100	—	—
1927	56	44	—
1928	36	64	—
1929	39	57	5
1930	54	41	5
1931	57	37	6
1932	53	42	5
1933	54	39	7
1934	54	38	8
1935	48	40	12

Sources: Japan Automobile Manufacturers Association; Nissan Jidōsha sanjū nen shi, *p. 16; Nihon Jidōsha Kaigi Sho,* Nihon jidōsha nenkan *(1947); Jerome Cohen,* Japan's Economy in War and Reconstruction, *p. 246.*

Appendix B: Japan—Domestic Sales and Imports, 1951-1984 (vehicles, %)

Year	Sales	Growth Rate (%)	Imports	$\dfrac{\text{Imports}}{\text{Sales}}$ (%)
1951	63,654	—	28,419	44.6
1952	57,491	−9.7	15,988	27.8
1953	76,185	32.5	27,406	36.0
1954	70,648	−7.3	16,317	23.1
1955	75,659	7.1	6,748	8.9
1956	133,050	75.9	9,103	6.8
1957	176,690	32.8	6,719	3.8
1958	198,285	12.2	6,702	3.4
1959	279,860	41.1	7,111	2.5
1960	407,963	45.8	4,329	1.1
1961	706,447	73.2	5,178	0.7
1962	899,952	27.4	12,228	1.4
1963	1,177,482	30.8	12,064	1.0
1964	1,471,581	25.0	12,913	0.9
1965	1,661,826	12.9	13,348	0.8
1966	2,046,261	23.1	15,754	0.8
1967	2,702,308	32.1	14,871	0.6
1968	3,303,134	22.2	15,571	0.5
1969	3,825,967	15.8	16,123	0.4
1970	4,097,361	7.1	19,552	0.5
1971	4,021,034	−1.9	19,047	0.5

Appendix B: Continued

Year	Sales	Growth Rate (%)	Imports	$\frac{\text{Imports}}{\text{Sales}}$ (%)
1972	4,367,276	8.6	25,324	0.6
1973	4,912,142	12.5	38,031	0.8
1974	3,849,547	−21.6	43,614	1.1
1975	4,309,016	11.9	46,145	1.1
1976	4,104,107	−4.8	41,028	1.0
1977	4,194,274	2.2	42,274	1.0
1978	4,681,893	11.6	55,429	1.2
1979	5,153,807	10.1	66,350	1.3
1980	5,015,628	−2.7	47,918	1.0
1981	5,127,412	2.2	33,366	0.7
1982	5,261,553	2.6	36,122	0.7
1983	5,382,225	2.3	38,013	0.7
1984	5,436,757	1.0	41,982	0.8

Sources: *Nihon Jidōsha Kōgyō Kai,* Jidōsha tōkei nenpyō; *Jidōsha Kōgyō Shinkō Kai,* Jidōsha kōgyō shiryō geppō; Automotive News; Japan Times, *12 January 1985.*

Appendix C: United States—Domestic Sales and Imports, 1951-1984 (vehicles, %)

Year	Sales	Imports	Imports ÷ Sales (%)	Imports from Japan	Percent of Sales	Percent of Imports
1951	6,064,753	23,951	0.4	0	—	—
1952	4,970,493	33,795	0.7	0	—	—
1953	6,669,301	29,842	0.4	0	—	—
1954	6,364,565	35,034	0.6	0	—	—
1955	8,126,909	58,425	0.7	0	—	—
1956	6,849,614	110,659	1.6	16	—	—
1957	6,840,427	267,775	3.9	13	—	—
1958	5,381,219	446,138	8.3	1,519	—	0.3
1959	6,983,408	689,833	9.9	3,539	—	0.5
1960	7,520,135	468,312	6.2	1,503	—	0.3
1961	6,773,355	288,741	4.3	1,806	—	0.6
1962	8,007,588	387,204	4.8	5,342	0.1	1.4
1963	8,800,941	426,658	4.8	7,517	0.1	1.8

389

Appendix C: Continued

Year	Sales	Imports	Imports / Sales (%)	Imports from Japan	Percent of Sales	Percent of Imports
1964	9,426,922	553,189	5.9	19,243	0.2	3.5
1965	10,842,771	590,323	5.4	34,441	0.3	5.8
1966	10,618,938	970,625	9.1	65,277	0.6	6.7
1967	9,875,847	1,109,095	11.2	82,035	0.8	7.4
1968	11,179,463	1,749,591	15.7	182,547	1.6	10.4
1969	11,335,336	2,017,885	17.8	281,162	2.5	13.9
1970	10,178,381	2,167,091	21.3	422,464	4.2	19.5
1971	11,823,812	2,826,421	23.9	813,779	6.9	28.8
1972	13,001,746	2,736,050	21.0	838,958	6.5	30.7
1973	14,380,069	2,626,929	18.3	823,041	5.7	31.3

1974	11,358,012	2,719,316	23.9	999,577	8.8	36.8
1975	10,659,257	2,199,909	20.6	919,949	8.6	41.8
1976	12,809,494	2,701,292	21.1	1,370,445	10.7	50.7
1977	14,335,562	3,016,828	21.0	1,714,572	12.0	56.8
1978	14,909,444	3,394,633	22.8	1,892,537	12.7	55.8
1979	13,828,904	3,281,087	23.7	2,072,666	15.0	63.2
1980	11,237,714	3,591,618	32.0	2,407,645	21.4	67.0
1981	10,629,408	3,737,271	35.2	2,304,814	21.7	61.7
1982	10,184,813	3,765,508	37.0	2,105,519	20.7	55.9
1983	11,900,742	4,475,799	37.6	2,234,375	18.8	49.9
1984	14,484,154	5,904,893	40.8	2,370,794	16.4	40.1

Sources: *Motor Vehicle Manufacturers Association of the U.S.; World Motor Vehicle Data; Ward's Automotive Yearbook, Automotive News.*

Note: *Sales indicate new vehicle registrations, except for 1984. Imports include vehicles from Canada.*

391

Appendix D: Japanese Automobile Production and Growth Rates, 1955-1984 (vehicles, %)

	Industry		Nissan		Toyota	
Year	Production	Growth Rate	Production	Growth Rate	Production	Growth Rate
1955	68,932	−1.6	21,767	9.8	22,786	0.3
1956	111,066	61.1	33,512	54.0	46,417	103.7
1957	181,977	63.8	58,940	75.9	79,527	71.3
1958	188,303	3.5	54,840	−7.0	78,856	−0.8
1959	262,814	40.0	77,822	41.9	101,194	28.3
1960	481,551	83.2	115,465	48.4	154,770	52.9
1961	813,879	69.0	165,737	43.5	210,937	36.3
1962	990,706	21.7	212,258	28.1	230,350	9.2
1963	1,283,531	29.6	268,315	26.4	318,495	38.3
1964	1,702,475	32.6	348,237	29.8	425,764	33.7
1965	1,875,614	10.2	345,165	−0.9	477,643	12.2
1966	2,286,399	21.9	471,598	36.6	587,539	23.0
1967	3,146,486	37.6	726,067	54.0	832,130	41.6
1968	4,085,826	29.9	979,834	35.0	1,097,405	31.9
1969	4,674,932	14.4	1,148,715	17.2	1,471,211	34.1
1970	5,289,157	13.1	1,374,022	19.6	1,609,190	9.4
1971	5,810,774	9.9	1,591,490	15.8	1,955,033	21.5
1972	6,294,438	8.3	1,864,244	17.1	2,087,133	6.8
1973	7,082,757	12.5	2,039,341	9.4	2,308,098	10.6
1974	6,551,840	−7.5	1,809,036	−11.3	2,114,980	−8.4

Appendix D: Continued

	Industry		Nissan		Toyota	
Year	Production	Growth Rate	Production	Growth Rate	Production	Growth Rate
1975	6,941,591	5.9	2,077,447	14.8	2,336,053	10.5
1976	7,841,447	13.0	2,303,703	10.9	2,487,851	6.5
1977	8,514,522	8.6	2,278,051	−1.1	2,720,758	9.4
1978	9,269,153	8.9	2,392,598	5.0	2,929,157	7.7
1979	9,635,546	4.0	2,337,821	−2.3	2,996,225	2.3
1980	11,042,884	14.6	2,644,052	13.1	3,293,344	9.9
1981	11,179,962	1.2	2,584,288	−2.3	3,220,418	−2.2
1982	10,731,794	−4.0	2,407,734	−6.8	3,144,557	−2.4
1983	11,111,659	3.5	2,482,540	3.1	3,272,335	4.1
1984	11,464,920	3.2	2,481,686	0.0	3,429,249	4.8

Sources: Japan Automobile Manufacturers Association; Motor Vehicle Manufacturers Association of the U.S.

Appendix E: Japanese Automobile Exports, 1957-1984 (A = Growth rate over previous year;
B = Exports as a % of total production; C = Company share of total industry exports)

Year	Industry			Nissan				Toyota			
	Exports	A(%)	B(%)	Exports	A(%)	B(%)	C(%)	Exports	A(%)	B(%)	C(%)
1957	6,554	167.8	3.6	739	32.7	1.3	11.3	4,117	373.8	5.2	62.8
1958	10,243	56.3	5.4	3,232	337.3	5.9	31.6	5,523	34.2	7.0	53.9
1959	19,285	88.3	7.3	6,219	92.4	8.0	32.2	6,134	11.1	6.1	31.8
1960	38,809	101.2	8.1	10,944	76.0	9.5	28.2	6,397	4.3	4.1	16.5
1961	57,037	47.0	7.0	15,535	41.9	9.4	27.2	11,675	82.5	5.5	20.5
1962	66,690	16.9	6.7	26,669	71.7	12.6	40.0	11,207	-4.0	4.9	16.8
1963	98,564	47.8	7.7	44,911	68.4	16.7	45.6	24,379	117.5	7.7	24.7
1964	150,421	52.6	8.8	68,389	52.3	19.6	45.5	42,785	75.5	10.0	28.4
1965	194,168	29.1	10.4	73,157	7.0	21.2	37.7	63,474	48.4	13.3	32.7
1966	255,734	31.7	11.2	98,219	34.3	20.8	38.4	105,145	65.7	17.9	41.1
1967	362,245	41.6	11.5	132,507	34.9	18.2	36.6	157,882	50.2	19.0	43.6
1968	612,429	69.1	15.0	206,657	56.0	21.1	33.7	279,087	76.8	25.4	45.6
1969	858,068	40.1	18.4	300,292	45.3	26.1	35.0	395,102	41.6	26.9	46.0

1970	1,086,776	26.7	20.5	395,300	31.6	28.8	36.4	481,892	22.0	29.9	44.3
1971	1,779,024	63.7	30.6	631,205	59.7	39.7	35.5	786,287	63.2	40.2	44.2
1972	1,965,245	10.5	31.2	715,770	13.4	38.4	36.4	724,552	−7.9	34.7	36.9
1973	2,067,556	5.2	29.2	710,624	−0.7	34.8	34.4	720,640	−0.5	31.2	34.9
1974	2,618,087	26.6	40.0	863,986	21.6	47.8	33.0	856,265	18.8	40.5	32.7
1975	2,677,612	2.3	38.6	884,864	2.4	42.6	33.0	868,352	1.4	37.2	32.4
1976	3,709,608	38.5	47.3	1,142,967	29.2	49.6	30.8	1,177,314	35.6	47.3	31.7
1977	4,352,817	17.3	51.1	1,216,986	6.5	53.4	28.0	1,413,235	20.0	51.9	32.5
1978	4,600,735	5.7	49.6	1,218,986	0.2	50.9	26.5	1,382,174	−2.2	47.2	30.0
1979	4,562,781	−0.8	47.4	1,134,191	−7.0	48.5	24.9	1,383,648	0.1	46.2	30.3
1980	5,966,961	30.8	54.0	1,465,827	29.2	55.4	24.6	1,785,445	29.0	54.2	29.9
1981	6,048,447	1.4	54.1	1,436,995	−2.0	55.6	23.8	1,716,486	−3.9	53.3	28.4
1982	5,590,513	−7.6	52.1	1,342,196	−6.6	55.7	24.0	1,665,793	−3.0	53.0	29.8
1983	5,669,510	1.4	51.0	1,359,724	1.3	54.8	24.0	1,664,361	−0.1	50.9	29.4
1984	6,109,184	7.8	53.3	1,403,386	3.2	56.5	23.0	1,800,923	8.2	52.5	29.5

Sources: Japan Automobile Manufacturers Association; Motor Vehicle Manufacturers Association of the U.S.; Japan Economic Review.

Appendix F: Vehicle Productivity at Nissan and Toyota, 1950-1983

FY	Toyota			Nissan		
	Vehicles	Employees	V/E	Vehicles	Employees	V/E
1950	11,706	5,887	2.0	12,458	6,599	1.9
1955	22,145	5,772	3.8	22,826	6,690	3.4
1956	43,289	5,693	7.6	42,177	7,069	6.0
1957	78,133	6,187	12.6	58,159	8,037	7.2
1958	78,187	6,453	12.1	57,624	7,714	7.5
1959	97,832	7,131	13.7	84,193	9,041	9.3
1960	149,694	10,091	14.8	129,893	11,008	11.8
1961	205,377	12,719	16.1	177,370	12,970	13.7
1962	230,297	14,242	16.2	223,871	15,247	14.7
1963	306,961	16,411	18.7	289,982	17,627	16.5
1964	418,270	20,504	20.4	351,625	19,984	17.6
1965	480,897	24,758	19.4	352,514	26,422	13.3
1966	565,904	26,853	21.1	548,583	30,291	18.1
1967	813,427	30,748	26.5	781,207	37,206	21.0
1968	1,072,977	35,267	30.4	1,026,112	43,529	23.6
1969	1,443,853	38,941	37.1	1,209,620	45,747	26.4
1970	1,592,888	41,720	38.2	1,421,142	46,986	30.2
1971	1,935,921	44,518	43.5	1,666,124	49,002	34.0
1972	2,062,776	45,110	45.7	1,903,414	51,060	37.3
1973	2,326,864	46,529	50.0	1,996,427	52,096	38.3
1974	2,160,350	48,320	44.7	1,851,271	52,146	35.5

Appendix F: Continued

	Toyota			Nissan		
FY	**Vehicles**	**Employees**	**V/E**	**Vehicles**	**Employees**	**V/E**
1975	2,463,623	49,090	50.2	2,111,957	51,654	40.9
1976	2,644,696	49,283	53.7	2,301,444	52,059	44.2
1977	2,804,303	49,721	56.4	2,353,729	53,539	44.0
1978	2,860,549	50,053	57.2	2,374,023	55,125	43.1
1979	3,249,271	51,125	63.6	2,412,069	56,270	42.9
1980	3,254,942	53,060	61.3	2,648,674	56,540	46.8
1981	3,158,547	55,279	57.1	2,575,110	57,091	45.1
1982	3,182,718	56,589	56.2	2,406,169	58,052	41.4
1983	3,376,224	58,706	57.5	2,518,491	59,335	42.4

Source: Yūka shōken hōkokusho.

Notes: The Toyota employee figures include Toyota Motor Sales. The figures for 1950 are for the calendar year. The fiscal years for Nissan and Toyota Motor Sales were from April of the year indicated through March of the following year. For Toyota, the fiscal year used above went from December through November of the year indicated from 1955 to 1974, and from July of the year indicated through June for 1975-1983. Employee figures include executives on the board of directors (full-time members only) and are averages for the 12-month period.

Appendix G: Capacity Utilization and Labor-Hour Differentials, 1965-1983

| | Capacity Utilization[a](%) | | | Annual Hours per Employee[b] | | |
| | United | | | | United | |
FY	States	Nissan	Toyota	Japan	States	(Japan = 100)
1965	96	89	103[c]	2370	2202	93
1970	81	82	101	2299	1991	87
1975	83	93	102	2191	1936	88
1979	84	96	117	2192	2011	92
1980	67	97	114	2170	1921	89
1981	63	94	109	2159	1929	89
1982	60	82	104	2172	1902	88
1983	76	85	100	2174	2033	94

Sources: U.S. Department of Commerce, Bureau of the Census, Statistical Abstract of the United States, 1984, *pp. 765, 793, and* Annual Survey of Manufacturers; *U.S. Department of Commerce, Bureau of Economic Analysis,* Survey of Current Business *and current telephone interview (for 1983 capacity figure), 5 March 1985; Nihon Kōgyō Ginkō,* Keizai tōkei nenkan; *Keizai Kikakuchō,* Nihon keizai shihyō; yūka shōken hōkokusho.

Notes: [a]Capacity utilization equals nominal capacity divided by actual production (see Chapter 4 and notes for additional explanations). For the U.S. auto industry, the figures refer to motor-vehicle body and components manufacturers.

[b]Average hours per employee reflect total hours worked per year (scheduled and overtime) for production workers in the U.S. auto industry and in the Japanese transportation and communication industries, the closest available comparison since actual company data on hours worked are not published in annual reports.

[c]The 1965 figure for Toyota is an estimate, based on the assumption (derived from comparisons from other years) that Toyota's actual capacity utilization was around 16% higher than Nissan's. It was necessary to make this adjustment since Toyota published a utilization figure for 1965 of 142.5%; this suggests that the company was using about 1½ shifts (or the equivalent in overtime) while calculating utilization on the basis of 1 shift.

Appendix H: Price Indexes and Purchasing-Power Parity (PPP) Rates

Consumer Price Indexes for Private Transportation (Automobiles and Related Expenses):

Year	Japan	United States	PPP Yen Rates (= $1.00)
1960	38.6	30.8	215
1965	40.6	32.8	213
1970	47.5	37.8	215
1975	77.8	51.0	260
1980	95.8	84.8	193
1981	97.9	94.4	177
1982	102.9	97.8	178
1983	100.0	100.0	170

General Consumer Price Indexes:

Year	Japan	United States	PPP Yen Rates (= $1.00)
1960	22.1	29.7	164
1965	29.5	31.7	203
1970	38.6	39.0	218
1975	66.5	54.0	271
1980	91.2	82.7	243
1981	95.6	91.3	231
1982	98.2	96.9	224
1983	100.0	100.0	220

Price Deflators for Domestic Non-Residential Fixed Investment:

Year	Japan	United States	PPP Yen Rates (= $1.00)
1960	53.1	35.1	331
1965	55.5	36.1	336
1970	61.8	44.1	303

Appendix H: Continued

Year	Japan	United States	PPP Yen Rates (= $1.00)
1975	88.3	63.9	299
1979	96.4	85.3	245
1980	102.2	90.0	245
1981	101.5	97.6	225
1982	100.7	101.4	214
1983	100.0[a]	100.0	217

Japanese Wholesale Price Index for Industrial Commodities:

1955	46.7
1960	47.2
1965	46.8
1970	51.3
1975	76.5
1980	99.2
1983	100.0

Sources: Bank of Japan; Economic Planning Agency (Japan); Prime Minister's Office; U.S. Departments of Labor and Commerce; Kravis et al., World Product and Income.

Note: [a]Based on first-quarter figure.

Appendix I: Fixed Assets (at Cost) per Employee, 1965-1983

FY	GM	Ford	Chrysler	Nissan	Toyota[a]
1983 Dollars					
1965	35,513	38,196	29,333	26,152	30,253
1970	45,188	39,923	32,781	38,756	57,287
1975	41,140	40,187	30,869	57,614[b]	72,336
1980	41,811	44,862	54,743	76,760	106,841
1983	57,142	52,100	62,090	119,137	150,649
Scale of Increase (Constant Dollar Values)					
1965	100	100	100	100	100
1970	127	105	112	148	189
1975	116	105	105	220	239
1980	118	117	187	294	353
1983	161	136	212	456	498
Relative Scale (GM = 100)					
1965	100	107	83	74	85
1970	"	88	73	86	127
1975	"	98	75	140	176
1980	"	107	131	184	256
1983	"	91	109	208	264

Source: Annual reports (English versions for Nissan and Toyota).

Notes: [a]*Figures for Toyota prior to 1983 are adjusted upward by 9% to account for the fixed assets of Toyota Motor Sales; this was the level of Toyota Motor Sales' fixed assets in the 2 years prior to the merger.*

[b]*Includes an estimate of 50% for accumulated depreciation not listed in Nissan's 1975 report. This estimate is based on data from other years.*

See Table 56 for an explanation of purchasing-power parity exchange rates.

NOTES

Introduction: A Half Century of Growth, Protection, and Promotion

1. Nissan Jidōsha Kabushiki Kaisha, *Nissan Jidōsha sanjū nen shi*, pp. 310-312; and *Tōyō keizai*, 23 May 1953, pp. 40-41.

2. *Nissan Jidōsha sanjū nen shi*, p. 134.

3. Mochikabu Kaisha Seiri Iin-kai, ed., *Nihon zaibatsu to sono kaitai*, I, 469 and 473.

4. Okumura Hiroshi, Hoshikawa Jun'ichi, and Matsui Kazuo, *Gendai no sangyō: jidōsha kōgyō*, p. 283.

5. This discussion is based on Arisawa Hiromi, ed., *Nihon sangyō hyaku nen shi*, I, 359-360; and Udagawa Masaru, "Nissan zaibatsu no jidōsha sangyō shinshutsu ni tsuite (1)," pp. 94-95.

6. Morikawa Hidemasa, *Zaibatsu no keiei shiteki kenkyū*, pp. 178-182; Okumura Shōji, "Jidōsha kōgyō no hatten dankai to kōzō," in Arisawa Hiromi, ed., *Gendai Nihon sangyō kōza* V, 269-270.

7. Tōyō Keizai Shimpōsha, ed., *Nihon no kaisha hyaku nen shi*, pp. 583-584. See also Isuzu Jidōsha Kabushiki Kaisha, *Isuzu Jidōsha shi*.

8. This discussion is based on Nihon Jidōsha Kōgyō Kai, ed., *Nihon jidōsha kōgyō shikō*, II, 20-45.

9. Udagawa Masaru, "Nissan zaibatsu no jidōsha sangyō shinshutsu ni tsuite (1)," pp. 97-99.

10. *Nissan Jidōsha sanjū nen shi*, pp. 96, 116.

11. The chairman in April 1985 was Nissan's Ishihara Takashi.

12. Interviews with Hara Teiichi, 12 May 1982, and Terazawa Ichibei, 31 May 1982. (Biographical data on interview subjects can be found in the bibliography.)

13. *Nissan Jidōsha sanjū nen shi*, p. 138.

14. This is discussed in Hiroya Ueno and Hiromichi Muto, "The Automobile Industry of Japan," in Kazuo Sato, ed., *Industry and Business in Japan*, pp. 148-155, and Masaru Udagawa, "Historical Development of the Japanese Automobile Industry, 1917-1971: Business and Government," pp. 37-39.

15. Ira C. Magaziner, "Japanese Industrial Policy: Source of Strength for the Automobile Industry," in Robert E. Cole, ed., *The Japanese Automobile Industry: Model and Challenge for the Future?*, pp. 79-83.

16. Chalmers Johnson's book *MITI and the Japanese Miracle: The Growth of Industrial Policy, 1925-1975*, presents an accurate history of MITI as an institution but, in doing so, the author tends to understate the enormous contribution of private firms to industrial development in Japan. Despite its importance to the growth of the domestic economy as well as to exports,

Johnson devotes scarce attention to the automobile industry—where he would have found less evidence pointing to a major role for MITI, except as a protector of local manufacturers.

17. *Nissan Jidōsha sanjū nen shi*, pp. 219-220, and Gendai Kigyō Kenkyū Kai, ed., *Nissan Jidōsha*, p. 19.

18. *Nissan Jidōsha sanjū nen shi*, pp. 349-350; and *Nihon sangyō hyaku nen shi*, II, 183-184.

19. Jidōsha Kōgyō Shinkō Kai, *Jidōsha hakubutsukan chōsa hōkokusho*, I, 16-19.

20. Nihon Jidōsha Kōgyō Kai, *Nihon no jidōsha kōgyō*.

21. Iwakoshi Tadahiro, *Jidōsha kōgyō ron*, p. 113. This study of the Japanese automobile industry in the mid-1960s, written for an academic audience, is particularly valuable because Iwakoshi (1937-1981) was an executive vice-president of Nissan at the time of its publication. The author wrote most of the book during 1962-1963 while he was a visiting lecturer in the economics division of the University of Tokyo, his alma mater. He entered Nissan in 1937 and later rose from director in 1952 to president of the company during 1973-1977. Until his death Iwakoshi served as vice-chairman.

22. *Nissan Jidōsha sanjū nen shi*, pp. 369-371.

23. Magaziner, pp. 81-82; and Tetsuo Sakiya, *Honda Motor: The Men, the Management, the Machines*, pp. 136-137.

24. These regulations are listed in *Jidōsha hakubutsukan chōsa hōkokusho*, I, 52-55.

25. Annual reports.

26. Nissan Jidōsha Kabushiki Kaisha Chōsa-bu, *Jidōsha kōgyō handobukku* (1983), p. 373.

27. *The Japan Times*, 27 March 1983, p. 1.

28. Nissan *Jidōsha kōgyō handobukku* (1984), p. 456.

Chapter 1: Company Origins and Truck Technology Transfer

1. Interview with former Nissan president Asahara Genshichi, "Nissan Jidōsha shi hanashi," recorded in Jidōsha Kōgyō Shinkō Kai, ed., *Nihon jidōsha kōgyō shi kōjutsu kiroku shū*, II, 98.

2. *Nihon zaibatsu to sono kaitai*, II, 383-384. These yen values should not be confused with the postwar currency. Between 1915 and 1931, 2 yen were worth about 1 dollar. This dropped to 3 or 4 per dollar during the mid-1930s. The yen was not readily convertible from the late 1930s until 1949 when, due to extreme inflation, GHQ fixed its value at 360 per U.S. dollar. It remained at this level until a 1971 revaluation and the adoption of floating exchange rates.

3. For a comprehensive list of combines and their investments, see Yamazaki Hiroaki, "Senji shita no sangyō kōzō to dokusen soshiki," in Tōkyō Daigaku Shakai Kagaku Kenkyūjo, ed., *Senji Nihon Keizai*, II, 236-237.

4. Aikawa Yoshisuke, *Watakushi no rirekisho*, XXIV, 277, 284-291.

5. Ibid., pp. 297-302; Ozawa Chikamitsu, *Aikawa Yoshisuke den*, pp. 39-41.

6. Udagawa Masaru, "Nissan zaibatsu keisei katei no keiei shiteki kosatsu," pp. 12-13; Aikawa, *Watakushi no rirekisho*, pp. 301-302; Ozawa, pp. 45-46.

7. Aikawa, *Watakushi no rirekisho*, pp. 305-308; Ozawa, p. 51.

8. Aikawa, *Watakushi no rirekisho*, p. 316; Udagawa, "Nissan zaibatsu keisei katei no keiei shiteki kōsatsu," pp. 26-21.

9. Udagawa Masaru, "Shinkō zaibatsu: Nissan o chūshin ni," in Yasuoka Shigeaki, ed., *Nihon no zaibatsu*, pp. 110, 112; also see Udagawa, "Nissan zaibatsu keisei katei no keiei shiteki kōsatsu," pp. 1-2.

10. Aikawa, *Watakushi no rirekisho*, pp. 317-319; Ozawa, pp. 58-59; Udagawa, "Nissan zaibatsu keisei katei no keiei shiteki kōsatsu," pp. 23-24.

11. Yoshisuke Aikawa, "New Capitalism and Holding Company" (text of a lecture to the Tokyo Bankers' Association on 6 and 7 November 1934, titled "Shinshihon-shugi to mochikabu kaisha" and translated into English in May 1935 by Nippon Industries), pp. 2-4.

12. Udagawa, "Nissan zaibatsu keisei katei no keiei shiteki kosatsu," p. 30.

13. Interview with Aikawa Yaichi, 7 September 1982. For a further discussion of the move to Manchuria, see Hara Akira, " 'Manshū' ni okeru keizai tōsei seisaku no tenkai—Mantetsu kaiso to Mangyō setsuritsu o megutte," in Andō Yoshio, ed., *Nihon keizai seisaku shiron*, II, 239-242; and Tomoda Jōichirō, ed., "Aikawa Yoshisuke kaisō to hōfu," pp. 36-38.

14. While Japanese life insurance companies were the main financial backers of Manchuria Investment Securities, Aikawa retained control by issuing them non-voting stock and placing ownership of the voting shares under a private research foundation he created in 1942, the Gisei Kai. The funds for establishing the foundation came from a retirement bonus of a reported 10,000,000 yen that Manchuria Development paid to Aikawa. See Ozawa, pp. 84-85, and *Nihon zaibatsu to sono kaitai*, I, 152-153. The latter source indicates that Manchuria Development transferred 13,500,000 yen to Aikawa in care of the Gisei Kai, and that the funds came from a profit of 70,000,000 yen earned by selling stocks to Manchuria Investment Securities at a premium.

15. *Nihon zaibatsu to sono kaitai*, I, 151-153; Hara, pp. 275-277.

16. See Udagawa Masaru, "Nissan zaibatsu no keiei soshiki (1)," pp. 62-66, for a discussion of how Aikawa controlled the domestic subsidiaries.

17. Interviews with Aikawa Yaichi and Katayama Yutaka (10 June 1982).

18. Gendai Kigyō Kenkyū Kai, ed., *Nissan Jidōsha*, pp. 4-5.

19. The following is based on *Nihon jidōsha kōgyō shikō*, II, 303-324.

20. The following is based on *Nihon jidōsha kōgyō shikō*, II, 403-414.

21. Asahara interview in *Nihon jidōsha kōgyō shi kōjutsu kiroku shū*, II, 93-99; *Nihon jidōsha kōgyō shikō*, II, 476-485, and III, 129-133.

22. William R. Gorham Shi Kinen Jigyō Iinkai, ed., *William R. Gorham den*, pp.353-360.

23. *Nissan Jidōsha sanjū nen shi*, data section.

24. Asahara interview in *Nihon jidōsha kōgyō shi kōjutsu kiroku shū*, II, 97-98.

25. Interview with Okumura Shōji, 10 June 1982.

26. Asahara interview in *Nihon jidōsha kōgyō shi kōjutsu kiroku shū*, II, 100.

27. Yoshisuke Aikawa, "New Capitalism and Holding Company, pp. 23-25. Also see Aikawa, *Watakushi no rirekisho*, p. 324.

28. Aikawa outlined these plans in a speech given in Tokyo during 1934 titled "Nissan no shimei ni tsuite" (Concerning the mission of Nissan). This is reprinted in *Nissan Jidōsha sanjū nen shi*, pp. 39-40.

29. *Nissan Jidōsha sanjū nen shi*, pp. 41-42, 45.

30. This objective is formally stated in Jidōsha Seizō Kabushiki Kaisha "Dai ikkai hōkokusho," December 1933 to April 1934. This was Nissan's first annual report (*eigyō hōkokusho*,) before the adoption of the modern company name.

31. Udagawa Masaru, "Nissan zaibatsu no jidōsha sangyō shinshutsu ni tsuite (1)," pp. 93-109, and "Nissan zaibatsu no jidōsha sangyō shinshutsu ni tsuite (2)," pp. 73-95.

32. *Nissan jidōsha sanjū nen shi*, pp. 77-78.

33. Asahara interview in *Nihon jidōsha kōgyō shi kōjutsu kiroku shū*, II, 111-113.

34. Interview with Kawazoe Sōichi, 2 June 1982.

35. *Nissan Jidōsha sanjū nen shi*, pp. 38, 51.

36. This discussion is based on interviews with Gotō Takashi, "Datsun no ryōsan-ka to gijutsu kakushin," pp.88-91, and with Hatamura Yasushi and Hosaka Tōru, "Nissan Jidōsha sōgyō toki no kikai setsubi to seizō gijutsu," recorded in *Nihon jidōsha kōgyō shi kōjutsu kiroku shū*, II. Also, "Nijū-go nen kan no omoide," pp. 12-13.

37. *Nissan Jidōsha sanjū nen shi*, p. 51.

38. After Tobata merged with Tōa Electric Machinery and became a subsidiary of Hitachi prior to being absorbed in 1937, Gorham remained in a precision-machinery and communications-equipment division created within Hitachi and also worked at Hitachi Seiki, a machine-tool manufacturing subsidiary established in 1936. He adopted Japanese citizenship and stayed in Japan during the 1940s, then returned to Nissan in 1945 as an executive director. He resigned in 1947 under the purge of business executives and went to work under Yamamoto Sōji as a vice-president of Fuji Motors. Gorham established his own consulting firm in 1948 but died the following year at the age of 61. See *William R. Gorham den*, pp. 353-360.

39. Katayama interview (31 May 1982).

40. Interview with Kubota Tokujirō, "Gorham-shiki san-rinsha kara Datsun made," recorded in *Nihon jidōsha kōgyō shi kōjutsu kiroku shū*, II, 68-70.

41. Asahara interview in *Nihon jidōsha kōgyō shi kōjutsu kiroku shū*, II, 105-106, and *Nissan Jidōsha sanjū nen shi*, pp. 61-62.

42. Asahara interview in *Nihon jidōsha kōgyō shi kōjutsu kiroku shū*, II, 107-108.

43. This discussion is based on the Kubota interview recorded in *Nihon jidōsha kōgyō shi kōjutsu kiroku shū*, II, 68-72; *Nihon jidōsha kōgyō shikō*, III, 314-316; *Nissan Jidōsha sanjū nen shi*, p. 62-64; and an interview with Sasaki Sadamichi, 18 May 1982.

44. Mitsubishi Shōji Kabushiki Kaisha, *Ritsugyō bōeki-roku*, pp. 228-229, 234.

45. Interviews with Sasaki and Kawazoe.

46. Sasaki interview.

47. Kawazoe interview; Hatamura and Hosaka, pp. 127-130.

48. Interview with Maeda Riichi, 21 May 1982.

49. Maeda interviews, 21 May and 22 July 1982. Also, Asahara interview recorded in *Nihon jidosha kōgyō shi kōjutsu kiroku shū*, II, 111-112, and Okumura, "Jidōsha kōgyō no hatten dankai to kōzō," pp. 295-296. Okumura, at the time, was making components for Nissan while employed by Hitachi.

50. Hatamura and Hosaka, p. 132.

51. *Nissan Jidōsha sanjū nen shi*, p. 362.

52. Maeda interview (21 May 1982). Also, Asahara interview recorded in *Nihon jidōsha kōgyō shi kōjutsu kiroku shū*, II, 113-114; and Okumura, "Jidōsha kōgyō no hatten dankai to kōzō," pp. 295-296.

53. Asahara interview recorded in *Nihon jidōsha kōgyō shi kōjutsu kiroku shū*, II, 115-116.

54. Interview with Asahara Hideo, 19 May 1982. Also, see the Asahara interview in *Nihon jidōsha kōgyō shi kōjutsu kiroku shū*, II, 93-95.

55. Udagawa, "Nissan zaibatsu no keiei soshiki (1)," pp. 50-51.

56. Interviews with Terazawa and Asahara Hideo.

57. This discussion is based on the Asahara interview recorded in *Nihon jidōsha kōgyō shi kōjutsu kiroku shū*, II, 119-123; *Nissan Jidōsha sanjū nen shi*, pp. 123-124, 132; and the Terazawa interview.

58. Interview with Aikawa Yaichi.

59. Interview with Asahara Hideo.

60. See "Nissan Konwa Kai kaihō."

61. Tōyō Keizai, *Kaisha shikihō*. This shareholding was also mutual: Nissan and Hitachi in 1983 were the fifth and seventh largest shareholders in the bank, owning 2.5% and 1.5% of its outstanding shares, respectively.

62. This organization, referred to as Chūseiren in Japanese, was the predecessor of Techno-Venture.

63. Ozawa, pp. 95-116.

64. Katayama interview (31 May 1982).
65. Aikawa, *Watakushi no rirekisho*, p. 288.
66. Katayama interview (10 June 1982).
67. Ibid.
68. Ozaki Masahisa, *Toyoda Kiichirō shi*, pp. 33-50.
69. Ōno Taichi, *Toyota seisan hōshiki*, pp. 143-144.
70. Morikawa Hidemasa, "Toyoda Kiichirō," in Morikawa Hidemasa et al., *Nihon no kigyōka* III, 16-18; Toyota Jidōsha Kabushiki Kaisha, *Toyota Jidōsha sanjū nen shi*, p. 11; and Ozaki, *Toyoda Kiichirō shi*, pp. 40, 49.
71. Morikawa, "Toyoda Kiichirō," pp. 34-35, and Okumura Shōji, "Jidōsha kōgyō no hatten dankai to kōzō," pp. 284-285.
72. Morikawa, "Toyoda Kiichirō," pp. 34-35.
73. Shotaro Kamiya, *My Life with Toyota*, p. 109.
74. Kamiya, p. 260, and Okumura, "Jidōsha kōgyō no hatten dankai to kōzō," pp. 284-285.
75. Toyoda Kiichirō, "Toyota Jidōsha ga konnichi ni itaru made," in Ozaki, *Toyoda Kiichirō shi*, p. 154; see also Morikawa, "Toyoda Kiichirō," pp. 38-41.
76. Toyoda Kiichirō in Ozaki, pp. 171-175.
77. Toyoda Kiichirō in Ozaki, pp. 172-173; Ozaki, pp. 152, 173-174; Kamiya, p. 107.
78. Toyoda Kiichirō in Ozaki, pp. 157-161.
79. Ozaki, pp. 54-55.
80. *Toyota Jidōsha sanjū nen shi*, pp. 51-55.
81. Ozaki, p.64
82. Toyoda Kiichirō in Ozaki, pp. 154-156. Chapter 4 discusses the establishment of this and other subsidiaries in more detail.
83. *Toyota Jidōsha sanjū nen shi*, pp. 41-42; Okumura, "Jidōsha kōgyō no hatten dankai to kōzō," pp. 271-273; Toyoda Kiichirō in Ozaki, pp. 163-164, 169-171.
84. *Toyota Jidōsha sanjū nen shi*, pp. 56-58.
85. Ibid., pp.59-67; Okumura, "Jidōsha kōgyō no hatten dankai to kōzō", pp. 277-288.
86. Toyoda Kiichirō in Ozaki, pp. 164-165; *Toyota Jidōsha sanjū nen shi*, pp. 57-58.
87. This discussion is based on Toyoda Kiichirō in Ozaki, pp. 166-171, and Okumura, "Jidōsha kōgyō no hatten dankai to kōzō," pp. 278-283.
88. *Toyota Jidōsha sanjū nen shi*, p. 67, and Ozaki, p. 90.
89. *Toyota Jidōsha sanjū nen shi*, p. 153.
90. Toyota Jidōsha Kōgyō Kabushiki Kaisha, *Toyota no ayumi*, pp. 189-190.
91. *Toyota Jidōsha sanjū nen shi*, pp. 202-204; and Ozaki, pp. 119-120.
92. *Toyota Jidōsha sanjū nen shi*, pp. 112-114, 353-355.
93. Maeda interview (21 May 1982).
94. Tōkai Aircraft switched to making automobile parts after 1945 and

changed its name to Aisin Seiki in 1965. See *Toyota Jidōsha sanjū nen shi*, pp. 205-210.

95. Ozaki, pp. 218-222; and Kamiya, p. 55.

Chapter 2: The Postwar Transition: Trucks to Cars

1. Eleanor Hadley, *Antitrust in Japan*, pp. 88-100.

2. Terazawa interview.

3. Shares held within the Mitsui group were sufficiently large for GHQ's Holding Company Liquidation Commission to designate Toyota as a Mitsui affiliate after World War II. Companies in the Mitsui group held a total of 12.2% of Toyota's outstanding shares at the end of the war, although the largest individual stockholders were Toyoda Automatic Loom (16.4%) and the family holding company, Toyoda Industries (12.0%). See *Nihon zaibatsu to sono kaitai*, II, 86 and 316.

4. *Toyota Jidōsha sanjū nen shi*, pp. 304-305.

5. *Yūka shōken hōkokusho.*

6. These historical ties with Mitsui were also reflected in the marriage of Toyoda Shōichirō to a member of the Mitsui family.

7. *Yūka shōken hōkokusho.*

8. *Nissan Jidōsha sanjū nen shi*, pp. 150-152, 208, 212, 249-250, and *yūka shōken hōkokusho.*

9. *Nissan Jidōsha sanjū nen shi*, pp. 160, 249; *Tōyō keizai*, 8 December 1951, pp. 48-49, and 26 April 1952, pp. 92-93.

10. Interview with Kawamata Katsuji, 8 June 1982; *Tōyō keizai*, 28 June 1952, p. 105; and *Nissan Jidōsha sanjū nen shi*, pp. 139, 160-161.

11. Kawamata interview. Also, Kawamata Katsuji, *Watakushi no rirekisho*, pp. 71-85.

12. Kawamata interview, and Kawamata, *Watakushi no rirekisho*, pp. 111-116.

13. Kawamata, *Watakushi no rirekisho*, pp. 115-117, and Miki Yōnosuke, *Nissan no chōsen*, pp. 73-74.

14. *Nissan Jidōsha sanjū nen shi*, pp. 169-175.

15. Kawamata Katsuji, "Atarashii shijō kaitaku e no mosaku," p. 159.

16. *Nissan Jidōsha sanjū nen shi*, pp. 225-226, and *Tōyō keizai*, 28 October 1950, p. 59.

17. *Tōyō keizai*, 6 October 1951, p. 50.

18. *Tōyō keizai*, 28 October 1950, p. 56, and *Nihon sangyō hyaku nen shi*, II, 63.

19. This discussion is based on interviews with Kawamata, Okumura (30 June 1982), Maeda (22 July 1982), and Matsuzaki Shirō (14 July 1982).

20. Interviews with Kawazoe, Asahara Hideo, and Okumura (30 June 1982). See also Yamamoto Sōji, *Nihon jidōsha kōgyō no seichō to nenbō.*

21. Interview with Asahara Hideo.

22. Kawamata interview.

23. Interviews with Kawazoe, Okumura, and Katayama.

24. Interviews with Asahara Hideo and Katayama (31 May 1982). Also see Masuda Tetsuo, *Ashita no hitotachi: Nissan rōdōsha no tatakai*, pp. 3-4.

25. Asahara interview recorded in *Nihon jidōsha kōgyō shi kōjutsu kiroku shū*, II, 116-117.

26. This discussion is based on the Hara interview, and Ikari Yoshirō, *Dai-Ichi Sharyō Sekkei-bu: Bluebird no otoko-tachi*, pp. 12-20.

27. *Nissan Jidōsha sanjū nen shi*, pp. 181, 210-212, and Ikari, p. 13.

28. Maeda interview (21 May 1982). I have checked this statement by examining accounts of the research conducted at Nissan and selected suppliers between 1947 and 1957 found in the in-house technical journal, *Nissan gijutsu* (Nissan engineering, volumes 1-29). More than 50% of the articles dealt specifically with manufacturing processes and only around 10% with vehicle designs. Approximately 20% were concerned with engines, transmissions, power-drive trains, and related components, 10% with steel materials, 5% with the testing of in-house models, and 2% with analyses of foreign vehicles, excluding the Austin.

29. Kawamata interview. Also, *Tōyō keizai*, 23 May 1953, pp. 40-41.

30. Kawamata interview. Also, *Tōyō keizai*, 1 November 1952, p. 50, and Kamiya, p. 114.

31. Interview with Asahara Hideo.

32. Interviews with Maeda (21 May 1982), Okumura (10 June 1982), Matsuzaki (14 July 1982), Katayama (31 May 1982), and Asahara Hideo.

33. Interviews with Maeda (21 May 1982) and Igarashi Tadashi, 11 June 1982.

34. Hara interview.

35. Kawamata interview. Also, Kawamata, "Atarashii shijō kaitaku e no mosaku," p. 161, and *Watakushi no rirekisho*, pp. 129-131.

36. *Nissan Jidōsha sanjū nen shi*, pp. 312-313. Also, interviews with Okumura (10 June 1982) and Sasaki.

37. Maeda interview (22 July 1982).

38. *Nissan Jidōsha sanjū nen shi*, pp. 312-313.

39. *Nissan Jidōsha sanjū nen shi*, pp. 313-314. Nissan also signed a 5-year agreement for service parts in 1960 with BMC that involved a single payment of 10,000 pounds and included manufacturing rights to components that Austin made in house. See *Nissan News*, July 1960, p. 2.

40. *Nissan Jidōsha sanjū nen shi*, pp. 331-333, and Iwakoshi, p. 92.

41. Sasaki interview.

42. *Nissan Jidōsha sanjū nen shi*, p. 297, and Harashina Kyōichi, "Austin kokusanka tassei ni atari," p. 1.

43. Calculated from Austin price data in Gendai Kigyō Kenkyū Kai, ed., *Nissan Jidōsha*, p. 107.

44. *Nissan Jidōsha sanjū nen shi*, data section.

45. Sasaki interview.

46. Fujita Shōjirō and Takagi Takeshi, "Austin A50 Cambridge no seinō ni tsuite," pp. 2-11.

47. Hara interview.

48. Ishida Takao, Nara Hideo, and Suzuki Kōzō, "Austin chūtetsu imono kokusanka no keika ni tsuite," pp. 44-54.

49. Interviews with Katayama (31 May 1982) and Okumura (10 June 1982).

50. Sasaki interview.

51. Endō Akira, "Body kokusanka no kaikoroku," pp. 18-21.

52. Ikari, pp. 39-41.

53. Kimura Hitoshi (Hitachi Ltd.), "A50 no kokusanka kikaki," pp. 26-31; Nihon Hatsujo Sekkei-bu Shasshi Sekkei-ka, "Austin yō supuringu no kokusanka ni tsuite," pp. 32-38; Tōkyō Kiki Kōgyō Jidōsha Sekkei-ka to Nissan Jidōsha Shasshi Sekkei-ka Sekkei-bu, "Austin shock-absorber no kokusanka," pp. 39-43.

54. Nissan Jidōsha Gijutsu-bu, "Austin cylinder block oyobi cylinder head yō transfer machines ni tsuite," p. 12. Also, *Toyota Jidōsha sanjū nen shi*, pp. 405-406.

55. Nissan Jidōsha Gijutsu-bu, "Austin cylinder block oyobi cylinder head yō transfer machines ni tsuite," p. 12-17, and Sasaki interview.

56. Also see *Nissan Jidōsha sanjū nen shi*, pp. 329-330.

57. *Nissan Jidōsha sanjū nen shi*, pp. 330, 425.

58. Hara interview.

59. Interviews with Okumura (10 June 1982) and Matsuzaki (19 January 1983); *Toyota Jidōsha sanjū nen shi*, p. 440.

60. Okumura interview (10 June 1982).

61. Interviews with Sasaki and Okumura (10 June 1983). Also, Okumura Shōji, "Concept of Technology Transfer as Reviewed from Japan's Experience," pp. 8-9.

62. Interviews with Kawamata, Sasaki, Matsuzaki (14 July 1982), and Okumura (10 June 1982).

63. Interviews with Hara, Maeda (21 May 1982), and Igarashi. Also, Endō, pp. 21-22.

64. *Nissan Jidōsha sanjū nen shi*, pp. 415-418.

65. Hara interview. Also, *Nissan Jidōsha sanjū nen shi*, pp. 362-363.

66. Nissan Jidōsha Kabushiki Kaisha, *Nissan Jidōsha shashi*, p. 355.

67. Hara interview.

68. Ibid.

69. See Fujita Shōtarō and Takagi Takeshi, "Austin A50 Cambridge no seinō ni tsuite."

70. *Nissan Jidōsha sanjū nen shi*, pp. 418-420.

71. *Nissan Jidōsha shashi*, p. 373.

72. Hara interview.

73. See Alfred P. Sloan, Jr., *My Years with General Motors*, pp. 192-193, 274-285, 309.

74. See Iwakoshi, pp. 231-234, and Shoichiro Toyoda, "Automotive Industry," in J.M. Juran, ed., *Quality Control Handbook*, Section 42, p. 6.

75. Katayama interview (31 May 1982).

76. Chapter 6 discusses this topic further under design quality.
77. This discussion is based on Kamiya, p. 70; *Toyota Jidōsha sanjū nen shi*, pp. 346-348; and an interview with Kamiya recorded in Morikawa Hidemasa, ed., *Sengo sangyō shi e no shōgen*, II, 31-32.
78. See also the Asahara interview recorded in *Nihon jidōsha kōgyō shi kōjutsu kiroku shū*, II, 111-113.
79. Kamiya, p. 61.
80. Interviews with Okumura (10 June 1982) and Maeda (21 May 1982). Also, Okumura, "Jidōsha kōgyō no hatten dankai to kōzō," p. 283.
81. *Toyota Jidōsha sanjū nen shi*, pp. 43, 168, 752; also, Kodaira Katsumi, *Jidōsha*, pp. 118-120.
82. *Toyota Jidōsha sanjū nen shi*, pp. 160-163, 193.
83. Ibid., pp. 249-252.
84. *Toyota Jidōsha sanjū nen shi* pp. 356, 844-845; also Kamiya, p. 121, and *Tōyō keizai*, 30 July 1955, p. 40.
85. Gendai Kigyō Kenkyū Kai, ed., *Toyota to Nissan*, pp. 89-91.
86. *Toyota Jidōsha sanjū nen shi*, p. 840; Kamiya, p. 123; Gendai Kigyō Kenkyū Kai, ed., *Nissan Jidōsha*, pp. 90-91.
87. Wakayama Fujio and Sugimoto Tadaaki, *Toyota no himitsu*, pp. 122-123.
88. This discussion is based on Kamiya, pp. 18-51.
89. Okumura interviews (10 June and 30 June 1982).
90. *Nissan Jidōsha sanjū nen shi*, p. 148.
91. Katayama interviews (31 May and 10 June 1982).
92. Kamiya, pp. 66-67; Wakayama and Sugimoto, p. 127; Okumura, "Jidōsha kōgyō no hatten dankai to kōzō," p. 357; Sakiya, pp. 84-85.
93. Kamiya, pp. 39-40, 57-58, 127; Katayama interview (31 May 1982); Wakayama and Sugimoto, pp. 141-142.
94. Kamiya, pp. 59-60, and Toyota Jidōsha Hanbai Kabushiki Kaisha, *Mōtarizeishon to tomo ni*, pp. 222-225. Also, interviews with Katayama and Okumura (10 June 1982).
95. Kamiya, pp. 56 and 117; Wakayama and Sugimoto, pp. 166-170; *Tōyō keizai*, 5 May 1956, p. 56.
96. Wakayama and Sugimoto, pp. 126-127, 143-144.
97. Kamiya, pp. 64-65, 117-119.
98. Ibid., pp. 62-64.
99. Interview with Kiyomasa Minoru, 11 March 1983.
100. *Jidōsha hakubutsukan chōsa hōkoku sho*, I, 52-55; Katayama interviews (31 May and 10 June 1982); Okumura, Hoshikawa, and Matsui, pp. 200-204; Wakayama and Sugimoto, pp. 128-129. The "price wars" were also followed by the leading business weekly. See *Tōyō keizai*, 19 November 1955, p. 114; 11 February 1956, p. 62; 2 March 1957, pp. 74-76; 18 May 1957, p. 111, 9 July 1960, p. 22; 12 November 1960, pp. 76-77.
101. *Yūka shōken hōkokusho*.

102. These comments are based on interviews with Katayama, Okumura, Maeda, and Matsuzaki.

103. *Mōtarizeishon to tomo ni*, p. 314; *Toyota no ayumi*, p. 360; Wakayama and Sugimoto, pp. 31, 160-165.

104. Interview with Kamio Takashi, 18 March 1983.

105. Wakayama and Sugimoto, p. 28-31.

106. *Nissan Jidōsha sanjū nen shi* pp. 253, 462-469; Toyota Jidōsha Kabushiki Kaisha, *Kōhō shiryō* (1982), p. 163; and Nissan Jidōsha Kabushiki Kaisha, "Nissan Jidōsha no gaiyō" (1981), p. 29.

107. This discussion is based on *Tōyō keizai*, 22 June 1957, pp. 62-63; 11 July 1959, p. 40; and summer supplement, No. 3, 1960, pp. 82-83.

108. See *Mōtarizeishon to tomo ni*, p. 250; *Nissan News* 79:3 (November 1958), and *Tōyō keizai*, 11 October 1958, pp. 106-109.

109. Kamiya, pp. 74-82; *Toyota Jidōsha sanjū nen shi*, pp. 456-457, and John B. Rae, *Nissan-Datsun: A History of Nissan Motor Corporation in U.S.A., 1960-1980*, pp. 15-18.

110. Kawazoe interview.

111. Katayama interview (31 May 1982). See also the company history written by John B. Rae.

112. Shibata Masaharu, "Amerika ni okeru mākettingu," p. 5; Wakayama and Sugimoto, p. 46.

113. Shibata, p. 5, and *Nissan News* 93:9 (January 1960).

114. Katayama interviews (31 May and 10 June 1982).

115. Interviews with Kawamata, and Okumura and Katayama (10 June 1982).

116. Interviews with Kamio, and Hamaguchi Haruo and Tsukioka Yukio, 22 November 1982.

Chapter 3: The Human Drama: Management and Labor

1. See Chapter 4 for figures on wage comparisons and vertical integration.

2. Nihon Seisansei Honbu, "Katsuyō rōdō tōkei" (Useful labor statistics), in Andō Yoshio, ed., *Kindai Nihon keizai shi yōran*, pp. 156, 183.

3. The following is based on Arisawa Hiromi, ed., *Shōwa keizai shi*, II, 224-226.

4. Kawamata, *Watakushi no rirekisho*, pp. 126-128.

5. *Nissan Jidōsha sanjū nen shi*, p. 259.

6. Chapter 5 will discuss this subject in more detail.

7. *Nissan Jidōsha sanjū nen shi*, pp. 162-163.

8. Kumagaya Tokuichi, "Zenjidōsha no rōdō undō to Nissan tōsō," p. 1.

9. Matsuzaki interview (14 July 1982).

10. Kumagaya, p. 2.

11. Ibid., pp. 1-3.

12. *Nissan Jidōsha sanjū nen shi*, pp. 165-166, 170-172, 196.

13. Strikes were not limited to the automobile industry but occurred

throughout Japan in nearly all major industries; they reached a peak in 1952. The annual average for working days lost to labor disputes between 1946 and 1951 was 6,000,000. This more than doubled in 1952 to 15,000,000 days—a record for Japan that had yet to be broken in the early 1980s. The end of the Korean War, and management efforts to oppose radical unions and replace them with second unions, contributed to a major reduction in this figure during 1953, when companies lost only 4,300,000 working days due to labor disputes. This level continued to be the annual average in Japan until companies lost nearly 10,000,000 days in 1974, following the first oil shock and retrenchment programs throughout the country. See Andō, pp. 156, 184.

14. *Nissan Jidōsha sanjū nen shi*, pp. 164-165, 176-177, 191-196, 291-293.

15. Ibid., pp. 212-216.

16. *Kumagaya*, pp. 1-3, and Masuda, p. 4.

17. Okumura interviews (10 June and 30 September 1982).

18. Kumagaya, p. 2.

19. Nissan Jidōsha Bunkai Kikanshi, *Heiwa: tokushū-go.*

20. Masuda, pp. 5-7.

21. Kumagaya, pp. 5-6.

22. *Nissan Jidōsha sanjū nen shi*, pp. 269-272.

23. Sasaki interview.

24. *Nissan Jidōsha sanjū nen shi*, pp. 270-273.

25. Ibid., pp. 264-278. See also Masuda, p. 7.

26. Kumagaya, p. 6.

27. Okumura interview (30 September 1982).

28. Matsuzaki interview (14 July 1983).

29. Kanagawa Ken Rōdō-bu Rōsei-ka, *Kanagawa ken rōdō undō shi*, II, 201, 215; and Miki, pp. 73-74.

30. *Nissan Jidōsha sanjū nen shi*, pp. 272-275. Also, interviews with Sasaki and Matsuzaki (14 July 1982) and Rōdō Sōgi Chōsa Kai, *Sengo rōdō jittai chōsa: rōdō sōgi ni okeru tokushū kesu*, XI, 99.

31. Okumura interview (30 June 1982).

32. *Nissan Jidōsha sanjū nen shi*, pp. 273-275.

33. Interviews with Maeda (22 July 1982), Matsuzaki (14 July 1982), Okumura (30 June 1982), and Ōta Hisakichi, 20 May 1982.

34. Masuda, pp. 12, 48-49.

35. Kawamata interview. See also Kawamata Katsuji et al., *Keiei no kokoro*, I, 113-115.

36. Kawamata interview.

37. Kawamata, *Watakushi no rirekisho*, p. 121.

38. Interviews with Matsuzaki (14 July 1982), Maeda (22 July 1982), and Okumura (30 June 1982).

39. Okumura interviews (10 June and 30 June 1982).

40. Rōdō Sōgi Chōsa Kai, pp. 99-103; Rōdō Sho, ed., *Shiryō: rōdō undō*

shi, pp. 856-857; *Tōyō keizai*, 14 November 1953, pp. 94-95; and Kumagaya, p. 6.

41. Rōdō Sōgi Chōsa Kai, p. 103.

42. Okumura interview (30 September 1982).

43. Masuda, pp. 12, 41-43. The issue of temporary workers was secondary in 1953 but became increasingly important. Temporary workers in the automobile industry rose from 0.3% in 1949, before the employee firings at Nissan, Toyota, and Isuzu, to 11.7% in 1952, out of a total work force of around 30,000. Management in effect replaced unionized employees, who received the high wages that Zenji won, with inexpensive help. Vigorous protests by union leaders brought temporary workers down to 7.3% by 1956, close to the average for all manufacturing industries in Japan, although their use subsequently increased as production levels rose dramatically. Toyota, for example, had used relatively few temporary workers during the early 1950s but, by 1960, they numbered 42% of the company's work force. This figure did not drop substantially until Toyota adopted a new apprentice system in 1967. At Nissan, temporary workers accounted for a quarter of the company's employees in 1959 and 44% in 1963. Management paid them between one-third and one-half the wages of regular employees. Although the number of temporary workers decreased during the late 1960s, for more than a decade temporary workers helped Nissan, Toyota, and other firms double production every few years while keeping down labor costs and the size of their permanent work forces. See Kodaira, p. 205; Gary D. Allinson, *Japanese Urbanism: Industry and Politics in Kariya*, p. 178; Yamamoto Kiyoshi, *Jidōsha sangyō no rōshi kankei*, pp. 59-60; and Takafusa Nakamura, *The Postwar Japanese Economy: Its Development and Structure*, pp. 166-167.

44. *Nissan Jidōsha sanjū nen shi*, pp. 275-276.

45. Ibid., pp. 276-280.

46. Rōdō Sōgi Chōsa Kai, pp. 107-114.

47. *Nissan Jidōsha sanjū nen shi*, pp. 277-280, 305-306.

48. Nissan Jidōsha Rōdō Kumiai, *Nissan sōgi hakusho*, pp. 14, 20, 25-26.

49. Masuda, pp. 34-36.

50. *Nissan sōgi hakusho*, pp. 25-26. See also Aoki Satoshi, *Nissan kyōeiken no kiki: rōshi nijū kenryoku shihai no kōzō*, p. 139. Aoki, who specialized in labor problems in the automobile industry, was perhaps the first journalist to investigate the story of the Nissan strike in detail. I am particularly grateful for his extensive research and generosity in sharing several published sources and additional information.

51. Kawamata, "Atarashii shijō kaitaku e no mosaku," p. 160, and Matsuzaki interview (14 July 1982).

52. Aoyama Shigeru, *Shioji Ichirō no ōinaru chōsen*, pp. 48-50.

53. Okumura interview (30 June 1982).

54. This chapter will later discuss the case of Shioji in more detail. Other

labor figures in Japan who went to the Institute included Kanesugi Hidenobu, head of the Japan Federation of Shipbuilding and Engineering Workers Unions (Zōsen Jūki Rōren); former Dōmei chairman Usami Tadanobu and vice-chairman Koga Atsushi; and Nakamura Mitoshi, a former editor of Dōmei's monthly journal. See Aoyama, pp. 48-50, and Aoki, *Nissan kyōeiken no kiki*, pp. 146-148.

55. Aoki Satoshi, *Gisō rōren: Nissan S-soshiki no himitsu*, pp. 42-45. "S" refers to Shioji Ichirō.

56. Ibid., pp. 138-141, and Nodani Mitsuru and Iwasaki Toshio, "Nissan Jidōsha no 'jinji' 'jinpa' sōran," pp. 64-76.

57. *Nissan Jidōsha sanjū nen shi*, pp. 281-285, 291-293.

58. *Tōyō keizai*, 14 November 1953, pp. 94-95.

59. This drop in compensation was especially severe, given that the average age of Nissan employees remained about the same through 1961, whereas the hiring of more new workers contributed to low wage averages in Toyota. At both companies, the rise in temporary workers tended to depress wage averages, although this appears to have been particularly true at Toyota.

60. Kumagaya, pp. 4-7.

61. *Heiwa: Tokushū-go*.

62. Kumagaya, pp. 5-7.

63. Rōdō Sōgi Chōsa Kai, pp. 100-104, 116-119.

64. Kumagaya, pp. 4-6.

65. Ibid., p. 6.

66. *Nissan Jidōsha sanjū nen shi*, pp. 480-482.

67. Kumagaya, pp. 2-3; Okumura interview (30 September 1982).

68. *Nissan sōgi hakusho*, pp. 14, 20.

69. A surprisingly large number of authors criticized management-labor relations in Nissan. See, for example, Saga Ichirō, "Tokui na jidōsha sangyō no rōshi kankei" (Saga was an assistant professor in the faculty of liberal arts at the University of Tokyo); Yamamoto Kiyoshi, *Jidōsha sangyō no rōshi kankei* (Yamamoto Kiyoshi was a professor of labor relations at the University of Tokyo's Institute of Social Science); "Nissan Jidōsha no higeki," an anonymous article published in a leading business magazine, *Purejidento*; Yasuda Yūzō, "Shioji ōkoku hōkai no jokyoku"; in addition to other publications cited in this chapter by Aoki, Nodani and Iwasaki, Takayama, and Akiyama.

70. Okumura interviews (10 June and 30 June 1982).

71. While the company did not publicize cases of this, in one example that occurred while I was in Japan studying Nissan during 1980, the union resorted to the union-shop clause to dismiss 7 employees of Atsugi Auto Parts who attempted to form a separate union. See Aoki Satoshi, *Aoi-tori wa doko e: Nissan Atsugi jomei kaiko jiken*, and Yamamoto Kiyoshi, pp. 178-182.

72. *Nissan sōgi hakusho*, pp. 7-10, 134.

73. Ibid., pp. 153-157; Yamamoto Kiyoshi, pp. 197-199, 280-282.

74. *Nissan Jidōsha sanjū nen shi*, p. 292; Kodaira, pp. 341-342.

75. Yamamoto Kiyoshi, p. 70, Table 70.

76. See Yamamoto Kiyoshi, pp. 313-318, especially Table 26 on p. 314, for a discussion of union demands and the percentages management granted.

77. Chapter 4 will discuss productivity, wages, and profitability in more detail.

78. Yamamoto Kiyoshi, pp. 139-141.

79. Hayashi Nobuo, " 'Rōshi kankei kindaika' no onkochishin," pp. 1-2. The association is also described in Miyake Masaru, *Kindaiteki rōshi kankei*, which includes a preface by Iwakoshi, and in Kawamata, *Keiei no kokoro*, p. 115.

80. Takayama Jirō, "Nissan Jidōsha zankoku monogatari," pp. 76-78.

81. Yamamoto Kiyoshi, pp. 261-263, 275-277.

82. Matsuzaki interview (14 July 1982).

83. Maeda interview (22 July 1982).

84. Matsuzaki interview (14 July 1982). See also Aoki, *Nissan kyōeiken no kiki*, pp. 153-159, and Nodani and Iwasaki, pp. 67-69.

85. Aoki, *Nissan kyōeiken no kiki*, p. 152, and *Gisō rōren*, p. 50. Also, interviews with Maeda (22 July 1982) and Matsuzaki (14 July 1982).

86. This discussion is based on interviews with Katayama (31 May 1982), Okumura (10 June 1982), Maeda (21 May and 22 July 1982), Matsuzaki (14 July 1982), Kawamata (8 June 1982), and *Tōyō keizai*, 4 January 1958, pp. 114-115.

87. " 'Kōkyō no jidōsha' koso shuntō no kikansha da," *Zaikai*, 1 April 1978, p. 32. This is the published version of an interview with Shioji by a reporter from this weekly business magazine.

88. Aoyama, pp. 74-75.

89. Shioji in the *Zaikai* interview, p. 32.

90. Aoyama, pp. 34-39.

91. Miki, pp. 48-50.

92. Aoyama, pp. 51-52, and Miki, pp 84-86.

93. Shioji in the *Zaikai* interview, p. 36. See also Aoki, *Nissan kyōeiken no kiki*, pp. 135-136.

94. Shioji in the *Zaikai* interview, p. 33.

95. Aoki, *Gisō rōren*, pp. 37-39, 55-62.

96. *Nissan Jidōsha shashi*, p. 418.

97. Unfortunately, I was not able to meet Mr. Shioji in person during my period of research in Japan. Nissan's Public Relations Department at first agreed and then declined to arrange an interview during 1983, because of tensions in management-labor relations at the time and a critique of the Nissan union published by a professor at the University of Tokyo, where I was affiliated. Two other attempts to arrange an interview with Mr. Shioji

through different intermediaries also failed. There were, however, sufficient secondary sources, newspaper reports, and published interviews with the union leader available to complete this section.

98. Shioji interview in *Zaikai*, pp. 33, 36.

99. This discussion is based on Miki, pp. 69-70; Kawamata, "Atarashii shijō kaitaku e no mosaku" pp. 163-164; Iwakoshi, p. 284; and *Nissan Jidōsha shashi*, pp. 18-20.

100. Union membership is reported each year in Nissan's *yūka shōken hōkokusho*.

101. This discussion is based on interviews with Katayama and Okumura (10 June 1982) and Matsuzaki (14 July 1982); "Nissan Jidōsha no higeki" pp. 237-241; Nodani and Iwasaki, p. 76; Aoki, *Nissan kyōeiken no kiki*, pp. 23-24; and articles in the *Asahi* newspaper on 13 February 1982, p. 3, and 20 October 1983, p. 14.

102. The new accord called for Nissan to assemble 24,000 cars annually from kits in a plant to be opened in 1986—compared to 200,000 cars per year in the initial proposal. Nissan expected to decide by the end of 1987 whether or not to upgrade the facility to produce 100,000 cars annually. See *The New York Times*, 2 February 1984, p. D-1, and "Nissan Decides on British Plant Location," *Business Japan*, May 1984, p. 109.

103. See Yasuda, pp. 16-21. I also confirmed the details of this incident through confidential interviews during December 1984 with Nissan workers from the Tokyo offices.

104. For an account of the change in top management at Nissan, see *The Wall Street Journal*, 2 April 1985, p. 33. Biographical details on Kume can be found in Nissan's *yūka shōken hōkokusho*.

105. *Kōhō shiryō* (1982), p. 78; Wakayama and Sugimoto, pp. 150-153.

106. Allinson, pp. 102-106.

107. Kodaira, p. 259.

108. Tsutsumi Shin'ichi, "Toyota shiki rōshi kankei no shushin,"pp. 99-100, and *Toyota Jidōsha sanjū nen shi*, pp. 300-303.

109. Okumura interview (10 June 1982).

110. Allinson, pp. 139-142, 175-180.

111. Chapter 6 will discuss this in more detail.

112. Allinson, p. 178. Also see Wakayama and Sugimoto, pp. 180-182, and *Toyota Jidōsha sanjū nen shi*, p. 499.

113. *Yūka shōken hōkokusho*.

114. Wakayama and Sugimoto, pp. 170-173.

115. *Yūka shōken hōkokusho*.

116. Wakayama and Sugimoto, pp. 170-173, and Toyota's Public Relations Department in Tokyo. These positions are accurate through June 1983.

117. Interviews with Hamaguchi, Kamio, and Tsukioka.

Chapter 4: Manufacturing: Strategy, Implementation, Performance

1. See the National Research Council, *The Competitive Status of the U.S. Auto Industry*, p. 177; William J. Abernathy, Kim B. Clark, and Alan M. Kantrow, *Industrial Renaissance: Producing a Competitive Future for America*, pp. 61-63; articles in *The New York Times*, such as on 1 February 1984, p. D-5, and 8 April 1984, p. F-1; and Alan Altshuler, Daniel Ross, et al., *The Future of the Automobile*, p. 161.

2. The standard 1984 Toyota Tercel, with a 1.5-liter engine and other basic equipment, listed for $5693 in the United States and 952,000 yen in Japan, which equaled $3886 at the general exchange rate of 245 yen to $1.00 in the fall of 1984.

3. Other Japanese automakers showed similar or lower rates of in-house manufacturing: Mazda (26%), Isuzu (26), Daihatsu (31), Fuji Heavy Industries (34), Suzuki (17). Data for other firms were not available. See Nissan's *Jidōsha kōgyō handobukku* (1983), p. 67.

4. Daihatsu assembled Starlet cars and Town-Ace trucks for Toyota, while Hino made Toyota's Corsa and Tercel cars and Hi-Lux pickups. Fuji Heavy Industries assembled Nissan Pulsar and Langley cars. Nissan and Toyota assembled some of these models in their own plants as well, but this number or the amount that they subcontracted was not publicly available information. See Nissan's *Jidōsha kōgyō handobukku* (1983), pp. 36-37.

5. This percentage was higher at Nissan than at Toyota beginning in 1977, despite the larger size of the Toyota group, also because Toyota relied more heavily on Hino and Daihatsu, which were not considered as subsidiaries in the annual reports, than Nissan relied on Fuji Heavy Industries.

6. Caution should be exercised regarding these numbers because of potential differences between Japan and the United States in definitions of automobile workers as well as coverage of employees. For example, the American productivity figure is slightly exaggerated because the total for autoworkers excludes automotive stamping operations. These figures, however, are the best estimates available, based on data provided by the Japan Automobile Manufacturers Association (1984) and the Motor Vehicle Manufacturers Association, *Motor Vehicle Facts and Figures* (1984), p. 65.

7. Sei Kōichirō, "Bungyō to rōdō no Nichi-Bei hikaku," p. 227.

8. These figures are rough estimates based on information I received in interviews with Kanao Kaiichi, 11 April 1983, and Ōno Taiichi, 18 March 1983.

9. Interviews with Ōno and Kiyomasu.

10. Kanao interview.

11. Tōyō Keizai, *Keizai tōkei nenkan*, p. 245.

12. Harbour and Associates, Inc., "Comparison of Japanese Car Assembly Plant Located in Japan and U.S. Car Assembly Plant Located in the U.S.," pp. 12-13. The figures on model combinations apply to the 1981 model year. For product-mix figures at General Motors and the other American automakers, see "Toyota 1984: Jidōsha sangyō no gaikyō,"p. 36.

420

13. Booz, Allen & Hamilton, which did this study, also maintained that the simplicity of the Japanese product lines accounted for $800 of Japan's $1500 cost advantage for small cars. See James Cook, "Where's the Niche?," pp. 54-55.

14. See the discussions of GM in *The New York Times,* 9 January 1984, p. D-1; 15 January 1984, p. F-1; and 5 February 1985, p. D-4.

15. Capacity utilization equals nominal capacity over a given period of time divided by actual production. In the U.S. automobile industry, these estimates are calculated quarterly; the yearly figure is an average of these, as reported to the U.S. Bureau of Economic Analysis (Department of Commerce). Individual company figures are not published. In Japan, automakers calculate capacity utilization by fiscal periods. For example, according to corporate reports submitted to the Ministry of Finance *(yūka shōken hōkokusho)*, Toyota estimates capacity for the first month of the fiscal year and then for the last (based on 21 working days), averages the two figures, and divides the result by average monthly production. Also see Table 65.

16. These figures are for production workers in the American automobile industry (bodies and components) compared to workers in the Japanese transportation and communication industries, the closest comparison available, since actual company figures are not published. See Appendix G. A company video describing the Toyota production system, which I viewed at Toyota headquarters in Japan during January 1985, claimed that employees were scheduled for 20 460-minute (7.7-hour) shifts per month, which works out to 1840 hours per year or 39 hours per week (47 working weeks per year). Actual hours worked at Toyota, including overtime, appear to be far in excess of this figure, especially in years when capacity utilization was over 100%

17. For a discussion of absenteeism, see the National Research Council, pp. 101-102. My thanks as well to Kim Clark of the Harvard Business School for pointing out the need to adjust for these differences in labor hours as well as capacity utilization.

18. These estimates do not adjust for differences in product mixes or non-automotive operations, which consume labor but do not show up in vehicles-per-worker statistics. Regarding non-automotive production, in 1983, 2% of Nissan's sales came from items such as textile machinery, rocket engines, marine craft, and forklifts. At Toyota, 16.6% came from petroleum products, forklifts, prefabricated housing, specialized machinery, and other products. Corporate reports list these figures without disclosing how many workers each operation required, although productivity in Toyota and the Toyota group is understated in comparison to Nissan as well as to the American firms. Non-automotive items accounted for 4% of General Motors' sales in 1983 and 8% of Ford's.

19. Other studies have confirmed the existence of a 2-fold productivity advantage in Japan but without pinpointing when it occurred, which is

useful when trying to identify the managerial and other practices that encouraged productivity to rise so rapidly in the Japanese automobile industry. A 1977 comparison of final assembly plants conducted by Toyota's production control department estimated that the company's Takaoka factory made 2.4 times as many cars, with the same amount of labor, as a major American assembly plant, was twice as productive as a representative factory in Sweden, and 70% more productive than another in West Germany. See Y. Sugimori, K. Kusunoki, F. Chō, and S. Uchikawa, "Toyota Production System and Kanban System of Materialization of Just-in-Time and Respect-for-Human System," p. 563. A 1982 American project sponsored by the National Research Council gave the Japanese a 2-fold productivity advantage in total hours needed to produce a small car, with the differential varying for specific processes such as assembly (2.2:1), body stamping (2.5), engine manufacturing and assembly (1.8), and axle production (1.7), even when the Japanese used equipment made in the United States. The National Research Council estimated as well that 60 to 85% of the Japanese productivity advantage over American automakers was due to factors other than higher levels of automation, such as greater process yield, much lower absenteeism, and more flexible job structures. See the National Research Council, pp. 101-107.

20. Both MITI and the Japan Productivity Center, founded in 1955, are major sources of value-added statistics for Japanese companies, based on the *yūka shōken hōkokusho*. The formula MITI uses measures "gross value added"; this subtracts, from the value of goods delivered (sales), the cost of materials, labor, average inventories, and other expenditures, including domestic consumption taxes incorporated into the value of the manufactured goods. It is a gross estimate because MITI does not consider depreciation as a cost. The Japan Productivity Center prefers "net value added," which subtracts depreciation. This is also simpler to calculate because it can be derived by adding total labor expenses to operating income, as well as by subtracting total costs from sales. I have followed the Japan Productivity Center formula in this section. For additional explanations see Tsūshō Sangyō Sho, *Sekai no kigyō no keiei bunseki*, and Nihon Seisansei Honbu, *Fuka kachi bunseki*.

21. Since Chrysler and General Motors do not report total labor costs in their annual reports, it is not possible to calculate net value added according to the formula used for Nissan and Toyota. Therefore, I have relied on comparisons with Ford. I did not generate these numbers from general exchange rates but used purchasing-power parity data for small cars and the Japanese and American consumer price indexes for private transportation (referred to in Japanese as "automobiles and related expenses"). This is noted in the tables for this section; Appendix H contains a list of price indexes and deflators. The reader should be aware that using the general exchange rate would result in different numbers, including lower value-added pro-

ductivity for Nissan in 1983, compared to Ford. Use of the general exchange rates is misleading, however, for several reasons. Most important, prior to 1971, the value of the dollar was fixed artificially at 360 yen, severely understating the "real" value (comparable purchasing power in Japan) of the Japanese currency. General exchange rates during the 1980s continued to understate the value of monetary productivity for Japanese autoworkers in their domestic market, which can be seen in the much lower prices of Japanese cars sold in Japan as compared to the United States. For example, dividing the list price in yen converted by the general exchange rate of a standard 1984 Toyota Tercel sold in Japan into its American list price produces a "parity" exchange rate of 167 yen per dollar (converted at 245 yen = $1.00).

22. The cost of labor at GM in the United States was slightly lower. Ford's American workers cost $23 an hour during 1982-1983, compared to $22 for GM workers, according to annual reports.

23. In MITI's annual series comparing firms in different countries, *Sekai no kigyō no keiei bunseki*, American automakers consistently appear to have more fixed assets per worker than Nissan or Toyota—which would mean truly extraordinary rates of capital productivity in the Japanese automobile industry! But MITI compares only the categories for plant, property, equipment, and construction in progress in the Japanese corporate reports submitted to the Ministry of Finance with listings on American annual reports that are not equivalent. About half of the Japanese firms' fixed assets appear on the balance sheets under a subcategory of fixed assets labeled "investments and other assets." These are actually stocks, bonds, or notes held as collateral for loans of plant and equipment; consequently, MITI compares "total" fixed assets in the American firms with "tangible" fixed assets in the Japanese firms. In the English versions of their annual reports, on the other hand, Nissan and Toyota combine tangible fixed assets with these other investments in plant, property, equipment, and construction in progress, producing figures (given in yen and dollars) that are more directly comparable with the numbers in American reports.

24. *Yūka shōken hōkokusho.* (By coincidence, perhaps, the Japanese list price of the standard 1984 Tercel was also 952,000 yen.) These estimates assume that the product mix and the average price of cars at Nissan and Toyota were similar; Toyota's actual cost advantage would be smaller if it sold more lower-priced cars than Nissan. To arrive at these figures, I multiplied car revenues times the overall cost of sales (sales minus operating profits), and divided by the number of cars produced in fiscal 1983. To get dollars, I used the general exchange rate of 224 yen to $1.00, which Nissan used to convert figures from the end of its fiscal year (31 March 1984). It might also be noted that, if the same relationship between Toyota's vehicle-productivity (adjusted only for vertical integration) and cost advantages over Nissan applied to the differentials between the Japanese and American automakers, then Nissan in 1983 had a "productivity-cost" advantage over

American automakers of about $1800 per small car, while Toyota's advantage was as high as $3000.

25. Chrysler, for instance, reduced its break-even point from 2,400,000 unit sales in 1980 to merely 1,100,000 in 1982, according to its 1982 annual report.

26. George Maxcy and Aubrey Silberston, *The Motor Industry*, pp. 79, 93.

27. "Nissan Jidōsha no gaiyō" (1982), pp. 19-20.

28. An analysis of the relationship between manufacturing costs and vehicle production at Toyota shows similar savings between 1955 and 1983. I have used Nissan for this example, however, since such a large percentage of Toyota's revenues during the early 1980s (and a related but unpublished portion of manufacturing expenses) came from non-automotive items.

29. Iwakoshi, p. 88.

30. *Nissan Jidōsha sanjū nen shi*, p. 142, and *Nissan News*, 86:12-13 (June 1959).

31. *Nissan Jidōsha sanjū nen shi*, p. 73.

32. Ibid. p. 141.

33. Terazawa interview.

34. Interviews with Okumura (10 June and 30 June 1982), as well as Igarashi, Sasaki, and Maeda (21 May 1982).

35. *Nissan Jidōsha sanjū nen shi*, pp. 141-145, 183-189.

36. Ibid., p. 182.

37. Kodaira, pp. 267-269.

38. *Nissan Jidōsha sanjū nen shi*, pp. 189, 235. Toyota received $56,000 and Isuzu $83,000 from the same fund, also to make vehicles for the American military.

39. Ibid., pp. 315-316.

40. Ibid., data section and p. 481, and *Tōyō keizai*, 5 May 1955, p. 56; 8 September 1956, p. 102; and 29 June 1957, p. 68.

41. *Nissan Jidōsha sanjū nen shi*, p. 434, and *yūka shōken hōkokusho*.

42. *Yūka shōken hōkokusho*. See also Table 65.

43. Interviews with Igarashi and Sasaki.

44. *Nissan Jidōsha sanjū nen shi*, pp. 428-436; *Nissan News* 83:2 (April 1959); and *yūka shōken hōkokusho*.

45. Interviews with Kawamata, Maeda (21 May 1982), Ōta, Kawazoe, Igarashi, and Matsuzaki (14 July 1982).

46. Kawamata interview, and "Atarashii shijō kaitaku e no mosaku," pp. 162-163.

47. Interviews with Kawazoe, Ōta, and Maeda (21 May 1982).

48. Matsuzaki interview (14 July 1982).

49. Interviews with Sasaki and Matsuzaki (19 January 1983).

50. Matsuzaki interview (19 January 1983); Nissan Jidōsha Kabushiki Kaisha, "Zama kōjō no gaiyō"; *Nissan Jidōsha shashi*, pp. 41-44.

51. Sasaki interview and *Nissan Jidōsha shashi*, pp. 44-46.

424

52. *Nissan Jidōsha shashi*, pp. 52-53.

53. Ibid., pp. 53-57.

54. *Sankei shimbun*, 4 October 1984, p. 7.

55. The Nissan Motor Company, "Data File 1984," p. 30.

56. Kanao interview; *Nissan Jidōsha shashi*, pp. 293-298; "Nissan Jidōsha no gaiyō" (1982), p. 57; and Ikari Yoshirō, "Seihin-seisan gijutsu no kakushinsei," pp. 290-291, 294.

57. *The Japan Times*, 8 March 1984, p. 6, and 31 March 1984, p. 10.

58. The price for a typical robot is from publicly available data at Toyota's Tsutsumi factory, as of January 1985. See also "Seihin-seisan gijutsu no kakushinsei," p. 292.

59. Nikkei Mechanical, *Robotto kakumei*, pp. 181-182.

60. *Toyota Jidōsha sanjū nen shi*, pp. 327-329, 342, 846; and *Tōyō keizai*, 30 July 1955, p. 56. Toyota increased its reliance on equity capital after the 1950s; in fact, in 1983, this constituted 63% of total assets. In comparison, equity-capital levels in 1983 were 47% at Nissan, 45% at General Motors, and 32% at Ford. Nissan and Toyota thus disprove the notion that equity-capital levels were necessarily low in Japan, although, at other Japanese automakers, equity averaged about 25%—ranging from 13% at Mitsubishi Motors to 38% at Honda. See Nissan's *Jidōsha kōgyō handobukku* (1984), pp. 115, 163, 167.

61. *Toyota Jidōsha sanjū nen shi*, pp. 333-336.

62. Ibid. pp. 337-340, and *Tōyō keizai*, 21 June 1952, pp. 60-61; 26 February 1955, p. 64; and 30 July 1955, p. 56.

63. *Toyota Jidōsha sanjū nen shi*, pp. 398-403.

64. Ōno, pp. 228-229, and Matsuzaki interview (19 January 1983).

65. *Toyota Jidōsha sanjū nen shi*, pp. 334-336, 404-414, 872, 874.

66. Ibid., pp. 466-477.

67. Ibid., pp. 854-874.

68. *Toyota no ayumi*, pp. 247-249.

69. Ibid., pp. 286-289, and *Toyota Jidōsha sanjū nen shi*, pp. 600-603.

70. Kanao interview. The figure for total robots at Toyota is from data at the Tsutsumi factory, as of January 1985.

71. Ikari, "Seihin-seisan gijutsu no kakushinsei," pp. 294-295.

72. Iwakoshi, pp. 187-189.

73. *Toyota Jidōsha sanjū nen shi*, p. 653. Actually, Japan had not achieved the American distribution of 1964, even by 1982. Japan had 1 vehicle per 2.8 people in 1982, half the U.S. ratio of 1.4:1 and less than Canada (1.7), Australia (1.9), France (2.3), West Germany (2.4), and Italy (2.7). See "Toyota 1984: Jidōsha sangyō no gaikyō," p. 42.

74. Iwakoshi, pp. 187-202.

75. Ibid., p. 84.

76. Wakayama and Sugimoto, pp. 135-137.

77. Kirk Monteverde and David J. Teece, "Supplier Switching Costs and Vertical Integration in the Automobile Industry," pp. 206-213.

78. Richard J. Schonberger, *Japanese Manufacturing Techniques: Nine Lessons in Simplicity*, pp. 174-176.

79. Executive dispatches were especially important because they usually preceded technical assistance, loans, or exclusive procurement contracts. Toyota led the industry with 98 of its current or former executives in top positions, ranging from director to chairman, at 29 related firms. Nissan was right behind with 97 executives placed in 22 companies. See Nodani and Iwasaki, pp. 70-72.

80. *Tōyō keizai*, 9 July 1960, p. 25, and *yūka shōken hōkokusho*.

81. The automakers that had the least success in finding suppliers during the 1950s were Isuzu and Hino. In addition to their lack of experience with cars, each had trouble moving out of the large truck field, despite tie-ups with Rootes and Renault, because they had to rely on too many small, expensive subcontractors for essential components and major processes such as casting and forging, which made it difficult for Isuzu and Hino to compete with Toyota and Nissan on the basis of quality or price. See *Tōyō keizai*, 3 March 1956, pp. 58-59.

82. Amagai Shōgo, *Nihon jidōsha kōgyō no shiteki tenkai*, p. 65; and Kodaira, p. 46.

83. Amagai, pp. 68-69, 107. Private businessmen formed a similar organization in 1948, the National Automobile-Parts Manufacturers Association (Zen-koku Jidōsha Buhin Kōgyō Kai).

84. Ibid., pp. 107-108.

85. Okumura, "Jidōsha kōgyō no hatten dankai to kōzō," pp. 324-325.

86. Magaziner, p. 80; Kodaira, p. 372; and *Nissan News*, April 1959, p. 4.

87. Amagai, p. 222.

88. Okumura, Hoshikawa, and Matsui, pp. 229-331.

89. *Toyota Jidōsha sanjū nen shi*, pp. 180-181.

90. Toyoda Kiichirō in Ozaki, pp. 154-156; and *Toyota Jidōsha sanju nen shi*, pp. 196-200. Aichi Steel continued to provide specialty steels to firms in the Toyota group through the early 1980s, although it sold half or more of its output to other companies after becoming an affiliate of Nippon Steel the world's largest steel manufacturer. See *Kaisha shikihō* (annual).

91. *Toyota Jidōsha sanjū nen shi*, pp. 200-202.

92. Ibid., pp. 272-273, 718.

93. Ibid., pp. 207-210, 226-229, 272-273, 718, and *Kaisha shikihō-* (annual).

94. This name combined the ideographs for "cooperation" and the "toyo" in "Toyota," read in this instance as "hō."

95. Toyota Motor Corporation, "Outline of Toyota," p. 27; and telephone interview conducted with an official in Toyota's Tokyo Public Affairs Department in June 1983. This total does not include 61 makers of dies, gauges, jigs, tools, and related equipment organized in Toyota's Eihō Kai, or secondary and tertiary subcontractors.

96. *Toyota Jidōsha sanjū nen shi*, pp. 685-692; *Toyota no ayumi*, pp. 274-275; and Kamiya, p. 135.

97. *Nissan Jidōsha sanjū nen shi*, pp. 340-341. See Table 71.

98. Matsuzaki interviews (14 July 1982 and 19 January 1983); and *Nissan Jidōsha shashi*, pp. 57-60.

99. *Nissan Jidōsha sanjū nen shi*, pp. 205-206, 478.

100. Ibid., pp. 239, 320-321, 342.

101. Ibid., p. 338, and Nihon Rajiēta Kabushiki Kaisha, *Ōinaru hishō: Nihon Rajiēta Kabushiki Kaisha yonjū nen shi*.

102. *Nissan Jidōsha sanjū nen shi*, pp. 339-342; *Tōyō keizai*, 3 March 1956, p. 58; and *Kaisha shikihō* (summer 1984).

103. *Nissan Jidōsha shashi*, pp. 76-79.

104. Ibid., pp. 31-33.

105. Okumura in "Jidōsha kōgyō no hatten dankai to kōzō," pp. 327-330.

106. *Nissan Jidōsha shashi*, pp. 60-61; Jidōsha Buhin Kōgyō Kai, *Nihon no jidōsha buhin kōgyō*, p. C-60; and Ōta interview.

107. Nissan Jidōsha shashi, pp. 74-76.

108. Ōta interview.

109. Hitachi Seisakujo Kabushiki Kaisha, *Hitachi Seisakujo shi*, III, 297-302.

110. *Nissan Jidōsha shashi*, pp. 55-56, 178-179, 222, 229, 262, 281-284.

Chapter 5: Production Management: Large Variety in Small (or Large) Volumes

1. These figures are from Martin Anderson, executive officer of the International Automobile Program at the Massachusetts Institute of Technology (1981-1984), telephone interview, 27 January 1984. For publication of the MIT data for individual nations, see Altshuler, p. 160. There is some discrepancy over how many hours are required to produce an automobile, due mainly to differences in methods of counting. *The Wall Street Journal*, for example, reported on 5 July 1984 (p. 7) that Japanese manufacturers took approximately 90 labor hours, compared to 120 for American automakers, to produce a small car. But, while the hour totals may differ, it appears that the Japanese required only 60 to 75% as long as American manufacturers.

2. I am referring to the book by Ōno Taiichi, *Toyota seisan hōshiki*, and the article by Y. Sugimori, K. Kusunoki, F. Chō, and S. Uchikawa, "Toyota Production System and Kanban System of Materialization of Just-in-Time and Respect-for-Human System."

3. Ōno interview; and Ōno, p. 139.

4. Ōno interview.

5. Ōno, pp. 20-21, 138-141.

6. Ibid., pp. 185-190.

7. For an account of the change in the American automobile market and the strategies of Ford and General Motors, see Sloan, especially pp. 190-193.

8. Ōno, pp. 175-179 189-193.

9. *Toyota Jidōsha sanjū nen shi*, pp. 265-271.

10. Ibid., pp. 379-380.

11. Ōno, pp. 39-44, 227; and Ōno interview.

12. Ōno interview.

13. Ōno, pp. 20-23.

14. *Toyota Jidōsha sanjū nen shi*, pp. 334-336; and Ōno, pp. 228-229.

15. Yasuhiro Monden, "Adaptable Kanban System Helps Toyota Maintain Just-in-Time Production," p. 34.

16. Matsuzaki interview (19 January 1983).

17. Ōno interview.

18. Ōno, pp. 36-38.

19. Ōno interview.

20. Sugimori et al., pp. 555-556; and *Toyota Jidōsha sanjū nen shi*, pp. 423-424.

21. *Toyota Jidōsha sanjū nen shi*, p. 422; and Ōno interview.

22. *Toyota Jidōsha sanjū nen shi*, p. 421.

23. Ōno interview; and Ōno, pp. 49-53.

24. Ōno, pp. 24-25, 222.

25. *Toyota Jidōsha sanjū nen shi*, p. 424.

26. Ōno, pp. 53 62-65.

27. Kodaira pp. 295-305.

28. *Toyota Jidōsha sanjū nen shi*, pp. 423-424.

29. Ōno, pp. 217, 228-229.

30. Ōno interview.

31. Ōno, pp. 11-12, 226.

32. Shingō Shigeo, *Toyota seisan hōshiki no IE-teki kosatsu*, pp. 131-133. Toyota video on the company's production system (January 1985); and interview with Uchida Ken'ichi, 22 January 1985.

33. Roger W. Schmenner, *Production/Operations Management*, p. 78.

34. Shingō, pp. 141-142; Yasuhiro Monden, "What Makes the Toyota Production System Really Tick?," pp. 40-42; and Harbour, p. 12.

35. Ōno interview; and Sugimori et al., p. 556.

36. Schonberger, pp. 119-121. See also Schmenner, p. 78.

37. The EOQ equation is Q = the square root of $2\,SD$ divided by I, where Q equals the optimal lot size to order (or produce) components in; S equals the fixed costs of ordering (or producing) the items; D equals demand (units per period); and I equals the cost per unit of holding inventory. For more detailed discussions of this formula, see Schmenner, pp. 217-220; and Harvard Business School, "Benson Electronics," pp. 15-16.

38. Ōno, pp. 70-72.

39. Interview with Ishikawa Kaoru (21 February 1983) and Shingō, pp. 64-67.

40. Kanao interview.

41. Sugimori et al., p. 563.

42. Ōno interview.

43. Ibid. See also a description of the author in Shingō's text.

44. This discussion is based on Shingō, pp. 70-77.

45. *Toyota no ayumi*, p. 342.

46. Ōno interview. Totota's lead-time formula was $x = s$ divided by T minus the sum of (tmi) (di), where x equals the lead time for all products; T equals the operating time per day (480 minutes); s equals the total setup time for all products, assuming that this is independent of the sequence of the products; tmi equals the unit processing time for the i-th product; and di equals demand for the i-th product per day. Toyota's lot-size formula was $Qi = (di) (x)$ for all $i = 1,2, \ldots n$. For a further discussion, see Sugimori et al., pp. 562-564.

47. Sugimori et al., pp. 560-561, contains a brief description of this. For a detailed treatment in Japanese, see Saitō Shigeru, *Toyota 'kanban' hōshiki no himitsu*. For accounts of this exchange in English see Schonberger, pp. 221-237, and the articles by Monden.

48. Ōno pp. 55-56, 74.

49. Ibid., pp. 55, 62-66, 228-229.

50. Sugimori et al., pp. 561-562; and Ōno interview.

51. Monden, "Adaptable Kanban System Helps Toyota Maintain Just-in-Time Production," p. 46.

52. Shingō, pp. 249-255.

53. Monden, "Adaptable Kanban System Helps Toyota Maintain Just-in-Time Production," p. 36.

54. Uchida interview. I am also indebted to Ramchandran Jaikumar of the Harvard Business School for initiating the questions during this interview.

55. Shingō, pp. 281-283.

56. For a discussion of MRP systems, see Schmenner, pp. 224-235. For a comparison of MRP and kanban systems, see Schonberger, pp. 219-233.

57. Ōno interview.

58. *Toyota Jidōsha sanjū nen shi*, pp. 427-430, 838, 840.

59. *Toyota no ayumi*, pp. 345-346.

60. Ōno interview.

61. Sugimori, p. 559.

62. Monden, "Adaptable Kanban System Helps Toyota Maintain Just-in-Time Production," pp. 39-40.

63. For a description of the problems suppliers faced, see Akamatsu Tokushi, *Toyota zankoku monogatari*, pp. 68-77.

64. Kanao interview.

65. National Research Council, p. 106; and General Motors Corporation, "The Framingham Plant." GM's assembly plant in Framingham, Massachusetts, carried components for approximately 5 days of production in October 1984, when I visited there, although 3 days was more common according to Richard Heithaus, a supervisor in the industrial engineering

department (interview, 12 October 1984). Also see Schmenner, p. 79, for a more detailed discussion of General Motors.

66. Harbour, pp. 83-84.

67. See Sugimori et al., p. 563.

68. Kanao interview.

69. For a discussion of Mazda (formerly Toyo Kogyo), see Harvard Business School, "Toyo Kogyo Co. LTD (A)"; and Richard Pascale and Thomas P. Rohlen, "The Mazda Turnaround."

70. Ōno interview.

71. Ibid.

72. Shingō, p. 113.

73. Akamatsu, pp. 12-18. Akamatsu claimed that Toyota group firms had an accident rate of 3.6 per million working hours in 1980, compared to an industry average of 2.19 (p. 18).

74. This discussion is based on Kamata Satoshi, *Jidōsha zetsubō kōjō: aru kisetsu-kō no nikki*. An English edition of this book came out in 1982 under the title *Japan in the Passing Lane* (Pantheon).

75. Sugimori et al., p. 558.

76. Ōno interview.

77. Ōno, p. 23.

78. Ōno interview.

79. Interviews with Kanao and Matsuzaki (19 January 1983).

80. Matsuzaki interview (19 January 1983), and Kanao interview.

81. Kanao interview.

82. Ibid.

83. Interviews with Kanao and Matsuzaki (19 January 1983).

84. Matsuzaki interview (19 January 1983).

85. *Nissan Jidōsha sanjū nen shi*, pp. 72-73.

86. Igarashi interview; and *Nissan Jidōsha sanjū nen shi*, p. 73.

87. *Nissan Jidōsha sanjū nen shi*, pp. 244-246.

88. Hosonoya Naoki, "WF gairon," pp. 44-47. The July 1954 volume of Nissan's technical journal, *Nissan gijutsu*, in which this article was published, was a special issue on production management techniques that Nissan studied and adopted between the early 1930s and mid-1954. The main articles dealt with standard operations, standard times, process analysis, conveyance, worker fatigue, time and motion studies, and cost control.

89. Matsuzaki interview (19 January 1983).

90. *Nissan Jidōsha sanjū nen shi*, pp. 330-331, 334-339.

91. Iwakoshi, pp. 236-237.

92. This discussion is based on *Nissan Jidōsha sanjū nen shi*, pp. 383-388.

93. Interviews with Matsuzaki (19 January 1983) and Kanao, and *Nissan Jidōsha shashi*, p. 44.

94. Matsuzaki interview (19 January 1983).

95. *Nissan Jidōsha shashi*, pp. 46-47.

96. Matsuzaki interview (19 January 1983).

97. *Nissan Jidōsha shashi*, pp. 375-376.

98. This discussion is based on interviews with Kanao and Matsuzaki (19 January 1983).

Chapter 6: Quality Control: Manufacturing and Design

1. For an account of the development of QC techniques and explanations of their use, see A.V. Feigenbaum, *Total Quality Control*; J.M. Juran, ed., *Quality Control Handbook* and George Foster, "Quality Control," in Carl Heyl, ed., *The Encyclopedia of Management*, pp. 796-806.

2. Interview with Ishikawa Kaoru (21 February 1983); Ishikawa Kaoru, *Nihon-teki hinshitsu kanri*, pp. 274-275; and Shindō Takezaemon, "Nihon Kagaku Gijutsu Renmei no koto," pp. 456-458.

3. Ishikawa interview; Ishikawa, pp. 262, 274-275; and W.E. Deming, "Hinshitsu kanri undō no idai na shidōsha," pp. 264-267.

4. Keidanren, *Ishikawa Ichirō tsuisōroku*, pp. 456-458, 695-711.

5. Ishikawa interview. See *Nihon-teki hinshitsu kanri*, pp. 290-292, for a bibliography of Ishikawa's major works.

6. Ishikawa interview; and Ishikawa, pp. 2-4.

7. See A.V. Feigenbaum, "Total Quality Control," and *Total Quality Control*, p. 16.

8. Ishikawa, pp. 106-110.

9. Ishikawa interview; and Ishikawa, pp. 26-30.

10. Ishikawa, pp. 110-112.

11. For a description of QC as American experts viewed it in the mid-1950s and early 1960s, see Feigenbaum's *Harvard Business Review* article and the first edition of his book, especially p. 16, as well as the Foster article.

12. Ishikawa, pp. 80-81, 224.

13. Ibid., pp. 126-130.

14. Ibid., pp. 45-46.

15. The figures that Harbour gives also correspond closely to the breakdown of workers at GM's assembly plant in Framingham, Massachusetts, where the ratio of production workers to inspection and QC staff was approximately 12 to 1 in October 1984 (Heithaus interview). According to Harbour's data, this ratio was 13.6:1 at American plants, and 8.5:1 at Japanese plants (see Table 79).

16. Foster, pp. 796-801; and Ishikawa, pp. 60-63, 103.

17. Ishikawa, p. 25.

18. Ibid., pp. 60-63, 103.

19. Ibid., pp. 33-41, 53-56.

20. Interviews with Ishikawa and Matsuzaki (19 January 1983); and Ishikawa, pp. 170-193.

21. Interviews with Matsuzaki (19 January 1983) and Ishikawa.

22. Ishikawa interview.

23. Ishikawa, pp. 250-251.

24. See Ishikawa, p. 99; Nihon Kagaku Gijutsu Renmei (JUSE), *QC sākuru katsudō un'ei no kihon*, p. 3; and Nissan Jidōsha Kabushiki Kaisha Hinshitsu Kanri-bu, "QC sākuru katsudō no ayumi," p. 18.

25. Ishikawa, pp. 29-31, 42.

26. Ishikawa interview.

27. This comment is based on several formal and informal discussions with managers and workers during the spring of 1983 at Nissan and Toyota. Robert Cole, in his 1979 study of Toyota Auto Body, also found that QC circles had a "negligible influence" on improving operations and productivity, and noted that union surveys in several companies reported that QC circles placed a psychological burden on employees, due to pressure from superiors to join and submit suggestions, and then to compete with other circles for project awards. Cole believed that QC circles helped Japanese companies solve some quality problems simply by having workers make adjustments in their job routines, whereas the common response of American industrial engineers to similar problems was to introduce complex technological solutions that might even make quality control more difficult. But he concluded that Japanese managers used QC circles mainly as tools for personnel administration and to improve worker training and participation. See Robert E. Cole, *Work, Mobility, and Participation: A Comparative Study of American and Japanese Industry*, pp. 166-167, 198-199.

28. It should be noted, however, that it was impossible to estimate these sums accurately and company policies toward these calculations differed. Toyota, for example, claimed that it did not even try to determine monetary savings. Interviews with Nonoguchi Junji, 18 May 1983, and Kawarada Shigeru, 4 April and 1 July 1983. For JUSE's survey see QC Sākuru Katsudō Kenkyū Sho-iinkai, Nihon Kagaku Gijutsu Renmei, "QC sākuru katsudō no jittai: anketo chōsa ni yoru," p. 26.

29. The following discussion is based on *Tōyō keizai*, 28 June 1969, pp. 60-64.

30. Telephone interviews with officials from the Japan Automobile Manufacturers Association, June 1983.

31. *Asahi shimbun*, 10 April 1983, p. 9.

32. *Nissan News* 5:3 (May 1960).

33. Matsuzaki interview (14 July 1982),

34. *Nissan Jidōsha sanjū nen shi*, pp. 404-405.

35. Yamashita Yoshitaka, "Hinshitsu kanri dōnyū kara konnichi made," p. 9; and Yasumaro Toshio (Inspection Department, Atsugi Plant), "Atsugi kōjō no hinshitsu kanri," pp. 58-59.

36. Ōkura Tsutomu, "QC are-kore," pp. 3-4.

37. Igarashi interview.

38. This discussion is based on Yamashita, pp. 9-12.

39. Shinoda Ken (Plating Section Chief, Yokohama Factory), "Hinshitsu kanri to sagyō hyōjun," pp. 33-37.

40. Yamashita, pp. 11-12.

41. For explanations of the different inspection techniques that Nissan used, see Miyashita Mutsuo (Materials Inspection Section, Yoshiwara Factory), "Nukidori kensa-hō ni tsuite," pp. 25-28, and Asano Shūzō and Aihara Giichi (QC Office), "Keisū senbetsu-gata ikkai nukidori kensa-zu," pp. 29-31.

42. Yamashita, pp. 9-12.

43. Odaira Kaoru (Purchasing Department), "Gaichū kankei e no jisshi," pp. 2-8; and Hori Kōjirō (Purchasing Department Manager), "Shitauke kōjō to hinshitsu kanri," p. 2.

44. Iwata Akira (Market Research Section), "Shijō chōsa to hinshitsu kanri," pp. 13-15; and Yamashita, p. 10.

45. Igarashi Tadashi, "Kantōgen," p. 1.

46. Yamashita, p. 9.

47. This discussion is based on "Saikin no hinshitsu kanri suishin jōkyō," *Nissan News* 92:7 (December 1959); *Nissan Jidōsha sanjū nen shi*, pp. 299, 380, 405; and interviews with Matsuzaki (14 July 1982) and Ishikawa.

48. *Nissan Jidōsha sanjū nen shi*, pp. 405-408.

49. This discussion is based on "Hinshitsu kanri o zensha-teki ni," *Nissan News* 90: 6-7 (October 1959).

50. *Nissan Jidōsha shashi*, pp. 301-302.

51. Igarashi interview.

52. *Nissan Jidōsha shashi*, p. 303.

53. Shoichiro Toyoda, Section 42, p. 23.

54. Interviews with Ishikawa, Nonoguchi, and Ōno.

55. Matsuzaki interview (19 January 1983).

56. *Nissan Jidōsha shashi*, p. 302.

57. Interviews with Kawarada (1 July 1983) and Nonoguchi.

58. Kawarada interview (1 July 1983).

59. Nonoguchi interview.

60. Shigeru Tsujita (Manager, Nissan Quality Control Department), "The Promoter's Role in QC Circle Activities," pp. 2, 7-8; *Nissan Jidōsha shashi*, pp. 302-303; and Yamamura Yoshiharu and Noguchi Noboru, *Nissan wa Toyota ni kateru ka*, p. 91.

61. Kanao interview. While there were many reasons for morale problems at Nissan, it was my impression that most stemmed from employees' dissatisfaction with the company union, management pressures to increase productivity, and Nissan's continued inability to match Toyota in sales or profitability. This situation appeared to be changing, however, at least according to statistics Nissan published. In 1983, only 2% of QC themes dealt with morale, while quality and efficiency accounted for 36% each, cost control 14%, and safety 11%. See Nissan Motor, "Data File 1984," p. 31.

62. Tsujita, pp. 4-5, 12.

63. Kawarada interview (1 July 1983); and Hinshitsu kanri-bu, Nissan Jidōsha Kabushiki Kaisha, "QC sākuru katsudō no ayumi," p. 3.

64. Toyota Jidōsha, *Kōho shiryō*, p. 34.

65. *Nissan Jidōsha sanjū nen shi*, pp. 295-296.

66. Kamata, pp. 236-237. See also Cole's *Work, Mobility, and Participation*, p. 162, for a description of the suggestion system at Toyota Auto Body.

67. Kawarada interview (1 July 1983).

68. *Nissan Jidōsha shashi*, pp. 72-74, 303-304.

69. Nihon Rajiēta, pp. 21-22.

70. Ibid., p. 210.

71. *Toyota Jidōsha sanjū nen shi*, pp. 43, 168, 318, 505-506, 752; and Kodaira, pp. 118-120. Also see Chapter 2.

72. *Toyota Jidōsha sanjū nen shi*, p. 500.

73. Ōno interview.

74. Interviews with Ōno and Ishikawa.

75. This discussion is based on Nippondensō Kabushiki Kaisha, *Nippondensō nijū-go nen shi*, pp. 68-74.

76. Shoichiro Toyoda, Sec. 42, p. 23; and *Toyota Jidōsha sanjū nen shi*, p. 508.

77. *Toyota Jidōsha sanjū nen shi*, pp. 508-511.

78. Ishikawa, pp. 160-166, 179.

79. *Toyota Jidōsha sanjū nen shi*, p. 512.

80. Ibid., p. 752.

81. Ibid., pp. 515-516; and Ishikawa interview.

82. *Toyota no ayumi*, pp. 358-360, 406.

83. Ishikawa interview.

84. Ibid.

85. Ibid.

86. Kanao interview. Also, interviews with Ishikawa and Matsuzaki (19 January 1983).

87. Matsuzaki interview (19 January 1983).

88. Igarashi interview.

89. Matsuzaki interview (19 January 1983)

Conclusion

1. If patents are indicative of innovativeness, then the Japanese are in good shape: They passed the United States and West Germany in motor-vehicle patents during the mid-1970s and maintained a significant lead through the early 1980s. Among the Japanese automakers, Toyota was first in automotive patents, and was followed by Nissan and Honda. See Altshuler, pp. 102-104.

BIBLIOGRAPHY

A Note on Sources:

The sources used in this study fall into four categories. Based on an analysis of footnotes and tables, approximately 36 percent of the text relies on published and unpublished primary sources: autobiographical materials, company annual reports, company technical reports and other in-house materials, published interviews, published industry statistics, and journals or newspapers cited as primary references. The next largest source, accounting for about 25 percent of the text, comes from approximately two dozen interviews conducted mainly in Japanese by this author, primarily with current or former managers at Nissan and Toyota. All major interviews were recorded. The next largest source, accounting for about 22 percent of the text, consists of company histories that Nissan, Toyota, and their subsidiaries or suppliers compiled. These are generally accurate and of a high scholarly quality, and rely mainly on primary documents used within the companies. On matters requiring interpretation, such as disputes with unions, the company histories usually present managers' versions of events, but much of the information they contain is not available elsewhere. The fourth source, accounting for about 17 percent of the text, consists of secondary materials—books and articles—published mainly in Japanese.

The place of publication for all works in Japanese is Tokyo unless noted. Publishers are not listed if they are identical to the author or editor. Japanese names are listed in the traditional style, with surnames preceding given names, unless the author published in English. This bibliography also contains several publications in English and Japanese which provide background material but are not cited in the text.

INTERVIEWS

Aikawa Yaichi *(7 September 1982).*
Yaichi, born in 1923, was the eldest son of Aikawa Yoshisuke and in 1982 the president of Techno-Venture, a venture-capital firm located in Tokyo which invested in small enterprises experimenting in bio-technology and other fields. He was graduated from the University of Tokyo in 1945 with a degree in agricultural science; later he received a PhD in biological engineering from the Massachusetts Institute of Technology, where he was also a university trustee in 1982.

Asahara Hideo *(19 May 1982).*
Hideo was the eldest son of Asahara Genshichi, a long-time Nissan executive and president of the company during the 1940s and 1950s. Hideo in

434

1982 was the chairman of Nippon Reizō, a frozen-foods processor that was formerly a subsidiary in the prewar Nissan group.

Hamaguchi Haruo *(22 November 1982).*
Hamaguchi formerly worked for Toyota's largest dealership, Aichi Toyota, and was the chief author of its company history. In 1982 he was also heading a company history project for another Toyota dealership.

Hara Teiichi *(12 May 1982).*
Hara, born in 1916, entered Nissan in 1939 after graduating from the mechanical engineering department of the University of Tokyo. During the 1950s, he was in charge of body design for the Datsun car line. Hara was named a company director in 1963, served as president of Nissan's subsidiary in Mexico during 1973-1978, and in 1982 was an executive director responsible for exports.

Heithaus, Richard *(12 October 1984).*
Heithaus in 1984 was a supervisor in the Industrial Engineering Department at the General Motors Assembly Division plant in Framingham, Massachusetts.

Igarashi Tadashi *(11 June 1982).*
Igarashi, born in 1906, studied industrial metallurgy at the Tokyo Higher Industrial School and joined Nissan in 1935. He was head of the Yokohama plant when named a company director in 1953, and later served as executive vice-president and vice-chairman. Igarashi was also the head of Nissan's quality control program from 1953 until he left Nissan in 1977 to become chairman of Atsugi Auto Parts.

Ishikawa Kaoru *(21 February 1983).*
Ishikawa, born in 1915, graduated from the University of Tokyo in 1939 and received a doctorate in engineering in 1958. He was one of the leaders of Japan's quality control movement after World War II and served as the chief quality consultant to Nissan from the late 1950s through the early 1980s. (For additional biographical details see Chapter 6.)

Kamio Takashi *(18 March 1983).*
Kamio was the manager of Toyota's No. 1 Public Affairs Section in Tokyo during 1983.

Kanao Kaiichi *(11 April 1983).*
Kanao, born in 1919, graduated from the mechanical engineering department of Waseda University in 1941. After serving in the army, he joined Nissan in 1946. He headed the Oppama factory during the early 1970s, became a company director in 1971, and in 1983 was the executive vice-president in charge of production management and manufacturing quality control.

Katayama Yutaka *(31 May and 10 June 1982).*
Katayama, born in 1909, was the nephew of Fujita Fumiko, one of Aikawa Yoshisuke's most important financial backers in his early years with Tobata

Casting and Nippon Industries. After graduating from the economics faculty of Keiō University in 1937, he joined Nissan Motor Sales and then another subsidiary, Manchuria Motors, in 1939. Katayama returned to Nissan Motor Sales after the war but entered Nissan when it absorbed the sales firm in 1949. After Nissan sent him to the United States in 1960 as one of two vice-presidents of Nissan Motor Corporation in U.S.A., Katayama served as president of the sales subsidiary from 1965 to 1975 and then as chairman until 1977. In 1977, Katayama became chairman of an advertising firm, Nippō, which did most of its business with Nissan.

Kawamata Katsuji *(8 June 1982)*.
Born in 1905, Kawamata was graduated from the prewar predecessor of Hitotsubashi University in 1929 and then joined the Industrial Bank of Japan. He entered Nissan in 1946 as a managing director, became president in 1957, and chairman in 1973, a position that he still held until mid-1985. (For additional biographical details see Chapter 2.)

Kawarada Shigeru *(4 April and 1 July 1983; 17 December 1984)*.
Kawarada in 1983 was the deputy general manager of Nissan's Public Affairs Department. In 1984, he was the deputy general manager of Nissan's Business Research Department.

Kawazoe Sōichi *(2 June 1982)*.
Kawazoe, born in 1907, graduated in 1930 with a degree in mechanical engineering from the University of Dayton in Ohio and followed this with a Masters Degree from the Massachusetts Institute of Technology. He then worked for Japan GM, served three years in Manchuria as an army conscript, and took a job with Japan Ford after returning home. He switched to Nissan in 1935 but later went back to Manchuria to run an assembly plant owned by Manchuria Motors. The Chinese captured him in 1945 and held him for eight years as a prisoner of war. He returned to Japan in August 1953 and worked for Fuji Motors, supervising the rebuilding of U.S. Army vehicles before rejoining Nissan in 1959. He then went to the United States in 1960 to open a new sales subsidiary and remained until 1977, when he retired from Nissan's American subsidiary as an executive vice-president. After returning to Japan, Kawazoe served as a consultant to Nissan's International Division.

Kiyomasa Minoru *(11 March 1983)*.
Kiyomasa was the assistant general manager of Toyota's Business Research Department in Tokyo during 1983.

Maeda Riichi *(21 May and 22 July 1982)*.
Maeda, born in 1896, was an associate professor of mechanical engineering at Osaka University when Nissan recruited him in 1937. Between 1929 and 1931, he studied at the Royal College of Mathematics in London, as well as at the Massachusetts Institute of Technology and in Detroit, where he learned automotive engineering. Maeda became a company director in 1946

responsible for research and development, an area still under his direction when he retired as a managing director in 1967. After retirement, he continued to serve Nissan as a technical advisor.

Matsuzaki Shirō *(14 July 1982 and 19 January 1983).*
Matsuzaki, born in 1911, entered Nissan in 1938 after graduating from the mechanical engineering department of the University of Tokyo. He served as a company director from 1961 to 1971, during which time he was responsible for planning the construction and then managing the Oppama and Zama factories. Matsuzaki left Nissan in 1971 to become president of a joint-venture subsidiary, Nihon Dia-Clevite (currently NDC, Inc.), which manufactured engine bearings and other metal components.

Nonoguchi Junji *(18 May 1983).*
Nonoguchi in 1983 was a junior official with Toyota's Public Affairs Department in Tokyo.

Okumura Shōji *(10 June, 30 June, and 30 September 1982).*
Okumura, born in 1913, was a 1937 graduate in mechanical engineering from Kyūshū University. He worked for Hitachi from 1937 to 1943 at a plant that made electrical components sold to Nissan, switched to the automobile company in 1943, and remained there until 1957. After leaving Nissan, he operated a patent examiner's office in Tokyo. Okumura also lectured at Chiba University and Senshū University and wrote extensively on technological development in the Japanese automobile industry, as well as on machine tools, special steels, and other engineering industries.

Ōno Taichi *(18 March 1983).*
Ōno, born in 1912, was the primary architect of Toyota's kanban system and the chief engineer in charge of production management after World War II. After graduating from the Nagoya Higher Industrial School in 1932, he entered Toyoda Spinning and Weaving. He switched to Toyota in 1943 and rose from company director in 1954 to executive vice-president in 1975. Ōno retired from Toyota in 1978 and returned to Toyoda Spinning and Weaving as chairman. (For more biographical details see Chapter 5.)

Ōta Hisakichi *(20 May 1982).*
Ōta, born 1912, graduated from the prewar predecessor of Hitotsubashi University in 1934 and entered Nissan in 1936. He rose from company director in 1958, responsible for sales and public relations, to executive director, before becoming the president of a major subsidiary in 1977, Nihon Radiator. In 1982, at the time of this interview, he was president of Nihon Radiator. Later in the year, he moved up to chairman.

Sasaki Sadamichi *(18 May 1982).*
Sasaki was born in 1911 and graduated from Kyoto University's department of mechanical engineering in 1937. He entered Nissan during the same year and worked in casting, forging, and other manufacturing operations, as well as production planning. During the 1950s, he headed Nissan's Austin de-

438

partment before being promoted to director in 1960. Sasaki also managed the Oppama plant during the 1960s, rose to executive vice-president in 1973, and then became president of Fuji Heavy Industries in 1978.

Terazawa Ichibei *(31 May 1982).*
Born in 1903, Terazawa in 1982 was a consultant to the Automobile Industry Promotion Association (Jidōsha Kōgyō Shinkō Kai). He graduated in 1925 from the mechanical engineering department of the Sendai Higher Industrial School (later Tōhoku University), and then entered the Ministry of Commerce and Industry in 1928. From 1936 to 1951, he was one of the main government officials in MCI and MITI responsible for supervising the automobile industry.

Tsukioka Yukio *(22 November 1982).*
Tsukioka in 1982 was the assistant general manager of Toyota's Business Research Department at the company's headquarters in Toyota City and a director of the company history office.

Uchida Ken'ichi *(22 January 1985).*
Uchida in 1985 was the assistant general manager of Toyota's Production Control Department.

WRITTEN MATERIALS

Abernathy, William J. *The Productivity Dilemma: Roadblock to Innovation in the Automobile Industry.* Baltimore, Johns Hopkins University Press, 1978.

———, Kim B. Clark, and Alan M. Kantrow. *Industrial Renaissance: Producing a Competitive Future for America.* New York, Basic Books, 1983.

Aikawa Yoshisuke. "New Capitalism and Holding Company." This was the text of a lecture to the Tokyo Bankers' Association on 6 and 7 November 1934, titled "Shinshihon-shugi to mochikabu kaisha" and translated into English in May 1935 by Nippon Industries.

———. *Mono no mikata kangaekata* (Ways of thinking and looking at things). Jitsugyō no Nihonsha, 1937.

———. *Watakushi no rirekisho* (My career). Nihon Keizai Shimbunsha, Vol. XXIV, 1965.

Akamatsu Tokushi. *Toyota zankoku monogatari* (The cruel story of Toyota). Eru Shuppansha, 1982.

Akiyama Tadashi. "N-Jidōsha Rōdō Kumiai no sugata" (The state of the N-Motor labor union), *Gekkan rōdō mondai* (Labor problems monthly) 257:94-99 (February 1979).

Allinson, Gary D. *Japanese Urbanism: Industry and Politics in Kariya.* Berkeley and Los Angeles, University of California Press, 1975.

Altshuler, Alan, Daniel Ross, et al. *The Future of the Automobile.* Cambridge, MIT Press, 1984.

Amagai Shōgo. *Nihon jidōsha kōgyō no shiteki tenkai* (The historical development of the Japanese automobile industry). Aki Shobō, 1982.

Andō Yoshio, ed. *Kindai Nihon keizai shi yōran* (An overview of modern Japanese economic history). University of Tokyo Press, 1981.

Aoki Satoshi. *Aoi-tori wa doko e: Nissan Atsugi jomei kaiko jiken* (To where the Bluebird: The Nissan Atsugi expulsion-dismissal incident). Rōdō Kuhosha, 1980.

―――. *Nissan kyōeiken no kiki: rōshi nijū kenryoku shihai no kōzō* (The crisis of the Nissan group: The structure supporting the dual authority of management and labor). Chōbunsha, 1980.

―――. *Gisō rōren: Nissan S-soshiki no himisu* (A labor federation in disguise: Secrets of the Nissan S-organization). Chōbunsha, 1981.

Aoyama Shigeru. *Shioji Ichirō no ōinaru chōsen* (The rising challenge of Shioji Ichirō). Nisshin Hōdō, 1982.

Arisawa Hiromi, ed. *Nihon sangyō hyaku nen shi* (A hundred-year history of Japanese industry). Nikkei Shinsho, 1967.

―――, ed. *Shōwa keizai shi* (An economic history of the Showa period). Nihon Keizai Shinbunsha, 1980.

Asahara Genshichi. "Nissan Jidōsha shi hanashi" (Discussion of the history of Nissan Motor). Interview, 13 May 1969, recorded in Jidōsha Kōgyō Shinkō Kai, ed., *Nihon jidōsha kōgyō shi kōjutsu kiroku shū* (Recordings of oral interviews on the history of the Japanese automobile industry). Vol. II, 1975.

Asahi shimbun (The Asahi newspaper).

Asano Shūzō and Aihara Giichi. "Keisū senbetsu-gata ikkai nukidori kensazu" (Inspection charts for counting selection and one-time sampling), *Nissan gijutsu* 26:29-31 (February 1956).

Automotive News. Weekly.

Chandler, Alfred D. *Giant Enterprise: Ford, GM, and the Automobile Industry.* New York, Harcourt, Brace, and World, 1964.

Chang, C.S. *The Japanese Auto Industry and the U.S. Market.* New York, Praeger, 1981.

Chrysler Corporation. *Annual Reports.*

Cohen, Jerome. *Japan's Economy in War and Reconstruction*. Minneapolis, University of Minnesota Press, 1949.

Cole, Robert E. *Japanese Blue Collar: The Changing Tradition*. Berkeley and Los Angeles, University of California Press, 1971.

——. *Work, Mobility, and Participation: A Comparative Study of American and Japanese Industry*. Berkeley and Los Angeles, University of California Press, 1979.

——, ed. *The Japanese Automobile Industry: Model and Challenge for the Future?* Ann Arbor, Michigan Papers in Japanese Studies, No. 3, 1981.

——, ed. *Automobiles and the Future: Competition, Cooperation, and Change*. Ann Arbor, University of Michigan Press, 1983.

Consumer Reports. Monthly.

Cook, James. "Where's the Niche?" *Forbes*, 24 September 1984.

Deming, William E. "Hinshitsu kanri undō no idai na shidōsha" (Prominent leaders of the quality control movement), in Keidanren (The Federation of Economic Organizations), ed., *Ishikawa Ichirō tsuisōroku* (Collection of reminiscences about Ishikawa Ichirō, 1971).

Diesel, Eugene, et al. *From Engines to Autos*. Chicago, H. Regnery, 1960.

Duncan, W.C. *U.S.-Japan Automobile Diplomacy*. Cambridge, Massachusetts, Ballinger, 1973.

Endō Akira. "Body kokusanka no kaikoroku" (Recollections on local manufacturing of the body), *Nissan gijutsu* 27:18-21 (November 1956).

Feigenbaum, A.V. "Total Quality Control," *Harvard Business Review* 34.6:93-101 (November-December 1956).

——. *Total Quality Control*. 3rd ed. New York, McGraw-Hill, 1983.

Ford Motor Company. *Annual Reports* (Including *10-K Reports*).

Form, William H. *Blue-Collar Stratification: Autoworkers in Four Countries*. Princeton, Princeton University Press, 1976.

Foster, George. "Quality Control," in Carl Heyl, ed., *The Encyclopedia of Management* (1963).

Fujita Shōjirō and Takagi Takeshi. "Austin A50 Cambridge no seinō ni tsuite" (On the performance of the Austin A50 Cambridge), *Nissan gijutsu* 27:2-11 (November 1956).

Gendai Kigyō Kenkyū Kai (Modern Business Research), ed. *Nissan Jidōsha* (Nissan Motor). Yunion Shuppansha, 1961.

——. *Toyota to Nissan* (Toyota and Nissan). Yunion Shuppansha, 1977.

General Motors Corporation. *Annual Reports* (Including *10-K Reports*).

————. "The Framingham Plant." Framingham, Massachusetts, GM Assembly Division, undated.

Gotō Hiroshi. *Fuka kachi bunseki no tehodoki* (An introduction to value-added analysis). Jitsugyō no Nihonsha, 1980.

Gotō Takashi. "Datsun no ryōsan-ka to gijutsu kakushin" (Datsun mass-production and technological innovations). Interview, 29 July 1964, recorded in *Nihon jidōsha kōgyō shi kōjutsu kiroku shū*, Vol. II, 1975.

Hadley, Eleanor. *Antitrust in Japan*. Princeton, Princeton University Press, 1970.

Hall, Robert W. *Zero Inventories*. Homewood, Illinois, Dow Jones-Irwin, 1983.

Hara Akira. " 'Manshū' ni okeru keizai tōsei seisaku no tenkai—Mantetsu kaiso to Mangyō setsuritsu o megutte" (The development of economic controls policy in Manchuria: The reorganization of the South Manchuria Railway and the establishment of Manchuria Development), in Andō Yoshio, ed., *Nihon keizai seisaku shiron* (A history of Japanese economic policy). University of Tokyo Press, Vol. II, 1976.

Harashina Kyōichi. "Austin kokusanka tassei ni atari" (Accomplishing local production of the Austin), *Nissan gijutsu* 27:1 (November 1956).

Harbour and Associates, Inc. "Comparison of Japanese Car Assembly Plant Located in Japan and U.S. Car Assembly Plant Located in the U.S." Berkley, Michigan, ca. 1980. This is a draft of a consultant's report on five assembly plants in Japan and the United States prepared for the U.S. Department of Transportation.

Harvard Business School. "Benson Electronics" (HBS Case Services No. 9-677-013). Boston, 1976 and 1978.

————. "Toyo Kogyo Co. LTD (A)" (HBS Case Services No. 9-682-092). Boston, 1982.

Hatamura Yasushi and Hosaka Tōru. "Nissan Jidōsha sōgyō toki no kikai setsubi to seizō gijutsu (Machinery, equipment, and manufacturing technology at the time of the founding of Nissan Motor). Interview, 29 August 1969, recorded in *Nihon jidōsha kōgyō shi kōjutsu kiroku shū*. Vol. II, 1975.

Hayashi Nobuo. " 'Rōshi kankei kindaika' no onkochishin" (Lessons from the "modernization of management-labor relations"), *Kindai rōken*, December 1979, pp. 1-4.

Hayes, Robert H., and Steven C. Wheelwright. *Restoring Our Competitive Edge: Competing Through Manufacturing*. New York, John Wiley and Sons, 1984.

"Hinshitsu kanri o zensha-teki ni" (Quality control throughout the company), *Nissan* News 90:6-7 (October 1959).

Hitachi Seisakujo Kabushiki Kaisha (Hitachi, Ltd.). *Hitachi Seisakujo shi* (A history of Hitachi, Ltd.). Vol. I (1949); Vol. II (1960); and Vol. III (1974).

Hori Kōjirō. "Shitauke kōjō to hinshitsu kanri" (Subcontracting factories and quality control), *Nissan gijutsu* 26:2 (February 1956).

Hoshino Yoshirō. *Nihon no gijutsu kakushin* (Japan's technological innovations). Keisei Shobō, 1966.

Hosonoya Naoki. "WF gairon" (A survey of work factor), *Nissan gijutsu* 24:44-47 (July 1954).

Igarashi Tadashi. "Kantōgen" (Foreword), *Nissan gijutsu* 26:1 (November 1956).

Ikari Yoshirō. *Dai-Ichi Sharyō Sekkei-bu: Bluebird no otoko-tachi* (The Number-One Chassis-Design Section: Men of the Bluebird). Bungei Shunshū, 1981.

————. *Nihon no jidōsha kōgyō* (The Japanese automobile industry). Nihon Nōritsu Kyōkai, 1981.

————. "Seihin-seisan gijutsu no kakushinsei" (Innovation in product and production technology), in Kyōikusha, ed., *Wārudo kā repōto 80s: masatsu to saihen no kōzu* (World car report for the 80s: The composition of trade friction and reorganization, 1981).

Ishida Takao, Nara Hideo, and Suzuki Kōzō. "Austin chūtetsu imono kokusanka no keika ni tsuite" (Concerning the progress of local production of Austin cast parts), *Nissan gijutsu* 27:44-54 (November 1956).

Ishikawa Kaoru. *Nihon-teki hinshitsu kanri* (Japanese-style quality control). Nihon Kagaku Gijutsu Renmei, 1981.

Isuzu Jidōsha Kabushiki Kaisha (Isuzu Motors). *Isuzu Jidōsha shi* (A history of Isuzu Motors). 1957.

Iwakoshi Tadahiro. *Jidōsha kōgyō ron* (A discussion of the automobile industry). University of Tokyo Press, 1968.

Iwata Akira. "Shijō chōsa to hinshitsu kanri" (Market research and quality control), *Nissan gijutsu* 26:13-15 (February 1956).

Japan Economic Review. Monthly.

Japan Times, The.

Jidōsha Buhin Kōgyō Kai (The Automobile-Parts Manufacturers Association). *Nihon no jidōsha buhin kōgyō* (The Japanese automobile parts industry). Annual.

Jidōsha Kōgyō Shinkō Kai (Automobile Industry Promotion Association). *Jidōsha kōgyō shiryō geppō* (Automobile industry monthly statistics).

———. *Nihon jidōsha kōgyō shi kōjutsu kiroku shū* (Recordings of oral interviews on the history of the Japanese automobile industry). Vol. II, 1975.

———. *Jidōsha hakubutsukan chōsa hōkokusho* (Automobile museum survey report). Vol. I, May 1978.

Johnson Chalmers. *MITI and the Japanese Miracle: The Growth of Industrial Policy 1925-1975.* Stanford, Stanford University Press, 1982.

Juran J.M. ed. *Quality Control Handbook.* New York, McGraw-Hill, 1974.

Kageyama Kiichirō. "Gijutsu shinpo to seizō genka kōsei ni miru kanren sangyō no yakuwari" (The function of related industries in technological progress and the composition of manufacturing costs), in Kyōikusha, ed., *Wārudo kā repōto 80s: masatsu to saihen no kōzu* (World car report for the 80s: The composition of trade friction and reorganization). 1981.

Kamata Satoshi. *Jidōsha zetsubō kōjō: aru kisetsu-kō no nikki* (The automobile factory of despair: Diary of a seasonal worker). Gendaishi Shuppan Kai, 1973.

———. *Japan in the Passing Lane.* New York, Pantheon, 1982.

Kamiya, Shotaro. *My Life with Toyota.* Nagoya, Toyota Motor Sales, 1976.

Kanagawa Ken Rōdō-bu Rōsei-ka (Kanagawa Prefecture, Labor Department, Labor Administration Section). *Kanagawa ken rōdō undō shi* (A history of the labor movement in Kanagawa prefecture). Kanagawa Prefecture, Vol. I (1953) and Vol. II (1959).

Kawamata Katsuji. *Watakushi no rirekisho* (My career). Nihon Keizai Shimbunsha, Vol. XX, 1964.

———. "Atarashii shijō kaitaku e no mosaku" (Reaching for a new market opening), *Chūō kōron,* Winter 1980, pp. 158-165.

———et al. *Keiei no kokoro* (The spirit of management). Nikkan Kōgyō Shimbunsha, Vol. I, 1973.

Keidanren (The Federation of Economic Organizations), ed. *Ishikawa Ichirō tsuisōroku* (Collection of Reminiscences about Ishikawa Ichirō). 1971.

Keizai Kikaku-chō (Economic Planning Agency). *Nihon keizai shihyō* (Japan Economic Indicators). Annual.

Kimura Hitoshi (Hitachi, Ltd.). "A50 no kokusanka kikaki" (The locally produced A50 carburetor), *Nissan gijutsu* 27:26-31 (November 1956).

Kodaira Katsumi. *Jidōsha* (Automobiles). Aki Shobō, 1968.

Kojima Naoki. *Aikawa Yoshisuke den* (Biography of Aikawa Yoshisuke). Nihon Keiei Shuppan Kai, 1967.

" 'Kōkyō no jidōsha' koso shuntō no kikansha da" ('A favorable atmosphere for automobiles' as the engine for the spring wage offensive), *Zaikai*, 1 April 1978, pp. 32-37 (Shioji Ichirō interview).

Kravis, Irving, Alan Heston, and Robert Summers. *World Product and Income: International Comparisons of Real Gross Product*. Baltimore, Johns Hopkins University Press (for the World Bank), 1982.

Kubota Tokujirō. "Gorham-shiki san-rinsha kara Datsun made" (From the three-wheel Gorham vehicle to the Datsun). Interview, 25 November 1970, recorded in *Nihon jidōsha kōgyō shi kōjutsu kiroku shū*. Vol. II, 1975.

Kumagaya Tokuichi. "Zenjidōsha no rōdō undō to Nissan tōsō" (The Zenji labor movement and the Nissan strike). This is an unpublished and undated manuscript, under consideration for publication, given to this writer by an associate of Kumagaya. Kumagaya was an Isuzu employee and a member of Zenji's executive committee.

Laux, James M. *The Automobile Revolution: The Impact of an Industry*. Chapel Hill, University of North Carolina Press, 1982.

Magaziner, Ira C. "Japanese Industrial Policy: Source of Strength for the Automobile Industry," in Robert E. Cole, ed., *The Japanese Automobile Industry: Model and Challenge for the Future?* Ann Arbor, Michigan Papers in Japanese Studies, No. 3, 1981.

Masuda Tetsuo. *Ashita no hitotachi: Nissan rōdōsha no tatakai* (Men of tomorrow: The struggle of Nissan workers). Gogatsu Shobō, 1954.

Matsuzaki, Shiro. "Metal Fabricating," in J.M. Juran, ed., *Quality Control Handbook*. New York, McGraw-Hill, 1974.

Maxcy, George. *The Multinational Automobile Industry*. New York, St. Martin's Press, 1981.

———and Aubrey Silberston. *The Motor Industry*. London, George Allen and Unwin, 1959.

Miki Yōnosuke. *Nissan no chōsen* (Nissan's challenge). Kōbunsha, 1969.

Mitsubishi Shōji Kabushiki Kaisha (Mitsubishi Trading). *Ritsugyō bōeki-roku* (Starting in the trading industry). 1958.

Miyake Masaru. *Kindaiteki rōshi kankei* (Modern management-labor relations). Yokohama, Kindaiteki Rōshi Kankei Kenkyū Kai, 1959.

Miyashita Mutsuo. "Nukidori kensa-hō ni tsuite" (Sampling inspection methods), *Nissan gijutsu* 26:25-28 (February 1956).

Mochikabu Kaisha Seiri Iin-kai (Holding Company Liquidation Commission), ed. *Nihon zaibatsu to sono kaitai* (The Japanese zaibatsu and their dissolution). Hara Shobō, 1951 (1973 reprint).

Monden, Yasuhiro. "What Makes the Toyota Production System Really Tick?" *Industrial Engineering*, January 1981, pp. 36-46.

————. "Adaptable Kanban System Helps Toyota Maintain Just-in-Time Production," *Industrial Engineering*, May 1981, pp. 29-46.

————. "How Toyota Shortened Supply Lot Production Time, Waiting Time, and Conveyance Time," *Industrial Engineering*, September 1981, pp. 22-30.

Monteverde, Kirk, and David J. Teece. "Supplier Switching Costs and Vertical Integration in the Automobile Industry," *The Bell Journal of Economics* 13.1:206-213 (Spring 1982).

Morikawa Hidemasa, ed. *Sengo sangyō shi e no shōgen* (Accounts of the history of postwar industry). Asahi Shimbunsha, 1977.

————. "Toyoda Kiichirō," in Morikawa Hidemasa et al., *Nihon no kigyōka* (Japanese entrepreneurs). Yūhikaku Shinsho, Vol. III, 1978.

————. *Zaibatsu no keiei shiteki kenkyū* (A business history study of the zaibatsu). Tōyō Keizai Shimpōsha, 1980.

Motor Vehicle Manufacturers Association of the U.S. *Motor Vehicle Facts and Figures*. Annual.

————. *World Motor Vehicle Data*. Annual.

Nakamura, Takafusa. *The Postwar Japanese Economy: Its Development and Structure*. University of Tokyo Press, 1981.

Nakane, Jinichiro and R.W. Hall. "Management Specs for Stockless Production," *Harvard Business Review* 61.3:84-91 (May-June 1983).

National Research Council. *The Competitive Status of the U.S. Auto Industry*. Washington, D.C., National Academy Press, 1982.

New York Times, The.

Nihon Hatsujo Sekkei-bu Shasshi Sekkei-ka (Japan Springs, Design Department, Chassis Design Section). "Austin yō supuringu no kokusanka ni tsuite" (Concerning the local manufacturing of the Austin springs), *Nissan gijutsu* 27:32-38 November 1956).

Nihon Jidōsha Kaigi Sho (Japan automobile council). *Nihon jidōsha nenkan* (Japan automobile annual). 1947.

Nihon Jidōsha Kōgyō Kai (Japan Automobile Manufacturers Association). *Jidōsha tōkei nenpyō* (Automobile statistics annual).

————. *Nihon no jidōsha kōgyō* (The Japanese automobile industry). Annual.

————, ed. *Nihon jidōsha kōgyō shikō* (A history of the Japanese automobile industry). Vol. II, 1967; Vol. III, 1969.

Nihon Kagaku Gijutsu Renmei (Japanese Union of Scientists and Engineers). *QC sākuru katsudō un'ei no kihon* (Fundamentals of managing the activities of QC circles). 1971.

———. "QC sākuru katsudō no jittai: anketo chōsa ni yoru" (The actual state of QC circle activities: according to the questionnaire survey). JUSE Subcommittee on QC Circle Activities Research, 1979.

Nihon Kōgyō Ginko (Bank of Japan). *Keizai tōkei nenkan* (Economic statistics annual).

Nihon Rajiēta Kabushiki Kaisha (Nihon Radiator, Inc.). *Ōinaru hishō: Nihon Rajiēta Kabushiki Kaisha yonjū nen shi* (The great flight: A forty-year history of Nihon Radiator). 1979.

Nihon Seisansei Honbu (The Japan Productivity Center). *Fuka kachi bunseki* (Value-added analysis). Annual since 1960.

"Nijū-go nen kan no omoide" (Twenty-five years of memories), *Nissan News* 86:12-13 (June 1959). This is a report on a conference marking Nissan's twenty-fifth anniversary, headed by Katsumata Shigeru, a forging section chief who entered the company in 1934 from Tobata Casting.

Nikkei Mechanical. *Robotto kakumei* (The robot revolution). 1981.

Nippondensō Kabushiki Kaisha (Nippon Denso, Inc.). *Nippondensō nijū-go nen shi* (A twenty-five year history of Nippon Denso). Kariya, 1974.

"Nissan Decides on British Plant Location," Business Japan, May 1984, p. 109.

Nissan Jidōsha Bunkai Kikanshi (Organ of the Nissan Motor Chapter). *Heiwa: tokushū-go* (Peace, special issue). Yokohama, 1953.

Nissan Jidōsha Gijutsu-bu (Nissan Motor, Engineering Department). "Austin cylinder block oyobi cylinder head yō transfer machines ni tsuite" (Concerning the transfer machines for the Austin cylinder block and cylinder head), *Nissan gijutsu* 27:12 (November 1956).

Nissan Jidōsha Kabushiki Kaisha (The Nissan Motor Company, Ltd.). *Eigyō hōkokusho* (Annual reports, prewar version.)

———. *Yūka shōken hōkokusho* (Annual reports, equivalent to American 10-K reports.)

———. *Annual Reports.*

———. *Nissan gijutsu* (Nissan Engineering).

———. *Nissan News.* Monthly, in Japanese.

———. *Nissan Jidōsha sanjū nen shi* (A thirty-year history of Nissan Motor). 1964.

————. *Nissan Jidōsha shashi* (Nissan Motor Company history). 1975.

————. "Zama kōjō no gaiyō" (An outline of the Zama factory). 1978.

————. "Nissan's Overseas Projects." International Division, July 1981.

————. "QC sākuru katsudō no ayumi" (The course of QC circle activities). Quality Control Department, 1981.

————. "Nissan Jidōsha no gaiyō" (An overview of Nissan Motor). 1982.

————. *Jidōsha kōgyō handobukku* (Automobile industry handbook). Business Research Department, 1983.

————. "Data File 1984."

————. *Nijū-ichi seiki e no michi: Nissan Jidōsha gojū nen shi* (The road toward the twenty-first century: A fifty-year history of Nissan Motor). 1983.

"Nissan Jidōsha no higeki" (The tragedy of Nissan Motor) *Purejidento* (President), December 1982, pp. 224-245.

Nissan Jidōsha Rōdō Kumiai (Nissan Motor Labor Union). *Nissan sōgi hakusho* (The Nissan strike white paper). Yokohama, June 1954.

Nissan Konwa Kai (Nissan Discussion Group). "Nissan Konwa Kai kaihō" (Nissan Discussion Group Bulletin).

Nodani Mitsuru and Iwasaki Toshio. "Nissan Jidōsha no 'jinji' 'jinpa' sōran" (A survey of Nissan Motor 'personnel' and 'factions'), *Zaikai tenbō* 26.4:64-76 (1 March 1982).

Odaira Kaoru. "Gaichū kankei e no jisshi" (Implementation related to outside orders), *Nissan gijutsu* 26:2-8 (February 1956).

Okumura Hiroshi, Hoshikawa Jun'ichi, and Matsui Kazuo. *Gendai no sangyō: jidōsha kōgyō* (Contemporary industries: The automobile industry). Tōyō Keizai Shimpōsha, 1965.

Okumura Shōji. *Jidōsha* (Automobiles). Iwanami Shinsho, 1954.

————. "Jidōsha kōgyō no hatten dankai to kōzō" (The developmental stages and structure of the automobile industry), in Arisawa Hiromi, ed., *Gendai Nihon sangyō kōza* (Series on contemporary Japanese industry). Iwanami Shoten, Vol. V, 1960.

————. "Concept of Technology Transfer as Reviewed from Japan's Experience," *Kenshū* (AOTS Quarterly) 77:8-9 (September 1980).

Ōkura Tsutomu. "QC are-kore" (This and that about QC), *Nissan gijutsu* 26:3-4 (February 1956).

Ōno Taichi., *Toyota seisan hōshiki* (The Toyota production system). Daiyamondo, 1978.

Oriental Economist. "Manchuria Industrial Development Corporation" (March 1938).

Ozaki Masahisa. *Toyoda Kiichirō shi* (Toyoda Kiichirō). Jikensha, 1955.

Ozawa Chikamitsu. *Aikawa Yoshisuke den* (A biography of Aikawa Yoshisuke). Yamaguchi, Yamaguchi Shimbunsha, 1974.

Pascale, Richard, and Thomas P. Rohlen. "The Mazda Turnaround," *Journal of Japanese Studies* 9.2:219-264 (Summer 1983).

Rader, James. *Penetrating the U.S. Auto Market: German and Japanese Strategies.* Ann Arbor, UMI Research Press, 1980.

Rae, John B. *Nissan-Datsun: A History of Nissan Motor Corporation in U.S.A., 1960-1980.* New York, McGraw-Hill, 1982.

Rōdō Sho (Ministry of Labor), ed. *Shiryō: rōdō undō shi* (Historical materials: Labor movement history). 1953.

Rōdō Sōgi Chōsa Kai (Labor Disputes Survey Association). *Sengo rōdō jittai chōsa: rōdō sōgi ni okeru tokushū kesu* (Survey of the actual state of postwar labor: Special cases among the labor disputes). Chūō Kōron, Vol. XI, 1956.

Saga Ichirō. "Tokui na jidōsha sangyō no rōshi kankei" (The peculiar management-labor relations in the automobile industry), *Ekonomisuto* (The Economist), 18 March 1980, pp. 20-25.

"Saikin no hinshitsu kanri suishin jōkyō" (The state of the recent quality control promotion effort), *Nissan News* 92:7 (December 1959).

Saitō Shigeru. *Toyota 'kanban' hōshiki no himitsu* (The secrets of the Toyota 'kanban' system). Kou Shobō, 1978.

Sakiya, Tetsuo. *Honda Motor: The Men, the Management, the Machines.* Kodansha International, 1982.

Salter, Malcom S., Alan M. Weber, and Davis Dyer, "U.S. Competitiveness in Global Industries: Lessons from the Auto Industry," in Bruce R. Scott and George C. Lodge, eds., *U.S. Competitiveness in the World Economy.* Boston, Harvard Business School Press, 1985.

Sankei shimbun (The Sankei newspaper).

Schmenner, Roger W. *Production/Operations Management.* Chicago, Science Research Associates, 1981.

Schnapp, John B. *Corporate Strategies of the Automobile Manufacturers.* Lexington, Mass., D.C. Heath and Co., 1979.

Schonberger, Richard J. *Japanese Manufacturing Techniques: Nine Lessons in Simplicity.* New York, The Free Press/Macmillan, 1982.

Sei Kōichirō. "Bungyō to rōdō no Nichi-Bei hikaku" (A comparison of specialization and labor in Japan and the United States), in Kyōikusha, ed., *Wārudo kā repōto 80s: masatsu to saihen no kōzu* (World car report for the 80s: The composition of trade friction and reorganization). 1981.

Shibata Masaharu. "Amerika ni okeru mākettingu" (Marketing in America), *Nissan News* 79:5 (November 1958).

Shindō Takezaemon. "Nihon Kagaku Gijutsu Renmei no koto" (The Japanese Union of Scientists and Engineers), in Keidanren (The Federation of Economic Organizations), ed., *Ishikawa Ichirō tsuisōroku* (Collection of reminiscences about Ishikawa Ichirō). 1971.

Shingō Shigeo. *Toyota seisan hōshiki no IE-teki kōsatsu* (An industrial engineering analysis of the Toyota production system). Nikkan Kōgyō Shimbunsha, 1980.

Shinoda Ken. "Hinshitsu kanri to sagyō hyōjun" (Quality control and work standards), *Nissan gijutsu* 26:33-37 (February 1956).

Sloan, Alfred P., Jr. *My Years with General Motors.* New York, Anchor/Doubleday, 1963.

Sugimori, Y., K. Kusunoki, F. Chō, and S. Uchikawa. "Toyota Production System and Kanban System of Materialization of Just-in-Time and Respect-for-Human System," *International Journal of Production Research* 15.6:553-564 (1977).

Takayama Jirō. "Nissan Jidōsha zankoku monogatari" (The cruel story of Nissan Motor), *Gekkan rōdō mondai* (Labor problems monthly), September 1964, pp. 76-78.

Tasugi Kyō and Mori Shunji. *Seisan kanri kenkyū* (A study of production management). Yūgendō, 1960.

Togai Yoshio. "Mangyō sanka kigyō no seisan katsudō" (The production activities of firms affiliated with Manchuria Development), *Matsuyama Shōdai ronshū* (Matsuyama Commercial University journal) 31.2:91-112 (June 1980).

Tōkyō Kiki Kōgyō Jidōsha Sekkei-ka to Nissan Jidōsha Shasshi Sekkei-ka Sekkei-bu (Tokyo Kiki Industries, Automobile Design Section, and Nissan Motor, Design Department, Chassis Design Section). "Austin shock-absorber no kokusanka" (Localizing production of the Austin shock absorbers), *Nissan gijutsu* 27:39-43 (November 1956).

Tomisawa, Konomi. "The Auto Parts Industry of Japan: Facing the Challenge of Internationalization and Technical Innovation," *LTCB Research*, No. 74 (July-August 1984).

Tomoda Jōichirō, ed. "Aikawa Yoshisuke kaisō to hōfu" (Aikawa Yoshisuke's recollections and aspirations). This is an unpublished manuscript, written around 1953, of an interview with Aikawa by a journalist from the *Oriental Economist.*

Tōyō keizai (The Oriental economist). Weekly.

Tōyō Keizai Shimpōsha, ed. *Nihon no kaisha hyaku nen shi* (A hundred-year history of Japanese companies). 1975.

————. *Keizai tōkei nenkan* (Economic statistics annual). 1982.

————. *Kaisha shikihō (Company quarterly reports).*

Toyoda Kiichirō. "Toyota Jidōsha ga konnichi ni itaru made" (Toyota Motor up to the present). September 1936 article reprinted in Ozaki Masahisa, *Toyoda Kiichirō shi.* Jikensha, 1955.

Toyoda, Shoichiro. "Automotive Industry," in J.M. Juran, ed., *Quality Control Handbook.* New York, McGraw-Hill, 1974.

Toyota Jidōsha Hanbai Kabushiki Kaisha (Toyota Motor Sales, Ltd.). *Mōtarizeishon to tomo ni* (Along with motorization). Nagoya, 1970.

Toyota Jidōsha Kabushiki Kaisha (Toyota Motor Corporation). *Yūka shōken hōkokusho* (Annual reports, equivalent to American 10-K reports).

————. *Annual Reports.*

————. *Toyota Jidōsha sanjū nen shi* (A thirty-year history of Toyota Motor). Toyota City, 1967.

————. *Toyota no ayumi* (The path of Toyota). Toyota City, 1978.

————. *Kōhō shiryō* (Public information materials). 1982.

————. *Kōhō handobukku* (Public information handbook). 1984.

————. "Toyota 1983: Jidōsha sangyō no gaiyō" (Toyota 1983: An overview of the automobile industry).

————. "Toyota 1984: Jidōsha sangyō no gaiyō" (Toyota 1984: An overview of the automobile industry).

————. "Outline of Toyota." 1984.

Tsujita, Shigeru. "The Promoter's Role in QC Circle Activities." JUSE Preconvention Seminar on QC Circles, Lecture 4. 1981.

Tsūshō Sangyō Sho (The Ministry of International Trade and Industry). *Waga kuni jidōsha kōgyō no shōrai* (The future of our country's automobile industry). 1957.

————. *Sekai no kigyō no keiei bunseki* (Management analysis of the world's companies). Annual since 1963.

Tsutsumi Shin'ichi. "Toyota shiki rōshi kaneki no shushin" (The guardian of Toyota-style management-labor relations), *Zaikai* 30.16:98-100 (15 July 1982).

Turner, M.A., et al. *Labor Relations in the Motor Industry.* London, George Allen and Unwin, 1967.

Udagawa Masaru. "Nissan zaibatsu keisei katei no keiei shiteki kōsatsu" (A business history inquiry into the formation process of the Nissan zaibatsu), *Keiei shigaku* 6.3:1-32 (March 1972).

———. "Shinkō zaibatsu: Nissan o chūshin ni" (The new zaibatsu: A focus on Nissan), in Yasuoka Shigeaki, ed., *Nihon no zaibatsu* (The Japanese zaibatsu). Nihon Keizai Shinbunsha, 1976.

———. "Nissan zaibatsu no jidōsha sangyō shinshutsu ni tsuite (1)" (The entrance of the Nissan zaibatsu into the automobile industry), *Keiei shirin* 13.4:93-109 (January 1977).

———. "Nissan zaibatsu no jidōsha sangyō shinshutsu ni tsuite (2)," *Keiei shirin* 14.1:73-95 (April 1977).

———. "Nissan zaibatsu no keiei soshiki (1)" (The management organization of the Nissan zaibatsu), *Keiei shirin* 15.3:43-52 (October 1978).

———. "Nissan zaibatsu no keiei soshiki (2)," *Keiei shirin* 15.4:55-67 (January 1979).

———. "Japan's Automobile Marketing: Its Introduction, Consolidation, Development, and Characteristics," in Akio Okochi and Koiichi Shimokawa, eds., *Development of Mass Marketing.* University of Tokyo Press, 1981.

———. "Historical Development of the Japanese Automobile Industry, 1917-1971: Business and Government," *Keiei shirin* 19.4:31-46 (January 1983).

———. *Shinkō zaibatsu* (The new zaibatsu). Nihon Keizai Shimbunsha, 1984.

———and Seishi Nakamura. "Japanese Business and Government in the Inter-war Period: Heavy Industrialization and the Industrial Rationalization Movement," in Keiichirō Nakagawa, ed., *Government and Business.* University of Tokyo Press, 1980.

Ueno, Hiroya, and Hiromichi Muto. "The Automobile Industry of Japan," in Kazuo Sato, ed., *Industry and Business in Japan.* New York and London, Croom-Helm, 1980.

U.S. Department of Commerce, Bureau of Economic Analysis. *Survey of Current Business.* Monthly.

452

U.S. Department of Commerce, Bureau of the Census. *Annual Survey of Manufacturers.*

―――. *Statistical Abstract of the United States, 1984.*

Wada Hidekichi. *Nissan kontsueron tokuhon* (Nissan concern reader). Shun-shūsha, 1937.

Wakayama Fujio and Sugimoto Tadaaki. *Toyota no himitsu* (Toyota secrets). Kou Shobō, 1977.

Wall Street Journal, The.

Ward's Automotive Yearbook. Annual.

White, Lawrence J. *The Automobile Industry Since 1945.* Cambridge, Harvard University Press, 1971.

William R. Gorham Shi Kinen Jigyō Iinkai (The William R. Gorham Memorial Committee), ed. *William R. Gorham den* (A biography of William R. Gorham). Fuji Jidōsha Kabushiki Kaisha, 1951.

Yamamoto Kiyoshi. *Jidōsha sangyō no rōshi kankei* (Management-labor relations in the automobile industry). University of Tokyo Press, 1981.

Yamamoto Sōji. *Jidōsha* (Automobiles). Daiyamondo, 1938.

―――. *Nihon jidōsha kōgyō no seichō to nenbō* (Growth and prospects for the Japanese automobile industry). San'ei Shobō, 1961.

Yamamura Yoshiharu and Noguchi Noboru. *Nissan wa Toyota ni kateru ka* (Can Nissan beat Toyota?). Kou Shobō, 1977.

Yamashita Yoshitaka. "Hinshitsu kanri dōnyū kara konnichi made" (From the introduction of quality control to the present), *Nissan gijutsu* 26:9-12 (February 1956).

Yamazaki Hiroaki. "Senji shita no sangyō kōzō to dokusen soshiki" (The wartime industrial structure and monopoly organization), in Tōkyō Daigaku Shakai Kagaku Kenkyūjo (Tokyo University Institute of Social Science), ed., *Senji Nihon Keizai*, (The wartime Japanese economy). University of Tokyo Press, Vol. II, 1979.

Yasudu Yūzō. "Shioji ōkoku hōkai no jokyoku" (Prelude to the collapse of the Shioji kingdom," *Keizai kai*, 27 November 1984, pp. 16-21.

Yasumaro Toshio. "Atsugi kōjō no hinshitsu kanri" (Quality control in the Atsugi factory), *Nissan gijutsu* 26:58-59 (February 1956).

Yates, Brock. *The Decline and Fall of the American Automobile Industry.* New York, Empire Books, 1983.

Yūka shōken hōkokusho (Japanese 10-K annual reports).

Zaikai (Financial World). Weekly.

INDEX

HARVARD EAST ASIAN MONOGRAPHS

Harvard East Asian Monographs

STUDIES IN THE MODERNIZATION OF THE REPUBLIC OF KOREA: 1945–1975

114. Joshua A. Fogel, *Politics and Sinology: The Case of Naitō Konan (1866–1934)*
115. Jeffrey C. Kinkley, ed., *After Mao: Chinese Literature and Society, 1978–1981*
116. C. Andrew Gerstle, *Circles of Fantasy: Convention in the Plays of Chikamatsu*
117. Andrew Gordon, *The Evolution of Labor Relations in Japan: Heavy Industry, 1853–1955*
118. Daniel K. Gardner, *Chu Hsi and the* Ta Hsueh: *Neo-Confucian Reflection on the Confucian Canon*
119. Christine Guth Kanda, *Shinzō: Hachiman Imagery and its Development*
120. Robert Borgen, *Sugawara no Michizane and the Early Heian Court*
121. Chang-tai Hung, *Going to the People: Chinese Intellectuals and Folk Literature, 1918–1937*
122. Michael A. Cusumano, *The Japanese Automobile Industry: Technology and Management at Nissan and Toyota*